MAIN

OXFORD

take off in

Greek

Athena Economides

OXFORD
UNIVERSITY PRESS

OXFORD
UNIVERSITY PRESS

Great Clarendon Street, Oxford OX2 6DP

Oxford University Press is a department of the University of Oxford.
It furthers the University's objective of excellence in research, scholarship,
and education by publishing worldwide in

Oxford New York

Athens Auckland Bangkok Bogotá Buenos Aires Calcutta
Cape Town Chennai Dar es Salaam Delhi Florence Hong Kong Istanbul
Karachi Kuala Lumpur Madrid Melbourne Mexico City Mumbai
Nairobi Paris São Paulo Shanghai Singapore Taipei Tokyo Toronto Warsaw

with associated companies in Berlin Ibadan

Oxford is a registered trade mark of Oxford University Press
in the UK and in certain other countries

Published in the United States
by Oxford University Press Inc., New York

British Library Cataloguing in Publication Data

Data available

Library of Congress Cataloging in Publication Data

Data available

ISBN 0–19–860316-9 (Book and cassettes)
ISBN 0–19–860317-7 (Book and CDs)
ISBN 0–19–860318-5 (Book only)

3 5 7 9 10 8 6 4 2

Commissioning and editorial development: Tracy Miller
Project management: Natalie Pomier
Audio production: Daniel Pageon, Actors World Production Ltd
Music: David Stoll
Design and typesetting: Oxford Designers & Illustrators

Every effort has been made to contact the copyright holders of the
illustrative material in this title. If notified, the publisher will be
pleased to amend the acknowledgement in any future edition.

Printed in Great Britain by
Cox and Wyman Ltd.
Reading Berks

Contents

	Introduction	iv
1	Starting out	1
	Τι κάνετε;	
2	Finding your way	15
	Πού είναι;	
3	Pleased to meet you	29
	Χαίρω πολύ	
	Review 1	43
4	Do you have rooms?	47
	Έχετε δωμάτια;	
5	Let's go to the shops	61
	Πάμε στα μαγαζιά	
6	Transport	75
	Συγκοινωνία	
7	Dates and celebrations	89
	Ημερομηνίες και γιορτές	
	Review 2	103
8	Entertainment	107
	Ψυχαγωγία	
9	Plans	121
	Σχέδια	
10	I want to do something else	135
	Θέλω να κάνω κάτι άλλο	
	Review 3	149
11	I went, I saw, I did	153
	Πήγα, είδα, έκανα	
12	The things we used to do	167
	Τι κάναμε	
13	Health	181
	Υγεία	
14	Which was the best?	195
	Ποιο ήταν το καλύτερο;	
	Review 4	209
	Answers	213
	Grammar Summary	222
	Vocabulary	238
	Glossary of Grammatical Terms	246
	Index	248

Introduction

Oxford Take Off In Greek is designed to help the beginner develop the basic language skills necessary to communicate in Greek in most everyday situations. It is intended for learners working by themselves, providing all the information and support necessary for successful language learning.

How to use the course
The book and the recording are closely integrated, as the emphasis is on speaking and listening. The course is led by the recording, which contains step-by-step instructions on how to work through the units. The presenter on the recording will tell you when to use the recording on its own, when to use the book, and when and how to use the two together. The book provides support in the form of transcriptions of the recording material, translations of new vocabulary, and grammar explanations. You'll find this icon  in the book when you need to listen to the recording.

1 (recording/book) Read the unit objectives on the first page telling you what you will learn in the unit, and then begin by listening to the **dialogue** on the recording. You may not understand everything the first time you hear it, but try to resist the temptation to look at the

transcript in the book. The first activity on the recording will help you develop your listening skills by suggesting things to concentrate on and listen out for. You'll be given the opportunity to repeat some of the key sentences and phrases from the dialogue before you hear it a second time. You may need to refer to the vocabulary list (book) before completing the second activity (book). Listen to the dialogue as many times as you like, but as far as possible try not to refer to the dialogue transcript (book).

2 (book) Once you have listened to all the new language, take some time to work through the **Vocabulary, Language Building,** and **activities** in the book to help you understand how it works.

3 (recording) Then it's time to practise speaking. First you'll find **Pronunciation practice** on the recording, focusing on an aspect of pronunciation that occurs in the dialogue. Next is the **Your turn** activity. You will be given all the instructions and cues you need by the presenter on the recording. The first few times you do this you may need to refer back to the vocabulary and language building sections in the book, but aim to do it without the book after that.

4 (book) The fourth learning section, **Culture** concentrates on reading practice. Try reading it first without referring to the vocabulary list to see how much you can already understand, making guesses about any words or phrases you are not sure of. The activities which accompany the text will help you develop reading comprehension skills.

5 (recording/book) For the final learning section, return to the recording to listen to the **Story**. This section gives you the opportunity to have some fun with the language and hear the characters in the story use the language you have just learnt in different situations. The aim is to give you the confidence to cope with authentic Greek. There are activities in the book to help you.

6 (book) Return to the book, and work through the activities in the **Test** section to see how well you can remember and use the language you have covered in the unit. This is best done as a written exercise. Add up the final score and, if it is not as high as you had hoped, try going back and reviewing some of the sections.

7 (recording/book) As a final review, turn to the **Summary** on the last page of the unit. This will test your understanding of the new situations, vocabulary, and grammar introduced in the unit. Use the book to prepare your answers, either by writing them down or speaking aloud, then return to the recording to test

yourself. You will be given prompts in English on the recording, so you can do this test without the book.

8 (book) At the very end of each unit you will find some suggestions for **revision** and ideas for extending your practice with the language of the unit.

Each unit builds on the work of the preceding units, so it's very important to learn the vocabulary and structures from each unit before you move on.

There are review sections after units 3, 7, 10, and 14 for you to test yourself on the material learnt so far.

Other support features
If you want a more detailed grammar explanation than those given in the *Language Building* sections, you will find a *Grammar Summary* at the end of the book. For a definition of the grammar terms used in the course, see the *Glossary of Grammatical Terms* on page 248.

The *Answers* section gives the answers to all the activities in the book. Some activities require you to give information about yourself, so you may also need to check some vocabulary in a dictionary.

At the end of the book you'll find a comprehensive Greek–English *Vocabulary*.

The Greek Language

Greek is not a widely used language, but it is spoken by over 13 million people. It is the official language of Greece, one of the two official languages of Cyprus, and, since 1981, has been one of the official languages of the European Union. Greek is also spoken by appreciable numbers of people of Greek origin living in communities in various parts of the world.

During the 19th and 20th centuries, the form of the Greek language was a highly contentious cultural and political issue. The question resolved itself into the tension between καθαρεύουσα (katharevousa) and δημοτική (demotiki). Katharevousa is the language the purists tried to reconstitute from 'archaic sources', particularly for formal, written use. Demotiki is the language spoken by the people, which its promoters and defenders argued was the the natural language of modern Greece, evolved through history and used by all. Demotic, under the name Neohellenic, was instituted by law in 1976, after the fall of the junta, and this is now the recognized common language of the Greeks. The formal codification of Neohellenic, allowing flexibility for spoken and regional variations, is still in process.

Even if you are a complete beginner, the number of Greek words you recognize will surprise you. Greek, like Latin, has had an enduring influence on English vocabulary and you will frequently come across words familiar from their English derivatives. μεγάλος, μικρός, μόνος – 'big', 'small', 'single' – are familiar in words like 'megalomania', 'microcosm', 'monotone'. φόβος – 'fear', is evident in 'phobia' and you can immediately begin to work out the Greek for 'spider' and 'foreigner' from this link: αράχνη and ξένος. As you progress through your studies, you will begin to identify prefixes, suffixes, and stems embedded in new words, that will make sense, and help you to remember.

Influences work in the opposite direction, too. Although purists resist the importation of foreign words, Greek has incorporated English words over the years. γκαράζ – 'garage', χάμπουργκερ – 'hamburger', and σουπερμάρκετ – 'supermarket' are obvious examples, and more recently, despite a lot of technical words in English being derived from the Greek, computer jargon has tended to enter modern Greek from English.

In Greek, as in many other languages, each noun has a gender. Greek nouns are masculine, feminine, or neuter. Greek also uses cases, a grammatical system where nouns, adjectives, pronouns, take different endings to show their function in the sentence. Also, there is more variation in the workings of Greek verbs than there is in English. Another detail that is immediately apparent is that Greek has two ways of addressing people: **σου** is the informal and **σας** the formal 'you' form.

Reading Greek is no real ordeal once you are used to the alphabet. Unlike English and French, Greek is a phonetic language. The written representation of a sound is standard: once you have learned what a letter or combination of letters sounds like, you know how to pronounce it.

Pronunciation

To achieve good pronunciation, there is no substitute for listening carefully to the recording and, if possible, to Greek native speakers, then trying to reproduce the sounds you hear. Here are a few guidelines to keep in mind as you do so. You will find this section most useful if you read while you listen to the Pronunciation section on the recording.

The Greek alphabet

There are 24 letters in the Greek alphabet. The chart should be used in conjunction with the pronunciation of the full alphabet given on the recording for Unit 1.

Capital	Lower-case	Letter name		Approximate pronunciation	IPA
A	α	alpha	άλφα	**ah**	/a/
B	β	beta	βήτα	**veer**	/v/
Γ	γ	gamma	γάμα	**hg** at the back of the throat before **α, ω, ο, ου**	/ɣ/
				yellow before **ε, η, ι, υ**	/j/
Δ	δ	delta	δέλτα	**these**	/ð/
E	ε	epsilon	έψιλον	**bell**	/ɛ/
Z	ζ	zeta	ζήτα	**zeal**	/z/
H	η	ita	ήτα	**leap** (but kept short)	/i/
Θ	θ	theta	θήτα	**thistle**	/θ/
I	ι	iota	γιώτα	**leap** (but kept short)	/i/
K	κ	kappa	κάπα	**kilt**	/k/
Λ	λ	lamda	λάμδα	**lamb**	/l/
M	μ	mi	μι	**milk**	/m/
N	ν	ni	νι	**need**	/n/
Ξ	ξ	ksi	ξι	**box**	/ks/
O	ο	omicron	όμικρον	**olive**	/ɔ/
Π	π	pi	πι	**pea**	/p/
P	ρ	ro	ρω	**rose**	/r/
Σ	σ, ς*	sigma	σίγμα	**see** or co**s**mos	/s/ /z/
T	τ	taf	ταυ	**tough**	/t/
Y	υ	ipsilon	ύψιλον	**leap** (but kept short)	/i/
Φ	φ	fi	φι	**feel**	/f/

X	χ	chi	χι	loch (as in Scottish pronunciation) at the back of the throat before α, ω, o, ου	/x/
				hue before ε, ι, αι	/ç/
Ψ	ψ	psi	ψι	perhaps	/ps/
Ω	ω	omega	ωμέγα	olive	/ɔ/

*at the end of words

Vowels

Note that there are only 5 vowel sounds, but that these can be written in a variety of ways.

Written form	Approx. pron.	Example		IPA
α	ah	καλά		/a/
ε, αι	eh	ένα, χαίρετε		/ɛ/
ι, η, υ, ει, οι	ee (short)	τι, καλησπέρα, κύριος, εντάξει, λοιπόν		/i/
o, ω	o (short)	ορίστε, παρακαλώ		/ɔ/
ου	oo	γειά σου		/u/

Vowel combinations

αι	e	χαίρετε	/ɛ/
αυ	af, av	αυτοκίνητο, αυγό	/af, av/
ευ	ef, ev	ευχαριστώ, Ευρώπη	/ɛf, ɛv/
ει	i	εντάξει	/i/
οι	i	λοιπόν	/i/
ου	oo	γειά σου	/u/

Where the 1st vowel in one of these combinations has a stress mark, the vowels are pronounced separately (e.g. τσάι). When the vowels are pronounced separately and the stress falls on the 2nd vowel, an accent (¨) is used to show the separate pronunciation (e.g. κανταΐφι).

Consonants

Note also the following *consonant combinations*.

Consonants	Approx. pron. (beginning of word)	Example	Approx. pron. (middle of word)	Example	
μπ	b	μπίρα	b, mb	λάμπα	/b/ /mb/
ντ	d	ντολμάδες	d, nd	εντάξει	/d/ /nd/
γκ	g	γκολφ	g, ng	πρίγκηπας	/g/ /ŋg/
γγ*	–	–	g, ng*	Αγγλία	/g/ /ŋg/
γχ	–	–	nh	άγχος	/ŋx/
τσ	ts	τσάι	ts	έτσι	/ts/
τζ	dz	τζάκι	dz	παντζούοι	/dz/

viii *Note that in the word συγγνώμη (excuse me) γγ is pronounced as /ɣ/: /siɣnɔmi/.

Starting out

Τι κάνετε;

OBJECTIVES

In this unit you'll learn how to:

- ✓ use the Greek alphabet
- ✓ greet people
- ✓ order snacks and drinks
- ✓ use simple everyday phrases

And cover the following grammar and language:

- ✓ the 24 letters of the alphabet: αΑ (alpha) to ωΩ (omega)
- ✓ stress
- ✓ different forms of address
- ✓ the definite and indefinite articles (ο, η, το and ένας, μία, ένα)
- ✓ masculine, feminine, and neuter nouns (ο κύριος, η κυρία, το σουβλάκι)

LEARNING GREEK 1

First become familiar with the Greek alphabet. Many of the letters look and sound like the English equivalents. Even the letters that are different are not difficult for English speakers to pronounce. Look at the chart in the Introduction, which names the letters, and gives a transcription and guide to pronunciation. Try writing your name in Greek letters! This first unit will give you various opportunities to familiarize yourself with the alphabet. The alphabet will appear at the bottom of each page, for quick reference. Once you know the sound of each letter and letter-combination, reading will be easy: the sounds do not vary – syllable for syllable, what you see is what you read, no matter how long the word!

Now start the recording for Unit 1.

Το αλφάβητο

Look at the chart of Greek letters on p. vii–viii of the Introduction and listen to the first part of the recording.

ACTIVITY 1

To practise the alphabet, write the following Greek words in lower-case letters. Then read them out loud: what do you think they mean in English?

ΜΑΜΑ   _____

ΤΑΞΙ   _____

ΣΙΝΕΜΑ   _____

ΣΑΛΑΤΑ   _____

ΛΕΜΟΝΑΔΑ   _____

ΤΑΡΑΜΟΣΑΛΑΤΑ   _____

ΑΕΡΟΠΛΑΝΟ   _____

ΓΙΑΟΥΡΤΙ   _____

ΠΡΟΒΛΗΜΑ   _____

ΤΗΛΕΦΩΝΟ   _____

ACTIVITY 2

Here are some more words for you to practise, this time involving some of the consonant and vowel combinations. You might want to look again at the chart in the Introduction before you do this. Write them in capitals. Then read them aloud and see if you can work out what they mean in English.

μπίρα   _____

γκαράζ   _____

τζατζίκι   _____

σάντουιτς   _____

ντομάτα   _____

τρένο   _____

ούζο   _____

μπάσκετ-μπολ   _____

μπαρ   _____

ΑΒΓΔΕΖΗΘΙΚΛΜΝΞΟΠΡΣΤΥΦΧΨΩ

The following are the Greek versions of English proper names. What are they in English? These are slightly more difficult – it will help to read them aloud.

Μπιλ	_____	Γκάρι	_____
Μπάρμπαρα	_____	Ουέλιγγτον	_____
Μπέτι	_____	Τσαρλς	_____
Ντόναλντ	_____	Τσίπερφιλντς	_____
Ντίλια	_____	Τζαμάικα	_____

ACTIVITY 3

How would you write the following in Greek?

1 the name of your street?
2 the names of your family?
3 the make of your car?

ACTIVITY 4

Here are some Greek greetings. Practise reading them aloud and learn what they mean. Then check your pronunciation using the recording.

γειά σας	hello, goodbye [*formal*]
γειά σου	hello, goodbye [*informal*]
χαίρετε	hello, goodbye N/D
καλημέρα	good morning
καλησπέρα	good evening, good afternoon
καληνύχτα	goodnight
αντίο*	bye, see you

*Note that this word is pronounced 'adio'.

Now try these words.

όχι	no	ευχαριστώ	thank you
ναι	yes	παρακαλώ	please

The Greek gestures for 'yes' and 'no' are not as you might expect. **όχι** ('no') is accompanied by a tilting upwards of the chin, and sometimes a low 'tut' sound. For **ναι** ('yes' – not to be confused with the English 'no'), the gesture is a downward diagonal movement of the head, often accompanied by a gentle dropping of the eyelids.

Now go to the recording.

α β γ δ ε ζ η θ ι κ λ μ ν ξ ο π ρ σ τ υ φ χ ψ ω   **3**

Γειά σας!

🔊 **ACTIVITY 5** is on the recording.

ACTIVITY 6
Are they meeting or parting? Decide for each of the four conversations.

DIALOGUE 1

○ Καλημέρα!
■ Καλημέρα! Τι κάνετε;
○ Καλά.

▼ Γειά σου, Σοφία, στο καλό.
● Γειά σου, Θανάση, να το ταξί!

○ Καλησπέρα, Κυρία Κατίνα.
■ Καλησπέρα, Γιάννη. Τι κάνεις;
○ Πολύ καλά, ευχαριστώ.

○ Χαίρετε, παιδιά!
■ Χαίρετε, Κυρ'Λάκη.
▼ Γειά σου.
● Αντίο!
○ Αντίο σας.

VOCABULARY	
τι κάνετε;	how are you? [*formal*]
καλά	fine
στο καλό	take care [*a phrase often used when parting*]
να το ταξί	there's the taxi
Κυρία	Mrs, Madam
τι κάνεις;	how are you? [*informal*]
πολύ	very
ευχαριστώ	thank you
παιδιά	everyone [*literally kids; here referring to a group of friends*]
Κυρ	Mr, Sir [*a contracted form of Κύριος, mostly heard in the villages and used for old men*]

Α Β Γ Δ Ε Ζ Η Θ Ι Κ Λ Μ Ν Ξ Ο Π Ρ Σ Τ Υ Φ Χ Ψ Ω

✓ Stress

Where you place the stress in a word is important in Greek as it affects meaning e.g. ταξί means 'taxi' whereas τάξη means 'class' or 'order'. Written Greek always shows with a mark where the word is stressed – be guided by that mark in your pronunciation and learn the stress for each new word. Note that the stress is not shown in words written entirely in capital letters.

✓ Punctuation

In Greek, the semi-colon is used as a question mark.

Τι κάνεις; How are you?

✓ Forms of address

Mr or Sir is Κύριος. When you address a man directly, however, you say Κύριε. Mrs, Ms, or Madam is Κυρία. Miss is Δεσποινίς.

You will have noticed the addition of σου and σας to some of the greetings. These are pronouns, meaning literally 'to you'. σου is the informal singular version used with friends and children. σας is the formal and plural version used with people you don't know or when talking to more than one person.
– σας can be added to all the greetings *except* χαίρετε

γειά σας, καλησπέρα σας, αντίο σας, etc.

ACTIVITY 7

Find the appropriate phrase (a–d) for each situation (1–4).

1 You're saying goodnight to a group of Greek friends.
2 You're greeting your Greek neighbour in the morning.
3 A Greek colleague in your office is going home at the end of the day.
4 You're arriving at your hotel and are greeting the receptionist.

a Καλημέρα, Κυρία Νίτσα, τι κάνετε;
b Χαίρετε.
c Καληνύχτα, παιδιά.
d Γεια σου, Περικλή, στο καλό.

ACTIVITY 8

Practise reading aloud the phrases a–d in Activity 7.

🎧 Now do activities 9 and 10 on the recording.

α β γ δ ε ζ η θ ι κ λ μ ν ξ ο π ρ σ τ υ φ χ ψ ω

1.3 Ordering in a taverna

Στην ταβέρνα

🔘 **ACTIVITY 11** is on the recording.

ACTIVITY 12

A Which of the following phrases do you hear in the dialogue?

1 ευχαριστώ	3 εντάξει	5 καλή όρεξη
2 καλημέρα	4 γειά σας	6 παρακαλώ

B Which of the phrases above would you use:

1 when you leave? 3 on starting a meal?
2 to thank someone?

DIALOGUE 2

○ Ορίστε;

■ Μια σαλάτα και μια πορτοκαλάδα, παρακαλώ.

○ Μάλιστα. Μια σαλάτα και μια πορτοκαλάδα για την κυρία. Και ο κύριος;

▼ Ένα σουβλάκι και μια μπίρα.

○ Ένα σουβλάκι και μια μπίρα. Εντάξει.

○ Λοιπόν. Η σαλάτα και η πορτοκαλάδα για την κυρία ...

■ Ευχαριστώ.

○ Το σουβλάκι και η μπίρα για τον κύριο.

▼ Ευχαριστώ.

○ Καλή όρεξη!

VOCABULARY

στην ταβέρνα	at the taverna
ορίστε	[*here*] may I help you?
μια/η σαλάτα	a/the salad
και	and
μια/η πορτοκαλάδα	an/the orange juice
για	for
μάλιστα	yes [*emphatic*], certainly, of course
ένα/το σουβλάκι	a/the souvlaki [*kind of kebab*]
μια/η μπίρα	a/the beer
εντάξει	OK
λοιπόν	so [*also* therefore]
καλή όρεξη	enjoy your meal

6 Α Β Γ Δ Ε Ζ Η Θ Ι Κ Λ Μ Ν Ξ Ο Π Ρ Σ Τ Υ Φ Χ Ψ Ω

✓ The definite and indefinite articles: ο/η/το – ένας/μια/ένα

In Greek every noun has a gender – it is either masculine, feminine, or neuter – and this affects the accompanying article ('the'/'a'). When you learn a new Greek word, always learn it with its article. This will tell you whether it is masculine, feminine, or neuter.

definite article ('the')

masculine		feminine		neuter	
ο		η		το	

masculine		feminine		neuter	
ο μπαμπάς	dad	η μαμά	mum, mom	το βράδυ	evening
ο κύριος	gentleman, Mr	η γυναίκα	woman	το σουβλάκι	souvlaki
		η μέρα	day	το παιδί	child
ο παπάς	priest	η μπίρα	beer	το ταξί	taxi
ο άνδρας	man			το αυτοκίνητο	car

indefinite article ('a'/'an')

masculine		feminine		neuter	
ένας		μια		ένα	
ένας παπάς	priest	μια σαλάτα	salad	ένα παιδί	child
ένας άνδρας	man	μια γυναίκα	woman	ένα σουβλάκι	souvlaki

ACTIVITY 13

Below are some things to eat and drink. Try recognizing them while reading aloud. Write them in groups according to gender, including the definite article ο, η, or το in each case.

το τζατζίκι, ο μεζές, η τυρόπιτα, το γιαούρτι, ο μουσακάς η ρετσίνα, το κρασί, ο καφές, το τσάι, η λεμονάδα, το ούζο, το σουβλάκι

Now match the Greek with its English equivalent from the following list.

tea, coffee, wine, retsina, ouzo, lemonade, moussaka, tzatziki, yoghurt, souvlaki, cheese pie, meze (snack)

ACTIVITY 14

Order the following using the correct form of the indefinite article (μια, or ένα).

1 A cheese pie and a beer.   2 A tea and a coffee.

🎧 Now do activities 15 and 16 on the recording.

α β γ δ ε ζ η θ ι κ λ μ ν ξ ο π ρ σ τ υ φ χ ψ ω

Let's go to the taverna!

Πάμε στην ταβέρνα!

Wherever you go in Greece, you will not be far from a local taverna, which, despite the trendier venues opening up all over, is still the most popular and established place to have an informal meal with your family or with guests. Food is usually simple, made from locally available seasonal produce, and you are welcome to inspect what's on offer in the kitchen before you make your choice.

There will be plenty of **λάδι** (olive oil), **ρίγανη** (oregano), and **λεμόνι** (lemon) in the cooking, and in the summer, **σαλάτες** (salads), including **μαρούλι** (lettuce) and **χωριάτικη** (a mixed 'Greek salad', with tomatoes, feta, and olives) are found in abundance. **μεζέδες** is an assortment of starters, and can include **ταραμοσαλάτα** (taramosalata) and **καλαμαράκια** (squid). Favourites like **κοτόπουλο** (chicken), **μακαρονάδα** or **παστίτσιο** (pasta dishes), **γεμιστά** (stuffed vegetables), **γιουβέτσι** or **στιφάδο** (meat casseroles), and **ντολμάδες** (stuffed vine leaves) will certainly be on the menu. Popular fish dishes include **μπαρμπούνι** (red mullet) and **μπακαλιάρος** (cod), served with **σκορδαλιά** (a garlic garnish). If you are having something grilled, you are often able to choose your cut of meat, and in **ψαροταβέρνες** (tavernas that specialize in seafood) you can select the particular fish you'd like cooked. The atmosphere is usually bustling and lively and enhanced with a touch of Greek music. To drink, besides water (**νερό**) and soft drinks, there will always be beer and house wine (**κρασί βαρελίσιο** – 'wine of the barrel'). Dessert is usually **φρούτα** (fruit) – perhaps **καρπούζι** (watermelon) or **σταφύλια** (grapes) – or, in winter, one of the honey-nut confections **μπακλαβάς** or **κανταΐφι** with coffee. For a more sophisticated meal, **το εστιατόριο** (the restaurant) is the place to go.

Greeks are accustomed to lunching at around 2 p.m. and they dine late. This accommodates summer working hours: most businesses shut down between 2 and 5 or 6 p.m. because of the heat and then reopen until about 9 p.m. (Banks and government departments, as well as larger companies, are gradually adapting to EU timetables.) Tavernas, however, usually serve food throughout the

Α Β Γ Δ Ε Ζ Η Θ Ι Κ Λ Μ Ν Ξ Ο Π Ρ Σ Τ Υ Φ Χ Ψ Ω

afternoon and evening. To attract the waiter's attention say
Παρακαλώ!

Tavernas do not usually include a standard service charge,
nor is a large tip (**πουρμπουάρ**) expected. Just round off the
amount shown on the bill.

ΤΑΒΕΡΝΑ ΑΦΡΟΔΙΤΗ

ΜΕΖΕΔΕΣ	ΖΕΣΤΑ	ΦΡΟΥΤΑ
Ταραμοσαλάτα	Μουσακάς	Καρπούζι
Καλαμαράκια	Παστίτσιο	Σταφύλια
Τζατζίκι	Ντολμάδες	
	Γεμιστά	ΠΟΤΑ
ΣΑΛΑΤΕΣ	Κοτόπουλο	Κρασί
Ντομάτα	Σουβλάκι	Μπίρα
Μαρούλι		Πορτοκαλάδα
Χωριάτικη		Λεμονάδα
		Κόκακόλα

ζέστα hot dishes   ποτά drinks

ACTIVITY 17

You're at the Taverna Aphrodite with a friend who's
forgotten his reading glasses. Look at the menu and answer
his questions in English.

1 Do they serve beer?
2 Do they only serve hot food?
3 What starters do they have?
4 What salads do they have?

ACTIVITY 18

Look at the menu again. You're at the taverna with two
friends who'd like something to eat and drink, but don't
speak any Greek at all. It's up to you to order for them.
There will be a number of things which are appropriate, so
give them a range to choose from.

Fiona – is not very hungry and she's a vegetarian. She's
very hot and thirsty. She decides to have some fruit and
something non-alcoholic to drink.

Donald – could eat a horse. He'll settle for fish as a starter,
meat as a main course, with a large mixed salad. He'd also
like something alcoholic to drink.

And finally order for yourself.

α β γ δ ε ζ η θ ι κ λ μ ν ξ ο π ρ σ τ υ φ χ ψ ω   **9**

1.5 Στο περίπτερο

 ΠΟ-ΠΟ, ΖΕΣΤΗ!
PHEW, IT'S HOT!

The story focuses on the daily life of a busy Athenian kiosk. It sells everything from newspapers to aspirins, from cold drinks to last-minute gifts. It is the site of all sorts of local gossip and a hub of activity.

In this episode, you'll meet three of the main characters: Kiria Vangelio, who owns the kiosk with her husband, Lakis; Pericles, a local taxi-driver; and Kiria Katina, who runs an office nearby, and is, like Pericles, a regular customer.

Katina has just stopped at the kiosk on her way home.

στο περίπτερο	at the kiosk
συγγνώμη	excuse me
πο-πο	*an expression of surprise*
ζέστη!	it's hot!
τίποτ'άλλο;	anything else?
το κρασί	wine

ACTIVITY 19

Listen to the recording and decide whether the following statements are true or false. Correct the statements which are false.

1 It's evening.	T / F
2 The male customer asks for lemonade.	T / F
3 He's rather rude.	T / F
4 Katina's mother is not well.	T / F
5 Katina has some wine.	T / F
6 Katina takes a taxi.	T / F

ACTIVITY 20

Who's speaking? Match the columns.

1 Αχ, συγγνώμη.		a	Pericles, the taxi-driver
2 Λοιπόν, Κατίνα, η μαμά σου;		b	The male customer
3 Τίποτ'άλλο;		c	Kiria Vangelio
4 Ευχαριστώ για το κρασί!		d	Katina
5 Α-αχ, η μαμά ...		e	Kiria Vangelio

Α Β Γ Δ Ε Ζ Η Θ Ι Κ Λ Μ Ν Ξ Ο Π Ρ Σ Τ Υ Φ Χ Ψ Ω

STORY TRANSCRIPT

Katina	Καλημέρα, κυρία Βαγγελιώ.
Vangelio	Καλημέρα, Κατίνα. Τι κάνεις;
Katina	Καλά …
Man	Αχ, συγγνώμη. Τι κάνετε, κυρία Βαγγελιώ, κυρία Κατίνα; Καλά; Πο-πο, ζέστη. Μία λεμονάδα, παρακαλώ!
Vangelio	Τίποτ'άλλο;
Man	Όχι, ευχαριστώ – αντίο σας!
Vangelio	Λοιπόν, Κατίνα, η μαμά σου;
Katina	Α-αχ, η μαμά …
Vangelio	Έναν καφέ, Κατίνα;
Pericles	Γειά σας, γειά σας! Κυρία Βαγγελιώ, ευχαριστώ για το κρασί!
A distant voice	Να το το ταξί. Ταξί, ταξί!

Test

Now it's time to test your progress in Unit 1.

1 Match the following words and phrases with their English equivalents.

1	ευχαριστώ	a	enjoy your meal
2	καλησπέρα	b	good evening
3	γειά σας	c	good night
4	εντάξει	d	thank you
5	αντίο	e	goodbye
6	καληνύχτα	f	please
7	καλή όρεξη	g	hello
8	παρακαλώ	h	OK

8

2 Pair up 1–6 with the correct response from a–f to make six mini-dialogues.

1 Τι κάνετε;
2 Αντίο!
3 Καλή όρεξη!
4 Καλησπέρα σας.
5 Ένα σουβλάκι;
6 Τίποτ'άλλο;

a Μάλιστα.
b Χαίρετε, κυρία Βαγγελιώ.
c Στο καλό!
d Πολύ καλά.
e Ευχαριστώ.
f Όχι, ευχαριστώ.

6

3 Use **ένα** or **μια**, as appropriate, to complete the following dialogue.

○ Η κυρία;
■ _____ γιαούρτι και _____ πορτοκαλάδα, παρακαλώ.
Όχι, _____ σουβλάκι και _____ κρασί.
○ Μάλιστα. Και ο κύριος;
▼ _____ παστίτσιο και _____ μπίρα, παρακαλώ.
■ Εντάξει.

6

4 Fill in the correct definite article, **o**, **η**, or **το** before each of the following nouns.

1 _____ κύριος
2 _____ κυρία
3 _____ βράδυ
4 _____ ταξί
5 _____ άνδρας
6 _____ ταβέρνα
7 _____ αυτοκίνητο
8 _____ γυναίκα

8

5 Complete the words.

1 ΤΑ-Ι   6 μπα- - άς
2 ΚΑ-ΗΜΕ-Α   7 - αίρετε
3 ΣΟΥ-ΛΑΚΙ   8 ε - χαριστώ
4 Ε- -ΑΞΕΙ   9 τ - ατ - ίκι
5 ΠΑ-ΑΚΑΛΩ

9

6 Give the appropriate Greek phrase.

1 Ask a friend how she is.
2 Order a salad and a coke in a taverna.
3 Order a souvlaki and a beer in a taverna.
4 Say 'goodbye' and 'take care' to someone.
5 Greet a group of Greek people in the evening and ask them how they are.
6 Greet the hotel receptionist in the morning and indicate that you're fine.
7 Thank somebody for the wine.
8 Say 'yes' emphatically.

8

TOTAL SCORE 45

If you scored less than 35, go through the dialogues and the Language Building sections again before completing the Summary on page 14.

Summary 1

Now try this final test summarizing the main points covered in this unit. You can check your answers on the recording.

How would you:
1. greet someone during the day? in the evening?
2. say 'good bye' and 'good night'?
3. say 'please' and 'thank you'?
4. order a cheese pie and a tea?
5. say 'enjoy your meal'?
6. spell your full name in Greek aloud? and write it out?

REVISION

Before moving on to Unit 2, play Unit 1 through again and compare what you can say and understand now with what you knew when you started. Go over any vocabulary you still feel unsure of. Check that you are comfortable with the Greek alphabet by reading out some Greek text from the dialogues in this unit.

Once you have worked through the next few units, come back to Unit 1 again. It will help you reinforce what you have learnt.

2

▷ ▷ ▷ ▷ ▷ ▷ ▷ ▷ ▷ ▷ ▷ ▷ ▷ ▷

Finding your way

Πού είναι;

> **OBJECTIVES**
>
> In this unit you'll learn how to:
>
> ✓ ask the way to various places
>
> ✓ ask if somewhere is open or closed
>
> ✓ understand and give simple directions
>
> ✓ say you don't know
>
> ✓ count from 1 to 10
>
> And cover the following grammar and language:
>
> ✓ the verb είμαι ('am')
>
> ✓ υπάρχει ('there is')
>
> ✓ the preposition στο ('in', 'on', 'at')
>
> ✓ negative forms
>
> ✓ the numbers 1–10 and 1st–10th

LEARNING GREEK 2

Each unit has been divided into manageable sections (2.1, 2.2, 2.3, etc.), so it is a good idea to aim to do one complete section at a time, then stop to practise and learn the vocabulary. You will find that you can learn more effectively that way.

It also helps if you can learn with someone else. If you can persuade a friend or family member to study with you, it will give you an extra impetus to keep working. Agree times to meet and goals for the week, and test each other regularly.

Now start the recording for Unit 2.

15

Το Ξενοδοχείο "Ο Θανάσης"

 **ACTIVITY 1** is on the recording.

ACTIVITY 2

Correct the statements which are false.

1 They drive past the taverna.	T / F
2 The bank is far away.	T / F
3 The Internet Café is near the Thanasis Hotel.	T / F

DIALOGUE 1

○ Α! Η πλατεία!

■ Ναι, και η εκκλησία.

○ Λοιπόν, πού είναι το ξενοδοχείο "Ο Θανάσης";

■ Είναι εδώ κοντά – νά το, εκεί, αριστερά.

○ Α, μάλιστα. Πού είναι η τράπεζα;

■ Δεν είναι μακριά – δυο-τρία λεπτά - εκεί, δεξιά.

○ Εντάξει, Ευχαριστώ πολύ. … Συγγνώμη, υπάρχει Internet Café εδώ κοντά;

■ Δυστυχώς, όχι . Αλλά υπάρχει ένα στο κέντρο.

VOCABULARY

η πλατεία	(town/city) square
η εκκλησία	church
πού είναι … ;	where is …?
εδώ	here
κοντά	near, nearby
νά το!	there it is!
εκεί	there
αριστερά	(on the) left
η τράπεζα	bank
δεν	(do) not [*used to make verbs negative*]
μακριά	far
δυο or δύο	two
τρία	three
λεπτά	minutes
δεξιά	(on the) right
συγγνώμη	excuse me
δυστυχώς	unfortunately
αλλά	but
στο κέντρο	in the centre

Α Β Γ Δ Ε Ζ Η Θ Ι Κ Λ Μ Ν Ξ Ο Π Σ Τ Υ Φ Χ Ψ Ω

LANGUAGE BUILDING

✓ **είμαι ('am') – irregular**

είμαι	I am	είμαστε	we are
είσαι	you are	είσαστε (είστε)	you are
είναι	he/she/it is	είναι	they are

Πού είσαι; Where are you?
Είμαι στο κέντρο. I am in the (town) centre.

✓ **υπάρχει ('there is')**

To ask if there is a bank/bakery/church/bookshop nearby, you simply say:

Υπάρχει τράπεζα/ φούρνος/εκκλησία/βιβλιοπωλείο εδώ κοντά;

Note that this structure needs no article in Greek.
You use the same phrase to reply:

Υπάρχει καφενείο δίπλα. There's a café next door.
Υπάρχει ξενοδοχείο εκεί, δεξιά. There's a hotel there, on the right.

To answer that there isn't a bank/bakery, etc., you add δεν before the verb: this is how to make any sentence negative in Greek.

Δεν υπάρχει σουπερμάρκετ/πάρκο στο κέντρο. There isn't a supermarket/park in the centre.
Δεν υπάρχει σταθμός/ ταχυδρομείο. There isn't a station/post office.

ACTIVITY 3

Write the following in Greek.

1 The church is there.
2 The hotel isn't far.
3 Where is the bank?
4 They're not here.
5 Where is the bookshop?

ACTIVITY 4

Imagine you're jotting down a brief note for a visitor to your neighbourhood. Write a couple of sentences about the facilities using Υπάρχει / Δεν υπάρχει and including some of the prepositions you have learned.
Example: Υπάρχει τράπεζα και δίπλα υπάρχει ταχυδρομείο, αλλά δεν υπάρχει περίπτερο.

🎧 Now do activities 5 and 6 on the recording.

α β γ δ ε ζ η θ ι κ λ μ ν ξ ο π ρ σ τ υ φ χ ψ ω

Αριστερά, δεξιά!

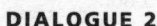 **ACTIVITY 7** is on the recording.

ACTIVITY 8
On the sketch, mark the
route to the chemist's
described by the couple.

Try also to identify
(1) the chemist's, (2) the
café, (3) the cinema.

DIALOGUE 2

○ Με συγχωρείτε, μήπως
ξέρετε πού είναι το φαρμακείο;

■ Κοντά είναι. Αλλά δεν ξερω αν είναι ανοιχτό.

▼ Θα πάτε ευθεία και θα στρίψετε αριστερά στο δεύτερο
στενό ... α, όχι, στο τρίτο – στη γωνία στο καφενείο.

■ Το φαρμακείο είναι δίπλα στο καφενείο ...

▼ Και υπάρχει ένα σινεμά απέναντι.

VOCABULARY	
με συγχωρείτε	excuse me
μήπως ξέρετε ... ;	do you know ...? [*formal*]
το φαρμακείο	chemist's, pharmacy, drugstore
αλλά	but
δεν ξέρω	I don't know
αν	if
ανοιχτό	open
θα πάτε	(you) go
ευθεία	straight
θα στρίψετε	(you) turn
στο	at [*with neuter nouns*]
δεύτερο	second
το στενό	side-street
τρίτο	third
στη	at [*with feminine nouns*]
η γωνία	corner
το καφενείο	café, coffee shop
το σινεμά	cinema, movies
απέναντι	opposite, across the road

Α Β Γ Δ Ε Ζ Η Θ Ι Κ Λ Μ Ν Ξ Ο Π Ρ Σ Τ Υ Φ Χ Ψ Ω

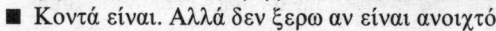

✓ στο ('in', 'on', 'at')

The preposition στο changes form to agree with the noun it accompanies. It takes the same ending as the definite article: στο(ν) / στη(ν) / στο.

ο σταθμός	στο σταθμό – *at* the station (the final 's' is dropped from the masculine noun); ν is added if the word following starts with a vowel, κ, τ, π, ψ, or ξ: στον κατάλογο
η γωνία	στη γωνία; + ν as above, e.g. στην εκκλησία
το στενό	στο στενό

✓ Negative forms

Verbs are made negative by the addition of δεν: δεν ξέρω ('I don't know').

Words other than verbs: όχι is used: όχι εδώ – έκει ('not here – there').

The negative imperative ('don't!') is μη! or μην! if the next word starts with a vowel or κ, τ, π, ψ, or ξ.

Μην πάτε έκει! Don't go there!   Μη στρίψετε εδώ! Don't turn here!

The word for nought or zero is μηδέν.

✓ Giving directions

In Greek, directions are usually given in the form θα + the verb.

Θα πάτε ίσια. (You) go straight.
Θα στρίψετε στο πρώτο στενό. (You) turn at the first side-street.
Θα πάρετε το δεύτερο δρόμο. (You) take the second road.

ACTIVITY 9

Match the phrase with the appropriate signpost.

1 ΑΡΙΣΤΕΡΑ
2 ΑΝΟΙΧΤΟ
3 ΜΗ ΣΤΡΙΨΕΤΕ ΔΕΞΙΑ

4 ΣΙΝΕΜΑ ΕΔΩ
5 ΜΗΝ ΠΑΤΕ ΕΥΘΕΙΑ

(a)   (b)   (c)

(d)   (e)

🎧 Now do activities 11 and 12 on the recording.

α β γ δ ε ζ η θ ι κ λ μ ν ξ ο π ρ σ τ υ φ χ ψ ω

Ένα, δύο, τρία, ...

 **ACTIVITY 12** is on the recording.

ACTIVITY 13

Three details in the following summary of Dialogue 3 are inaccurate. Listen and correct them

Two people are standing on Alexandras Avenue and Pedhion tou Areos is up on the left. To get to the Archaeological Museum they should go straight until they reach the corner – Polytechneio Street. There they turn right. Then they go straight down. It's quite far. The Archaeological Museum is next to the Polytechnic.

DIALOGUE 3

○ Πού είμαστε;

■ Φφ, Λεωφόρος Αλεξάνδρας – το Πεδίον του Άρεως είναι εκεί πάνω, δεξιά.

○ Και πού είναι το Αρχαιολογικό Μουσείο;

■ Θα πάμε ευθεία μέχρι τη γωνία ...οδός Πατησίων.

○ Α, ναι, η οδός Πατησίων.

■ Εκεί θα στρίψουμε αριστερά.

○ Α, μάλιστα ... και θα πάμε ίσια κάτω ...δεν είναι μακριά.

■ Το Αρχαιολογικό Μουσείο είναι δίπλα στο Πολυτεχνείο.

VOCABULARY	
η λεωφόρος	avenue
το Πεδίον του Άρεως	*a park, named* Field of Ares
πάνω	up
εκεί πάνω,	up there
το Αρχαιολογικό Μουσείο	the Archaeological Museum
θα πάμε	we go
μέχρι	as far as, until
η οδός	street
θα στρίψουμε	we turn
κάτω	down
ίσια κάτω	straight down
μακριά	far
το Πολυτεχνείο	the Polytechnic

Α Β Γ Δ Ε Ζ Η Θ Ι Κ Λ Μ Ν Ξ Ο Π Ρ Σ Τ Υ Φ Χ Ψ Ω

✓ The numbers 1 to 10

1 ένα	3 τρία	5 πέντε	7 εφτά	9 εννιά
2 δύο	4 τέσσερα	6 έξι	8 οχτώ	10 δέκα

✓ The numbers 1st to 10th

Like other adjectives, ordinal numbers change ending depending on the noun they accompany. Adjective agreement will be covered in detail in the section on adjectives on page 63.

1st	πρώτος	ο **πρώτος** δρόμος
2nd	δεύτερος	η **δεύτερη** γωνία
3rd	τρίτος	το **τρίτο** στενό

4th	τέταρτος	8th	όγδοος
5th	πέμπτος	9th	ένατος
6th	έκτος	10th	δέκατος
7th	έβδομος		

✓ Street names

Note that streets are often referred to by name alone, i.e. without the word Street or Avenue (η οδός / η λεωφόρος).

Το σουπερμάρκετ είναι **στην Πατησίων**. The supermarket is on Patision (Street).

Θα πάρετε τη Σταδίου. You take Stadiou (Street).

ACTIVITY 14

Match 1–5 with the appropriate Greek version from a–e.

1 We're at the station.

2 Don't turn here!

3 He's at the corner.
4 At the first road on the right.
5 The pharmacy is closed.

a Στο πρώτο δρόμο δεξιά.

b Το φαρμακείο είναι κλειστό

c Μη στρίψετε εδώ!
d Είμαστε στο σταθμό.
e Είναι στη γωνία.

ACTIVITY 15

The following throws were made in a game of backgammon (τάβλι) in your local καφενείο. What are the totals in Greek?

1 Petros: 4 + 6   3 Vangelis: 2 + 5
2 Spiros: 7 + 1   4 Kostas: 6 + 3

Now do activities 16 and 17 on the recording.

21

α β γ δ ε ζ η θ ι κ λ μ ν ξ ο π ρ σ τ υ φ χ ψ ω

2.4 On the road

Στο δρόμο

On entering Greece, depending on your citizenship, you will require a passport (**διαβατήριο**) or some other form of travel ID (**ταυτότητα**). Once you have passed though customs (**τελωνείο**), found the toilets (**τουαλέτες** or **αποχωρητήρια**), and sorted out some foreign exchange (**συνάλλαγμα**), you will probably be ready to take to the road. If you are driving, remember to drive on the right (**δεξιά**) and be prepared for hair-raising traffic conditions. **ΕΛΠΑ** is the Greek Automobile Association. International roadsigns apply, but look out for warnings in Greek.

| It is forbidden | **ΑΠΑΓΟΡΕΥΕΤΑΙ** |
| Danger | **ΚΙΝΔΥΝΟΣ** |

Also useful:

Entrance	**ΕΙΣΟΔΟΣ**
Exit	**ΕΞΟΔΟΣ**
Open	**ΑΝΟΙΧΤΟ**
Closed	**ΚΛΕΙΣΤΟ**

Although it may appear haphazard, public transport is fairly efficient, extensive, and inexpensive. If you are going to travel by boat, but have not arranged your tickets (**εισιτήρια**) beforehand, information (**πληροφορίες**) on destinations, fares, departure times, and the like is available at the small agencies (**πρακτορεία**) set up on the waterfront at the harbour (**λιμάνι**).

ACTIVITY 18

You are taking your friends out on Saturday. Carol is interested in Greek antiquities – particularly the Minoan civilization of Crete, **η Μινωική Κρήτη**. Bill would like to try Greek cuisine – he enjoys seafood. Look at the selection opposite and decide which outing would best suit (1) Carol and (2) Bill.

(a)

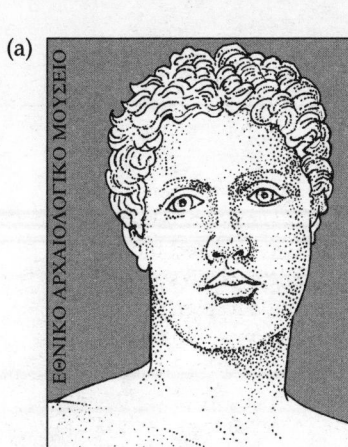

ΕΘΝΙΚΟ ΑΡΧΑΙΟΛΟΓΙΚΟ ΜΟΥΣΕΙΟ

Πατησίων 44   τηλ. 8217717
Αρχαία ελληνική τέχνη

(b)

ΕΛΛΗΝΙΚΗ ΚΟΥΖΙΝΑ

Ταβέρνα *Ο Γλάρος*
         τηλ. 3637905

Ψάρι και θαλασσινά

(c)

ΔΙΕΘΝΗΣ ΚΟΥΖΙΝΑ

Μεζεδοπωλείο *Ελ Τόρο*   τηλ. 6320910
Μεζέδες από τη Μεσόγειο - Αφρική

(d)

ΜΟΥΣΕΙΟ ΚΥΚΛΑΔΙΚΗΣ ΤΕΧΝΗΣ

Νεοφύτου Δούκα 4, Κολωνάκι   τηλ. 7228321 - 3

Η Μινωική Κρήτη στην Αθήνα 3 - 31 Μαΐου
Μεγάλη έκθεση με αντικείμενα από το
μουσείο Ηρακλείου

η τέχνη	art
από όλες τις εποχές	from all ages
το ψάρι	fish
διεθνής	international
το μεζεδοπωλείο	place that sells/serves mezedes
η Μεσόγειο(ς)	Mediterranean
η έκθεση	exhibition
αντικείμενα	articles
το μουσείο Ηρακλείου	the museum of Iraklio

α β γ δ ε ζ η θ ι κ λ μ ν ξ ο π ρ σ τ υ φ χ ψ ω

2.5 Στο περίπτερο

 ΕΙΣΤΕ ΞΕΝΟΣ;
ARE YOU FOREIGN?

Pericles is talking to the passenger he's just picked up.

ο ξένος	foreigner
ο φίλος	friend
ο Σκοτσέζος	a Scot
ο φίλος μου	my friend
βεβαίως	of course

ACTIVITY 19

Listen to the recording and write down whether the following statements are true or false. Correct the statements which are false.

1 They are a long way from the museum.	T / F
2 The man is from Scotland.	T / F
3 The man's name is Petros.	T / F
4 Pericles has a friend in Loch Ness.	T / F
5 Kiria Vangelio's kiosk is opposite the museum.	T / F
6 Craig and Pericles have a mutual friend.	T / F

ACTIVITY 20

Choose the correct answer.

1 Ο Κραίηγκ είναι
   a στο ταξί.
   b στο Αρχαιολογικό Μουσείο.

2 Το Αρχαιολογικό Μουσείο
   a είναι μακριά.
   b είναι κοντά.

3 Ο Περικλής είναι
   a Σκοτσέζος.
   b Έλληνας.

4 Ο Πέτρος είναι
   a στο Λοχ-Νες.
   b στο Εδιμβούργο.

Α Β Γ Δ Ε Ζ Η Θ Ι Κ Λ Μ Ν Ξ Ο Π Ρ Σ Τ Υ Φ Χ Ψ Ω

STORY TRANSCRIPT

Man [Craig]	Ταξί!
Pericles	Ορίστε, πού πάτε;
Craig	Στο Αρχαιολογικό Μουσείο, παρακαλώ.
Pericles	Εντάξει.
Craig	Η οδός Πατησίων είναι μακριά;
Pericles	Εδώ κοντά είναι.
	...
Pericles	Είστε ξένος;
Craig	Μάλιστα, Σκοτσέζος.
Pericles	Αα, ναι – Λοχ-Νες!
Craig	Όχι, Εδιμβούργο.
Pericles	Εδιμβούργο, ε; Ο φίλος μου, ο Πέτρος, είναι στο Εδιμβούργο.
Craig	Μμμμ; .... Μήπως ξέρετε ένα περίπτερο εδώ κοντά – η κυρία Βαγγελιώ ...
Pericles	Βεβαίως – εκεί κάτω είναι, στο τρίτο στενό - στη γωνία. Η Βαγγελιώ είναι η μαμά ...
	...
Craig	Και νάτο το μουσείο ... Ξέρετε, ο Πέτρος, είναι φίλος μου στο Εδιμβούργο ...

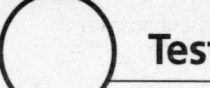

Test

Now it's time to test your progress in Unit 2.

1 Match the 1–10 with the appropriate English translation from a–j.

1	η τράπεζα	a	hotel
2	το καφενείο	b	chemist's
3	ο φούρνος	c	café
4	το ξενοδοχείο	d	post office
5	το βιβλιοπωλείο	e	bakery
6	ο σταθμός	f	church
7	το Πολυτεχνείο	g	bank
8	το φαρμακείο	h	station
9	το ταχυδρομείο	i	bookshop
10	η εκκλησία	j	polytechnic

10

2 Which of the words in Activity 1 are feminine and which are masculine?

4

3 Match the words with the appropriate direction.

1 ίσια   2 δεξιά   3 αριστερά

A ⟵ _____

B ⟶ _____

C ⟶ _____

3

4 Complete the sentences with the correct form of **είμαι**.

1 Ο φούρνος _____ στη γωνία.
2 Χαίρετε. _____ καλά;
3 Με συγχωρείτε, το ταχυδρομείο _____ ανοιχτό;
4 Αχ, Πέτρο, εγώ δεν _____ καλά!
5 Ο Περικλής και η Κατίνα _____ στο περίπτερο.

5

5 Complete the sentences with the appropriate word from the box.

> Συγγνώμη μέχρι Δυστυχώς νάτο Μήπως

1 _____ ξέρετε πού είναι η πλατεία;
2 Το φαρμακείο δεν είναι μακριά – _____ εκεί πάνω.
3 Υπάρχει τουαλέτα εδώ κοντά; _____ δεν ξέρω.
4 _____, πού είναι το ταχυδρομείο;
5 Θα πάτε _____ το φούρνο και θα στρίψετε δεξιά.

5

6 Decide whether you need the definite article, **στο**, or nothing at all to complete the sentences. Remember to supply the correct form of the article/**στο** as necessary.

1 _____ μουσείο είναι _____ οδό Πατησίων.
2 _____ τράπεζα είναι _____ γωνία.
3 Πού είναι _____ λεωφόρος Αλεξάνδρας;
4 Είσαστε _____ σταθμό;
5 Υπάρχει _____ φούρνος δίπλα.

7

7 How would you say the following in Greek?
(2 points for each answer, 1 if you make one mistake)

1 Where is the bank, please?
2 Is there a post office nearby?
3 Do you know where the Barbara Hotel is?
4 You take the first side-street on the right.
5 There's a bank next door.
6 You go left.

12

TOTAL SCORE **46**

If you scored less than 36, go through the dialogues and the Language Building sections before completing the Summary on page 28.

Summary 2

Now try this final test summarizing the main points
covered in this unit. You can check your answers on the
recording.

How would you:
1 ask the way to the station?
2 ask whether there is a post office nearby?
3 say there's a bookshop on the corner?
4 say that the bank is opposite?
5 tell someone to turn left at the second side-street?
6 tell someone to go as far as the park?
7 tell someone not to go straight on?
8 count from one to ten?

REVISION

A considerable amount of vocabulary has been covered in
this unit. To practise both your writing and reading skills, it
would be useful to start a vocabulary file. The way you
manage your vocabulary is up to you. Decide whether you
want a portable notebook, for quick and easy reference, or
a box of cards or a file on your computer to use for more
detailed review at home. You'll probably order the words
alphabetically, but you may also find it useful to group
them by topic, as a context can make memorizing
vocabulary easier.

Pleased to meet you

Χαίρω πολύ

OBJECTIVES

In this unit you'll learn how to:

- ✓ introduce yourself, tell people your name
- ✓ say where you live and where you come from
- ✓ say what you do for a living
- ✓ count from 11 to 20

And cover the following grammar and language:

- ✓ the present tense of Group 1 verbs
- ✓ the question form τι; ('what?')
- ✓ adjectives of nationality
- ✓ the question πόσον καιρό; ('how long?')
- ✓ the prepositions από ('from') and σε ('in')

LEARNING GREEK 3

Before attempting the dialogue activities, always try listening to the recordings several times and only then look at the transcript in your book. This will give you a feel for the language and train you to listen to detail. Even when you feel you haven't understood very much, try doing the activities anyway. Write down some kind of answer, and don't look at the answer section until you've had a go, even if you consider it only to be a guess. Guesswork is an important strategy in learning a new language and it is no use learning parrot-fashion, relying on memory alone. The key to communicating is always to understand the gist of the situation and say as much as you can in response.

Now start the recording for Unit 3.

29

Πώς σας λένε;

🔊 **ACTIVITY 1** is on the recording.

ACTIVITY 2

1 The man lives
   a next door   b opposite   c in the town centre.
2 The man works
   a at the university   b in an office in Athens
   c in an office in Galatsi.
3 The man's name is
   a Takis Eleftheros   b Takis Eleftheriou.
4 Christina is
   a a lawyer   b an office worker   c a student.

DIALOGUE 1

○ Μένετε εδώ κοντά;
■ Ναι, μένω ακριβώς απέναντι.
○ Πώς σας λένε;
■ Με λένε Τάκη Ελευθερίου.
○ Και τι δουλειά κάνετε;
■ Είμαι δικηγόρος.
○ Δουλεύετε στην Αθήνα;
■ Ναι – δουλεύω στο κέντρο. Έχω γραφείο εκεί.
   Αλλά μένω εδώ στο Γαλάτσι. Κι εσείς;
○ Με λένε Χριστίνα και είμαι φοιτήτρια στο πανεπιστήμιο.
■ Χαίρω πολύ.

VOCABULARY	
μένω	I live
ακριβώς	exactly, right
τι;	what?
η δουλειά	work
κάνω	I do, I make
ο δικηγόρος	lawyer
δουλεύω	I work
έχω	I have
το γραφείο	office
εσείς	you [formal or plural]
η φοιτήτρια	student [female]
το πανεπιστήμιο	university

LANGUAGE BUILDING

✓ Group 1 verbs

There are 2 kinds of regular verbs in Greek – Group 1 and Group 2. *Group 2* consists of (a) all verbs that end in -άω, such as μιλάω ('speak', 'talk'), αγαπάω ('love'), and πονάω ('hurt') and (b) verbs that end in –ώ, such as οδηγώ ('drive'), αργώ ('delay'), and καλώ ('invite'). (See Unit 5.) *Group 1* consists of all other regular verbs: that is, verbs which are not stressed on the last syllable. You have already met κάνω ('do'), μένω ('stay'), έχω ('have'), and δουλεύω ('work'). There are a few *irregular* verbs (listed separately in the glossary). You will need to learn these individually.

The Greek present tense can be translated in one of two ways, depending on the context, either 'I work' or 'I'm working'.

Greek verbs are made up of a *stem + endings*. The ending tells you who is doing the action so that the subject pronoun is not generally needed. To form the present tense of Group 1 verbs add the following endings to the stem (the 'I' form without the -ω ending).

ξέρω – I know

ξέρω	I know	ξέρουμε	we know
ξέρεις	you know [*sing., informal*]	ξέρετε	you know [*pl., formal*]
ξέρει	he/she/it knows	ξέρουν(ε) *	they know

*Note that the final ε is often dropped here.

- In the dictionary, Greek verbs are given in the 'I' form (which always ends in -ω), thus κάνω, θέλω, έχω, and so on.
- Regular verbs have 2 stems. The second stem is used to form other tenses and constructions, which will be introduced later in the course. Irregular verbs sometimes have a third stem.
- There are two ways of addressing people directly: For children and people you know well, you use the 'you' singular form (ξέρεις). For people you don't know well, you use the 'you' plural (ξέρετε).

✓ Question forms

τι; means 'what?' **Τι δουλειά κάνετε;** What work do you do? However, to ask a person's name, you say **Πώς σας λένε;** or, informally, **Πώς σε λένε;** The answer to both questions is **Με λένε** ...

Note that as the *subject* of the sentence, masculine names end in 's'. In all other cases they lose the 's'. e.g. **Με λένε Τάκη.**

ACTIVITY 3

Identify the stem in: θέλω, έχω, δουλεύω
Now write out in Greek the full versions of these verbs.

 Now do activites 4 and 5 on the recording.

Από πού είσαστε;

🔊 **ACTIVITY 6** is on the recording.

ACTIVITY 7

Correct the statements which are false.

1 Christina is a Greek.	T / F
2 Christina is from far away.	T / F
3 Christina is studying in Athens.	T / F
4 Christina is studying modern Greek and philosophy.	T / F
5 Takis lives in Cyprus.	T / F

DIALOGUE 2

○ Είσαστε Αμερικανίδα;

■ Όχι, δεν είμαι από τόσο μακριά!

○ Αλήθεια; Από πού είσαστε;

■ Είμαι από την Αγγλία αλλά σπουδάζω εδώ, στην Αθήνα.

○ Έτσι ε; Και τι ακριβώς σπουδάζετε;

■ Σπουδάζω αρχαία ελληνικά και φιλοσοφία.

○ Πολύ ωραία. Και μένετε μακριά;

■ Μένω στο Κουκάκι, κοντά στην Ακρόπολη. ... Εσείς από πού είσαστε;

○ Τώρα μένω στην Αθήνα, αλλά είμαι από την Κύπρο.

VOCABULARY

Αμερικανίδα	American woman
αλήθεια;	really? is that true?
από	from
τόσο μακριά	so far (away)
έτσι, ε;	is that so?
σπουδάζω	I study, I am studying
πολύ ωραία	very nice
αρχαία ελληνικά	ancient Greek
φιλοσοφία	philosophy
Κουκάκι	Koukaki [*an area in the centre of Athens*]
η Ακρόπολη	the Acropolis
τώρα	now
η Κύπρος	Cyprus

✓ Saying where you come from

Country		Nationality (m/f)	Language
England	η Αγγλία	ο Άγγλος / η Αγγλίδα	αγγλικά
America	η Αμερική	ο Αμερικάνος / η Αμερικανίδα	αγγλικά
Australia	η Αυστραλία	ο Αυστραλός / η Αυστραλέζα	αγγλικά
France	η Γαλλία	ο Γάλλος / η Γαλλίδα	γαλλικά
Germany	η Γερμανία	ο Γερμανός / η Γερμανίδα	γερμανικά
Greece	η Ελλάδα	ο Έλληνας / η Ελληνίδα	ελληνικά
Ireland	η Ιρλανδία	ο Ιρλανδός / η Ιρλανδέζα	ιρλανδικά
Spain	η Ισπανία	ο Ισπανός / η Ισπανίδα	ισπανικά
Italy	η Ιταλία	ο Ιταλός / η Ιταλίδα	ιταλικά
Canada	ο Καναδάς	ο Καναδός / η Καναδέζα	αγγλικά / γαλλικά
China	η Κίνα	ο Κινέζος / η Κινέζα	κινέζικα
Cyprus	η Κύπρος	ο Κύπριος / η Κύπρια	ελληνικά / τούρκικα
Russia	η Ρωσία	ο Ρώσος / η Ρωσίδα	ρωσικά

To say which country you come from, you use the preposition από. This is followed by the object-form of the definite article and the noun (with the appropriate ending, depending on the gender). This object-form, known as the accusative case, will be covered in detail later in the course. For now learn the following common forms.

Είμαι από την Αμερική. I'm from America.
Είμαι από την Βρετανία. I'm from Britain.
Είμαι από τον Καναδά. I'm from Canada.

✓ Talking about what you do

Είμαι γιατρός/διευθυντής/γραμματέας/μηχανικός. I'm a doctor/manager/teacher/engineer.

Note that there's no article in this structure.
To say 'in a bank', 'in a factory', etc., you use σε without an article, in place of στο ('in *the* bank, etc.). (You might also hear σε μία τράπεζα.)

Δουλεύω σε τράπεζα/εργοστάσιο/νοσοκομείο/ γραφείο. I work in a bank/factory/hospital/office.

ACTIVITY 8

Write down the following sentences in Greek.

1 I'm English.
2 She's Greek.
3 I know French.
4 Canada is far.
5 He doesn't know Greek.
6 Do you live in Ireland?

 Now do activities 9 and 10 on the recording.

Πόσον καιρό;

🎧 **ACTIVITY 11** is on the recording.

ACTIVITY 12

1 How long has Takis lived in Greece?
2 Does Christina know Greek well?
3 Which is better, her modern or her ancient Greek?
4 How long has she been studying ancient Greek?
5 Where has she studied ancient Greek?

DIALOGUE 3

- ■ Πόσον καιρό μένετε στην Ελλάδα;
- ○ Ου – πολύ καιρό. Είκοσι χρόνια, και. Εσείς;
- ■ Εγώ μένω στην Αθήνα δύο χρόνια.
- ○ Και ξέρετε καλά ελληνικά!
- ■ Αα, όχι, ξέρω μόνο λίγα νέα ελληνικά.
- ○ Αλλά αρχαία ... ;
- ■ Αρχαία ελληνικά ξέρω καλύτερα.
- ○ Πόσον καιρό σπουδάζετε αρχαία ελληνικά;
- ■ Δώδεκα χρόνια.
- ○ Στο πανεπιστήμιο στο Μπέρμιγκχαμ και στην Αθήνα;
- ■ Ναι. Και τρία χρόνια στην Θεσσαλονίκη.
- ○ Μπράβο! Ξέρετε την Ελλάδα αρκετά καλά!
- ■ Ίσως.

VOCABULARY	
πολύ καιρό	a long time
είκοσι χρόνια, και	twenty years plus
μόνο	only
λίγα	a little, a few
νέα	modern, contemporary
αρχαία	ancient
καλύτερα	better
δώδεκα χρόνια	twelve years
Θεσσαλονίκη	Salonica
μπράβο!	well done!
αρκετά καλά	quite well
ίσως	perhaps

✅ Numbers 11 to 20

11	έντεκα	16	δεκαέξι
12	δώδεκα	17	δεκαεφτά
13	δεκατρία	18	δεκαοχτώ
14	δεκατέσσερα	19	δεκαεννέα
15	δεκαπέντε	20	είκοσι

✅ πόσον καιρό; ('how long?')

πόσον καιρό + the present tense is used to ask about an action which began in the past and which continues in the present.

Πόσον καιρό μένετε εδώ; How long have you lived here?
Πόσον καιρό δουλεύετε εδώ; How long have you worked here?

The present tense is used in reply to these questions too. Note that the English word 'for' is not translated.

Μένω εδώ τρία χρόνια. I've lived here for three years.

λίγο καιρό	a little while
πολύ καιρό	a long while
αρκετό καιρό	quite a while
δέκα χρόνια	ten years

ACTIVITY 13

Choose the right number from the box.

δεκαέξι δεκαεννέα έντεκα δεκατρία
είκοσι δεκαεφτά δεκαοχτώ

1 8 + 9 =   5 1 + 19 =
2 17 + 2 =   6 7 + 4 =
3 11 + 5 =   7 5 + 8 =
4 6 +12 =

ACTIVITY 14

Answer the following questions about yourself.
Example: Πόσον καιρό μένετε εδώ;
           Μένω εδώ δύο χρόνια.

1 Πόσον καιρό δουλεύετε εδώ;
2 Πόσον καιρό μένετε στην Αγγλία;
3 Πόσον καιρό σπουδάζετε ελληνικά;
4 Πόσον καιρό ξέρετε το δικηγόρο σας;

 Now do activities 15 and 16 on the recording.

35

3.4 Come to Greece

Ελάτε στην Ελλάδα

η **φιλοξενία** is the Greek for 'hospitality', derived from the words **φίλος** 'friend', and **ξένος** 'stranger/foreigner'. Greeks generally treat the reception of visitors seriously, perhaps because of their history as a sea-faring people (**ναυτικός λαός**) and thus their status as strangers abroad themselves. They have come to pride themselves on their hospitality. Whether tucked away on some distant, 'undiscovered' island (**το νησί**) or in the hub of downtown Athens, Greeks tend to be curious about and to welcome strangers. **Καλώς ήρθατε** or **Καλώς ορίσατε** are the much-used phrases of welcome.

Travellers' tales over the ages tell of the tasty morsel (**το μεζεδάκι**) and the shelter (**το καταφύγιο**) offered by local people to visitors. This hospitable impulse manifests itself today in the contemporary tourist industry (**ο τουρισμός**). While often generous to an embarrassing fault, a Greek is aware of unwritten codes of interaction. Abuse of hospitality is treated with some contempt. An idea associated with **φιλοξενία** is **φιλότιμο**. Literally, it means 'love of honour/trust/value'. It involves mutual respect and 'doing the right thing' as the situation requires.

ACTIVITY 17

Look at this selection from a book catalogue. It includes Greek books and British books in translation.

1 Match the English translation with the book cover.
2 Write down the author in each case.

1 *I, Victoria*
2 *The Van*
3 *My Sweet Loula*
4 *The House of Death*
5 *The Information*
6 *The Thieving Magpie (The Robber Bride)*

CULTURE

A

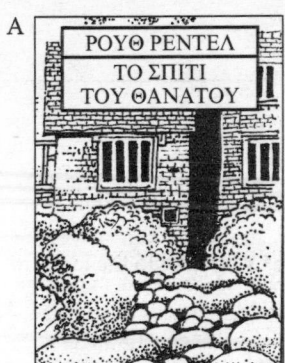

ΡΟΥΘ ΡΕΝΤΕΛ
ΤΟ ΣΠΙΤΙ
ΤΟΥ ΘΑΝΑΤΟΥ

B

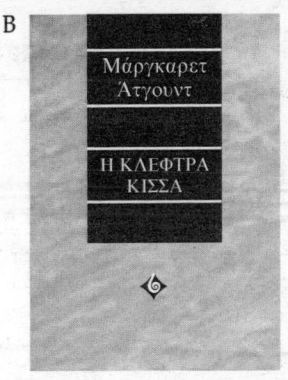

Μάργκαρετ
Άτγουντ

Η ΚΛΕΦΤΡΑ
ΚΙΣΣΑ

C

Μάρτιν Έϊμις
Η ΠΛΗΡΟΦΟΡΙΑ

D

ΣΥΝΘΙΑ ΧΑΡΡΟΝΤ-ΗΓΚΛΖ
ΕΓΩ
Η ΒΙΚΤΩΡΙΑ

E

ΡΟΝΤΥ ΝΤΟΥΛ
TO BAN

F

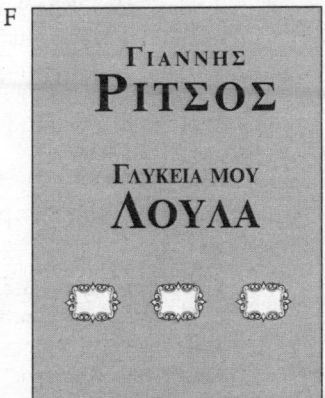

ΓΙΑΝΝΗΣ
ΡΙΤΣΟΣ

ΓΛΥΚΕΙΑ ΜΟΥ
ΛΟΥΛΑ

3.5 Στο περίπτερο

 ΞΕΡΩ ΤΟΝ ΓΙΟ ΣΑΣ
I KNOW YOUR SON

After getting out of Pericles' taxi, Craig goes to the kiosk to meet Vangelio.

Σκοτία	Scotland
αμάν	good grief
το γράμμα	letter
καθίστε	sit down
αρχαιολογία	archaeology
οικονομικά	economics
ο γιος μου	my son
μια χαρά	just fine
σας στέλνει χαιρετίσματα	he sends you greetings
το παγωτό	ice-cream
ωραία	nice, good
περίπου	about, approximately
εβδομάδες	weeks
μήνες	months

ACTIVITY 18

Listen to the story and answer the following questions.

1 Who is Petros?
2 How does Vangelio know about Craig?
3 What is Petros studying?
4 What is Craig studying?
5 What refreshments does Vangelio offer Craig ?
6 How long will Craig be staying in Greece?

ACTIVITY 19

Match 1–4 with the appropriate response from a–d.

A	B
1 Ορίστε ένα παγωτό.	a Μια χαρά.
2 Πόσον καιρό είσαστε εδώ;	b Οχτώ εβδομάδες.
3 Τι κάνει ο Πέτρος;	c Χαίρω πολύ.
4 Με λένε Κραίηγκ.	d Ευχαριστώ πολύ.

STORY TRANSCRIPT

Craig	Είσαστε η Κυρία Βαγγελιώ;
Vangelio	Μάλιστα.
Craig	Με λένε Κραίηγκ, Κραίηγκ ΜακΦέρσον.
Vangelio	Χαίρω πολύ.
Craig	Ξέρω τον Πέτρο. Τον γιο σας. Ο Πέτρος είναι φίλος μου.
Vangelio	Από πού είσαστε;
Craig	Από το Εδιμβούργο, στη Σκοτία. Σπουδάζω εκεί.
Vangelio	Α! Σας ξέρω, από ένα γράμμα! Καλώς ήρθατε! Ορίστε, καθίστε!
Craig	Ευχαριστώ πολύ.
Woman	Λοιπόν, εσείς σπουδάζετε αρχαιολογία, και ο γιος μου οικονομικά ...
Man	Ακριβώς.
Vangelio	Τι κάνει ο γιος μου;
Craig	Μια χαρά. Σας στέλνει χαιρετίσματα.
Vangelio	Α, ευχαριστώ, ευχαριστώ! Θέλετε μια κοκα κόλα, μια λεμονάδα, ένα παγωτό;
Craig	Μμμ, ωραία.
Vangelio	Πόσον καιρό θα μείνετε στην Ελλάδα;
Craig	Δυο-τρεις μήνες.

Now it's time to test your progress in Unit 3.

1 Supply the Greek questions for the following answers.
  Use the informal form of the verbs.

  1 Με λένε Ουίλιαμ.
  2 Είμαι από την Αγγλία.
  3 Όχι, δεν είμαι Γερμανός, είμαι Ολλανδός.
  4 Είμαι νοσοκόμα.
  5 Δουλεύω σε γραφείο.

  10

2 Put the following statements in the right order to make a
  conversation.

  • Δέκα χρόνια.
  • Όχι, είμαι Αμερικανίδα.
  • Από πού είσαστε;
  • Πόσον καιρό μένετε στο Μάντσεστερ;
  • Από το Σικάγο.
  • Είσαστε Αγγλίδα;

  6

3 Complete Louisa's description of herself by inserting the
  words in the box in the appropriate gaps.

λίγα στην Τώρα σε από Με εδώ

  (1) _____ λένε Λουίζα και είμαι (2) _____ την
  Αυστραλία. (3) _____ μένω στην Ελλάδα. Είμαι
  (4) _____ έντεκα χρόνια. Δουλεύω (5) _____ Πάτρα,
  (6) _____ μία τράπεζα. Ξέρω (7) _____ ελληνικά.

  7

4 Supply the correct form of the appropriate nationality,
  country or language, as required.

  1 Η Έλλη είναι από την _____ , είναι Ελληνίδα.
  2 Ο Καρλ είναι από την Γερμανία, είναι _____ .
  3 Η Μαργαρίτα είναι από την Ιρλανδία, είναι
    _____ .

  4 Ο Μάρκος είναι από την Ιταλία, είναι _____ .

5 Η Ιζαμπέλα ξέρει γαλλικά, αλλά δεν είναι
_____ .

6 Ο Γιάννης μένει στην Αυστραλία και ξέρει
_____ .

| | 6 |

5 Complete the sentences with the correct form of the verb.

1 Ο Γιάννης και η Έλλη _____ στον Πειραιά. (μένω)
2 Η Ιζαμπέλα _____ από την Ισπανία. (είμαι)
3 Ο Μάρκος _____ σκοτσέζικα. (ξέρω)
4 Εσείς _____ σε πανεπιστήμιο; (δουλεύω)
5 Η Χριστίνα _____ φιλοσοφία. (σπουδάζω)
6 Ο Κραίηγκ _____ αρχαιολόγος. (είμαι)

| | 6 |

6 Fill in the missing numbers.
έντεκα, _____ , δεκατρία, δεκατέσσερα, _____ ,
δεκαέξι, _____ , _____ , δεκαεννέα, _____

| | 5 |

7 You have a Greek friend who does not know you have started learning Greek. Write a short postcard to him or her, saying:

– you're in Scotland
– you're working in an office there for two months
– you're staying in the Hotel Charles
– you know a little Greek!

begin: **Αγαπητέ** (with a man's name)   *or* **Αγαπητή** (with a woman's name)

end: **Χαιρετίσματα** + your name

| | 10 |

TOTAL SCORE | 50 |

If you scored less than 40, go through the dialogues and the Language Building sections again, before completing the Summary on page 42.

Summary 3

 Now try this final test summarizing the main points covered in this unit. You can check your answers on the recording.

You have just met two people.
How would you:
1 ask his name?
2 ask where she lives?
3 ask what work he does?
4 ask where she works?
5 ask if he is a Greek?
6 say you know a little Greek?
7 say you live in England?
8 say you work in an office?

REVISION

Besides covering conversational openings, this unit has introduced you to Greek verbs. It is a good idea to make up simple sentences in your head using verbs you know, to practise the different forms. For example, think about how you would say: 'we work', 'they study', 'he lives', 'I want', 'she has', 'Maria and Sophocles know', and so on.

Before moving on to the first Review, take the time to organize and revise thoroughly everything you have covered so far. Play all three units through again and check that you remember the vocabulary you have acquired. Test yourself on the grammar points explained in the Language Building sections. For light relief you could make a list of idiomatic expressions, such as 'It's hot!', 'Good grief!' 'Really?', 'Exactly', and so on. Using phrases like these confidently in conversation will help to make you sound more fluent.

Review 1

There are four Review sections in the course. These consist of activities which will test you on the language introduced up to that point. Answers to the activities can be found in the Answer section that starts on page 213.

VOCABULARY

1 Put the following words into the appropriate groups.

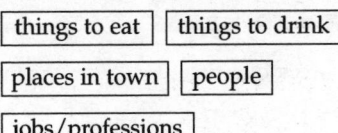

| things to eat | things to drink |
| places in town | people |
| jobs/professions |

παγωτό, άνδρας, γιαούρτι, κρασί, φοιτήτρια, βιβλιοπωλείο, ούζο, πλατεία, ταχυδρομείο, φίλος, εκκλησία, τζατζίκι, γιος, τράπεζα, μπίρα, ταραμοσαλάτα, φούρνος, Γαλλίδα, δικηγόρος, περίπτερο

2 Add the correct article **ο, η**, or **το** before each word.

1 ξενοδοχείο	5 πανεπιστήμιο	9 λάδι
2 Άγγλος	6 Ιταλίδα	10 μαμά
3 τυρόπιτα	7 καφενείο	11 ταξί
4 αρχαιολόγος	8 θάλασσα	12 ντομάτα

3 Choose from the directions below, to label the diagrams A–E.

A   B   C   D   E

1 θα πάτε ευθεία.
2 θα πάρετε το πρώτο στενό δεξιά.
3 θα στρίψετε αριστερά.
4 θα πάρετε το δεύτερο στενό αριστερά.
5 το σινεμά είναι εδώ.

4 Match the Greek expressions 1–10 with the correct English version from a–j.

1	πο-πο ζέστη	a	so
2	με συγχωρείτε	b	sit down
3	ορίστε	c	OK
4	δυστυχώς	d	excuse me
5	χαίρω πολύ	e	very nice
6	καλή όρεξη	f	phew, it's hot
7	λοιπόν	g	pleased to meet you
8	εντάξει	h	here you are
9	καθίστε	i	enjoy your meal
10	πολύ ωραία	j	unfortunately

GRAMMAR AND USAGE

5 Match the Greek questions 1–10 with the English a–j.

1 Τι θέλετε;
2 Πού είναι το ταχυδρομείο;
3 Υπάρχει τουαλέτα εδώ κοντά;
4 Πώς σας λένε;
5 Τι δουλειά κάνετε;
6 Τι κάνετε;
7 Πού δουλεύετε;
8 Πόσον καιρό μένετε στην Ελλάδα;
9 Από πού είστε;
10 Μήπως ξέρετε τον φίλο μου;

a What's your name?
b Where are you from?
c How are you?
d Is there a toilet nearby?
e Perhaps you know my friend?
f What work do you do?
g How long have you stayed in Greece?
h Where's the post office?
i What do you want?
j Where do you work?

6 Supply the correct form of the verb in the following sentences.

1 Ο Αντώνης δεν _____ εδώ. (είμαι)
2 Ο Τάκης και η Χριστίνα _____ στην Αθήνα. (μένω)
3 Εγώ _____ μία πορτοκαλάδα. (θέλω)

4 Αλίκη, μήπως _____ πού είναι το διαβατήριό μου; (ξέρω)

5 Εμείς δεν _____ ισπανικά. (ξέρω)

6 Η Έλλη _____ στο πολυτεχνείο. (σπουδάζω)

7 Πού _____ τώρα, Γιάννη; (δουλεύω)

7 Complete the sentences with the correct preposition, **σε**, **στο(ν) / στη(ν) / στο**, or **από**.

1 Μένω _____ Ελλάδα.

2 Είμαι _____ το Σικάγο.

3 Δουλεύω _____ εργοστάσιο.

4 Είμαι _____ ξενοδοχείο.

5 Η Άννα είναι _____ γραφείο.

🔊 LISTENING

8 You'll hear a woman introducing herself on the recording. Listen and then answer the following questions.

1 What is her name?

2 Where does she come from?

3 Where does she live?

4 How long has she lived there?

5 What work does she do?

6 Does she speak any foreign languages?

9 You'll hear four exchanges on the recording. Listen to the exchanges and correct the error in each in the transcript below.

1 Woman   Γειά σου, Γιώργο, πού είσαι;
   Man   Είμαι εδώ, στην οδό Πατησίων, κοντά στο σταθμό.

2 Man   Πόσον καιρό μένετε στην Κύπρο;
   Woman   Δέκα χρόνια.

3 Man   Από πού είστε;
   Woman   Είμαι από την Κρήτη.

4 Woman   Μήπως ξέρετε πού είναι το ταχυδρομείο;
   Man   Δεν είναι μακριά.

10 You're trying to find your way to the Archaeological Museum and have stopped a passerby to ask for directions.

You	Say 'excuse me'.

Passerby	Ορίστε;
You	Ask where the Archaeological Museum is.

Passerby	Είναι στην οδό Πατησίων.
You	Ask if it's far.

Passerby	Θα πάτε ίσια, και θα στίψετε αριστερά – εκεί, πάνω.
You	Ask 'at the kiosk?'.

Passerby	Μάλιστα.
You	Say 'fine'.

You	Now ask if there's a bookshop nearby.

Passerby	Υπάρχει βιβλιοπωλείο στο δεύτερο στενό δεξιά. Στη γωνία.
You	Confirm what she said: On the corner, on the second side-street to the right?

Passerby	Ακριβώς.
You	Say 'thanks a lot'.

11 You've started talking to a Greek woman at a party. She's going to ask you about yourself: prepare your responses and then join in the dialogue on the recording. Try to do it without using your notes. She'll ask (though not in this order):

– where you live
– where you're from
– what your job is
– your name

Do you have rooms?

Έχετε δωμάτια;

> **OBJECTIVES**
>
> In this unit you'll learn how to:
>
> ✓ make a hotel reservation
>
> ✓ talk about rooms and amenities
>
> ✓ say how long you'll be staying
>
> ✓ count from 21 to 100
>
> ✓ tell the time
>
> And cover the following grammar and
> language:
>
> ✓ plurals
>
> ✓ diminutive forms
>
> ✓ the definite article as object
>
> ✓ πόσο '(how much?, 'how many?')

LEARNING GREEK 4

When learning a language, use different strategies to best
effect: work out how (and when) to use the book, listen to
the recordings, practise dialogues and reading aloud, learn
vocabulary, write things down, and so on, so that you can
practise the four basic skills of listening, speaking, reading,
and writing. Discover your own particular learning style.
Do you learn better when you write things down? How
often do you need to hear something before you know it?
Does the idea of learning rules appeal to you or turn you
off completely? Does it help you to remember if you link
learning to some other activity? Do you already have your
own methods and how can you adapt them to the course?
Structure your learning to focus on what best suits you –
but remember that it's important not to neglect any of the
skills completely.

🎧 Now start the recording for Unit 4. 47

Στο τηλέφωνο

(🎧) **ACTIVITY 1** is on the recording.

ACTIVITY 2

1 What sort of room does the man want?
2 How long does he want it for?
3 Where in the building is the room located?
4 Does the price include a bath? Dinner?
5 Does the man take the room on offer?

DIALOGUE 1

○ Εμπρός, λέγετε.
■ Χαίρετε. Θα ήθελα να κλείσω ένα δωμάτιο.
○ Μάλιστα, τι δωμάτιο θέλετε;
■ Ένα δίκλινο, αν υπάρχει.
○ Με μπάνιο ή με ντουζ;
■ Δεν με πειράζει ...
○ Για πόσες μέρες το θέλετε;
■ Για δύο μέρες – το Σαββατοκύριακο.
○ Εντάξει. Έχω ένα δίκλινο με ντουζ στον πρώτο όροφο.
■ Ωραία ...
○ Και πρωινό, αν θέλετε.
■ Και με θέα;
○ Το δωμάτιο έχει μπαλκόνι με θέα προς τη θάλασσα.
■ Ευχαριστώ πολύ.

VOCABULARY	
εμπρός, λέγετε	*phrases used on answering telephone*
θα ήθελα να κλείσω	I'd like to book, I'd like to reserve
το δωμάτιο	room
ένα δίκλινο	double room (with two beds)
το μπάνιο	bath
το ντουζ	shower
δεν με πειράζει	it doesn't matter (to me), I don't mind
για πόσες μέρες;	for how many days?
το Σαββατοκύριακο	weekend
ο όροφος	floor (level)
το πρωινό	breakfast
η θέα	view
το μπαλκόνι	balcony
προς	towards

✓ Plurals

Most nouns form the plural as follows.

Masculine nouns ending in:

singular	plural		
-ος	-οι	ο Άγγλος	οι Άγγλοι
-ας	-ες	ο Έλληνας	οι Έλληνες
-ης	-ες	ο φοιτητής	οι φοιτητές (male student)

Feminine nouns ending in:

singular	plural		
-α	-ες	η σαλάτα	οι σαλάτες
-η	-ες	η δραχμή	οι δραχμές (drachma)

Neuter nouns ending in:

singular	plural		
-ι	-ια	το σουβλάκι	τα σουβλάκια
-ο	-α	το τηλέφωνο	τα τηλέφωνα
-μα	ματα	το πρόβλημα	τα προβλήματα (problem)

Words imported from other languages are normally neuter and do not change in the plural: το ντουζ / τα ντουζ, το σινεμά / τα σινεμά.

✓ Booking a room

ένα μονόκλινο	single room		
ένα δίκλινο	double room (with two beds)		
ένα τρίκλινο	room with three single beds		
το πρωινό	breakfast	το μεσημεριανό	lunch
το βραδινό	dinner	το γεύμα	meal

Note the word order of the form Τον/Την/Το θέλω. I want it. Note also that the pronoun has a different form, depending on the gender of the noun it replaces.

> θέλω τον χάρτη/την σαλάτα/το δωμάτιο. *Τον/ την/ το θέλω.*

ACTIVITY 3

Make the following plural.

1 η πλατεία	5 το δωμάτιο	9 η τουαλέτα
2 το λεμόνι	6 ο δικηγόρος	10 το μπάνιο
3 ο Ιταλός	7 η τράπεζα	11 το κομπιούτερ
4 η φίλη	8 το διαβατήριο	

Now do activities 4 and 5 on the recording.

4.2 In the village

Στο χωριό

 **ACTIVITY 6** is on the recording.

ACTIVITY 7

1 Paul arrives on	a Saturday	b Sunday.
2 Paul is expecting a	a male friend	b a female friend.
3 The bathroom is	a beside Paul's room	
	b behind the house.	

DIALOGUE 2

○ Καλησπέρα σας. Μήπως υπάρχουν δωμάτια;
■ Ορίστε, περάστε, καθίστε εδώ έξω στην αυλή.
○ Α! Ευχαριστώ. Τι μέρα έχουμε σήμερα;
■ Σήμερα είναι Κυριακή.
○ Θα ήθελα ένα δωμάτιο για μερικές μέρες.
■ Εντάξει! Μέχρι την Τετάρτη ... Πέμπτη;
○ Ναι, ναι. Και περιμένω έναν φίλο μου.
■ Ένα δωμάτιο για δύο άτομα λοιπόν ... Έχω ένα, πίσω, με θέα το βουνό.
○ Ωραίο κήπο έχετε ... Πού είναι η τουαλέτα;
■ Η τουαλέτα είναι δίπλα στο δωμάτιό σας – πηγαίνετε μέσα. Θέλετε νεράκι; ... Κάτι να φάτε;

VOCABULARY

περάστε	come through, come in
έξω	outside, out
η αυλή	yard, courtyard
η μέρα	day
σήμερα	today
μερικές μέρες	a few days
μέχρι	until
περιμένω	wait (for), expect
το άτομο	person
πίσω	at the back, behind
το βουνό	mountain
ο κήπος	garden
πηγαίνω	go
μέσα	inside, in
το νεράκι	water [*diminutive*]
κάτι να φάτε	something to eat

✅ Days of the week

η Δευτέρα	Monday	η Παρασκευή	Friday
η Τρίτη	Tuesday	το Σάββατο	Saturday
η Τετάρτη	Wednesday	η Κυριακή	Sunday
η Πέμπτη	Thursday	το Σάββατοκύριακο	the weekend

Note that all are feminine except Saturday and the weekend. To say 'on Monday', etc. you use the definite article.

Σήμερα είναι Πέμπτη. Today is Thursday. [*no article*]

την Τρίτη – on Tuesday   το Σαββατοκύριακο – at the weekend

To say 'for Monday', and so on, the definite article is also included.

Θα ήθελα ένα δωμάτιο για τη Δευτέρα. I'd like a room for Monday.

✅ Diminutive forms

Greeks often apply a diminutive ending to nouns, frequently as a sign of affection (such as το παιδάκι from το παιδί ('child'), but also simply as a familiar form: thus το νεράκι as a variant for 'water' (το νερό). The usual diminutive ending for masculine and neuter nouns is -άκι: το παιδάκι, το νεράκι. For feminine nouns, it is -ούλα or -ίτσα: η πατάτα ('potato') – η πατατούλα, η μπίρα ('beer') – η μπιρίτσα.

Diminutive endings are also added to proper names: ο Γιάννης – ο Γιαννάκης, ο Παναγιώτης – ο Παναγιωτάκης, η Σοφία – η Σοφούλα, η Ελένη – η Ελενίτσα. Hence the many people called Akis, Takis, Loula, Nitsa, and so on.

✅ The object form of the definite article

The definite article changes when the noun it accompanies is the object of a verb. ο becomes το(ν) and η becomes τη(ν). το remains το.

The final ν appears when the next word begins with a vowel or the letters κ, τ, π, ψ, or ξ.

την Έλλη, την Κυριακή, την τράπεζα, τον Παύλο, τον ψαρά, τον ξένο

✅ πόσο ('how much?', 'how many?')

πόσο changes to match the number and gender of the thing referred to. More details on how adjectives in general change are given in Unit 5. For now, note the following forms.

πόσες (feminine plural)
Για πόσες μέρες/εβδομάδες ...; For how many days/weeks?
πόσα (neuter plural)
Για πόσα άτομα ...; For how many people?

 Now do activities 8 and 9 on the recording.

4.3 At the Poseidon Hotel

Στο Ξενοδοχείο "Ποσειδώνας"

🔊 **ACTIVITY 10** is on the recording.

ACTIVITY 11

1 Which floor is the tourist's room on?
2 Where are her suitcases?
3 When is the meal served?

DIALOGUE 3

○ Το 47 είναι στον τέταρτο όροφο.
■ Έχει μπάνιο και τηλεόραση;
○ Βεβαίως, και διπλό κρεβάτι. Αλλά είναι χωρίς τηλέφωνο. Το θέλετε;
■ Μάλιστα.
○ Το διαβατήριό σας, παρακαλώ, και μία υπογραφή.
■ Ορίστε.
○ Το κλειδί σας, μαντάμ. Πού είναι οι βαλίτσες σας;
■ Στο αυτοκίνητο, έξω. Υπάρχει ασανσέρ;
○ Το ασανσέρ είναι εκεί, δεξιά.
■ Α, ωραία. ... ... Σερβίρετε βραδινό γεύμα;
○ Βεβαίως – από τις οχτώ η ώρα το βράδυ.
■ Αχ, το κινητό μου! Λέγετε! ... Τι τηλέφωνο έχετε εδώ;
○ 39 72 0 96.

VOCABULARY	
η τηλεόραση	television
βεβαίως	certainly
διπλός/ή/ό	double
το κρεβάτι	bed
χωρίς	without
το διαβατήριο	passport
η υπογραφή	signature
το κλειδί	key
η βαλίτσα	suitcase
το αυτοκίνητο	car
το ασανσέρ	lift, elevator
σερβίρω	serve
το κινητό	mobile (phone), cell phone
το τηλέφωνο	telephone; telephone number

✓ Numbers 21–100

20	είκοσι	21	είκοσι ένα
30	τριάντα	32	τριάντα δύο
40	σαράντα	43	σαράντα τρία
50	πενήντα	54	πενήντα τέσσερα
60	εξήντα	65	εξήντα πέντε
70	εβδομήντα	76	εβδομήντα έξι
80	ογδόντα	87	ογδόντα εφτά
90	ενενήντα	98	ενενήντα οχτώ
100	εκατό		

Greek telephone numbers are given in twos, as far as possible. If the number is uneven, the odd number is given just before the last pair
96 34 4 58 ενενήντα έξι, τριάντα τέσσερα, τέσσερα, πενήντα οχτώ.

✓ Τι ώρα είναι; ('What time is it?')

Είναι πέντε η ώρα. It's five o'clock.

As η ώρα ('hour') is feminine, the feminine μία is used for 'one'. Gender also affects two other numbers: 'three' and 'four'. The feminine plural form is used with the hours: τρεις and τέσσερις.
μία η ώρα – one o'clock
τρεις η ώρα – three o'clock   τέσσερις η ώρα – four o'clock
Midday is το μεσημέρι and midnight is τα μεσάνυχτα.

With times involving 'to' or 'past', the hour is given first;
'to' is παρά and 'past' is και.
έξι παρά είκοσι – twenty to six
εννιά και δέκα – ten past nine

'quarter' is τέταρτο and 'half' is μισή.
έξι παρά τέταρτο – a quarter to six
έντεκα και μισή – half past eleven

The twenty-four hour clock is also used, mainly in official contexts. Note the use of και in these times. δεκατρείς *και* σαράντα – 13.40, δεκαοχτώ *και* πενηνταπέντε – 18.55.

ACTIVITY 12
Give the time in Greek.

1	11.20	3	14.35	5	16.55
2	10.00	4	13.50	6	20.15

 Now do activities 13 and 14 on the recording.

4.4 Books

Βιβλία

Beyond tourist guides, there are plenty of travellers' tales through the ages which include descriptions, humorous and otherwise, of places stayed at and conditions experienced in Greece. Well-known among these are Patrick Leigh Fermor's *Mani* and *Roumeli* and Peter Levi's *The Hill of Kronos*.

There are also a number of novels situated in Greece that you might like to read.
The strange and beguiling setting of John Fowles's *The Magus* is the mysterious island of Phraxos. Here a British teacher becomes embroiled in a complex world of staged tableaux and myth-laden real-life events.

The events of *Captain Corelli's Mandolin* by Louis de Bernières centre on the occupation of Greece by Italian and German forces during the Second World War.

Anne Michaels's *Fugitive Pieces* involves an interplay of past and present time, following the story of Jakob, a survivor of persecution whose journey takes him from Eastern Europe to the island of Zakinthos, then Athens, and later to Canada.

Lawrence Durrell's *Bitter Lemons* (set in Cyprus), *Reflections on a Marine Venus* (set in Rhodes), and *Prospero's Cell* (set in Corfu) are based on his experiences before and during the Second World War. His younger brother, Gerald, wrote amusingly about animal life in Corfu where he grew up, most famously in *My Family and Other Animals*.

Virginia Woolf, in *Jacob's Room*, takes her characters to Greece and lets them wander, if briefly, among the Greeks, acting out their seductions among the cafés and the ruins – her story is set in the early twentieth century.

Many Greek writers are now available in translation. Short and accessible novels include: Alki Zei *Achilles' Fiancée*, Eugenia Fakinou *The Seventh Garment*, Menis Koumandareas *Koula*, Alexandros Kotsias *Jaguar*.

ACTIVITY 15

A Your friend Marika, a writer, is looking for accommodation for a few weeks. You see these notices pinned up on the local kiosk. Read through the notices and answer the following questions.

1 Which of the two places is more self-contained?
2 Where is each located?
3 What is the greatest advantage of each?

1

Ενοικιάζονται Δωμάτια

Δύο δωμάτια, με τουαλέτα, στον πέμπτο όροφο, ένα μονό και ένα διπλό. Και τα δύο με μπαλκόνι. Υπάρχει ασανσέρ. Είμαστε κοντά στο κέντρο. Τηλ. 737041.

2

Θέλετε Γκαρσονιέρα;

Μία ωραία γκαρσονιέρα με κήπο. Καλό για δύο άτομα. Έχει δροσιά και ζεστό νερό. Δίπλα στο σταθμό Λαρίσης και απέναντι απο το Σινεμά Άστορ. Τηλ. 7215980.

B Decide which of the two is more suitable for a writer, then write a note to your friend briefly describing the one you have chosen.

Τρίτη
Αγαπητή Μαρίκα,
Υπάρχει _____

Χαιρετίσματα,
(Your name)

4.5 Στο περίπτερο

 ΠΑΜΕ ΜΙΑ ΒΟΛΤΑ
LET'S GO FOR A DRIVE

Vangelio is eager to make sure that Craig is settled in and feels at home in Athens.

νοικιάζω	rent
η γκαρσονιέρα	studio flat
η Σχολή	School (as in Business School)
η βόλτα	stroll, ride
το πεύκο	pine
η δροσιά	cool(ness)
βλέπω	see
όλη την Αθήνα	all of Athens
έλα να σε συστήσω	let me introduce you
από πάνω	from above
η κόρη μου	my daughter
έλα μαζί μας	come with us
η εξοχή	countryside, outdoors
κάνω μπάνιο	bathe
το δέντρο	tree
πάλι	again

ACTIVITY 16

Listen to the story and decide whether the following are true or false. Correct those which are false.

1 Ο Κραίηγκ μένει σε ένα δωμάτιο στην
  Αμερικανική Αρχαιολογική Σχολή.   T / F
2 Ο Κραίηγκ πηγαίνει βόλτες στο Λυκαβηττό. T / F
3 Η Σοφία είναι στο χωριό.   T / F
4 Το σπίτι έχει πεύκα.   T / F
5 Το σπίτι στο χωριό είναι κοντά στη θάλασσα. T / F

ACTIVITY 17

Listen again and answer the following questions.

1 What does Craig like about Lycabettos?
2 When are Vangelio and her family going to the village?
3 What exactly does Vangelio say when she invites Craig to the village?

4 What does Sophia tell Craig about the village, to encourage him to join them?
5 What does Vangelio say when Craig tries to say he has work to do?

STORY TRANSCRIPT

Vangelio	Έχεις δωμάτιο εδώ στην Αθήνα;
Craig	Ναι, νοικιάζω μία γκαρσονιέρα κοντά στην Αμερικανική Αρχαιολογική Σχολή.
Vangelio	Α! Προς το Λυκαβηττό …
Craig	Μάλιστα - όταν δεν έχω πολλή δουλειά, πηγαίνω βόλτα εκεί.
Vangelio	Ωραία είναι. Ο Λυκαβηττός έχει πεύκα και δροσιά.
Craig	Και υπέροχη θέα – βλέπεις όλη την Αθήνα από πάνω.
Sofia	Γειά σου, Μαμά.
Vangelio	Σοφία! Έλα να σε συστήσω. Κραίηγκ, η Σοφία είναι η κόρη μου.
Craig	Χαίρω πολύ
Vangelio	Ο Κραίηγκ είναι ο φίλος του Πέτρου - απο το Εδιμβούργο.
Sofia	Α! Γειά σας!
Vangelio	Κραίηγκ, την Κυριακή πάμε μια βόλτα στο χωριό. Έλα μαζί μας!
Craig	Μμ, δεν ξέρω …
Sofia	Είναι ωραία στο χωριό, στην εξοχή. Κάνουμε μπάνιο στη θάλασσα, το σπίτι έχει κήπο με δέντρα – λεμονιές, πορτοκαλιές, ελιές …
Craig	Αλλά έχω δουλειά …
Vangelio	Δεν πειράζει – δουλεύεις πάλι την Δευτέρα.

Now it's time to test your progress in Unit 4.

1 Match 1–10 with the appropriate translation from a–j.

1	υπογραφή	a	meal
2	διαβατήριο	b	key
3	κήπος	c	bathroom
4	τουαλέτα	d	mobile phone
5	βαλίτσα	e	passport
6	γεύμα	f	garden
7	αυτοκίνητο	g	car
8	κλειδί	h	signature
9	ελιά	i	olive
10	κινητό	j	suitcase

10

2 Give the plural forms of 1–10 in activity 1, including the correct form of the definite article.
Example: **οι** υπογραφές

10

3 Complete the days of the week and then put them in order, starting with Monday.

– Υ– ΙΑΚ–
Τ– Ι– Η
– Α– Β– – Ο
Π– – – Σ– Ε– –
Τ– – Α– Τ–
– – Υ– ΕΡ–
– Ε– Π– Η

14

4 Supply the correct time for each of the clocks. Write out the time in full in Greek.

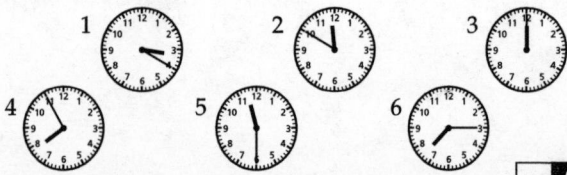

6

5 Complete the conversation with the words/phrases in the box. You won't need all of them.

> χωρίς   καθίστε   βραδινό   σερβίρετε
> όροφο   διπλό   δίκλινο   κλείσω   με
> εμπρός   θέα   δροσιά   υπάρχει

○ (1) _____ , λέγετε.

■ Θα ήθελα να (2) _____ ένα δωμάτιο.

○ Τι δωμάτιο θέλετε;

■ Ένα (3) _____ , παρακαλώ.

○ Μάλιστα. (4) _____ μπάνιο ή (5) _____ μπάνιο.

■ Με ντούζ, αν (6) _____ .

○ Εντάξει. Το δωμάτιό σας είναι στον τρίτο(7) _____ , με (8) _____ το βουνό.

■ Ωραία. Μήπως (9) _____ γεύματα;

○ Βεβαίως. Έχουμε πρωινό στις οχτώ και μισή, και (10) _____ στις εννιά το βράδυ.

| | 10 |

6 Supply the diminutive form for each of the following.

1 το μπαλκόνι
2 το κρεβάτι
3 το δωμάτιο
4 η κόρη
5 η βόλτα
6 η δροσιά

| | 6 |

| **TOTAL SCORE** | 56 |

If you scored less than 46, go through the Dialogues and the Language Building sections again, before completing the summary on page 60.

Summary 4

 Now try this final test summarizing the main points covered in this unit. You can check your answers on the recording.

How would you:
1 ask what time it is?
2 say it's half-past four?
3 say it's five to ten?
4 say 'on Friday'?
5 say 'here you are' as you hand over your passport?
6 say you'd like a double room please?
7 ask what the telephone number is here?
8 give the following telephone number? 23 61 4 97

REVISION

Remember to update your vocabulary lists and make sure you know the new verbs introduced in this unit.

The next unit focuses on shopping, so prepare to think more about expressing prices and amounts in Greek. Why not set yourself some simple arithmetic questions giving the answers in Greek? Can you tell people your phone/mobile number?

Look at your diary and try to work out what you're doing and when in Greek, reviewing the days of the week and how to give times.

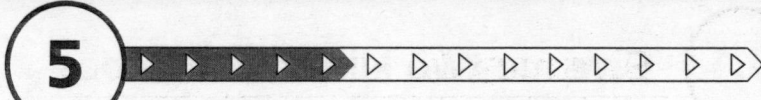
Let's go to the shops
Πάμε στα μαγαζιά

OBJECTIVES

In this unit you'll learn how to:

- ✓ ask for and describe items
- ✓ express quantities
- ✓ ask about prices
- ✓ use larger numbers

And cover the following grammar and language:

- ✓ adjectives (1)
- ✓ Group 2 verbs

LEARNING GREEK 5

Make the most of the time you have available to study. You need to set time aside to go through the material in the book and the recording, but you can make use of other opportunities – perhaps when you are travelling to work or to the shops or doing household chores – to do less demanding but nonetheless essential exercises. You could, for example, do some pronunciation practice, memorize vocabulary and structures, or listen again to some of the audio material.

Practise speaking Greek as often as you can – even speaking to yourself is good practice. If you can, record yourself regularly. This way you will become more aware of your pronunciation and by playing it back will be able to improve on your performance.

🎧 Now start the recording for Unit 5.

Δώστε μου δύο κιλά ντομάτες

 **ACTIVITY 1** is on the recording.

ACTIVITY 2

1 The woman buys a   a kilo   b two kilos
                               c half a kilo of tomatoes.

2 The vendor encourages   a more vegetables   b fruit
   her to buy   c cheese.

3 Finally the vendor   a her goods   b her change
   hands her   c a thousand drachmas.

DIALOGUE 1

○ Ελάτε! Ορίστε! Όλα φρέσκα, όλα νόστιμα!

■ Χαίρετε, κύριε Αντώνη. Θέλω ντομάτες για σαλάτα.

○ Έχω ντομάτες λουκούμι! Μεγάλες, κόκκινες, νόστιμες ...

■ Δώστε μου δυό κιλά και ένα μάτσο μαϊντανό.

○ Τίποτ' άλλο, κυρία μου - κολοκυθάκια, πιπεριές,
μελιτζάνες, κρεμμύδια, σκόρδο;

■ Μου δίνετε ένα κιλό μελιτζάνες; Για μουσακά ... Και
ξέρετε πού υπάρχει καλό τυρί εδώ στη λαϊκή;

○ Στη λαϊκή, όχι. Πηγαίνετε στον Κώστα, εκεί πάνω.

■ Εντάξει, ευχαριστώ ... Ορίστε χίλιες δραχμές.

○ Χίλιες δραχμές – ορίστε και τα ρέστα σας.

VOCABULARY

φρέσκος/ια/ο	fresh
νόστιμος/η/ο	tasty, delicious
η ντομάτα	tomato
λουκούμι	delicious [*idiomatic*]
τίποτ' άλλο	anything else?
ο μαϊντανός	parsley
το μάτσο	bunch
κολοκυθάκι	courgette, zucchini
η πιπεριά	pepper [*vegetable*]
η μελιτζάνα	aubergine, egg plant
το κρεμμύδι	onion
το σκόρδο	garlic
μου δίνετε	give me [*formal*]
το τυρί	cheese
χίλια	thousand
τα ρέστα σας	your change

✓ Adjectives (1)

Adjectives agree in gender, number, and case with the nouns they describe. Adjectives used in this course take the following endings in the *nominative* (the case used for the subject of a sentence). Notice that adjectives ending in -ιος in the masculine singular form have the feminine singular in -α.

singular	*masculine*	*feminine*	*neuter*
yellow	κίτρινος	κίτρινη	κίτρινο
small	μικρός	μικρή	μικρό
beautiful	ωραίος	ωραία	ωραίο

plural			
yellow	κίτρινοι	κίτρινες	κίτρινα
small	μικροί	μικρές	μικρά
beautiful	ωραίοι	ωραίες	ωραία

ο **μεγάλος** κήπος – the large garden
οι **πράσινες** πιπεριές – the green peppers

Some adjectives in -ος, derived from different older forms, also use -ιά for the feminine: for example, the adjective γλυκός ('sweet') – γλυκός, γλυκιά, γλυκό, γλυκοί, γλυκές, γλυκά. You need to learn these as you go.

When adjectives describe the noun or pronoun which is the object of the sentence (*accusative case*), they take the following endings.

singular	*masculine*	*feminine*	*neuter*
yellow	κίτρινο	κίτρινη	κίτρινο
small	μικρό	μικρή	μικρό
beautiful	ωραίο	ωραία	ωραίο

plural			
yellow	κίτρινους	κίτρινες	κίτρινα
small	μικρούς	μικρές	μικρά
beautiful	ωραί ους	ωραίες	ωραία

Έχουμε **καλούς** δασκάλους. We have good teachers.
Δώστε μου έξι **φρέσκα** αυγά. Give me six fresh eggs.

ACTIVITY 3

Complete the sentences with the correct form of the adjective in brackets.

1 Πού είναι η _____ τσάντα; (κόκκινος)
2 Θα ήθελα τον _____ χάρτη. (μεγάλος)
3 Έχω τρεις _____ φίλους στον Καναδά. (καλός)

🎧 Now do activites 4 and 5 on the recording.

Πόσο κάνει;

🎧 **ACTIVITY 6** is on the recording.

ACTIVITY 7
Correct the statements which are false.

1 The black bag costs 35,000 GDR   T / F
2 The black bag is cheaper than the blue one.   T / F
3 The man takes a size 32.   T / F

DIALOGUE 2

○ Πόσο κάνει η δερμάτινη τσάντα στη βιτρίνα;
■ Η μαύρη κάνει τριάντα πέντε χιλιάδες δραχμές.
○ Ακριβή είναι. Αυτή η μπλε είναι ωραία. Πόσο κάνει;
■ Αυτή είναι πιο φτηνή. Κάνει είκοσι οχτώ χιλιάδες.
○ Πουλάτε καλά παπούτσια ... Αυτά τα καφετί πέδιλα;
■ Αυτά κάνουν είκοσι τέσσερις χιλιάδες. Είναι άνετα, στη μόδα, και τα έχουμε σε όλα τα χρώματα.
○ Καλή τιμή. Φοράω νούμερο σαράντα δύο. Έχετε;
■ Βεβαίως. Ορίστε. Δοκιμάστε τα.

VOCABULARY

δερμάτινος/η/ο	leather
η βιτρίνα	shop window
μαύρος/η/ο	black
ακριβός/ή/ό	expensive
αυτός/ή/ό	this (one)
μπλε	blue
πιο φτηνός/ή/ό	cheaper
πουλάω	sell
το παπούτσι	shoe
καφετί	brown
η τιμή	price
άνετος/η/ο	comfortable
στη μόδα	in fashion, fashionable
το χρώμα	colour
το πέδιλο	sandal
το νούμερο	size [*shoes, clothes*]
φοράω	wear
δοκιμάζω	try, try on

✅ Group 2 verbs

The second group of regular verbs are stressed in the final syllable (-άω) of the first person. For the present tense, the following endings are added to the stem (the 'I' form without the -ω ending). These verbs are often contracted to end in ώ in the first person form.

Group 2a verbs

φοράω – I wear

| φορώ | I wear | φοράει | he/she/it wears | φοράτε | you wear |
| φοράς | you wear | φοράμε | we wear | φοράν(ε) | they wear |

Other useful Group 2a verbs: αγαπώ (-άω) ('love'), μιλώ (-άω) ('speak'), βοηθώ (-άω) ('help')

Group 2b verbs (verbs ending in –ώ) are slightly different.

οδηγώ – I drive

| οδηγώ | I drive | οδηγεί | he/she/it drives | οδηγείτε | you drive |
| οδηγείς | you drive | οδηγούμε | we drive | οδηγούν(ε) | they drive |

Other useful Group 2b verbs: καλώ ('invite'), ζω ('live')

Group 2 verbs such as τρώω ('eat'), λέω ('say'), and πάω* ('go') are slightly irregular, taking the following contracted endings.

τρώω	τρώμε	λεω	λέμε	πάω	πάμε
τρώς	τρώτε	λες	λέτε	πάς	πάτε
τρώει	τρών(ε)	λέει	λέν(ε)	πάει	πάν(ε)

(*Note that 'go' has another form – πηγαίνω – which is a Group 1 verb.)

✅ Numbers 200+

200 διακόσια	800 οχτακόσια	5000 πέντε χιλιάδες	
300 τριακόσια	900 εννιακόσια	10,000 δέκα χιλιάδες	
400 τετρακόσια	1000 χίλια	20,000 είκοσι χιλιάδες	
500 πεντακόσια	2000 δυο χιλιάδες	100 000 εκατό χιλιάδες	
600 εξακόσια	3000 τρεις χιλιάδες	1,000,000 εκατομμύριο	
700 εφτακόσια	4000 τέσσερις χιλιάδες	50,000,000 πενήντα εκατομμύρια	

ACTIVITY 8

Complete with the correct form of the verb in brackets.

1 Το κατάστημα _____ ωραία πέδιλα. (πουλάω)

2 Ο Γιάννης και η Ρένα _____ σοκολάτες. (τρώω)

3 Η Σοφία και εγώ _____ λίγα αγγλικά. (μιλάω)

4 Τα παιδιά _____ στη λαϊκή σήμερα. (πάω)

 Now do activities 9 and 10 on the recording.

Λίγο κρασί;

ACTIVITY 11 is on the recording.

ACTIVITY 12

How much of each of the following is required?

1 macaroni   2 oil   3 mince   4 olives   5 tarama

DIALOGUE 3

○ Αμάν! Το σουπερμάρκετ είναι κλειστό. Πάω στο μπακάλη.

■ Πάω εγώ. Τι θέλουμε;

○ Θέλω δύο πακέτα μακαρόνια, ένα κουτί ρύζι, μισό κιλό φέτα και δυό μπουκάλια λάδι.

■ Κιμά έχουμε για τους κεφτέδες;

○ Όχι. Πάρε ένα κιλό. Και μερικά αυγά.

■ Λίγο κρασί;

○ Υπάρχει κόκκινο στο σπίτι. Πάρε μερικές μπίρες.

■ Άλλο τίποτα;

○ Λίγες ελιές ... α, και ταραμά – ένα τέταρτο, για ταραμοσαλάτα. ... Μα είναι δυνατόν; Περιμένουμε κόσμο, και δεν έχουμε τίποτα στο σπίτι!

VOCABULARY	
Αμάν!	Good grief!
το σουπερμάρκετ	supermarket
ο μπακάλης	grocer
το πακέτο	packet, pack(age)
το μακαρόνι	macaroni, spaghetti
το κουτί	box
το ρύζι	rice
το μπουκάλι	bottle
το λάδι	oil
ο κιμάς	mince, ground meat
κεφτέδες	meatballs
πάρε	get, take [*imperative*]
μερικά αυγά	a few eggs
ο ταραμάς	tarama
είναι δυνατόν;	is it possible?
ο κόσμος	people

✓ Quantities

To ask 'how much?' or 'how many?', you use **πόσο;** or **πόσα;**

> **Πόσο** κάνουνε; How much are they?
> **Πόσα μπουκάλια υπάρχουν;** How many bottles are there?

With containers/measures, there is no word for 'of'
> a box of matches – **ένα κουτί σπίρτα**
> a bottle of water – **ένα μπουκάλι νερό**
> a glass of wine **ένα ποτήρι κρασί**   a cup of tea – **ένα φλιτζάνι τσάι**

μερικοί/ές/ά ('a few', 'some') is used with items which can be counted. It is always in the plural: **μερικοί άνθρωποι** ('a few people'), **μερικές πατάτες** ('a few potatoes'), **μερικά κουτιά** ('a few boxes').

λίγος ('a little', 'a few') is used both with items that can be counted and with uncountable quantities – **λίγος καφές, λίγα κουτιά.**

To say 'there isn't/aren't any ...', you use **δεν υπάρχει/ υπάρχουν καθόλου** ... Note the double negative.

> **Δεν υπάρχουν καθόλου πορτοκάλια.** There aren't any oranges.

ACTIVITY 13
Label the pictures with the help of the words in the box.

ένα κουτί ένα πακέτο ένα μπουκάλι ένα ποτήρι	σπίρτα καραμέλες ουίσκι πορτοκαλάδα

1

2

3

4

Now do activities 14 and 15 on the recording.

Το εμπόριο

Supermarkets notwithstanding, the tradition of street markets continues to flourish in Greek cities and towns, and **η λαϊκή**, supplying regularly available fresh produce, **φρέσκα προϊόντα**, at reasonable prices, **λογικές τιμές**, is part of everyday life. Besides foodstuffs and household wares, many of these markets also accommodate traders (**εμπόρους**) from beyond Greece bringing exotic goods.

Beyond the neighbourhood cut and thrust lie the labyrinthine arcades of the general downtown shopping area, **η αγορά**, teeming with their own brand of life-meets-commerce. More upmarket shopping is also available and is just as versatile. It offers the finest merchandise designed and produced by local manufacturers, as well as a vast and growing range of items from all over the world. There is something to suit every pocket and for bargain-hunters the January and August sales (**εκπτώσεις**) are a must.

Climate (**το κλίμα**) has, to a large degree, dictated working hours in Greece for centuries: the heat in summer makes it virtually impossible to function in the afternoon and the timetable is adjusted to allow for the afternoon rest. However, air-conditioning and membership of the EU (**Ευρωπαϊκή Ένωση**) are gradually asserting themselves, and Greek business hours are responding to the call for greater global efficiency.

το ευρώ euro

ACTIVITY 16

Look at the promotional flyer and then answer the following questions.

1 What kind of oil is in the bottle? What is the special offer with the oil?
2 What is the special offer on the price of the macaroni?
3 Is the chicken frozen? How much does it cost?
4 What flavours of jam (**μαρμελάδα**) do you see?
5 Which dairy products are advertised?
6 Find the Greek for:
   a only   c strained
   b free gift   d long life

ΕΥΚΑΙΡΙΕΣ

ΕΥΚΑΙΡΙΕΣ

1.

ΔΩΡΟ ελιές

Μόνο!! **4,25€**

Ελαιόλαδο **XENIA EXTRA** παρθένο 750 ml

2.

ΜΙΣΗ ΤΙΜΗ

Μόνο!! **0,65€**

Μακαρόνια **STELLA No 6**, 1 κιλό

3.
Μόνο!! **1,70€**

Κοτόπουλο φρέσκο το κιλό

4.

Μόνο!! **1,90€**

2 μαρμελάδες **NONA**

2 = 3

+1 ΔΩΡΟ

5.

ΤΟ γνήσιο **ΚΕΡΚΥΡΑΣ** ΦΡΕΣΚΟ ΒΟΥΤΥΡΟ **Αλπίνο**

Μόνο!! **2,10€** φρέσκο βούτυρο

ΚΕΡΚΥΡΑΣ ΑΛΠΙΝΟ 250 γρ.

Μόνο!! **0,60€**

Γιαούρτι ΜΕΒΓΑΛ **HARMONY** στραγγιστό 200 γρ.

Γάλα ΜΕΒΓΑΛ

Μόνο!! **0,90€**

5.5 Στο περίπτερο

 ΕΝΑ ΔΩΡΟ
A PRESENT

Katina, who works in an office nearby, is back at the kiosk.
She is looking for a last minute gift for Cosma, who is
celebrating. (It must be his nameday.)

γιορτάζω	celebrate
ίσως	maybe
το στιλό	pen
η ζώνη	belt
το κομπολόι	set of worry beads [*beads on a string, usually played with by men in the kafeneion*]
το κεχριμπάρι	amber
μπα	[*here*] hardly, not a chance [*used to express surprise or a negative response*]
δεν νομίζω	I don't think so
η εφημερίδα	newspaper
εξαρτάται	it depends
η γραβάτα	tie
βρε	expression of exasperation
το Βέλγιο	Belgium
το χαρτί	paper
τυλίγω	wrap
η παρέα	company
εμείς	we

ACTIVITY 17

Listen to the story then answer the following questions.

1 Does Vangelio have a wide range of gifts?
2 What is her first suggestion?
3 Are the worry beads amber?
4 Which newspaper does the passing customer buy?
5 What does Katina eventually choose?
6 What does Vangelio do with the gift?
7 Where is Katina going over the weekend?
8 During the conversation Katina says Τι ζώνη τι γραβάτα;
  What is the implication of her remark?

STORY TRANSCRIPT

Katina	Γειά σου, Βαγγελιώ! Θέλω ένα μικρό δώρο για τον Κοσμά – γιορτάζει .
Vangelio	Δεν έχω πολλά δώρα ... Ίσως ένα στιλό; Μία δερμάτινη ζώνη;
Katina	Αυτό το κομπολόι – είναι κεχριμπάρι;
Vangelio	Μπα, δεν νομίζω. Ορίστε, κύριε:
Male customer	Πόσο κάνουν οι ξένες εφημερίδες;
Vangelio	Εξαρτάται – η αγγλική κάνει χίλιες δραχμες, η γερμανική οχτακόσιες πενήντα.
Male customer	Μου δίνετε την αγγλική;
Katina	Γραβάτες πουλάς;
Vangelio	Γραβάτες; Περίπτερο είμαστε βρε Κατίνα!
Katina	Ε, τι ζώνη, τι γραβάτα;
Vangelio	Έλα τώρα Κατίνα – πάρε σοκολάτες. Είναι από το Βέλγιο. Έχω ωραίο χαρτί για δώρα.
Katina	Εντάξει. Δώσ' μου τις σοκολάτες. Τυλίγεις το κουτί;
Vangelio	Βέβαια.
Katina	Τι κάνετε το Σαββατοκύριακο;
Vangelio	Πάμε στο χωριό. Έχουμε παρέα τον Κραίηγκ από το Εδιμβούργο.
Katina	Με τον Κραίηγκ, ε; Εμείς πάμε στο θέατρο.

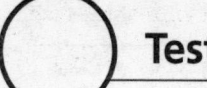

Test

Now it's time to test your progress in Unit 5.

1 Complete the sentences with the correct form of the adjective in brackets (and article, where shown).

   1 Το κατάστημα έχει _____ παπούτσια. (καλός)
   2 Θέλω μία/ένα _____ κοτόπουλο. (μικρός)
   3 Βλέπεις _____ δώρα; (ο ωραίος)
   4 Ο μουσακάς είναι _____. (νόστιμος)
   5 Ο λαϊκή δεν έχει _____ φρούτα σήμερα. (φρέσκος)
   6 Πουλάτε _____ εφημερίδες εδώ; (ξένος)
   7 Βλέπουμε τους _____ κήπους στην Αγγλία. (μεγάλος)

   7

2 Find the answers, writing them out in full in Greek.
   a 500 + 499   c 8 × 30   e 7000 + 20000
   b 1000000 − 500000   d 4 × 4 × 10

   5

3 Fill in the missing words on your list. Choose from the box.

   | μπουκάλι ντομάτες |
   | μάτσο πακέτο |
   | κρεμμύδια κιλό |

   ΜΑΚΑΡΟΝΑΔΑ
   • ένα ____ μακαρόνια
   • μισό ____ κιμά
   • ένα ____ μαϊντανό
   • ένα ____ λάδι (2 λίτρα)

   • δυο κιλά κόκκινες ____
   • μερικά ____

   6

4 Complete the sentences with the correct form of the verb.

1 Η Ελένη _____ γιαούρτι για πρωινό. (τρώω)
2 Ο μπακάλης δεν _____ φρέσκο βούτυρο. (πουλάω)
3 Τα παιδιά _____ λίγα γαλλικά. (μιλάω)
4 Τι _____ , Γιάννη, είναι δυνατόν; (λέω)
5 Δεν _____ κεφτέδες στη ταβέρνα. (υπάρχω)

6

5 Match 1–3 with the correct response from a–c.

1 Πόσο κάνουν τα κολοκυθάκια;
2 Μου δίνετε ένα τέταρτο φέτα;
3 Πάρτε μια πορτοκαλάδα!
a Δυστυχώς, δεν πουλάμε τυρί.
b Διακόσιες είκοσι το κιλό.
c Όχι ευχαριστώ.

6

6 Aliki is at the fruit market. Complete her conversation with the vendor. Remember to make the adjectives agree.

| δώστε μου | όλα μαζί | Ορίστε | μικρός | μέλι |
| Πουλάω | Τίποτ' άλλο; | γλυκός | φρέσκος | Μου δίνετε |

Αλίκη   Αα, φρούτα!
Πωλητής (1 I sell) _____ πορτοκάλια, μήλα, φράουλες, όλα τα φρούτα μου είναι (2 fresh) _____!
Αλίκη   Κυρ' Γιάννη, γειά σου. (3 Give me) _____ μισό κιλό ροδάκινα;
Πωλητής Πάρτε και ένα καρπούζι – είναι (4 sweet) _____ σαν το _____ (5 honey)!
Αλίκη   Εντάξει, (6 give me) _____ ένα (7 small) _____.
Πωλητής (8 Anything else?) _____
Αλίκη   Όχι ευχαριστώ. Πόσο κάνουνε (9 all together) _____;
Πωλητής Οχτακόσιες πενήντα.
Αλίκη   (10 Here's) _____ χίλιες.

10

TOTAL SCORE 40

If you scored less than 35, go through the Dialogues and the Language Building sections again, before completing the summary on page 74.

73

Summary 5

 Now try this final test summarizing the main points
covered in this unit. You can check your answers on the
recording.

How would you:
1 ask for a kilo of tomatoes?
2 ask for a glass of water?
3 ask 'Anything else?'?
4 ask how much the yellow bag is?
5 ask how much the shoes are?
6 say that the sandals are very expensive?
7 say you want a few tasty strawberries?
8 say there's no coffee at all?

REVISION

Go over all new items of vocabulary. Make sure you can
handle both first and second conjugation verbs. Also, to
review what you learned in earlier units, try various
conversational strategies – try to remember how you invite
someone to come in, to sit down, to speak up on the phone,
to get something from a particular shop. Make time to
'think Greek' – try to make up basic conversations around
the situations you have dealt with so far. Set the scene –
where are you? Name the characters – can you think of
Greek names? Use questions and answers, and the odd
exclamation.

▶ ▶ ▶ ▶ ▶ ▶ ▶ ▷ ▷ ▷ ▷ ▷ ▷ ▷ ▷ ▷ ▷

Transport

Συγκοινωνία

OBJECTIVES

In this unit you'll learn how to:

- ✓ book and buy tickets
- ✓ ask about plane/train/boat/bus times
- ✓ cope when you go to a garage
- ✓ read road signs

And cover the following grammar and language:

- ✓ the preposition **με** + means of transport
- ✓ more on time
- ✓ **αυτός** ('this') and **εκείνος** ('that')
- ✓ **πολύς** a lot, much
- ✓ **κάθε πότε;** ('how often?')
- ✓ adverbs

LEARNING GREEK 6

It is important to practise speaking aloud as often as possible. Besides improving your pronunciation and developing your fluency, this activity will help you memorize vocabulary and structures. Going through the same dialogue several times is also a good idea. You might try varying the tones – play the role happy, sad, shy, angry, young, old, and so on, as if you were auditioning for a part.

🎧 Now start the recording for Unit 6.

At the travel agency

Στο ταξιδιωτικό γραφείο

ACTIVITY 1 is on the recording.

ACTIVITY 2

Answer the following questions in both Greek and English.

1 How does the man want to travel?
2 When does he want to travel?
3 What leaves at 10.30?
4 What time does it arrive?
5 How much are the tickets?

DIALOGUE 1

○ Θα ήθελα να κλείσω δύο εισιτήρια για την Καβάλα.
■ Πώς θέλετε να πάτε;
○ Με το αεροπλάνο.
■ Για πότε τα θέλετε;
○ Για την Παρασκευή το πρωί.
■ Η πρώτη πτήση φεύγει στις δεκάμισι – σας κάνει;
○ Τι ώρα φτάνει;
■ Κάτα τις έντεκα και τέταρτο – αν δεν έχει καθυστέρηση.
○ Εντάξει. Πόσο κάνουν τα εισιτήρια;
■ Τα μονά κάνουν είκοσι τρεις χιλιάδες το ένα. Με επιστροφή κάνουν σαράντα πέντε χίλιάδες.
○ Α, ωραία, δεν είναι ακριβά. Δώστε μου δύο μονά παρακαλώ.

VOCABULARY

κλείνω	book, reserve (*lit.* close)
το εισιτήριο	ticket
το αεροπλάνο	aeroplane
πότε	when?
η πτήση	flight
φεύγω	leave
σας κάνει;	does it suit you?
φτάνω	arrive
κατά	towards, at about
η καθυστέρηση	delay
μονός/ή/ό	single, one way
η επιστροφή	return, round-trip
το ένα	each

✅ με + means of transport

The preposition με ('with') is used with all means of transport. It is followed by the appropriate accusative (object) form of the noun.

by bicycle	με το ποδήλατο	by motorbike	με τη μοτοσυκλέτα
by plane	με το αεροπλάνο	(idiomatically:	με το παπάκι)
by boat	με το καράβι	by ship	με το πλοίο
by bus	με το λεωφορείο	by taxi	με ταξί
by car	με το αυτοκίνητο	by train	με το τρένο
by coach	με το πούλμαν	on foot	με τα πόδια

✅ πότε/ποτέ

πότε; (stress in the first syllable) means 'when?'.
ποτέ (stress in the second syllable) means 'never'.

✅ στη μία/στις δύο

To say 'at' a particular time you use στις. στις δύο και είκοσι ('at 2.20'). The only exception to this is 'at one o'clock': στη μια.

When giving the half-hour, the word και is often lost: μιάμισι, δυόμισι, εννιάμισι, δωδεκάμισι, and so on. Remember that three and four change form (see page 53): τρεισήμισι, τεσσερισήμισι.

✅ από ('from'), για ('for')

The prepositions από and για are used to refer to the place of departure and the destination.

Το πούλμαν φεύγει **από** την Αθήνα **για** την Καβάλα στις εννιά η ώρα.
The coach leaves from Athens for Kavala at 9 o'clock.

✅ κάθε ('every')

Έχει λεωφορείο κάθε ώρα/μέρα/Σάββατο. There's a bus every hour/day/Saturday.

ACTIVITY 3

Write out the sentences in full, making any changes to the endings as necessary.
Example: αεροπλάνο / φεύγω / 6:00
Το αεροπλάνο φεύγει στις έξι η ώρα.

1 τρένο / φτάνω / 4:30
2 καράβι / φεύγω / 1:15
3 πάω / αγορά / πόδια / κάθε Τρίτη

Now do activities 4 and 5 on the recording.

At the harbour

Στο λιμάνι

ACTIVITY 6 is on the recording.

ACTIVITY 7

1 Where do the boats for Aegina leave from?
2 How far along Akti Poseidon is Karaiskaki Square?
3 How does the news vendor suggest the woman get to her departure point?
4 Where does the woman finally say she'll go?

DIALOGUE 2

○ Από πού φεύγει το καράβι για την Αίγινα;

■ Από την Ακτή Ποσειδώνος – εκεί, ευθεία, δεν είναι μακριά.

○ Μήπως ξέρετε κάθε πότε φεύγουνε τα φεριμπότ για το νησί;

■ Α, κυρία μου, αυτό δεν το ξέρω – αλλά πάνε τακτικά.

○ Και για τις Κυκλάδες, από πού φεύγουν τα πλοία;

■ Από την Πλατεία Καραϊσκάκη – λίγο πιο πέρα.

○ Είναι μακριά με τα πόδια;

■ Έχετε πολλές αποσκευές;

○ Όχι – μόνο αυτό το μπλε σακ βουαγιάζ, αυτή τη βαλίτσα και εκείνο το κουτί.

■ Πάρτε καλύτερα ένα ταξί.

○ Ωραία λοιπόν. Με ταξί στο Πασαλιμάνι και από εκεί με το δελφίνι στην Ύδρα.

■ Καλό ταξίδι!

VOCABULARY	
κάθε πότε;	how often?
το φεριμπότ	ferry
το νησί	island
τακτικά	regularly
λίγο πιο πέρα	a little further on
οι αποσκευές [pl.]	luggage
το σακ βουαγιάζ	travel bag
το δελφίνι	dolphin [type of hydrofoil]
καλό ταξίδι!	have a good journey!

✓ αυτός ('this') and εκείνος ('that')

αυτός and εκείνος agree in number, gender, and case with the noun they refer to or replace. They have the same endings as common adjectives. (See page 63.) When accompanying a noun, αυτός and εκείνος are followed by the definite article in its appropriate form.

αυτός ο άνθρωπος – this person   εκείνοι οι άνθρωποι – those people
εκείνη η τιμή – that price   αυτές οι τιμές – those prices
αυτό το λεωφορείο – this bus   εκείνα τα λεωφορεία – those buses

The following adjectives / pronouns agree with the noun but are not followed by the definite article:
πόσος ('how much?', 'how many?'), ποιος ('who'), λίγος ('a little', 'a few').

✓ πολύς ('a lot', 'much', 'many')

the adjective πολύς takes the following forms:

	masculine	*feminine*	*neuter*
singular	πολύς	πολλή	πολύ
plural	πολλοί	πολλές	πολλά

When πολύς describes the noun or pronoun which is the object of the sentence (accusative case), it takes the following endings.

	masculine	*feminine*	*neuter*
singular	πολύ	πολλή	πολύ
plural	πολλούς	πολλές	πολλά

Υπάρχει **πολύς** καφές. There is a lot of coffee.
Δεν θέλω **πολύ** κρασί. I don't want much wine.
Η Ελλάδα έχει **πολλά** νησιά. Greece has many islands.

πολύ is also an adverb meaning 'very'.

πολύ αργά – very late   ευχαριστώ πολύ – thank you very much

✓ Travelling around

arrivals	αφίξεις	(bus) stop	η στάση
departures	αναχωρήσεις	airport	το αεροδρόμιο
station	ο σταθμός	harbour/port	το λιμάνι

ACTIVITY 8

Choose the correct form

1 Πότε φεύγει εκείνος/εκείνη/εκείνο το πούλμαν;
2 Πηγαίνουμε στην Ελλάδα με αυτούς τους/αυτές τις/αυτά τα Αμερικάνους.

(🔊) Now do activities 9 and 10 on the recording.

Οι δρόμοι είναι επικίνδυνοι!

ACTIVITY 11 is on the recording.

ACTIVITY 12

Correct the statements which are false.

1 They are in a hurry to go to the village.   T / F
2 Irini refers to a specific example of Yorgos'
   careless driving.   T / F

DIALOGUE 3

○ Γιώργο, το αυτοκίνητο θέλει βενζίνη.

■ Καλά – πάω σε λίγο.

○ Κοίταξε και τα λάστιχα, το λάδι και το νερό.

■ Εντάξει. Αύριο φεύγουμε για το χωριό, γιατί βιάζεσαι;

○ Γιατί όλα τα αφήνεις μέχρι την τελευταία στιγμή!

■ Ησύχασε βρε Ειρήνη ...

○ Και μετά τρέχεις – σαν τρελός!

■ Οδηγώ πολύ προσεκτικά – δεν υπάρχει κίνδυνος ...

○ Γιώργο, θέλω να οδηγείς πιο αργά – σε παρακαλώ.

■ Μα δεν πάω πολύ γρήγορα – με τόση κίνηση;

VOCABULARY

η βενζίνη	petrol, gas
κοίταξε	see to, look at [*imperative*]
το λάστιχο	tyre
γιατί βιάζεσαι;	why are you in a hurry?
αφήνω	allow, let happen
όλος/η/ο	all, every
τελευταία στιγμή	last moment, second
ησύχασε	calm down, relax [*imperative*]
τρέχω	speed [*also* run]
σαν τρελλός	like a madman/lunatic
οδηγώ	drive
προσεκτικά	carefully
πιο αργά	more slowly
μα	but
γρήγορα	quickly, fast
τόση κίνηση	so much traffic

LANGUAGE BUILDING

✓ γιατί; /γιατί

γιατί means both 'why' and 'because'.

Γιατί τρέχει; Γιατί βιάζεται. Why is he running? Because he is in a hurry.

✓ Adverbs

Adverbs (words such as 'quickly', 'well', etc.) generally end in -α or -ώς. They do not change form.

Adjectives ending in -ος form the corresponding adverb with the ending -α: γρήγορος – γρήγορα ('quickly'), αργός – αργά ('slowly'), ήσυχος – ήσυχα ('quietly'). Adjectives ending in -ής form the corresponding adverb with the ending -ώς: δυστυχής – δυστυχώς ('unfortunately'). The first group is much more common than the second.

Other adverbs that do not follow the above pattern:

δωρεάν	free of charge	περίπου	approximately
καθόλου	not at all	πουθενά	nowhere
μήπως	by any chance, perhaps	πριν	previously, before
μόλις	just now, a moment ago	σχεδόν	almost
ξανά or πάλι	again	τώρα	now

✓ Places

You can usually work out the gender of places from their endings:
η Αθήνα, ο Βόλος, τα Ιωάννινα, οι Δελφοί

Islands, however, even when they end in -ος, are usually feminine:
η Ζάκυνθος, η Μύκονος, η Θάσος, η Κέρκυρα, η Θήρα, η Ιθάκη.

Foreign places, like other foreign words, are usually neuter: το Παρίσι, το Λονδίνο, το Βερολίνο. For some places an attached Greek ending determines the gender: η Νέα Υόρκη, η Ρώμη, οι Βρυξέλες (pl.).

✓ The imperative

Dialogue 3 contained examples of the imperative, the verb form used to give instructions: ησύχασε ('calm down') and κοίταξε ('look at/see to'). Other examples in earlier units include: ορίστε ('come through'), περάστε ('come in'), καθίστε ('sit down'). More details will be given in Unit 9.

ACTIVITY 13
Write in Greek:
1 My mother drives carefully.
2 Calm down, these tickets are free of charge.

🎧 Now do activities 14 and 15 on the recording.

Λόγια, λόγια, λόγια

To the chagrin of many a purist, more and more anglicized words are entering the Greek language, and there is much debate about the imported forms.

Although **ηλεκτρονική** and **τεχνολογία** are Greek, the more popular form for 'a computer' is **το κομπιούτερ** (rather than the more Greek **ο ηλεκτρονικός υπολογιστής/εγκέφαλος**). A hybrid is the phonecard, **η τηλεκάρτα**. More hellenic in flavour, although new world in style, is **το κινητό**, the mobile.

Most Greeks go to the **βενζινάδικο** ('place that sells petrol') – more formally known as **το πρατήριο βενζίνης** ('the petrol shop'). The petrol tank is **το ντεπόζιτο βενζίνης** (literally, 'the petrol deposit') and parking is **το πάρκιγκ** or **το γκαράζ**. Gear is **η ταχύτητα** (literally 'speed'), with top gear **μεγαλύτερη** (that is, 'biggest') and bottom gear **μικρότερη** (that is, smallest); 'reverse' is **όπισθεν**. Occasionally other languages slip in: in this context, for example, from French come **παρ-μπριζ** ('windscreen'), **μπουζί** ('spark-plug'), and **αμπραγιάζ** ('clutch').

ACTIVITY 16

Try guessing the match between the following Greek words and their English counterparts, then label the sketch of a car at a garage.

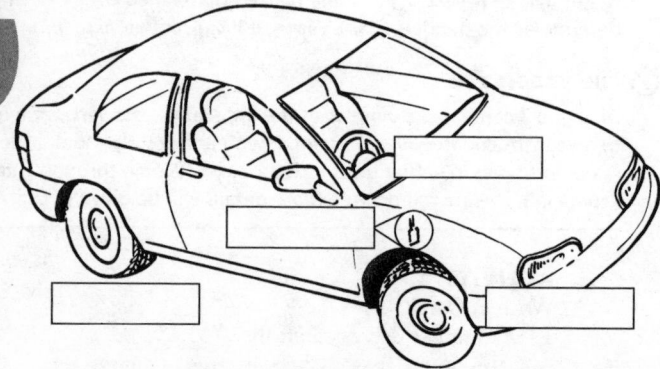

τροχός, προβολέας, τιμόνι, φρένο
headlight, steering wheel, brake, wheel

ACTIVITY 17

Find the correct signpost from 1–5 for each of the
instructions in a-e.

a ΑΠΑΓΟΡΕΥΕΤΑΙ ΤΟ ΚΑΠΝΙΣΜΑ
b ΑΠΑΓΟΡΕΥΕΤΑΙ Η ΣΤΑΘΜΕΥΣΗ
c ΚΙΝΔΥΝΟΣ
d ΟΔΗΓΕΙΤΕ ΑΡΓΑ
e ΜΗ ΜΙΛΑΤΕ ΣΤΟΝ ΟΔΗΓΟ

6.5 Στο περίπτερο

 ΕΝΑ ΜΙΚΡΟ ΑΤΥΧΗΜΑ
A LITTLE ACCIDENT

Vangelio's efforts to prepare for the weekend are interrupted by a sudden crash.

σταματάω	stop
το τάβλι	backgammon
ο αέρας	air
η μπαταρία	battery
η βέσπα	scooter
χριστιανέ μου	term of address used when outraged in some way
χτύπησες;	are you hurt?
σωστά	correctly
ξαναλέω	repeat
η γειτονιά μας	our neighbourhood
απόψε	tonight, this evening
προσοχή	be careful, beware
τα φανάρια	traffic lights
η συναυλία	concert
το Ολυμπιακό Στάδιο	the Olympic Stadium

ACTIVITY 18

Listen to the story and answer the following questions.

1 How many men are involved in the episode?
2 Can you name the men?
3 What vehicles are named?
4 What was the problem with the faulty vehicle?
5 What does Vangelio say the problem is?
6 What does Thanasis tell Sophia?

STORY TRANSCRIPT

Vangelio	Λάκη! Σταμάτα το τάβλι. Το βράδυ φεύγουμε και το αυτοκίνητο δεν έχει καθόλου βενζίνη!
Lakis	Καλά, καλά, και τα λάστιχα θέλουν αέρα, και η μπαταρία νερό...
Vangelio	Αμάν! Το ταξί του Περικλή! ... Και ο Θανάσης με τη βέσπα!
Pericles	Μα, χριστιανέ μου! Δεν βλέπεις μπροστά σου;
Vangelio	Θανάση, παιδί μου, χτύπησες;
Thanasis	Αχ! Αυτά τα φρένα - δεν δουλεύουν σωστά!
Vangelio	Το λέω και το ξαναλέω - αυτή η γωνία είναι επικίνδυνη.
Sofia	Θανάση - τι κάνεις εδώ;
Lakis	Βόλτα κάνει το παιδί ...
Pericles	Πολλή κίνηση έχει η γειτονιά μας απόψε ...
Vangelio	Ελάτε όλοι γρήγορα - προσοχή τα φανάρια!
Thanasis	Σοφία, έχω δύο εισιτήρια γιά την συναυλία στο Ολυμπιακό Στάδιο το Σάββατο ...

Now it's time to test your progress in Unit 6.

1 Match 1–5 with the correct ending from a–e.

1 Φεύγω από το λιμάνι	a με το πλοίο
2 Φεύγω από το σταθμό	b με τα πόδια
3 Φεύγω από το αεροδρόμιο	c με το τρένο
4 Φεύγω από τη στάση	d με το λεωφορείο
5 Φεύγω από το σπίτι	e με το αεροπλάνο

5

2 Find the correct Greek word/phrase for the following situations.

1 Where would you wait for a friend arriving by plane?
2 What would you be told if there had been a delay?
3 How would you ask for a return ticket?
4 What sign would you look for, for departures?
5 What is the Greek word for transport?

a συγκοινωνία	d υπάρχει καθυστέρηση
b αφίξεις	e με επιστροφή
c αναχωρήσεις	

5

3 Use the appropriate form of αυτός or εκείνος to complete the sentences.

1 _____ (αυτός) το αυτοκίνητο θέλει βενζίνη, _____ (εκείνος) θέλει αέρα στα λάστιχα.
2 _____ (αυτός) οι αποσκευές είναι για το Παρίσι, _____ (εκείνος) η βαλίτσα είναι για την Μαδρίτη.
3 Δεν ξέρω _____ (εκείνος) τους μεγάλους σταθμούς στο Λονδίνο.
4 _____ (εκείνος) τα φανάρια είναι κόκκινα.

6

4 Complete the following sentences by filling in the correct form of πολύς.

1 Η Ελλάδα έχει _____ νησιά.
2 Η μοτοσυκλέτα δεν θέλει _____ βενζίνη.

3 Ο Γιώργος τρέχει _____ γρήγορα.
4 Έχουμε _____ φωτογραφίες από το ταξίδι μας.

| | **4** |

5 You're at the information counter at the station. Ask the
   following questions:

1 At what time does the train leave for Volos?
2 Where does it leave from?
3 When does the bus from Salonica arrive?
4 Is there a delay?

Now say to the platform attendant:

5 I don't have a lot of luggage.

| | **10** |

6 Match 1–5 with the correct response from a–e.

1 Από πού φεύγει το   a Στις τεσσερισήμισι.
   καράβι για τη Ρόδο;
2 Χτύπησες;   b Από την Ακτή Μιαούλη.
3 Πότε φτάνει το τρένο;   c Γιατί άργησα.
4 Γιατί τρέχεις;   d Όχι, είμαι εντάξει.
5 Γιατί σταματάς;   e Γιατί τα φανάρια
                                είναι κόκκινα.

| | **10** |

7 Match 1–5 with the correct opposite from a–e.

1 δυστυχώς   a φεύγω
2 σιγά   b αργά
3 νωρίς   c εκείνος
4 φτάνω   d ευτυχώς
5 αυτός   e γρήγορα

| | **5** |

TOTAL SCORE | **45** |

If you scored less than 38 go through the Dialogues and the
Language Building sections again, before completing the
summary on page 88.

Summary 6

 Now try this final test summarizing the main points covered in this unit. You can check your answers on the recording.

How would you:
1 say you'd like to go by plane?
2 ask when the first flight is?
3 ask what time the bus leaves for Patras?
4 ask for a return ticket?
5 say the train arrives at 9.30?
6 ask where the boat for Tinos leaves from?
7 say 'this is my luggage'?

REVISION

In this unit you have again accumulated quite a lot of new vocabulary. To fix it in your mind, put it into action. Imagine a conversation with a travel agent in which you are booking tickets to the island of Amorgos: ask how often the boats go, where they leave from, how much the tickets are, and so on.

Dates and celebrations

Ημερομηνίες και γιορτές

OBJECTIVES

In this unit you'll learn how to:

- ✓ ask about birthdays and other special occasions
- ✓ give dates
- ✓ express your good wishes
- ✓ talk about people's ages
- ✓ talk about family relationships

And cover the following grammar and language:

- ✓ the genitive case
- ✓ adjectives (2)
- ✓ possessives

LEARNING GREEK 7

You should now be expanding your stock of common expressions to include everyday things that do not appear in this book. Make a mental note of subjects you discuss at work, at home, and with your friends. Be alert to phrases that come up again and again in conversation, and try to work out how you would say them in Greek. This way you will be able to respond more quickly, and participate in speaking situations, even if it is just with a short phrase.

If you do not know any native speakers you can consult, make use of a good dictionary. Look for one which not only gives translations of single words, but also provides examples of common phrases and expressions showing the fuller meaning of the word when seen in different contexts.

🎧 Now start the recording for Unit 7.

7.1 How time passes

Πώς περνάει ο καιρός

🎧 **ACTIVITY 1** is on the recording.

ACTIVITY 2

1 On what date does the conversation take place?
2 What has Stella brought?
3 What does Kirios Andreas offer Stella?
4 What does Kirios Andreas say about time passing?

DIALOGUE 1

○ Γειά σας, Κύριε Ανδρέα! Χρόνια πολλά!

■ Τι ημερομηνία έχουμε σήμερα;

○ Τριάντα Νοεμβρίου! Γιορτάζετε! Να ένα μικρό δώρο – ένα κασκόλ για το χειμώνα.

■ Α, Ευχαριστώ πολύ, Στέλλα μου. Έλα, πάρε ένα κονιάκ.

○ Λοιπόν. Χρόνια πολλά, κύριε Ανδρέα.

■ Νά'σαι καλά, παιδί μου, και ό,τι ποθείς.

○ Επίσης, κυρ' Ανδρέα, επίσης.

■ Αχ, Ο Νοέμβριος τελειώνει, και αύριο αρχίζει ο Δεκέμβριος. Πολύ γρήγορα φεύγει ο χρόνος. Πώς περνάει ο καιρός!

○ Δεν πειράζει – απόψε γλεντάμε μαζί – να και η παρέα!

VOCABULARY

η ημερομηνία	date
ο Νοέμβριος	November
γιορτάζω	celebrate
περνάω	pass
το κασκόλ	scarf
ο χειμώνας	winter
το κονιάκ	cognac, brandy
νά'σαι καλά	may you be well/may you keep well
τελειώνω	finish, end
αύριο	tomorrow
αρχίζω	start, begin
ο χρόνος	year
ο καιρός	time
απόψε	tonight
γλεντάω	have fun

✓ The months

'month' is ο μήνας and 'year' is ο χρόνος.
The months are all masculine and take the article. To say 'in' a month, use the accusative: τον Ιούνιο – in June. In the dialogue you heard the form τριάντα Νοεμβρίου '30 November'. In this construction, the month is in the genitive case – more details on this in section 7.2 on page 93.

To say 'on' a particular date you use στις + the normal number + the genitive case: στις εφτά Ιανουαρίου – on 7 January. There are a few exceptions: for the 3rd and 4th use τρεις and τέσσερις: στις τρεις Απριλίου – on 3 April. For the first of the month use την + πρώτη: την πρώτη Ιανουαρίου.

nominative	accusative	genitive
ο Ιανουάριος	τον Ιανουάριο	(του) Ιανουαρίου
ο Φεβρουάριος	τον Φεβρουάριο	(του) Φεβρουαρίου
ο Μάρτιος	τον Μάρτιο	(του) Μαρτίου
ο Απρίλιος	τον Απρίλιο	(του) Απριλίου
ο Μάιος	τον Μάιο	(του) Μαΐου
ο Ιούνιος	τον Ιούνιο	(του) Ιουνίου
ο Ιούλιος	τον Ιούλιο	(του) Ιουλίου
ο Αύγουστος	τον Αύγουστο	(του) Αυγούστου
ο Σεπτέμβριος	τον Σεπτέμβριο	(του) Σεπτεμβρίου
ο Οκτωβρίος	τον Οκτώβριο	(του) Οκτωβρίου
ο Νοέμβριος	τον Νοέμβριο	(του) Νοεμβρίου
ο Δεκέμβριος	τον Δεκέμβριο	(του) Δεκεμβρίου

✓ να

να is used to express good wishes 'May you …'/'I hope that …'

Να'σαι καλά. May you always be well.

It can also be used to mean 'there's … '.

Να το ταξί. There's the taxi.

Other uses of να will be shown in later units.

ACTIVITY 3

Put in the correct form of the date given in brackets:
e.g. Ο Κώστας γιορτάζει **στις** είκοσι μία Μαΐου (on 21/5)

1 Ο Γιάννης γιορτάζει _____ . (on 7/1)

2 Η Κατερίνα γιορτάζει _____ . (on 25/11)

3 Πάω στη Ζάμπια _____ . (in September)

4 Δεν πάμε στο σχολείο _____ . (on 1 May)

 Now do activities 4 and 5 on the recording.

How old are you?

Πόσων χρονών είσαι;

ACTIVITY 6 is on the recording.

ACTIVITY 7

Correct the statements which are false.

1 They are going to five parks today.   T / F
2 There are fifteen balloons in the room.   T / F
3 The birthday present is a hot-air balloon ride.   T / F
4 Dad asks about going to the wine festival later.   T / F

DIALOGUE 2

○ Μαμά, μαμά! Ξύπνα! Είναι τα γενέθλιά μου!

■ Χρόνια πολλά, λεβέντη μου! Και πόσων χρονών είσαι σήμερα;

○ Είμαι πέντε χρονών – και ο μπαμπάς λέει ότι στις πέντε η ώρα πάμε στο λούνα παρκ με την Νίκη και τον Θωμά!

■ Και τώρα, τι κάνουμε;

○ Μία τούρτα, με πέντε αυγά, και πέντε κεριά!

▼ Βλέπω πέντε μπαλόνια ...

■ Ακούω ένα κουδούνι ...

○ Ποδήλατο! Ένα μεγάλο ποδήλατο!

■ Το μεγάλο ποδήλατο του μεγάλου παιδιού!

▼ Πάμε μαζί στη γιορτή του κρασιού;

○ Όχι, μαμά, μπαμπά, πάμε στην παιδική χαρά!

VOCABULARY	
ξυπνάω	wake up
τα γενέθλιά μου	my birthday
ο λεβέντης	fine young man
ο μπαμπάς	dad
το λούνα παρκ	amusement park
η τούρτα	birthday cake
το κερί	candle
το μπαλόνι	balloon
το κουδούνι	bell
η παιδική χαρά	playground

✓ The genitive case

The genitive case is used to show possession: the doctor's house το σπίτι *του γιατρού*. Anna's friend – ο φίλος *της Άννας*.

It is also used for the indirect object ('to whom' or 'to which' something is done) of the verb.

Δίνω **του Γιάννη** ένα βιβλίο. I am giving John a book / I am giving a book *to John*.

Nouns

The genitive singular of masculine nouns ending in -ος, and of neuter nouns, ends in –ου; other masculine nouns simply drop the final -ς. For feminine nouns -ς is added. The plural ending for all forms is -ων and the stress usually moves on a syllable.

singular	*masculine*	*feminine*	*neuter*
nominative	ο άνθρωπος, ο άνδρας	η γυναίκα	το σπίτι
genitive	*του ανθρώπου, του άνδρα*	*της γυναίκας*	*του σπιτιού*
plural			
nominative	οι άνθρωποι	οι γυναίκες	τα σπίτια
genitive	*των ανθρώπων*	*των γυναικών*	*των σπιτιών*

Adjectives

	masculine	*feminine*	*neuter*
singular	*του καλού άνδρα/ανθρώπου*	*της καλής γυναίκας*	*τού καλου σπιτιού*
plural	*των καλών ανδρών/ανθρώπων*	*των καλών γυναικών*	*των καλών σπιτιών*

Other examples of the genitive

– in dates, as seen in 7.1.

– to talk about age in the phrase **πόσων χρονών είσαι;** ('how old are you?') and in the response: Είμαι είκοσι δύο **χρονών.** I'm 22.
Note the forms of one, three, and four: **ενός χρονού** (singular), **τριών χρονών, τεσσάρων χρονών.** (χρονών = years *of* age)

ACTIVITY 8

Complete the sentences with the genitive case of the nouns.
Example: Η μπανάνα είναι *του παιδιού*. (το παιδί)

1 Τα παπούτσια είναι _____ . (οι γυναίκες)
2 Τα μπαλόνια είναι _____ . (ο Γιάννης)
3 Ο καφές είναι _____ . (η Μαρία)

 Now do activities 9 and 10 on the recording.

93

7.3 Are you ready?

Είσαι έτοιμη;

🔊 **ACTIVITY 11** is on the recording.

ACTIVITY 12

1 Η Νίκη **a** είναι έτοιμη **b** φοράει αθλητικά ρούχα.
2 **a** Ο Ολυμπιακός υπάρχει για τριάντα χρόνια.
  b Η γιαγιά είναι παντρεμένη για τριάντα χρόνια.
3 Η επέτειος είναι **a** ομάδα. **b** γιορτή. **c** ημερομηνία.
4 **a** Ο Ολυμπιακός **b** Ο παππούς παίζει μπάλα σήμερα.

DIALOGUE 3

○ Νίκη, είσαι έτοιμη; Φεύγουμε.
■ Όχι ακόμα.
○ Μπα, τι είναι αυτά;
■ Τα καινούρια αθλητικά μου ρούχα – σήμερα παίζει ο Ολυμπιακός. Πού είναι η μπάλα μου;
○ Σήμερα έχουν επέτειο η γιαγιά και ο παππούς.
■ Πόσα χρόνια είναι παντρεμένοι;
○ Τριάντα.
■ Και πόσα χρόνια υπάρχει η ομάδα του Ολυμπιακού;
○ Δεν ξέρω. Ρώτα τον πατέρα. Να η γιαγιά και ο παππούς!
■ Γειά σας, γειά σας! Γιαγιά! Παππού! Να ζήσετε! Χρόνια πολλα και ευτυχισμένα!

VOCABULARY	
έτοιμος/η/ο	ready
όχι ακόμα	not yet
καινούριος/ια/ο	new
το ρούχο	item of clothing [*usually* τα ρούχα clothes]
παίζω	play
ο Ολυμπιακός	Olympiakos [*here: a top sports club*]
η γιαγιά	granny, grandma
ο παππούς	grandad, grandpa
η επέτειος	anniversary
παντρεμένος/η/ο	married
η ομάδα	team
ρωτάω	ask
ο πατέρας	father
η μπάλα	ball
ευτυχισμένος/η/ο	happy

✅ Adjectives (2)

Adjectives can come before or after the noun.

> Έχω κόκκινες ντομάτες/Έχω ντομάτες κόκκινες. I have red tomatoes.
> Χρόνια Πολλά και Ευτυχισμένα! Many happy returns!

Note that when the adjective is placed *after* a noun with a definite article, the article is repeated.

> οι ντομάτες οι κόκκινες – the red tomatoes

✅ Negatives

Remember that δεν is used to make verbs negative.
> Δεν καταλαβαίνουμε. We don't understand.
> Δεν πειράζει. It doesn't matter.

όχι is used to make words other than verbs negative.

> Όχι τώρα! Not now! Όχι ακόμα. Not yet.

✅ Possessives

As in English, the form of the possessive ('my', 'your', etc.), is determined by the number and gender of the possessor.

μου	my	το όνομά **μου** – my name
σου	your	το αυτοκίνητό **σου** – your car
του	his	η ομάδα **του** – his team
της	her	τα ρούχα **της** – her clothes
του	its	η ουρά **του** – its tail
μας	our	η μπάλα **μας** – our ball
σας	your	τα σπίτια **σας** – your houses
τους	their	η δουλειά **τους** – their work

ACTIVITY 13

1 ο άνδρας   2 η γυναίκα   3 τα παιδιά

a   b   c   d   e   f   g

Write a sentence matching 1, 2, and 3 with their belongings.
Example: 1a Το διαβατήριό του.

 Now do activities 14 and 15 on the recording.

95

Καλές γιορτές

The Greeks have always prided themselves on maintaining a healthy balance between work and play. While the culture is not short of rigour, life would lose its gusto (**το κέφι**) if there were not at least one generally celebrated feast day a month. Here is a selection:

1 Ιανουαρίου	**Πρωτοχρονιά** (New Year): a special cake, **Βασιλόπιτα**, is baked
6 Ιανουαρίου	**Θεοφάνια** (Epiphany): the public blessing of the waters: seas, lakes, rivers, wells, reservoirs
Φεβρουάριο/Μάρτιο	**Απόκριες** (depending on when Easter is): pre-Lent carnival season
Μάρτιο	**Καθαρή Δευτέρα** ('Clean' Monday, i.e. Shrove Monday): picnics and kite-flying all over Greece
25η Μαρτίου	national holiday celebrating independence (parades) as well as the Annunciation
Μάρτιο/Απρίλιο	**Πάσχα** (Easter): the most important series of services in the Greek Orthodox calendar
Πρωτομαγιά	May Day: public holiday and the gathering of flowers all over Greece
Δεκαπενταύγουστος	**Της Παναγίας** (Assumption Day: 15 August): universally celebrated
8 Σεπτεμβρίου	**Γενέσιο της Θεοτόκου** (Birth of the Virgin Mary): major feasts/services, followed by fasting for the Exaltation of the Cross on 14 September
28η Οκτωβρίου	**Το Μεγάλο Όχι**: celebrates Greece's refusal to capitulate to Mussolini; feasts as well as military parades and remembrance services
25 Δεκεμβρίου	**Χριστούγεννα** (Christmas)

Each month also has its share of name days, each with its steady stream of gift-wrapped flowers, cakes, chocolates, spirits, and gifts. A person's name day used to be his/her main annual celebration. Most Greek names come from the Orthodox calendar, so a name day is celebrated on the matching saint's day. For names with a 'pagan' source, such as Artemis, Socrates, etc., there is no assigned date.

In summer there are many additional outdoor events –
festivals of song, dance, theatre, wine, and so on. Many
islands, villages, and even urban communities have their
own local traditions, often traceable back to antiquity.

ACTIVITY 16

Look at the poster and answer the following questions.

1 What kind of festival is being advertised?
2 When does the festival take place?
3 Where are the festivities going to be held?
4 What is being offered free?
5 What will be available at the kiosks?
6 What kind of entertainments will be available?
7 Who is sponsoring the event?
8 What is the festival motto at the bottom of the poster?

ΓΙΟΡΤΗ ΚΡΑΣΙΟΥ

15–23 ΣΕΠΤΕΜΒΡΙΟΥ

ΚΑΘΕ ΑΠΟΓΕΥΜΑ
ΣΤΟ ΔΗΜΟΤΙΚΟ ΚΗΠΟ ΠΑΦΟΥ

ΟΛΑ ΤΑ ΚΡΑΣΙΑ ΤΗΣ ΚΥΠΡΟΥ—*ΔΩΡΕΑΝ!*

Δοκιμάστε τα όλα!

ΜΕΖΕΔΕΣ ΣΤΑ ΠΕΡΙΠΤΕΡΑ
Σουβλάκια, λουκάνικα παστουρμά, σαλάτες, λούντσα,
κεφτεδάκια, ντολμαδάκια, χαλούμι, ελιές, πιτάκια - απ'όλα!

Φάτε σουτζούκι!

ΠΑΡΑΔΟΣΙΑΚΗ ΜΟΥΣΙΚΗ, ΧΟΡΟΙ, ΘΕΑΤΡΟ,
ΚΑΡΑΓΚΙΟΖΗΣ

Χορέψτε, τραγουδήστε, διασκεδάστε!

ΕΛΑΤΕ ΝΑ ΓΙΟΡΤΑΣΕΤΕ ΜΑΖΙ ΜΑΣ!

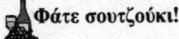 "ΠΙΝΕ ΚΡΑΣΙ ΝΑ'ΧΕΙΣ ΖΩΗ!"

ΔΗΜΟΣ ΛΕΜΕΣΟΥ ● *ΤΟΥΡΙΣΤΙΚΟΣ ΟΡΓΑΝΙΣΜΟΣ ΚΥΠΡΟΥ*

ACTIVITY 17

Read through the poster material again and try to find the
Greek for the following:

1 Try them all!   2 Dance, sing, have fun!
3 Eat must-sausage!   4 Come and celebrate with us.

7.5 Στο περίπτερο

Η NONA
THE GODMOTHER

Katina has dropped by to talk about a christening. Today she has something new to complain about.

βαφτίζω	baptize, christen
το μωρό	baby
αλλά	but
το όνομα, ονοματάκι	name
άλλος/η/ο	other
μαθαίνω	learn
παίρνω	take
η εποχή	time, period
το έθιμο	custom, practice
τόσος/η/ο	so much, so many
η χάρη	grace, charm
δίκιο έχεις	you're right
η μπεμπέκα	baby girl
να 'ναι καλά	may (s)he be well

ACTIVITY 18

Listen to the story and answer the following questions.

1 When is the christening?
2 What is the problem?
3 Who is called Amalia?
4 What is the baby's name to be?
5 Who is to be the godmother?
6 What kind of name would Katina prefer?

STORY TRANSCRIPT

Vangelio	Γειά σου, Κατινάκι. Πότε βαφτίζετε το μωρό;
Katina	Την Κυριακή – αλλά έχω πρόβλημα με το όνομα.
Vangelio	Γιατί;
Katina	Το όνομα της γιαγιάς είναι Αμαλία, αλλά σήμερα μαθαίνω ότι το παιδί θα το λένε Μονίκ ...
Vangelio	Ωραίο ονοματάκι - Μονί-ικ.
Katina	Καλό είναι, αλλά ξένο. Γιατί δεν παίρνει το όνομα της γιαγιάς της;
Vangelio	Άλλες εποχές, άλλα έθιμα.
Katina	Ναι, αλλά τι έχει το 'Αμαλία'; Αμαλία, Λία, Λιλί, Λιλίκα ...
Vangelio	Κατίνα, εσύ είσαι η νονά ...
Katina	Υπάρχουν τόσα ωραία ελληνικά ονόματα ...
Vangelio	Και τα ξένα ονόματα έχουν τη χάρη τους. Να σας ζήσει η μικρή!
Katina	Α-α-χ, δίκιο έχεις Βαγγελιώ μου ... Να μας ζήσει η μπεμπέκα μας, και να'ναι καλά η γιαγιά της.

Test

Now it's time to test your progress in Unit 7.

1 Give the following dates in Greek.

    1 14 February
    2 31 August
    3 4 July
    4 today's date
    5 the date of your birthday

5

2 Complete the sentences with the correct form of the verb in brackets.

    1 Ο Πέτρος _____ μπάσκετ κάθε Σάββατο. (παίζω)
    2 Πότε _____ η Ράνια; (γιορτάζω)
    3 Η νονά και ο νονός _____ το μωρό την Κυριακή. (βαφτίζω)
    4 Τα παιδιά _____ αγγλικά στο σχολείο. (μαθαίνω)
    5 Αχ! Σήμερα _____ τα προβλήματά μας. (αρχίζω)

5

3 How would you do the following in Greek?
(2 points for each correct answer, 1 point if you make one mistake)

    1 Say 'Here's the gang.'
    2 Tell a friend 'It's our anniversary.'.
    3 Say, the end of the year.
    4 Say you have a little gift for your godmother.
    5 Ask where the doctor's house is.

10

4 Choose from the following to complete the dialogue.

    a Μάλιστα. Με λένε Αριάνα.
    b Ευχαριστώ πολύ. Νά 'στε καλά.
    c Είσαστε παντρεμένη;
    d Ο άνδρας μου; Απόψε παίζει ποδόσφαιρο.
    e Πόσων χρονών είναι;
    f Όχι ακόμα, αλλά έχουν μερικές μέρες.

Άνδρας: 1 _____

Γυναίκα: Βεβαίως, και έχω δύο παιδιά.

Άνδρας: 2 _____

Γυναίκα: Η Βάλια είναι έξι χρονών, και ο Τάκης εννιά.

Άνδρας: Α! Είσαστε η γυναίκα του Οδυσσέα;

Γυναίκα: 3 _____

Άνδρας: Χαίρω πολύ. Πού είναι ο άνδρας σας;

Γυναίκα: 4 _____

Άνδρας: Α, ναι, έχουν μεγάλο παιχνίδι στις τρεις
          Δεκεμβρίου ... Είναι έτοιμοι;

Γυναίκα: 5 _____

Άνδρας: Καλή επιτυχία τους!

Γυναίκα: 6 _____

| 6 |

5 Complete the sentences with the correct genitive form of
  the words in brackets.

  1 Το χρώμα _____ . (ο Ολυμπιακός)
  2 Η γιορτή _____ . (τα παιδιά)
  3 Τα γενέθλια _____ . (ο παππούς)
  4 Η επέτειος _____ . (η μαμά και ο μπαμπάς)
  5 Το όνομα _____ . (ο φίλος μου)

| 5 |

6 Match the greeting with the appropriate card.

  a Καλό Πάσχα   d Να σας ζήσει
  b Καλά Χριστούγεννα   e Χρόνια Πολλά – να ζήσετε
  c Καλή Χρονιά

| 5 |

TOTAL SCORE | 36 |

If you scored less than 28 go through the dialogues and the
Language Building sections again, before completing the
summary on page 102.

Summary 7

Now try this final test summarizing the main points covered in this unit. You can check your answers on the recording.

How would you:
1 ask someone's age?
2 ask someone when her birthday is?
3 ask someone when he celebrates?
4 say on 4 July?
5 say 'Happy Birthday!'?
6 say 'It's Maria's baby'?
7 ask a colleague where his team is playing on Saturday?

REVISION

In preparation for Review 2, dip into some of the earlier units again. Listen to some of the dialogues. Go over the vocabulary lists you have been putting together. Imagine yourself in various situations, to revise the key language you'll need. Could you book a room in a hotel? shop for food, a gift, an item of clothing, things at a kiosk? buy a ticket for the ferry, use local transport? These are the situations you'll need to cope in if you go to Greece, so make sure you're familiar with the vocabulary and structures required.

Review 2

VOCABULARY

1 δίκλινο / γκαρσονιέρα / τρίκλινο
  Θέλω ένα δωμάτιο με τρία κρεβάτια - ένα _____
  – Υπάρχει;

2 κόρη / γιαγιά / αδελφή
  Η μητέρα της μητέρας μου, η _____ μου, είναι
  στην κουζίνα.

3 εισιτήριο / εφημερίδα / διαβατήριο
  Το Σεπτέμβριο φεύγω για την Ινδία - θέλω καινούριο
  _____ .

4 παίζει / περιμένει / φοράει
  Ο Λουίζος δεν _____ ποτέ γραβάτα.

5 θέα / θάλασσα / βουνό
  Απόψε πάω στη _____ για μπάνιο.

6 κατάστημα / λαϊκή / αγορά
  Η Νίκη ξυπνάει νωρίς και πηγαίνει πρωί-πρωί στη
  _____ για φρέσκα φρούτα και λαχανικά.

7 μεγάλος / καινούριος / έτοιμος
  Γρήγορα! Δεν είσαι _____ ακόμα; Το μάθημα
  αρχίζει στις εννιά.

8 λεωφορείο / πλοίο / πτήση
  Η _____ από το Λονδίνο, ΟΑ 301, φτάνει στις
  έντεκα και τέταρτο.

9 πακέτο / μπουκάλι / κουτί
  Φέρε μου ένα _____ σπίρτα, παρακαλώ.

10 κλειδί / κινητό / καράβι
  Το _____ μου δεν δουλεύει — πού υπάρχει
  τηλέφωνο;

2 Match the comments 1–5 with the appropriate response from a–e.

1
> Θα ήθελα τρία εισιτήρια για τη Νάξο.

a
> Την Τετάρτη – δεκαεννιά Ιουνίου.

2
> Χρόνια Πολλά! Καλό Πάσχα!

b
> Μονά ή με επιστροφή;

3
> Μου δίνετε τη ζώνη που έχετε στη βιτρίνα;

c
> Θα ήθελα τον γιατρό, παρακαλώ

4
> Πότε γιορτάζετε;

d
> Τη μαύρη ή την καφετιά;

5
> Εμπρός, λέγετε.

e
> Ευχαριστώ, επίσης.

GRAMMAR AND USAGE

3 Complete the sentences with the verbs from the box: the verbs need to be changed to the appropriate form.

> φοράω   τυλίγω   πουλάω   οδηγώ   σερβίρω
> παίζω   μαθαίνω   νοικιάζω

1 _____ μία μεγάλη, μαύρη Κάντιλακ. (εγώ)
2 Το κατάστημα _____ ιταλικές ζώνες.
3 Ο άνδρας μου _____ ακριβές γραβάτες.
4 _____ τα δώρα με ωραίο χαρτί εδώ;
5 Δυστυχώς, δεν _____ κρασί - πάτε στην ταβέρνα δίπλα.
6 Τα παιδιά _____ τένις κάθε Παρασκευή.
7 Δεν πάω βόλτα με τα πόδια, _____ μια βέσπα – μόνο χίλιες δραχμές την ημέρα!
8 _____ ισπανικά τα βράδια στο πολυτεχνείο. (εγώ)

4 Complete the sentences with the correct word from the box.

> στις   στο   από   την   στα   για   στην   τον   στις

1 Το λεωφορείο _____ τη Ραφήνα φτάνει εδώ _____ δυόμισι.

2 _____ Αύγουστο πηγαίνουνε πολλά ταξίδια _____ νησιά.

3 Η μαμά γιορτάζει _____ 11 Απριλίου.

4 _____ πού φεύγει το τρένο _____ τη Λάρισα;

5 Πότε πάμε _____ Ιταλία;
_____ Τετάρτη.

5 Change the nouns and adjectives given in brackets into the plural.

1 Ο Μίμης έχει εφτά _____ . (κόκκινος, μπαλόνι)

2 Η Δανάη περιμένει _____ . (πολύς, φίλος)

3 _____ υπάρχουν για το σπιτι μας; (πόσος, κλειδί)

4 Δώστε μου _____ παρακαλώ. (τρία, πράσινα, πιπεριά)

5 Α- α! Τι _____ . (ωραίος, δέντρο)

🎧 LISTENING

6 Your friend Michalis has left a message on your answerphone, inviting you out later this week. Listen to it, noting down the missing information.

Καλημέρα παιδιά! (1) _____ είμαι. Ξέρετε ότι ο Παναθηναϊκός παίζει μπάλα την (2) _____ στο Στάδιο ... Λοιπόν - έχω (3) _____ εισιτήρια! Οχι μπάσκετ - (4) _____! Πάμε μαζί; Τα εισιτήρια κάνουν (5) _____, και το παιχνίδι αρχίζει (6) _____. Θέλετε να πάμε με το λεωφορείο; Φεύγουμε από την (7) _____ στις έξι η ώρα την Τρίτη, δεκατρείς Φεβρουαρίου! Πάρτε με τηλέφωνο στο (8) _____. Γειά σας!

7 Roula is chatting to her friend about tonight's meal. Listen to their conversation and then answer the following questions.

1 What is the name of the dish she is planning?

2 What does her friend have reservations about?

3 When is Roula leaving the office?

4 Where is she going first?

5 What is she going to get at the grocer's?

6 What else does her friend want her to pick up?

7 What will her friend bring?

8 You're on the phone to your travel agent. Prepare your answers here, then join in the activity on the recording. Try to do it without looking at your notes.

You   1 Ask what time the flight leaves for Rethymnon.

You   2 Ask what time it arrives there.

You   3 Ask how often there's a boat to Crete.

You   4 Ask how much the taxi is to the airport.

9 You're booking a room in a hotel in Athens. Prepare your answers and then join in the dialogue on the recording. Try to do it without looking at your notes.

Receptionist	Καλησπέρα σας
You	Say good evening. Say you'd like to reserve a room.

Receptionist	Τι δωμάτιο θέλετε;
You	Say you want a double, with bath.

Receptionist	Για πότε;
You	Say for 1 August.

Receptionist	Εντάξει - έχουμε ένα άνετο δωμάτιο στον δεύτερο όροφο.
You	Ask if it has a nice view

Receptionist	Βεβαίως!
You	Ask how much it costs.

Receptionist	Για το Σαββατοκύριακο, για δύο, κάνει τριανταπέντε χιλιάδες – με πρωινό.
You	Say that's fine, thank you.

Entertainment

Ψυχαγωγία

OBJECTIVES

In this unit you'll learn how to:

- ✔ express likes and dislikes
- ✔ express preferences
- ✔ talk about some kinds of entertainment
- ✔ ask about people

And cover the following grammar and language:

- ✔ the construction **μ'αρέσει / μ'αρέσουν** ('I like')
- ✔ **ούτε … ούτε** ('neither … nor)
- ✔ **ότι** ('that')
- ✔ **ποιος, ποια, ποιο** ('who', 'which')

LEARNING GREEK 8

Try to get access to satellite television or videos in Greek. Don't worry about trying to understand everything, but get used to hearing everyday Greek spoken at normal speed. International news is a good thing to listen to, particularly if you have already heard the news in English and have an idea of what the Greek speaker may be talking about. Soaps and TV series are also fun to watch. Their language is usually not too elaborate, and the contexts will often give you clues as to what is being said.

If you can find Greek films with subtitles, these are also useful learning tools. You'll find that you can pick up a lot of vocabulary by making use of the subtitles, especially for words and expressions that occur regularly. Don't forget to use your dictionary too.

Now start the recording for Unit 8.

Καλή όρεξη!

ACTIVITY 1 is on the recording.

ACTIVITY 2

Correct the statements which are false.

1 Η κυρία θέλει ψάρι απόψε.   T / F
2 Ο κύριος δεν είναι χορτοφάγος.   T / F
3 Η κυρία και ο κύριος θέλουνε μια ποικιλία.   T / F

DIALOGUE 1

○ Έχουν ωραίο ψάρι εδώ. Τι σ'αρέσει; Το μπαρμπούνι, ο
   ξιφίας, ο μπακαλιάρος με σκορδαλιά, ...
■ Αα, μπα, δεν θέλω ούτε ψάρι, ούτε κρέας.
○ Γιατί – είσαι χορτοφάγος;
■ Όχι, αλλά προτιμώ κάτι άλλο απόψε.
○ Γκαρσόν, τον κατάλογο, παρακαλώ! ... Θέλεις γεμιστά;
■ Μμμ! Έχουν κοτόπουλο αυγολέμονο ... μμμ ....
○ Αρνάκι με πατάτες! Όχι. ... Εγώ θα πάρω χταπόδι.
■ Πώς μ'αρέσει η φάβα, ... αχ, και χόρτα! Τι δύσκολο.
○ Λοιπόν, αρχίζουμε με μία ποικιλία ορεκτικά ...
▼ Είσαστε έτοιμοι;

VOCABULARY

το μπαρμπούνι	red mullet
ο ξιφίας	swordfish
ο μπακαλιάρος	cod, haddock
η σκορδαλιά	*a potato-garlic purée, served with cod*
το κρέας	meat
ο χορτοφάγος	vegetarian
προτιμώ	I prefer
ο κατάλογος	menu
γεμιστός/ή/ό	stuffed, filled
κοτόπουλο αυγολέμονο	chicken in egg-lemon sauce
αρνάκι με πατάτες	lamb with potatoes
εγώ θα πάρω	I'll take
χταπόδι	octopus
η φάβα	pea purée
τα χόρτα	greens
δύσκολος/η/ο	difficult
ποικιλία ορεκτικά	selection of appetizers

LANGUAGE BUILDING

✅ μ'αρέσει / μ'αρέσουνε ('I like')

To say you *like something*, you use the structure μ'αρέσει (it appeals to me). The thing liked is the subject of the sentence.

> **Μ'αρέσει** το ελληνικό φαγητό. I like Greek food.
> **Μ'αρέσει** η κιθάρα σου. I like your guitar.

To talk about what someone else likes (or doesn't like) exactly the same verb is used, but the pronoun changes. The pronoun used in this construction is the indirect object pronoun.

μου αρέσει [μ'αρέσει]	I like	*μας* αρέσει	we like
σου αρέσει [σ'αρέσει]	you like	*σας* αρέσει	you like
του/της/του αρέσει	he/she/it likes	*τους* αρέσει	they like

> Τι σ'αρέσει; What do you like?
> Δεν **μας** αρέσει η τηλεόραση. We don't like television.

If you want to say someone *likes more than one thing*, the verb changes to αρέσουνε (accompanied by the appropriate pronoun).

> Της **αρέσουνε** οι γάτες. She likes cats.
> Δεν τους **αρέσουνε** τα ζώα. They don't like animals.
> Σας **αρέσουνε** οι γαλλικές ταινίες; Do you like French films?

Notice that whatever is liked can appear before or after μ'αρέσει.

> **Το θέατρο** μ'αρέσει. *or* **Μ'αρέσει το θέατρο**. I like the theatre.
> **Το αρνάκι** μ'αρέσει αλλά προτιμώ το κοτόπουλο. I like lamb, but I prefer chicken.

✅ ούτε ... ούτε ('neither ... nor')

Remember that Greek uses the double negative, so in this construction the negative δεν is included with the verb.

> Δεν θέλω **ούτε** ψάρι, **ούτε** κρέας. I want neither fish nor meat.
> 'either ... or' is **ή ... ή**.
> Θέλουμε **ή** σούπα **ή** μεζέδες – όχι και τα δυό. We want either soup or starters – not both.

ACTIVITY 3

How would you write the following in Greek?

1 I like black cats.
2 He doesn't like large animals.
3 They like neither cars nor buses – they prefer taxis.
4 We like Italian shoes.
5 Do you like Helen's bicycle?

🎧 Now do activities 4 and 5 on the recording.

Have a good time!

Καλή διασκέδαση!

ACTIVITY 6 is on the recording.

ACTIVITY 7

1 Which orchestra is playing Mahler tonight?
2 What sort of performance is *Το Κλουβί με τις Τρελές*?
3 Which play would Marina prefer to see?
4 What is the film they finally agree on?

DIALOGUE 2

○ Τι θα κάνουμε απόψε, Μαρίνα; Η Φιλαρμονική Ορχήστρα του Βερολίνου παίζει Μάλερ στο Μέγαρο Μουσικής.

■ Στο Θέατρο Αλίκη παίζει *Το Κλουβί με τις Τρελές*. Ο Νίκος λέει ότι είναι υπέροχη κωμωδία.

○ Αν μιλάμε για θέατρο, γιατί δεν πάμε στο *Αγαμέμνων*;

▼ Κορίτσια – Ελάτε, πάμε στο σινεμά – όλοι λένε ότι το *Μπουένα Βίστα* είναι καταπληκτικό έργο! Σας αρέσει η μουσική της Κούβας;

○ Α, ναι! Η τελευταία ταινία του Βιμ Βέντερς …

▼ Έγινε! Βλέπουμε την ταινία, και μετά πάμε για φαγητό.

■ Καλή μας διασκέδαση!

▼ Και άλλη φορά στα μπουζούκια!

VOCABULARY

το κλουβί	cage
Το Κλουβί με τις Τρελές	*The Birdcage*
υπέροχος/η/ο	marvellous, excellent
η κωμωδία	comedy
Αγαμέμνων	*Agamemnon* [*play by Aeschylus*]
το κορίτσι	girl
λέω	say, tell
καταπληκτικός/ή/ό	amazing, fantastic
το έργο	film, movie [*also* work]
τελευταίος/α/ο	last, latest
η ταινία	film, movie
έγινε!	done!
μετά	after(wards)
άλλη φορά	another time, next time

✅ ό*τι* ('that')

ότι is used in constructions such as λέω ότι ('I say that'), νομίζω ότι ('I think that'), ξέρω οτι ('I know that'), and είμαι βέβαιος ότι ('I'm sure that ... ').

Ο Νίκος λέει ότι είναι υπέροχη κωμωδία Nikos says it's an excellent comedy.

Νομίζω ότι ο καινούριος διευθυντής είναι απαίσιος. I think that the new manager is horrible.

✅ Giving your opinion

απίθανος/η/ο	fantastic
εξαιρετικός/ή/ό	exceptional, excellent
θαυμάσιος/η/ο	wonderful
καλός/ή/ό	good
καταπληκτικός/ή/ό	amazing, fantastic
υπέροχος/η/ο	marvellous, excellent
φοβερός/ή/ό	awful, awesome
φριχτός/ή/ό	terrible
απαίσιος/α/ο	horrible

Η γιαγιά έχει **θαυμάσια λουλούδια** στον κήπο της. Granny has wonderful flowers in her garden.

Ο σεισμός είναι **φριχτό πράγμα**. An earthquake is a terrible thing.

ACTIVITY 8

Complete the sentences with the correct form of the verb 'like'.

Example: _____ πολύ οι γεμιστές ντομάτες. (η Ελένη)
  Της αρέσουνε πολύ οι γεμιστές ντομάτες.

1 Δεν _____ καθόλου οι κωμωδίες. (εγώ)
2 Τα μπουζούκια _____. (η Ισαμπέλα)
3 _____ πολύ τα έργα του Αριστοφάνη. (εγώ και ο πατέρας μου)

ACTIVITY 9

Complete the sentences with the correct form of the adjective.

1 Το καινούριο τραγούδι του Πέτρου είναι _____ .
  (απίθανος)
2 Οι δύο ταινίες που παίζουν στο σινεμά είναι _____ .
  (καινούριος)

Now do activities 10 and 11 on the recording.

Ποιος είναι αυτός;

ACTIVITY 12 is on the recording.

ACTIVITY 13

1 The man in white is **a** a footballer **b** called Pavlos
  c a photographer.
2 The man in white is also wearing **a** sandals **b** a scarf
  c a watch.
3 Yvonni is: **a** from Thessaloniki **b** an actor.
4 Stavros **a** likes what Katie has bought **b** doesn't like
  what Katie has bought **c** puts on what Katie has bought.

DIALOGUE 3

○ Ποιος είναι αυτός με το άσπρο πουκάμισο;
■ Ποιος; Αυτός που μιλάει με τον ποδοσφαιριστή;
○ Όχι, καλέ! Αυτόν τον ξέρω! Είναι ο Παύλος.
■ Για ποιον ρωτάς, λοιπόν;
○ Μα δεν τον βλέπεις; Αυτός που φοράει γυαλιά ηλίου και
  ρολόι στο δεξί χέρι.
■ Α! Αυτός είναι φωτογράφος – από την Θεσσαλονίκη –
  και δίπλα του είναι η Υβόνη.
○ Ποια Υβόνη;
■ Η ηθοποιός – δεν την γνωρίζεις; Από την τηλεόραση.
○ Ωραίο παντελόνι φοράει ...
■ Άσε τους! Τι έχεις στην τσάντα;
○ Μμμ! ... Σ'αρέσει το καινούργιο μου μαγιό;
■ Δεν είναι άσχημο ... Έλα πάμε για μπάνιο!

VOCABULARY

το πουκάμισο	shirt
ο ποδοσφαιριστής	footballer, soccer player
τα γυαλιά (ηλίου)	(sun)glasses
το ρολόι	watch, clock
το (δεξί) χέρι	(right) hand
ο φωτογράφος	photographer
ο/η ηθοποιός	actor, actress
γνωρίζω	recognize, know
το παντελόνι	trousers, pants
το μαγιό	bathing suit, swimsuit
άσχημος/η/ο	ugly, bad

✅ *Ποιος είναι αυτος;* ('Who's that?')

Like αυτός ('this' or 'that'), ποιος ('who', 'which') changes to agree with the gender, number, and case of what it refers to.

singular	masculine	feminine	neuter
nominative	ποιος	ποια	ποιο
accusative	ποιον	ποια	ποιο

plural	masculine	feminine	neuter
nominative	ποιοι	ποιες	ποια
accusative	ποιους	ποιες	ποια

If the people or things referred to are of more than one gender, the masculine form is used.

Ποιοι στην παρέα είναι φωτογράφοι; Who in the group are photographers?

Ποιες είναι αυτές οι γυναίκες; Who are these women?

Ποια ειναι τα γυαλιά σου; Which are your glasses?

Ποιο σπορ προτιμάς; Which sport do you prefer?

Ποιους θέλεις; Who/ Which do you want? (*acc. pl. – m.*)

✅ Occupations and professions

With the names of occupations and professions in Greek, in many cases there is just a single (masculine) form: only the article, ο or η, reveals the gender of the person. Examples already used include ο ηθοποιός / η ηθοποιός ('actor'), ο γιατρός / η γιατρός (doctor), ο συγγραφέας / η συγγραφέας ('writer'), and ο δικηγόρος / η δικηγόρος ('lawyer').

Occupations with a different form for masculine/feminine include:

ο καθηγητής / η καθηγήτρια – professor, lecturer

ο δάσκαλος / η δασκάλα – teacher

ο φοιτητής / η φοιτήτρια – student

ο μαθητής / η μαθήτρια – scholar

ο πωλητής / η πωλήτρια – salesman/saleswoman

ACTIVITY 14

Complete the following sentences with the correct form of **ποιος** (+ **αυτός**, if necessary).

1 _____ είναι αυτά τα κορίτσια;

2 _____ ταινίες προτιμάς;

3 _____ είναι η γυναίκα με το ροζ πουκάμισο;

4 _____ από _____ τους κατάλογους θέλεις;

5 _____ ζώα προτιμάς - τις γάτες ή τους σκύλους;

🎧 Now do activities 15 and 16 on the recording.

8.4 Tonight

Απόψε

To get information on what's happening in Athens, you'll find the following publications useful: the weekly *Αθηνόραμα*, available from most kiosks, and the monthly *ΜονοΠόλη*, available free from bookshops. Not only do they offer wide-ranging information about things such as what's on, who's in, where it's at, they also include a critical article or two on the current cultural scene, as well as book reviews.

Newspapers, especially the Sundays, are also a rich source of information, although it must be said that the still fairly formal language of Greek newspapers tends to be something of a challenge if you're a learner.

Here is a selection of events on offer. Read them and try to get the gist of what they're about and then try Activity 17.

1

ΑΘΗΝΩΝ
Βουκουρεστίου 10, τηλ. 3235524

Μικρές Αλεπούδες
Ένα έργο της Λίλιαν Χέλμαν

5 Απριλίου μέχρι 23 Μαΐου
Παίζουν: Κ. Μαραγκού, Τ. Χρυσικάκος,
Κ. Αθανασόπουλος, και άλλοι.
Παραστάσεις: Βράδυ - Πέμ. - Κύρ. 9:15 μ.μ.
Απόγ. - Δευ., Σαβ., Κύρ. 6:15 μ.μ.
Εισιτήρια: 14,60€, 10,20€, 8,20€ (φοιτητές)

2
ΜΕΓΑΡΟ
ΜΟΥΣΙΚΗΣ

14 Μαΐου 8 : 00 μ.μ.

Μοντσερát Καμπάλ
Μοντσερát Μάρτι

Οι μεγάλες ισπανίδες
ντίβες του κλασικού
τραγουδιού ερμηνεύουν
άριες των Ντονιζέτι,
Μπελίνι, Ροσίνι, κ. ά.

Δωρεά προς ΕΛΠΙΔΑ,
Σύλλογος Υποστήριξης
Φορέων του Ιού του AIDS

3
ΡΑΔΙΟ ΣΙΤΥ
ΑΣΣΟΣ ΟΝΤΕΟΝ
Πατησίων 240, τηλ. 8674832

Μεγάλες Προσδοκίες

Το υπέροχο έργο του
Κάρολου Ντίκενς σε
ελεύθερη διασκευή.
Ηθοποιοί: Γκουίνεθ
Πάλτρόου, Ρόμπερτ ντε
Νίρο, Αν Μπάνκροφτ

Εισιτήρια: 8,20€
6 : 00, 8 :15, 9 :30
Αιρ Κοντίσιον

οι παραστάσεις	performances
ερμηνεύω	interpret
η αλεπού	fox
η δωρεά	donation
ΕΛΠΙΔΑ	HOPE
Σύλλογος Υποστήριξης Φορέων του Ιού του AIDS	*Association for the Protection of the Carriers of the AIDS Virus*
η προσδοκία	expectation
ελεύθερη διασκευή	free adaptation

ACTIVITY 17

1 a What's on at the Athenon?
  b Name the days when there are two performances.
  c Who is entitled to the lowest priced tickets?

2 a What sort of performance is on at the Megaro Mousikis?
  b Which composers are featured?
  c What are they raising money for?

3 a What is the address of the cinema?
  b Which actors are featured?
  c Is the Odeon a hot, stuffy building?

ACTIVITY 18

Your holiday rep is arranging some evening entertainment for you. Choose one of the performances opposite and complete the form she has given you, showing your preference for:

1 date (day and time)   2 place (name)
3 which (name of performance)   4 price

1 ΠΟΤΕ: μέρα και ώρα _____

2 ΠΟΥ: _____

3 ΠΟΙΟ: όνομα παράστασης _____

4 ΤΙΜΗ: σε ευρώ _____

115

POK ΕΛΛΗΝΙΚΟ
GREEK ROCK

Sofia is looking after the kiosk for an hour, while her mother, Vangelio, has her hair cut. Thanasis has just dropped by.

πώς από 'δώ	what brings you this way?
έτσι περαστικός	just passing
τα νέα	news
σπουδαίος/α/ο	superb, excellent
το γκρουπ	group, band
είναι κάτι άλλο	is something else

ACTIVITY 19

Listen to the story and answer the following questions.

1 Where and with whom was Sophia over the weekend?
2 What is the name of the rock group in question?
3 Does Sophia think they are any good?
4 Is Sophia interested in going to their next concert with Thanasis?
5 Who does she suggest they invite along?
6 According to Thanasis, what is the foreigner's idea of Greek music?

ACTIVITY 20

Read the following summary of the story episode. There is one inaccuracy in it: can you find it?

Thanasis is interested to know what kind of weekend Sophia had. She tells him they had a wonderful time at the village with Craig, a friend of her brother, Peter. Thanasis then asks Sophia whether she likes rock music, and mentions the group Pix Lax. She is very enthusiastic about them. He tells her they're playing at the AN Club and he can get tickets if she likes. She agrees and wants him to get a ticket for Craig, too. Thanasis is reluctant. He says visitors only like to hear bouzoukis and drink ouzo.

Sofia	Πώς από 'δώ, Θανάση;
Thanasis	Γειά σου, Σοφούλα! Έτσι, περαστικός είμαι. Τι νέα; Καλό το Σαββατοκύριακο;
Sofia	Σπουδαίο! Ήμασταν με έναν φίλο του Πέτρου. Το χωριό του αρέσει πάρα πολύ ...
Thanasis	Σοφία, σ'αρέσει η ροκ;
Sofia	Η ροκ μουσική; Δεν είναι άσχημη ...
Thanasis	Σ'αρέσουν οι Πυξ Λαξ;
Sofia	Α! Τώρα μιλάς - φοβερό γκρουπ!
Thanasis	Παίζουν σε λίγες μέρες στο AN CLUB.
Sofia	Έχεις εισιτήρια;
Thanasis	Όχι ακόμα, αλλά αν θέλεις ...
Sofia	Ναι, ναι! Πάρε και ένα για τον Κραίηγκ ...
Thanasis	Ποιος είναι αυτός ο Κραίηγκ;
Sofia	Ο φίλος του Πέτρου απο το Εδιμβούργο!
Thanasis	Τι ξέρουν οι ξένοι για την ελληνική μουσική; Μπουζούκι και ούζο σε ταβέρνα!
Sofia	Ε! Οι Πυξ Λαξ μας είναι κάτι άλλο - πάμε όλοι παρέα, ή όχι;

Now it's time to test your progress in Unit 8.

1 Match 1–4 with the correct response from a–d.

  1 Σ'αρέσουν τα φρούτα;
  2 Του αρέσουν τα σκυλιά;
  3 Μ'αρέσει η λαϊκή μουσική.
  4 Δεν σας αρέσει το ούζο;

  a Όχι, προτιμάει τις γάτες.
  b Μ'αρέσει και η τζαζ.
  c Ναι, αλλά προτιμώ τα γλυκά.
  d Δυστυχώς, όχι. Δεν μας αρέσει καθόλου.

    5

2 Vocabulary check
  1 Which one of these is a fruit?
    μεζέδες / ποικιλία / φράουλες / ορεκτικά
  2 Which one of these is not a profession?
    ηθοποιός / διευθυντής / μουσικός / μπακαλιάρος
  3 Which one of these adjectives communicates a
    negative response?
    φριχτό / καταπληκτικό / θαυμάσιο / υπέροχο
  4 Which one of these is not a type of performance?
    κωμωδία / φάβα / άρια / τραγωδία
  5 Which one of these words / phrases is not about time?
    άλλη φορά / κάτι άλλο / μετά / τώρα

    5

3 Match each of the speakers 1–3 with the correct response
  from a–c.

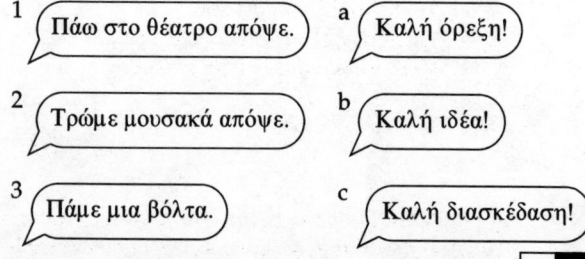

1 Πάω στο θέατρο απόψε.   a Καλή όρεξη!

2 Τρώμε μουσακά απόψε.   b Καλή ιδέα!

3 Πάμε μια βόλτα.   c Καλή διασκέδαση!

    5

4 Complete the sentences with the appropriate phrase from the box.

> άλλη φορά ποιος ... αυτός
> λέει ότι άσε τους ούτε ... ούτε

1 Η Μαρίκα _____ το χταπόδι είναι πολύ νόστιμο.
2 _____ Μπαμπά! Δεν θέλουν. Πάμε εμείς στο λούνα παρκ.
3 Ο παππούς μου δεν είναι _____ δάσκαλος _____ γραμματέας, είναι συγγραφέας.
4 _____ είναι _____ ο δικηγόρος που φοράει γυαλιά ηλίου;
5 Αχ! Τελειώσαν τα εισιτήρια. Δεν πειράζει, πάμε _____.

`10`

5 Read the following piece which advertises music lessons, then answer the questions.

> ## ΠΙΑΝΟ   ΚΙΘΑΡΑ   ΜΠΟΥΖΟΥΚΙ
>
> Με το σύστημά μας, παιδιά από τεσσάρων χρονών μαθαίνουν και παίζουν μουσική.
>
> ### *Κλείστε θέση τώρα!*
>
> Δευτέρα, Τετάρτη ή Σάββατο
> Από 3000 δρχ την ώρα - Τιμές που σας αρέσουν!
>
> ## ΕΥΚΟΛΑ   ΓΡΗΓΟΡΑ   ΣΩΣΤΑ

1 What instruments are taught?
2 What does the system promise?
3 What should you do now?
4 Which days can you choose from?
5 What are you told about price?

`10`

TOTAL SCORE `35`

If you scored less than 28 go through the Dialogues and the Language Building sections again, before completing the summary on page 120.

Summary 8

Now try this final test summarizing the main points covered in this unit. You can check your answers on the recording.

How would you:
1 say you don't like meat at all?
2 say you're a vegetarian?
3 say he doesn't like his boss?
4 say they like all sports?
5 say 'let's go to the cinema'?
6 say this film is awful?
7 say John's new car is amazing?
8 ask who the woman in the black bathing suit is?

REVISION

Make sure you are comfortable with the structures and vocabulary in this unit. To practise, list some of the things you like and dislike; think of some of the things that people you know like and dislike; mention what you/they prefer.

To practise the new adjectives you have learnt, go over some of the most recent productions/events/people you have seen at the cinema, theatre, concert hall, on the television, at work, and so on, expressing your appreciation – or otherwise. As you go on your way, ask yourself who that is, who they are.

You will probably find that writing things down, as well as repeating them as often as possible, helps you to remember and fixes vocabulary in your mind.

Plans

Σχέδια

OBJECTIVES

In this unit you'll learn how to:

- ✓ make arrangements
- ✓ give instructions
- ✓ understand the weather forecast

And cover the following grammar and language:

- ✓ the future tense
- ✓ formation of the second stem
- ✓ the imperative

LEARNING GREEK 9

Practise improvising ways of getting your meaning across when speaking spontaneously, even if you don't know the exact words or phrases in Greek. With practice, you'll find that you improve your ability to express yourself and to describe things. Use facial expressions, gestures, anything to communicate. The important thing is to build up confidence so that you're not afraid of getting involved in a conversation.

Now start the recording for Unit 9.

What shall we do?

Τί θα κάνουμε;

🎧 **ACTIVITY 1** is on the recording.

ACTIVITY 2

1 Πού θα πάει ο Αλέκος για τις διακοπές του;
2 Ποιος τον περιμένει;
3 Πόσον καιρό θα μείνουν;
4 Πού θα κάνουνε μπάνιο;

DIALOGUE 1

○ Πού θα πάτε για τις διακοπές σας;
■ Θα κάνουμε διακοπές στο Βανκούβερ φέτος. Μας περιμένει η αδελφή μου.
○ Α, θαυμάσια πόλη! Ξέρετε τι θα κάνετε εκεί;
■ Απ' όλα! Θα δούμε μουσεία και αγορές, θα κάνουμε βόλτες στα βουνά, σκι, εγώ θα παίξω γκολφ ... Και για πρώτη φορά θα κάνουμε μπάνιο στον Ειρηνικό Ωκεανό.
○ Πόσον καιρό θα μείνετε;
■ Τρεις εβδομάδες. Θα φύγουμε στις 22 Ιουλίου και θα γυρίσουμε στις 12 Αυγούστου.
○ Εγώ θα είμαι στα Καμένα Βούρλα για τις διακοπές μου. Θα κάνω θεραπευτικά λουτρά και ηλιοθεραπεία – τίποτ'άλλο!
■ Μέχρι τότε, τι θα κάνουμε;
○ Θα δουλέψουμε, αλλιώς πώς θα τα πληρώσουμε!

VOCABULARY	
οι διακοπές	holidays, vacation
φέτος	this year
η αδελφή	sister
η πόλη	city
η αγορά	shopping centre, market
η πρώτη φορά	first time
κάνω μπάνιο	have a swim
ο Ειρηνικός Ωκεανός	Pacific Ocean
θεραπευτικά λουτρά	spa baths
η ηλιοθεραπεία	sunbathing
αλλιώς	otherwise
πληρώνω	pay

⊘ The future tense

To express the future ('will' or 'going to'), you use **θα** + the second stem of the verb (see below). The endings are the same as those for the present tense: -ω, -εις, -ει, -ουμε, -ετε, -ουν(ε).

e.g. **Θα ξέρετε** αύριο. You'll know tomorrow.

⊘ Formation of the second stem

There are no hard and fast rules about the formation of the second stem. Here, however, are a few guidelines to help you.

1 For the following verbs the 1st and 2nd stem are the same: **κάνω** – **θα κάνω** ('do'), **έχω** – **θα έχω** ('have'), **θέλω** – **θα θέλω** ('want'), **ξέρω** – **θα ξέρω** ('know'), **περιμένω** – **θα περιμένω** ('wait'), **είμαι** – **θα είμαι** ('am').

2 Group 1 verbs that follow certain patterns:
  (a) ζ > σ e.g., **αγοράζω** – **θα αγοράσω** ('buy'), **διαβάζω** – **θα διαβάσω** ('read'), **γυρίζω** – **θα γυρίσω** ('return', 'come back')
  (b) ν > σ e.g. **φτάνω** – **θα φτάσω** ('arrive'), **κλείνω** – **θα κλείσω** ('close'), **πληρώνω** – **θα πληρώσω** ('pay')
  (c) φ / ευ > ψ e.g. **γράφω** – **θα γράψω** ('write'), **χορεύω** – **θα χορέψω** ('dance'), **μαγειρεύω** – **θα μαγειρέψω** ('cook')
  (d) γ/ζ/χ > ξ e.g., **ανοίγω** – **θα ανοίξω** ('open'), **παίζω** – **θα παίξω** ('play'), **τρέχω** – **θα τρέξω** ('run')

3 Group 2 verbs that follow certain patterns:
  (a) first stem + –ησ–: **μιλ(ά)ω** – **θα μιλήσω** ('speak'), **ρωτ(α)ώ** – **θα ρωτήσω** ('ask')
  (b) first stem + –ασ–: **περν(ά)ω** – **θα περάσω** ('pass'), **ξεχν(ά)ω** – **θα ξεχάσω** ('forget')
  (c) first stem + –εσ–: **φορ(ά)ω** – **θα φορέσω** ('wear'), **καλώ** – **θα καλέσω** ('invite')

There are many verbs that do not conform strictly to any category, but are 'standard', for example, **ακούω** – **θα ακούσω** ('hear', 'listen to'), **μένω** – **θα μείνω** ('stay', 'live'). There are also many exceptions.

4 Irregular verbs include: **τρώω** – **θα φάω** ('eat'), **βλέπω** – **θα δω** ('see', 'watch'), **δίνω** – **θα δώσω** ('give'), **λέω** – **θα πω** ('say')

There is a list of all the verbs contained in this course on pages 234–37.

 Now do activities 3 and 4 on the recording.

Θα κάνω δίαιτα

ACTIVITY 5 is on the recording.

ACTIVITY 6
Correct the statements which are false.

1 Θα αγοράσουνε μήλα στο δρόμο.	T / F
2 Το παστίτσιο είναι εύκολο φαγητό.	T / F
3 Η κυρία Πόπη θα κάνει δίαιτα.	T / F
4 Θα φάνε χόρτα σήμερα.	T / F
5 Η κυρία Πόπη δεν θα μαγειρέψει αύριο.	T / F

DIALOGUE 2

○ Φάε κάτι – θα πάμε βόλτα σε λίγο;
■ Δεν θέλω τίποτα.
○ Έλα, πάρε λίγο παστίτσιο που σ'αρέσει.
■ Όχι λέω! Κοίταξε εδώ – το παντελόνι μου δεν κλείνει.
○ Δεν πειράζει – παλιό είναι. Θα αγοράσουμε καινούριο.
■ Δώσε μου ένα μήλο και φεύγουμε.
○ Βρε παιδάκι μου, θα πεινάσεις στο δρόμο και θα θέλεις σοκολάτα – κρίμα ο κόπος μου!
■ Άφησέ με, Μαμά. Θα κάνω δίαιτα.
○ Εντάξει. Κάνε δίαιτα από αύριο. Κάνε και γυμναστική.
■ Καλά … Τι θα μαγειρέψεις αύριο;
○ Εγώ δεν θα μαγειρέψω τίποτα – ούτε βραστά χόρτα! Εσύ μαγείρεψε ό,τι θέλεις.
■ Μαμά … το νερό έχει πολλές θερμίδες;

VOCABULARY

τσ παστίτσιο	*a baked pasta dish*
σου λέω	*I tell you*
παλιός/α/ο	*old*
το μήλο	*apple*
πεινάω	*I am hungry*
κρίμα ο κόπος μου	*a pity about my hard work/effort*
αφήνω	*leave (alone)*
η γυμναστική	*(physical) exercise*
βραστός/ή/ό	*boiled*
ό,τι	*whatever*
η θερμίδα	*calorie*

✓ The imperative

The imperative is the form of the verb used to give orders, instructions or advice, or to suggest that someone does something. It is widely used in such situations in Greek, without sounding abrupt.

To form the imperative, simply add to the second stem of the verb: -ε (singular, informal) or -ετε (often contracted to -τε) (plural, formal).

1st stem	2nd stem	imperative	
	θalva	singular	plural
παίρνω	πάρω	πάρε	πάρ(ε)τε
δίνω	δώσω	δώσε	δώσ(ε)τε
κοιτάζω	κοιτάξω	κοίταξε	κοιτάξ(ε)τε
μαγειρεύω	μαγειρέψω	μαγείρεψε	μαγειρέψ(ε)τε
αφήνω	αφήσω	άφησε	αφήσ(ε)τε
ακούω	ακούσω	άκουσε	ακούσ(ε)τε
τρώω	φάω (irregular)	φάε	φά(γε)τε

Φάε κάτι πριν φύγουμε. Eat something before we go.
Δώσε μου τα κλειδιά. Give me the keys.

You've already come across another form which can be used to give instructions: the future tense. (Unit 2)

Θα στρίψετε δεξιά στην πρώτη γωνία. Turn right at the first corner.

✓ The negative imperative

To give a command or instruction in the negative, you use the future tense of the verb with μη(ν) before it.

Μη φας (you singular) εκείνα τα αυγά. Don't eat those eggs.

✓ ότι/ό,τι

Note the difference between ότι ('that') and ό,τι ('what(ever)'):

Ξέρω ότι η Άννα είναι καλά. I know that Anna is well.

Κάνε ό,τι θέλεις. Do what(ever) you want.

ACTIVITY 7

Give the following instructions in Greek using the imperative.

1 Don't come back by taxi!
2 Read your book.
3 Pay the bill, please.
4 Write a letter to granny.
5 Wait here. (polite form)
6 Don't leave!
7 Take whatever you like.
8 Don't talk English!

Now do activities 8 and 9 on the recording.

Τι καιρό θα μας κάνει;

🎧 **ACTIVITY 10** is on the recording.

ACTIVITY 11

Select the option that does *not* agree with what you hear.
1 Σήμερα   **a** θα βρέξει   **b** είναι καλοκαίρι.
2 Η γυναίκα θα   **a** πάρει γάντια   **b** αναπτήρα
              c ομπρέλα.
3 Ο άνδρας δεν   **a** η τσέπη   **b** το κασκόλ
   ξέρει πού είναι   **c** ο χαρτοφύλακας του.
4 Θα φύγουν   **a** τώρα   **b** σήμερα   **c** αύριο.

DIALOGUE 3

○ Κάνει κρύο σήμερα, έχει πολύ αέρα. Τι καιρό θα κάνει;
■ Βάλε το παλτό σου, πάρε και μία ομπρέλα – θα βρέξει.
○ Νοέμβριος – πάει το καλοκαίρι!
■ Στη βόρεια Ελλάδα χιονίζει στα βουνά ...
○ Θα πάρω και γάντια.
■ Πού είναι το κασκόλ μου;
○ Είμαστε έτοιμοι; Θα αργήσουμε αν δεν φύγουμε αμέσως.
■ Πού είναι τα κλειδιά μου;
○ Κοίταξε στην τσέπη σου ...
■ Πορτοφόλι, μαντήλι, αναπτήρας ...
○ Να τα κλειδιά σου! Κάτω από την εφημερίδα – Πάμε!
■ Αμάν – να η βροχή! Πού είναι ο χαρτοφύλακας μου;

VOCABULARY	
το κρύο	cold
ο αέρας	wind
βάζω	put, put on
το παλτό	coat
βρέχει	it's raining
το γάντι	glove
αργώ	delay, am late
η τσέπη	pocket
το πορτοφόλι	wallet, purse
το μαντήλι	handkerchief
ο αναπτήρας	lighter
η βροχή	rain
ο χαρτοφύλακας	briefcase

✓ οι εποχές (the seasons)

η άνοιξη	spring	την άνοιξη	in spring
το καλοκαίρι	summer	το καλοκαίρι	in summer
το φθινόπωρο	autumn, fall	το φθινόπωρο	in autumn, fall
ο χειμώνας	winter	το(ν) χειμώνα	in winter

To say 'in spring', and so on, you just use the accusative.
This is also true for the months and for times of day: το πρωί
('in the morning'), το βράδυ ('in the evening'), τη νύχτα ('at night').

✓ Talking about the weather

κάνει κρύο	it's cold	έχει δροσιά	it's cool (weather)
κάνει ζέστη	it's hot	έχει λιακάδα	it's warm and sunny
έχει ήλιο	it's sunny	βρέχει	it's raining
έχει αέρα	it's windy	χιονίζει	it's snowing
έχει συννεφιά	it's cloudy	φυσάει	it's windy

ο βορράς	north	βόρειος/βορεινός	northern/northerly
ο νότος	south	νότιος	southern/southerly
η ανατολή	east	ανατολικός	eastern/easterly
η δύση	west	δυτικός	western/westerly

βόρειοι άνεμοι – northerly winds
Σήμερα θα έχει ήλιο και η θερμοκρασία θα φτάσει 39 βαθμούς.
Today it will be sunny and the temperature will reach
39 degrees.

ACTIVITY 12

Read this postcard and answer the questions.

26 Νοεμβρίου

Αγαπητή Μαρία,

Ο καιρός εδώ στην Αλεξάνδρεια είναι
υπέροχος σήμερα. Κάνει ζέστη, αλλά όχι
πολλή – η θερμοκρασία είναι γύρω στους
32 βαθμούς. Αύριο λένε ότι θα βρέξει λίγο
το πρωί, αλλά εμείς θα είμαστε στο Κάιρο.
Θα σε δω την επόμενη Κυριακή
Χαιρετίσματα.
Γιάννης

1 Πού είναι ο Γιάννης;
2 Ποια εποχή του χρόνου είναι;
3 Πόση ζέστη κάνει στην Αίγυπτο; Πώς το ξέρετε;
4 Πότε θα είναι οι φίλοι πάλι μαζί;

🎧 Now do activities 13 and 14 on the recording.

9.4 The weather in Greece

Ο καιρός στην Ελλάδα

To think of Greece is to think at once of sea and sun – an extraordinary range of crystalline blues and the incomparable quality of the light, a contrast reflected in the blue and white of the national flag. But that is not the whole story. The sun can be blistering, the sea violent, the heat intolerable, and the winters bitter, if relatively short. The Greek climate, **το κλίμα**, has its extremes, with local variations, and it covers the gamut of weathers, including winter rainfall and hot summer winds, ανέμους: **μελτέμια** is the name for summer winds in particular.

ACTIVITY 15

Read the following weather report and answer the questions on it.

1 Which days are featured in the weather report?
2 What direction(s) will the winds come from today?
3 Where is rain expected?
4 What is the expected temperature range tomorrow:
 a in Athens? b in the north? c in the rest of Greece?
5 In which part of the country is it going to be sunny?
6 What is said about travelling on the Mediterranean?

Ο ΚΑΙΡΟΣ
ΣΗΜΕΡΑ – ΚΥΡΙΑΚΗ 23 ΜΑΙΟΥ

Λίγες συννεφιές θα υπάρχουν, που το μεσημέρι και το απόγευμα θα δώσουν ψιλές βροχές, κυρίως στο βόρειο Αιγαίο. Η θερμοκρασία θα πέσει, και θα φυσούν βόρειοι άνεμοι με ένταση 3-5 μποφόρ.

ΑΥΡΙΟ – ΔΕΥΤΕΡΑ 24 ΜΑΙΟΥ

Θα υπάρχει ηλιοφάνεια σε όλη σχεδόν τη χώρα, με λίγη συννεφιά στην ανατολική Ελλάδα. Η θάλασσα θα είναι καλή για ταξίδια σε όλη τη Μεσόγειο.

CULTURE

Θερμοκρασία:
Αττική: από 17 έως 34 βαθμούς.
Θεσσαλονίκη: από 15 έως 29 βαθμούς.
Βόρεια Ελλάδα: από 12 έως 30 βαθμούς.
Υπόλοιπη Χώρα: από 15 έως 35 βαθμούς.

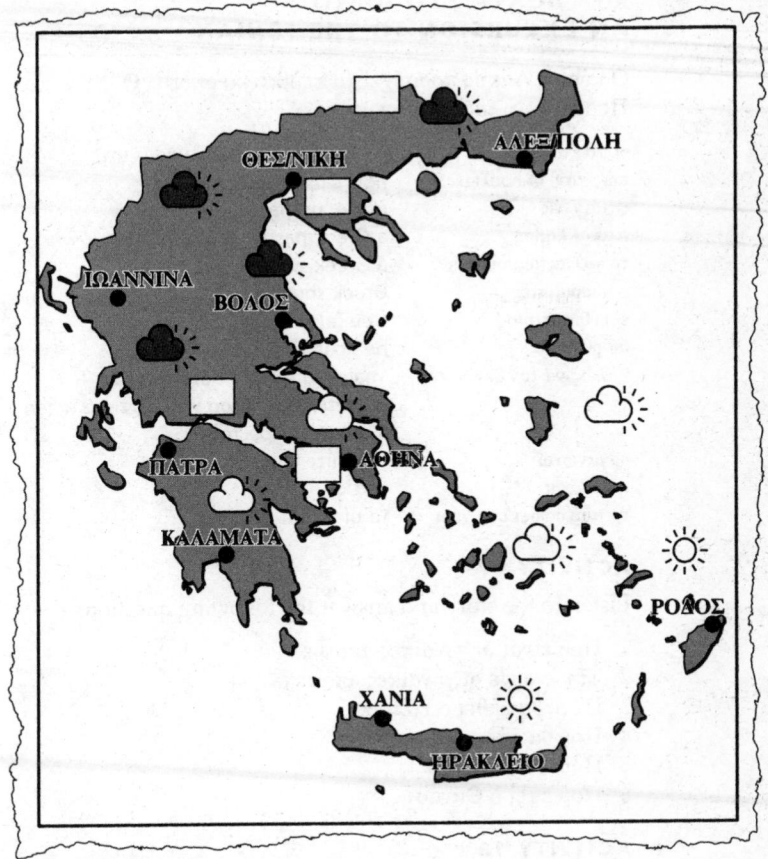

ACTIVITY 16

Fill in the temperature ranges given in the correct places on
the map.

ΜΙΑ ΒΟΛΤΑ ΣΤΟ ΙΟΝΙΟ
AN EXCURSION TO THE IONIAN

Ο κύριος Λάκης προσέχει το περίπτερο απόψε. Ο Περικλής, ο ταξιτζής, σταματάει.

τι γίνεται;	what's happening?, what's up?
πώς πάν' οι δουλειές;	how's business?
φτιά(χ)νω	make, prepare
ο μπακλαβάς	a Greek pastry
το γαλακτομπούρικο	a Greek sweet
ο κουραμπιές	Greek shortbread
ελεύθερος/η/ο	free [also single]
θά'ρθει	he's coming
καλώς να τον δεχθείτε	'may you receive him well' [an expression of good wishes, used when a guest is expected]
οργανώνω	organize
η χελώνα	turtle
να σου δώσει ενα χέρι	to give you a hand

ACTIVITY 17

Listen to the story and answer the following questions.

1 Πού είναι οι γυναίκες απόψε;
2 Τι κάνουνε οι γυναίκες απόψε;
3 Πότε θα έρθει ο Πέτρος;
4 Πού θα πάει η παρέα;
5 Ποιοι θα πάνε μαζί;
6 Πού πάει ο Θανάσης;

ACTIVITY 18

Listen to the story again and answer the following questions in English.

1 Why are the women preparing pastries?
2 Who has organized the excursion?
3 Why is Pericles pleased for Vangelio?
4 Why is Lakis a little concerned?
5 In which area of Greece is Cephalonia?

STORY TRANSCRIPT

Pericles   Τι γίνεται, Λάκη; Πώς πάν' οι δουλειές; Μόνος σου, ε;

Lakis   Έτσι είναι. Οι γυναίκες πάνε σπίτι. Θα φτιάξουν γλυκά ...

Pericles   Τι γλυκά; Κανένα μπακλαβά, γαλακτομπούρικο, κουραμπιέ; Ποιος γιορτάζει;

Lakis   Κανένας. Ο Πέτρος έχει μερικές μέρες ελεύθερες – θά'ρθει αύριο.

Pericles   Μπράβο. Από το Εδιμβούγο, ε; Καλώς να τον δεχθείτε!

Lakis   Ναι. Και η Σοφία θα οργανώσει ένα ταξιδάκι στην Κεφαλλονιά.

Pericles   Μπα; Για πόσον καιρό; Ποιος θα πάει;

Lakis   Ποιος θα μείνει εδώ; Η Βαγγελιώ θα πάει μαζί τους.

Pericles   Καλά θα κάνει! Θα δει κι αυτή καμιά χελώνα.

Lakis   Θα πάρουν και τον Κραίηγκ μιά βόλτα στο Ιόνιο.

Pericles   Εσύ ... δεν λες του Θανάση να σου δώσει ενα χέρι; Καλό παιδί είναι.

Lakis   Θα πάει κι αυτός παρέα!

Test

Now it's time to test your progress in Unit 9.

1 Complete the sentences with the correct form of the future tense.

1 Το τρένο _____ απο το Ηράκλειο στη μία. (φεύγω)
2 Αύριο _____ τους λογαριασμούς μου. (πληρώνω)
3 Εμείς τι _____ στο σινεμά απόψε; (βλέπω)
4 Ποιος _____ μας _____ στο αεροδρόμιο; (περιμένω)
5 _____ εγώ τον γιατρό τι έχει ο πατέρας. (ρωτώ)

5

2 Give the Greek for the following:

1	a diet	b calorie	c boiled greens
2	a old	b ready	c free
3	a tomorrow	b tonight	c after
4	a I'll run	b I'll speak	c I'll write
5	a coat	b glove	c pocket

15

3 Complete Lela's note to her friend using the verbs in the box: you will need to change them to imperatives.

```
περιμένω   φεύγω   δεν   διαβάζω   τηλεφωνώ
```

Τζένη

(1) _____ αυτό το γράμμα και μετά (2) _____ του Μιχάλη.
(3) _____ από το σπίτι στις τρεισήμισι και (4) _____ στο σταθμό –
εκεί θα δεις εναν παλιό φίλο - ποιον νομίζεις; (5) _____ πεις σε
κανέναν τίποτα..

Λέλα

5

4 Sort the following into words matching the descriptions a–e.

1 ΕΚΑΝΣΟΩ   2 ΑΝΓΣΥΤΙΚΗΜ   3 ΛΝΕΩΧΑ
4 ΠΕΙΔΑΚΟΣ   5 ΟΡΦΤΟΠΛΙΟ

132

a time away from work/school
b something that holds money
c large sea
d form of exercise
e a sea creature

[ ] 5

5 Complete the sentences with either ότι or ό,τι, as appropriate.

1 Θα κάνω _____ θέλω.
2 Ο Πέτρος λέει _____ η Σκοτία είναι καταπληκτική.
3 Θα τηλεφωνήσω _____ ώρα γυρίσω.
4 Νομίζετε _____ θα έρθει σήμερα ο Θανάσης;
5 Η Έλλη θα δει _____ παίζει στο θέατρο. Της αρέσει πολύ.

[ ] 5

6 How would you make the following comments on the weather in Greek?
(2 points for each correct answer, 1 point if you make only one error)

1 It's going to be hot tomorrow.
2 The temperature will be 40 degrees.
3 It's cold today.
4 Take your umbrella – it's raining.
5 It's windy. The weather's not very good. Where's the sun?

[ ] 10

7 Give the second stem for the following verbs:

Present	θα/να
1 πληρώνω	
2 δουλεύω	
3 θέλω	
4 διαβάζω	
5 φοράω	

[ ] 5

TOTAL SCORE [ ] 50

If you scored less than 42 go through the dialogues and the Language Building sections again before completing the summary on page 134.

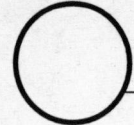

Summary 9

  Now try this final test summarizing the main points covered in this unit. You can check your answers on the recording.

How would you:
1 ask a friend where she's going for her holidays?
2 say 'we'll play tennis later'?
3 ask a new acquaintance when he'll be leaving?
4 tell a friend to invite Helen?
5 say she'll be in Athens next week?
6 ask a friend to make you a snack?
7 say it's hot?
8 say 'we'll swim and eat ice-creams'?

REVISION

It is important that you learn the second stem of each verb as you go. This stem is used in many other constructions, to express different functions – it is an essential tool in your acquisition of the language. You'll find a list of all the verbs used in this course in the Grammar Summary for reference.

If memorizing a list is not the most effective way for you to remember, try using the different forms in realistic situations. Go over your plans for the future – for example, for later in the day: what you will do, see, buy, pay, play, etc. Think about your holidays: where you will go, when you will leave, arrive, return, and so on. Try using the imperative to give some instructions with the verbs you have learnt.

I want to do something else

Θέλω να κάνω κάτι άλλο

OBJECTIVES

In this unit you'll learn how to:

- ✓ express your intention to do something
- ✓ make offers
- ✓ give and accept invitations
- ✓ ask for and give permission
- ✓ express necessity and obligation

And cover the following grammar and language:

- ✓ the subjunctive after **θέλω να** ('want to'), **μπορώ να** ('can', 'am able to'), and **πρέπει να** ('I must', 'it is necessary that I ... ')
- ✓ direct and indirect object pronouns

LEARNING GREEK 10

When learning a foreign language, it is not feasible to translate everything word for word. You will have noticed some examples of this already in the course: for example, Greek has no word for 'of' in phrases like ένα κουτί σοκολάτες ('a box of chocolates'). There are also variations in word order. What becomes more and more important is that when speaking Greek, you try to think directly in Greek. Try to think in terms of contexts and functions – which phrases are you likely to need when looking for accommodation or planning a trip? If you're prepared with the kind of language you need, you're less likely to try to translate.

Now start the recording for Unit 10.

I want to see other places

Θέλω να δω άλλα μέρη

ACTIVITY 1 is on the recording.

ACTIVITY 2

Correct the statements which are false.

1 Ο Μπεν θέλει να πάει στο Πέραμα. T / F
2 Θα μείνει εκεί για μερικούς μήνες. T / F
3 Ξέρει λίγα ελληνικά. T / F
4 Έχει έναν φίλο Έλληνα. T / F
5 Του αρέσει το ελληνικό φαγητό. T / F

DIALOGUE 1

○ Σε λίγες μέρες φεύγω για τον Πειραιά.
■ Στην Ελλάδα! Τι θα κάνεις εκεί;
○ Θα μείνω μερικές εβδομάδες. Θέλω να δω πώς πάνε οι δουλειές σε εκείνη τη χώρα ...
■ Πας να δεις αν υπάρχουν ευκαιρίες; Και μετά;
○ Αν μ'αρέσει αρκετά, θα ανοίξω ταξιδιωτικό γραφείο.
■ Ξέρεις καθόλου ελληνικά;
○ Δύο-τρεις λέξεις μόνο, αλλά θέλω να μάθω λίγα.
■ Νομίζω ότι είναι πολύ δύσκολη γλώσσα.
○ Ο φίλος μου, ο Χαράλαμπος, λέει ότι θα με βοηθήσει.
■ Καλή επιτυχία!
○ Θέλεις να βγούμε για ελληνικό φαγητό απόψε; Ο Φοίνικας είναι υπέροχο εστιατόριο.
■ Γιατί όχι – κάλεσε και τον Χαράλαμπο – θέλω να μιλήσω ελληνικά μαζί του!

VOCABULARY

εκείνος/η/ο	that
η χώρα	country
η ευκαιρία	opportunity
αρκετά	enough
το ταξιδιωτικό γραφείο	travel agency
η λέξη	word
η γλώσσα	language
βοηθάω	help
βγαίνω	go, get out
μαζί του	with him

✅ The subjunctive

In Greek, the subjunctive form of the verb is used in certain constructions, including θέλω να ('I want to'), μπορώ να ('I can'), and πρέπει να ('I must'). It is mainly used to present an action or state as an expectation or a wish.

The subjunctive, exactly like the future tense, is formed with the second stem of the verb and takes the standard present tense endings. It uses *να* in place of *θα*.

μαθαίνω – θα/να μάθω ('learn', 'find out'), μάθω, μάθεις, μάθει, μάθουμε, μάθετε, μάθουνε

✅ *θέλω να* ('want to')

θέλω να ('want to') is followed by the subjunctive. The verb in the subjunctive is in the same person ('I', 'you', etc.) as the one in the verb 'want'.

Θέλω να διαβάσω την εφημερίδα. I want to read the newspaper.
Θέλει να φτιάξει κουραμπιέδες. She wants to make shortbread.
Δεν θέλει να μιλήσει τώρα. He doesn't want to talk now.
Τα παιδιά θέλουν να πάνε στο πάρκο. The children want to go to the park.

If, however, you're talking about what you/someone want(s) *someone else* to do, the verb in the subjunctive changes form accordingly.

Θέλω να μάθεις ελληνικά. *I* want *you* to learn Greek.
Δεν θέλει να φύγουμε. *He* doesn't want *us* to go.

Other verbs, including πάω and περιμένω, are also followed by να + the subjunctive.

(Δεν) Πάω να δω τον πατέρα. I'm (not) going to see father.
(Δεν) Περιμένουν' να ακούσουν' τα νέα. They're (not) waiting to hear the news.

ACTIVITY 3

Write out the following in full using θέλω να.
Example: γράφω/γράμμα/μητέρα   *Θέλω να γράψω ένα γράμμα στην μητέρα.*

1 Η Λιλίκα/δεν πιω/πορτοκαλάδα
2 αγοράζω/καινούριο σπίτι/του χρόνου
3 Ο Τάκης/τρώω/έξω/παρέα του
4 Τα παιδιά/παίζω/ποδόσφαιρο/το απόγευμα
5 Ο Μάνος/φεύγω/πρώτη πτήση/αύριο

 Now do activities 4 and 5 on the recording.   137

10.2 I can't

Δεν μπορώ

ACTIVITY 6 is on the recording.

ACTIVITY 7

There are 4 errors in the following description of the flat the woman shows the man. What are they?

Το διαμέρισμα είναι στον τρίτο όροφο και έχει τέσσερα κύρια δωμάτια. Μπαίνουνε από δεξιά. Η κουζίνα είναι δίπλα στο μπάνιο. Οι κρεβατοκάμαρες βλέπουν τον ήλιο, αλλά δεν υπάρχει κεντρική θέρμανση. Το ενοίκιο είναι εκατόν πενήντα χιλιάδες δραχμές, με τα κοινόχρηστα.

DIALOGUE 2

○ Μπορώ να σας βοηθήσω;

■ Θέλω να νοικιάσω ένα διαμέρισμα. Βλέπω ότι διαφημίζετε ένα τεσσάρι στον πρώτο όροφο.

○ Βεβαίως. Ελάτε – θα σας το δείξω. Έχει δύο κρεβατοκάμαρες, τραπεζαρία και σαλόνι. Μπαίνουμε από το χολ. Δεξιά είναι η κουζίνα και δίπλα το μπάνιο ... Φωτεινά υπνοδωμάτια, κεντρική θέρμανση ...

■ Μ'αρέσει. Πότε μπορεί να το δει και η γυναίκα μου;

○ Ελάτε το απόγευμα ... Θέλετε να ρωτήσετε τίποτα άλλο;

■ Μπορείτε να μου πείτε την τιμή;

○ 140.000 το μήνα, χωρίς τα κοινόχρηστα.

VOCABULARY

το διαμέρισμα	flat, apartment
διαφημίζω	advertise
το τεσσάρι	*house or flat with four main rooms*
δείχνω	show
η κρεβατοκάμαρα	bedroom
η τραπεζαρία	dining room
το σαλόνι	living room, lounge
η κουζίνα	kitchen
μπαίνω	go, get in
φωτεινός/ή/ό	bright
το υπνοδωμάτιο	bedroom
η κεντρική θέρμανση	central heating
τα κοινόχρηστα	communal charges

✅ μπορώ να ('can', 'am able to')

μπορώ να ('can', 'am able to') is also followed by the subjunctive. The verb in the subjunctive is in the same person ('I', 'you', etc.) as the verb 'can'.

Μπορώ να τρέξω δέκα χιλιόμετρα. I can run ten kilometres.

μπορώ να is also used to ask for permission and, in the negative, to prohibit something.

Μπορούμε να κλείσουμε την πόρτα; Can/May we shut the door?
Δεν **μπορείτε να** παίξετε εδώ. You can't play here.

Note that πω, πιω and δω, like μπορώ, are declined like Group 2b verbs (see p.65).

✅ Object pronouns

Object pronouns are pronouns affected by the action of the verb: this can be *direct* ('I saw *him*') or *indirect* ('I spoke *to him*'). You have already come across the indirect object pronoun in the phrase μ(ου)'αρέσει.

Μπορώ να **σας** βοηθήσω; - Can I help you? [*direct object*]
Μπορώ να **του** στείλω **το γράμμα**. I can send the letter to him.

Note the position of the object pronoun: it comes between να (or θα) and the verb. The indirect pronoun always comes before the direct pronoun in Greek.

Θέλω να **σας το** φέρω. I want to bring it to you. [το – *direct object*;
σας – *indirect object*]

Direct		*Indirect*	
με	μας	μου	μας
σε	σας	σου	σας
τον/την/το	τους/τις/τα	του/της/του	τους

Verbs often followed by the indirect object pronoun: δίνω ('give'), λέω ('say'), μιλ(α)ώ ('speak'), γράφω ('write'), διαβάζω ('read'), στέλνω ('send'), ρωτ(α)ώ ('ask'), απαντ(α)ώ ('answer'), τηλεφωνώ ('telephone')

ACTIVITY 8

Write out complete sentences using **μπορώ να**.
Example: δεν/τρώω *Δεν μπορώ να φάω*.

1 Η Αννα/μαγειρεύω/μεξικάνικο φαγητό
2 Εμείς/δεν γράφω/κινέζικα γράμματα
3 Οι φοιτητές/νοικιάζω/ένα αυτοκίνητο
4 Ο γιατρός/δεν βλέπω/ο Κώστας/ σήμερα

🔊 Now do activities 9 and 10 on the recording.

Μεγάλη ταλαιπωρία

🎧 **ACTIVITY 11** is on the recording.

ACTIVITY 12

Correct the statements which are false.

1 Η γυναίκα πάει στον οδοντίατρο κάθε έξι μήνες.   T / F
2 Δεν είναι εύκολο να φύγει από την δουλειά της.   T / F
3 Το ιατρείο είναι κοντά στο γραφείο.   T / F
4 Θέλει να πάει με το λεωφορείο.   T / F
5 Ο άνδρας πρέπει να πάει στο καθαριστήριο.   T / F

DIALOGUE 3

○ Πρέπει να κλείσω ραντεβού με τον οδοντίατρο.
■ Πονάει το δόντι σου;
○ Όχι ακριβώς. Θέλω να πάω για γενική εξέταση.
■ Πηγαίνεις κάθε έξι μήνες;
○ Όχι. Πρέπει να ζητήσω άδεια και είναι δύσκολο.
■ Ξέρω, ξέρω. Δεν πρέπει να είναι έτσι, αλλά ...
○ Δεν μπορώ να αφήσω τη θέση μου γιά πολλή ώρα, το ιατρείο είναι μακριά από το γραφείο, δεν υπάρχει πάρκιν.
■ Μεγάλη ταλαιπωρία, ε;
○ Τι να σου πω!
■ Και εγώ θέλω να πάω - Πρέπει να μου καθαρίσει τα δόντια ... άντε, θέλεις να πάμε μαζί;
○ Δεν νομίζω ότι πρέπει να φύγουμε και οι δύο ...

VOCABULARY	
η ταλαιπωρία	trouble, bother
το ραντεβού	appointment
ο οδοντίατρος	dentist
πονάω	hurt, be in pain
το δόντι	tooth
η γενική εξέταση	general examination
ζητώ	ask for
άδεια	permission
έτσι	like that, so
η θέση	place, seat
το ιατρείο	surgery, consulting room, doctor's office
καθαρίζω	clean

✓ πρέπει να ('it is necessary')

πρέπει να ('it is necessary') is also followed by a subjunctive. Unlike θέλω and μπορώ, πρέπει is an impersonal verb: that is, it always uses the third person. The verb in the subjunctive gives the details of who has to do/must avoid the action recommended/prohibited.

Πρέπει να φύγουμε γρήγορα. We must leave quickly.

Πρέπει να ξυπνήσω τον μπαμπά. I must wake dad.

Δεν πρέπει να μπούμε εκει χωρίς άδεια. We shouldn't go in there without permission.

ACTIVITY 13

Using **πρέπει να**, respond to the person making the following statements. Use the words in brackets to help you.

Example: Το τηλέφωνο δεν δουλεύει! (πληρώνω, λογαριασμός)

Πρέπει να πληρώσεις *τον λογαριασμό.*

1 Δεν έχω καθόλου φαγητό στο σπίτι. (πάω, μπακάλη)
2 Θέλω να δω τον γιατρό. (κλείνω ραντεβού)
3 Δεν υπάρχει πλοίο για την Μόσχα. (πηγαίνω, αεροπλάνο)
4 Κάνει ζέστη. (ανοίγω, παράθυρο)
5 Η μαμά έχει πολύ δουλειά. (την, βοηθάω)
6 Πεινάω πολύ. (δεν κάνω δίαιτα)

ACTIVITY 14

Complete these sentences about yourself.

1 Αυριο θέλω να _____ .
2 Κάθε βράδυ πρέπει να _____
_____ .
3 Το καλοκαίρι μπορούμε να _____
_____ .
4 Στο εστιατόριο απόψε δεν θέλω να _____
_____ .
5 Όταν διαβάζω ελληνικά δεν πρέπει να _____
_____ .

🎧 Now do activities 15 and 16 on the recording.

10.4 Greek songs

Τα Ελληνικά τραγούδια

With a strong oral tradition behind it, Greek poetry lives on in song. To this day, there is a lively collaboration between musicians and the works of the poets. The names of the twentieth-century composers Mikis Theodorakis and Manos Hadjidakis have become internationally recognized, as have some of their many chosen singers. Their work, while alert to emerging talent, also includes musical settings of established poets like Sikelianos, Kalvos, Kavadias, Seferis, Elytis, and Ritsos. Choosing from many contemporary artists, Nena Venetsanou recently produced an acclaimed collection starting with fragments from Delphic hymns and Sappho, through island songs (**Νησιώτικα** continue to be very popular genre) to more contemporary pieces. A certain wandering urban spirit is captured in **Ρεμπέτικα** which has a strong demotic flavour and its own major stars, including Markos Vamvakaris, Rosa Eskenazi, Vassilis Tsitsanis, and Sotiria Bellou. The supply of popular Greek song is ongoing, inexhaustible, and responsive to the moment. It now reaches well beyond its own traditional forms and instruments.

Here is a song – **Υπομονή** 'Patience' – made famous by **Μαρινέλλα** in the 1960s.

As this is a song, rhyme effects might help you.

ACTIVITY 17

Read it through, trying to make sense of it, and then choose from the words in the box to fill in the gaps.

βράδυ	γειτονιά
δρόμος	γαλανός
λεμονιά	

ΥΠΟΜΟΝΗ

Γειτονιά και (1) _____ σου στενός
Παγωνιά και γκρίζος ουρανός
Μαύρη ζωή, (2) _____, πρωί
Μία συντροφιά, μία συννεφιά

Υπομονή, Υπομονή, Υπομονή,

Κάντε υπομονή, και ο ουρανός
Θα γίνει πιο (3) _____
Κάντε υπομονή, μία (4) _____
Ανθίζει στη (5) _____

Γειτονιά και ο _____ σου στενός
Παγωνιά και γκρίζος ουρανός
Μαύρη ζωή, _____ πρωί
Μία συντροφιά, μία συννεφιά

Υπομονή, Υπομονή, Υπομονή,
Αλέκος Σακελλάριος

η γειτονιά	neighbourhood
στενός/ή/ό	narrow
γκρίζος/α/ο	grey
η συντροφιά	companionship
ανθίζω	blossom

ACTIVITY 18

Now focus on the lyrics and answer these questions about the song.

1 Why is the singer cast adrift? Two things are mentioned.
2 What kind of neighbourhood is described?
3 What does the song say will be the rewards if you have patience?

10.5 Στο περίπτερο

 ΠΡΕΠΕΙ ΝΑ ΠΕΡΑΣΩ
I MUST PASS

Η Σοφία περνάει από το περίπτερο να πάρει ένα στυλό. Ο Θανάσης την σταματάει.

περνάω	pass
ερχόμενος/η/ο	next, coming
δίνω εξετάσεις	sit examinations
το μέρος	part
η άδεια οδηγήσεως	driver's licence
ίσως	perhaps
το πράγμα	thing
αλήθεια	really

ACTIVITY 19

Listen to the story again and answer the following questions.

1 Πού θέλει να πάει ο Θανάσης αύριο το βράδυ;
2 Γιατί δεν μπορεί να βγει η Σοφία;
3 Πότε αρχίζουν οι εξετάσεις της στα αγγλικά;
4 Σε τι άλλο θα την βοηθήσει ο Κραίηγκ;
5 Τι θέλει η Σοφία από τον πατέρα της;
6 Τι σχέδια έχει η Σοφία για όταν τελειώσει το σχολείο;
7 Τι της λέει ο Θανάσης για το Internet;

ACTIVITY 20

A Match the Greek expressions 1–5 with the correct English version from a–e.

1 Τι να σου πω;
2 Είναι μια χαρά.
3 Ποιος ξέρει;
4 Έτσι, ε;
5 Δυστυχώς, δεν μπορώ.

a Who knows?
b Is that so?
c Unfortunately I can't.
d What can I say?/What can I tell you?
e It's just fine

B Identify who says 1–5 during this episode of the story.

STORY TRANSCRIPT

Thanasis	Σοφία, θέλεις να πάμε στη Βουλιαγμένη αύριο το βράδυ;
Sophia	Δυστυχώς, δεν μπορώ. Πρέπει να διαβάσω. Έχω εξετάσεις την ερχόμενη εβδομάδα.
Thanasis	Τι εξετάσεις θα δώσεις;
Sophia	Δίνω Proficiency στα αγγλικά φέτος, και το πρώτο μέρος είναι την Πέμπτη.
Thanasis	Καλή επιτυχία! Τα αγγλικά σου είναι μια χαρά. ... Θα σε βοηθήσει καθόλου ο Κραίηγκ;
Sophia	Αυτός θα με βοηθήσει σήμερα στο αυτοκίνητο – θέλω να πάρω την άδεια οδηγήσεως, και θα βγούμε λιγάκι το απόγευμα να μου δείξει μερικά πράγματα ...
Thanasis	Έτσι, ε; Πολλές ώρες περνάς με τον Κραίηγκ.
Sophia	Τι να σου πω; Πρέπει να περάσω – θέλω να μου πάρει ο μπαμπάς αυτοκίνητο, και θέλω αργότερα να πάω στην Αγγλία.
Thanasis	Πότε; Τι θα κάνεις στην Αγγλία;
Sophia	Ίσως να πάω στο πανεπιστήμιο εκεί, ποιος ξέρει ...
Thanasis	Το ξέρεις ότι μπορείς να δεις όλα τα πανεπιστήμια στο Internet από το σπίτι μου;
Sophia	Αλήθεια; Πότε μπορώ να περάσω να τα δω;

Test

Now it's time to test your progress in Unit 10.

1 Give the future/subjunctive of each of the following verbs.

θα/να

1 διαφημίζω
2 πληρώνω
3 φοράω
4 μιλάω
5 μένω
6 τρώω
7 βλέπω
8 λέω
9 μαθαίνω
10 ακούω

`10`

2 Match 1–12 with the correct Greek translation from a–l.

1 heating	a κοινόχρηστα
2 word	b τραπεζαρία
3 tooth	c χώρα
4 bedroom	d μέρος
5 trouble/bother	e εξέταση
6 part	f λέξη
7 flat	g γλώσσα
8 examination	h θέρμανση
9 communal charges	i δόντι
10 dining room	j υπνοδωμάτιο
11 language	k διαμέρισμα
12 country	l ταλαιπωρία

`12`

3 Complete the sentences with the correct form of the verb.

1 Ο Θανάσης θέλει να _____ τη Σοφία. (βοηθάω)
2 Οι φοιτητές πρέπει να _____ γαλλικά (μαθαίνω)
3 Ποιος μπορεί να _____ γρήγορα; (τρέχω)
4 Η Βιβή θέλει να _____ τα γενέθλια της στο Βερολίνο. (γιορτάζω)
5 Τα παιδιά δεν μπορούν να _____ εδώ. (παίζω)

`5`

4 Complete the sentences with the pronouns in the box. There is one more than you need.

> τους   της   μου   μας   με   του

1 Φέρε _____ κάτι να φάω, σε παρακαλώ.
2 Να ο Πέτρος - μπορείς να _____ πεις τα νέα.
3 Πότε θα _____ πληρώσεις; Θέλουν να ξέρουν.
4 Πάμε! Η παρέα _____ περιμένει στην πλατεία.
5 Η Βάλια θέλει να _____ στείλεις ένα βιβλίο.

| 5 |

5 Read the following piece about Valentina abroad, then answer the questions that follow.

ΜΙΑ ΕΛΛΗΝΙΔΑ ΣΤΟ ΕΞΩΤΕΡΙΚΟ

Η Βαλεντίνα είναι φοιτήτρια - σπουδάζει ιατρική στο πανεπιστήμιο Θεσσαλονίκης. Του χρόνου θέλει να πάει στην Αγγλία. Θέλει να δουλέψει σε ένα ξένο νοσοκομείο για λίγους μήνες να δει τι κάνουν εκεί. Έχει φίλους στο Λονδίνο, και αν πάνε όλα καλά, θα νοικιάσουν ένα διαμέρισμα μαζί. Ξέρει αρκετά αγγλικά, αλλά δεν τα μιλάει καλά. Επίσης θα πρέπει να μάθει πώς οδηγούν στα αριστερά του δρόμου. Τον καιρό που θα είναι εκεί, ίσως να κάνει μερικά ταξίδια. Της Βαλεντίνας της αρέσει πολύ το Λονδίνο αλλά όταν πάει, δεν θα μπορεί να βγαίνει κάθε βράδυ: ή παιδίατρος, ή γλέντι.

1 What and where is Valentina studying? (2)
2 Where does she want to spend some time next year? (1)
3 Why does she want to do this? (2)
4 Who will she live with and where? (2)
5 Is she concerned about the language there? Why? (2)
6 What is the one thing she will have to learn? (2)
7 What else might she do while she's there? (1)
8 What will she not be able to do there? (2)
9 As what does she hope to specialize? (1)

| 15 |

TOTAL SCORE | 47 |

If you scored less than 37 go through the dialogues and the Language Building sections again, before completing the Summary on page 148.

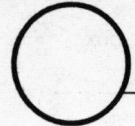

Summary 10

 Now try this final test summarizing the main points covered in this unit. You can check your answers on the recording.

How would you:
1 say 'she wants to read the newspaper'?
2 ask a friend 'Do you want us to go out together this evening?'?
3 say 'we're waiting to see the manager'?
4 ask the receptionist if you have to make an appointment?
5 say you can't pay your bill?
6 tell someone who asks for directions he can't stop here?
7 say 'she must leave immediately'?
8 say 'we have to ask for permission'?

REVISION

In preparation for Review 3, revise all of the verbs, first and second stem, so that you can work with the future tense, and say what you want to, can, and must do. Go over the vocabulary you have covered, particularly in Units 8, 9, and 10, to do with holidays, eating, other leisure activities, the weather, clothes, houses, workplaces, and so on. Remind yourself of the various questions you are now able to formulate: for example, Who is that? How much must I pay? Do you like Greece? Can we see the new French film? Is it going to rain? Do you want to sing?

Once through the review, take a breather before you gear up for the past tense.

Review 3

1 Sort the following words into the given categories.
  There are 5 in each group.

τραγούδι	οδοντίατρος	αρνάκι	διαμέρισμα
παλτό	κρεβατοκάμαρα	ποδοσφαιριστής	ταινία
παπούτσια	κουζίνα	καθηγητής	χόρτα
κουραμπιέδες	θέατρο	γυαλιά	παντελόνι
καλαμαράκι	σαλόνι	μπουζούκι	κασκόλ
συγγραφέας	γκαρσονιέρα	ορχήστρα	κοτόπουλο
δασκάλα			

Ρούχα Clothes	Φαγώσιμα Food	Επαγγέλματα Occupations	Ψυχαγωγία Entertainment	Στέγαση Accommodation

2 Find the right word.

1 Which of the following is not an animal?
   a σκύλος b χελώνα c έργο d γάτα

2 Which of the following words does not refer to a woman?
   a τσέπη b κυρία c αδελφή d γυναίκα

3 Which of the following adjectives would you use to describe something unpleasant?
   a σπουδαίος b θαυμάσιος c απαίσιος d απίθανος

4 Which of the following verbs is a second stem?
   a φοράω b φτάνω c φεύγω d φάω

5 Which of the following weather words is a verb?
   a λιακάδα b βρέχει c άνοιξη d χειμώνας

3 Choose the correct expression from a–d for the following situations.

1 You are at a party and think you recognize the person across the room. What do you ask?

2 Your neighbour tells you her son is arriving home from a year abroad. What do you say?

3 You wonder how well the new florist is doing. What would be an appropriate question to ask her?

4 Your children are unappreciative about the meal that has taken you all afternoon to prepare. What's your reaction?

5 Your friends are going to the ballet for the first time. What do you wish them?

a Πώς πάνε οι δουλειές;
b Καλώς να τον δεχθείτε!
c Κρίμα ο κόπος μου!
d Ποιος είναι αυτός;
e Καλή διασκέδαση!

GRAMMAR AND USAGE

4 Complete the sentences with the correct form of **αρέσει** + the relevant pronoun. In each case, the speaker is addressing the person(s) named in the sentence.

1 Νίκη, _____ τα ζώα;

2 _____ αυτή η μουσική, μαμά και μπαμπά;

3 Αντωνία, γιατί δεν _____ οι διακοπές στα βουνά;

4 Κύριε Αγγέλου, οι φίλοι σας πίνουν ούζο, ή δεν _____.

5 Γειά σου Λάκη! _____ το καινούριο πουκάμισό σου!

5 Complete the sentences with the correct form of the verbs in brackets.

1 Ο Ηλίας θέλει να _____ τις φωτογραφίες. (βλέπω)

2 Έχω δουλειά και πρέπει να την _____. (τελειώνω)

3 Ο Φίλιππος δεν μπορεί να _____ την Μαργαρίτα. (ξυπνάω)

4 Παππού, πότε θα _____ τα παιδιά στο πάρκο; (πάω)

5 Η γιαγιά θέλει να _____ την εφημερίδα. (διαβάζω)

6 Complete the sentences with the correct form of the imperative.

1 _____ την κουζίνα. (καθαρίζω)

2 _____ το παράθυρο, σε παρακαλώ. (κλείνω)

3 _____ τα βιβλία εδώ. (φέρνω)

4 _____ μου ένα ψωμί και μισή ντουζίνα αυγά. (δίνω)

5 _____ τα ρέστα σου. (ζητάω)

7 Complete the text with the correct form of the appropriate adjective.

ΠΟΙΟΣ ΕΙΝΑΙ Ο ΜΑΓΚΑΣ;

' _____ (Σπουδαίος) ηθοποιός,' λέει η μία εφημερίδα. _____ '(Απαίσιος) έργο,' λέει η άλλη. Όλη η οικογένεια είναι _____ (έτοιμος) να δει την ταινία. Ο Μπαμπάς φοράει το _____ (καινούριος) παλτό του, η Μαμά έχει ωραία _____ (δερμάτινος) παπούτσια, η Νίτσα θα πάρει τα _____ (κόκκινος) γάντια της, και ο Γρηγόρης θα είναι

_____ (φοβερός) - τα ρούχα του είναι το κάτι άλλο! Έχουν κλείσει εισιτήρια, και το ταξί περιμένει. Το μόνο _____ (άσχημος) πράγμα είναι ότι ο Μάγκας, ο σκύλος τους, πρέπει να μείνει στο σπίτι.

 LISTENING

8 Georgia has just called her mother from France. Listen to the message left on the answerphone then answer the following questions.

1 Πού είναι η Γιωργία τώρα;
2 Πώς διασκεδάζουν σήμερα;
3 Ποιον ηθοποιό βλέπει;
4 Τι θα κάνουνε αύριο;
5 Τι πρέπει να κάνει όταν τελειώσουν οι διακοπές;
6 Τι ώρα θα γυρίσουνε στην Ελλάδα την Κυριακή;
7 Τι θα γιορτάσουνε;

9 Nina is talking to a salesman in a shop. Listen and read the dialogue below. There are 10 differences between this and what you hear.

Nina   Χαίρετε. Θέλω να αγοράσω ένα μαγιό.
Salesman Α, μάλιστα. Ελάτε από 'δώ. Τι χρώμα σας αρέσει;
Nina   Δεν ξέρω ... μπορώ να τα δω;
Salesman Βεβαίως. Έχουμε όλα τα νούμερα.
Nina   Το κίτρινο, με τα λουλούδια είναι ωραίο ...
Salesman Θέλετε να το δοκιμάσετε ...
Nina   Μφφ ... προτιμώ το μαύρο ... α, και εκείνο το πορτοκαλί ... μπορώ να τα φορέσω;
Salesman Φυσικά. Μπείτε σ'αυτό το δωμάτιο.
Nina   Μ'αρέσουν και τα δύο - Πόσο κάνουν;
Salesman Το μαύρο είναι τριάντα χιλιάδες ... Το άλλο, ε-ε-ε, είκοσι εφτά.
Nina   Εντάξει - θα πάρω το μαύρο.

10 Read the following out loud and listen to the recording
to check your pronunciation.

1 Η ψυχαχωγία
2 Ο χορτοφάγος
3 Φριχτό πράγμα
4 Καταπληκτικός ποδοσφαιριστής
5 Σας γνωρίζω από κάπου.
6 Θα βγούμε μαζί.

11 You're speaking to somebody about renting a house for
the autumn. Prepare your answers then join in the
dialogue on the recording. Try to do it without looking
at your notes.

Say you have to rent a house for the autumn.

You _____

Agent Πού το θέλετε;
Say, near the sea, but not too far from the airport.

You _____

Agent Σας αρέσει η βόρεια Ελλάδα;
Say you like northern Greece – on an island,
perhaps?

You _____

Agent Υπάρχει ένα σπουδαίο σπίτι στη Μυτιλήνη –
παλιό αλλά άνετο.
Say you want it to have two bathrooms.

You _____

Agent Έχει δύο, και ντουζ στον κήπο.
Ask if you can see photographs of the house.

You _____

Agent Βεβαίως. Ορίστε.
Say it's excellent. Ask how much it is a month.

You _____

Agent Δεν είναι καθόλου ακριβό – 80.000 – και δεν έχει
κοινόχρηστα.
Έχει όλες τις μοντέρνες ανέσεις.
Say you have to speak to your wife first, but you
think you'll take it.

You _____

Agent Ό,τι θέλετε. Μπορείτε να μου τηλεφωνήσετε
όταν είσαστε έτοιμοι.

I went, I saw, I did

Πήγα, είδα, έκανα

OBJECTIVES

In this unit you'll learn how to:

- ✓ talk about what you did in the past
- ✓ discuss further indoor and outdoor pursuits
- ✓ tell a story

And cover the following grammar and language:

- ✓ the simple past tense
- ✓ the question **πώς περάσατε;** to ask how something went
- ✓ **όταν** and **πότε** (both meaning 'when')
- ✓ the pronoun **ο άλλος** ('the other')

LEARNING GREEK 11

When learning a language, it is important that you recycle material so that you can use what you have learnt in as many different contexts as possible. The course itself is structured to do this, but you can do more yourself to suit your own needs and interests. At the end of each unit, think of ways to combine what you have just learnt with what you already know. For example, once you have learnt the past tense in this unit, you can combine it with the language in Unit 9 and say what you did on holiday and what the weather was like, or with the language in Unit 5 and say what you bought recently when you went shopping.

Now start the recording for Unit 11.

11.1   What did you do last night?

Τι κάνατε χθες το βράδυ;

ACTIVITY 1 is on the recording.

ACTIVITY 2 Correct the answers which are false.

1 Ο άνδρας περίμενε τηλεφώνημα από την Αγγλία.	T / F
2 Η κυρία έφυγε από την δουλειά το βράδυ.	T / F
3 Η έκθεση βιβλίου είναι στο Ζάππειο.	T / F
4 Στην έκθεση έχει ελληνικά και ξένα βιβλία.	T / F

DIALOGUE 1

○ Τι κάνατε χθές το βράδυ; Πήγατε πουθενά;

■ Αμέ, και περάσαμε πολύ ωραία.

○ Εμείς μείναμε σπίτι – περιμέναμε τηλεφώνημα από την Αυστραλία.

■ Εγώ έφυγα νωρίς από τη δουλειά. Πήγαμε με τα παιδιά στην έκθεση βιβλίου.

○ Α, ναι, στο Ζάππειο. Το διάβασα στην εφημερίδα.

■ Αξίζει. Να πάτε. Είχε απ' όλα τα βιβλία – χιλιάδες! Παιδικά, τεχνικά, ελληνικά, ξένα ...

○ Είχε και ηλεκτρονικά υλικά;

■ Απ' όλα σου λέω – λογοτεχνία σε βίντεο, εγκυκλοπαίδειες σε σι-ντί, παιχνίδια για κομπιούτερ ...

○ Είδατε πολλά, ε;

■ Καταπληκτική έκθεση – για όλα τα γούστα. Μετά κάναμε μια βόλτα στο Μοναστηράκι για φαγητό.

○ Α! Δεν σας είπα να πάτε στην καινούργια ταβέρνα που άνοιξε ...

■ Εκεί πήγαμε – απίθανοι μεζέδες!

VOCABULARY

(ε)χθές	yesterday
πήγατε πουθενά;	did you go anywhere?
η έκθεση	exhibition, display
αξίζει	it's worth it
παιδικός/ή/ό	child's, childlike
τεχνικός/ή/ό	technical
η λογοτεχνία	literature
η εγκυκλοπαίδεια	encyclopaedia
το παιχνίδι	game
το γούστο	taste

✓ The simple past tense

In Greek, the simple past tense is used to relate completed actions in the past.

Ο Πέτρος **αγόρασε** ένα βιβλίο χθες. Peter bought a book yesterday.
Πέρσι **πήγαμε** στην Αμερική. Last year we went to America.

The simple past is formed using the relevant stem plus the endings -α, -ες, -ε, -αμε, -ατε, -αν(ε). For regular verbs, the stem is the one used for the future and subjunctive forms: so δουλεύω – δούλεψα, διαβάζω – διάβασα, and so on. Verb list showing both stems starts on page 234.

δουλεύω – work
I: δούλεψα   you: δούλεψες   he/she/it: δούλεψε
we: δουλέψαμε   you: δουλέψατε   they: δούλεψαν(ε)

Some irregular verbs have a variations in the stem, for example: λέω / θα πω ('say') becomes: είπα, είπες, είπε, είπαμε, είπατε, είπαν(ε). More details are in the verb tables on pages 229–234.

Important: the stress in the simple past falls on the third syllable from the end. Look at δούλεψα (above) again.

When a simple past verb does not have three syllables, an extra syllable (known as an *augment*) is added to the front of the stem to supply the need. The standard augment is ε-, as in γράφω – έγραψα, φεύγω – έφυγα, τρώω – έφαγα (the γ is inserted to separate the two α's). πάω – (ε)πήγα ('go') is an irregularity: the ε is usually dropped and the stress has come to rest on the second syllable from the end.

Other augments:
η- θέλω – ήθελα, ξέρω – ήξερα, πίνω – ήπια.
ει- έχω – είχα, βλέπω – είδα, λέω – είπα.

ACTIVITY 3

Rewrite the sentences, putting the underlined verbs into the past tense.

1 Ο Γιάννης <u>λέει</u> όχι.
2 Τα παιδιά <u>παίζουν</u> στο πάρκο.
3 Η Ελένη δεν <u>θέλει</u> να πάει μαζί μας.
4 Δεν <u>ξέρω</u> τι να πω.
5 Μαρίκα, τι ώρα <u>φεύγεις</u> απο το γραφείο;
6 <u>Κάνει</u> πολλή ζέστη το Σαββατοκύριακο.
7 <u>Βλέπεις</u> τη θάλασσα;

🎧 Now do activities 4 and 5 on the recording.

Περνάν τα χρόνια

(🔊) **ACTIVITY 6** is on the recording.

ACTIVITY 7

1 Πού έμενε η κυρία Μαρία όταν ήταν παιδί;
2 Τι δουλειά έκανε ο παππούς της;
3 Τι ήταν ο πατέρας της;

DIALOGUE 2

○ Ήμασταν πολύ ευτυχισμένοι στο νησί τότε. Η ζωή ήταν απλή και λίγα θέλαμε.
■ Μιλάτε για τα χρόνια πριν τον πόλεμο;
○ Ωραία χρόνια, εκείνα τα παλιά ...
■ Ήσαστan, λοιπόν, μεγάλη οικογένεια, και το σπίτι σας ήταν κοντά στη θάλασσα ...
○ Μάλιστα. Ο παππούς ήταν ναυτικός – γύρισε όλον τον κόσμο. Η γιαγιά είχε πολλά χωράφια. Δουλέψανε σκληρά για να σπουδάσουν τα παιδιά τους.
■ Ο πατέρας σας ήταν ο διευθυντής του σχολείου;
○ Για σαράντα χρόνια. Η μητέρα ήταν νοσοκόμα αλλά δεν δούλεψε πολλά χρόνια. Σταμάτησε όταν έκανε το πρώτο παιδί.
■ Εσείς κυρία Μαρία;
○ Α, όχι, εγώ ήμουν το τελευταίο.
■ Πόσα αδέλφια ήσαστan;
○ Ήμασταν εφτά, αλλά τώρα είμαστε τρεις ... όλοι συνταξιούχοι ... περνάν τα χρόνια, περνάνε οι ζωές ...
■ Εσείς πόσα παιδιά έχετε;
○ Μία κόρη, έναν γιο, και τρία εγγόνια.

VOCABULARY

τότε	then
η ζωή	life
απλός/η/ο	simple
ο πόλεμος	war
ο ναυτικός	sailor
γύρισε όλον τον κόσμο	went all over the world
το χωράφι	field
η νοσοκόμα	nurse
συνταξιούχος	pensioner, senior citizen
το εγγόνι	grandchild

✅ The simple past tense of *είμαι* ('am')

The simple past of είμαι is irregular.

I: ήμουν(α)	we: ήμασταν *or* ήμαστε
you: ήσουν(α)	you: ήσασταν *or* ήσαστε
he/she/it: ήταν(ε)	they: ήταν(ε)

> Ο Αλέκος **ήταν** στην Γερμανία πέρσι. Alekos was in Germany last year.
> Δεν **ήμουν** καλά το Σάββατο. I wasn't well on Saturday.

The simple past of υπάρχω ('exist', 'be') is υπήρχα.

> Πριν το 1980, δεν **υπήρχε** κανένα ξενοδοχείο εδώ. Before 1980, there wasn't a single hotel here.

✅ The simple past of *πρέπει*, *μ'αρέσει*, and *μπορώ*

The simple past of πρέπει is έπρεπε (with an augment).

> Χθες **έπρεπε** να φύγουμε νωρίς. Yesterday we had to leave early.

The simple past of μ'αρέσει is μ'άρεσε.

> Οταν ήμασταν παιδιά, **μας άρεσε** ο Καραγκιόζης. When we were children we liked Karagiozis [*Greek shadow-puppet theatre*].

μπορώ changes like a standard Group 2 verb. For the past, use the second stem (with -εσ- in this case) + past endings: μπόρεσα, μπόρεσες, μπόρεσε, μπορέσαμε, μπορέσατε, μπόρεσαν (or μπόρεσάνε).

> Δεν **μπόρεσα** να βρω το μαύρο στιλό μου. I couldn't find my black pen.

✅ *όταν* and *πότε*

όταν and πότε both mean 'when'. πότε is the word for 'when' used in questions, both direct and indirect.

> Ξέρεις **πότε** έφτασε ο εργάτης προχθές; Do you know when the workman arrived the day before yesterday?
> Η γιαγιά έμενε στη βόρειο Ελλάδα **όταν** ήταν μικρή. Granny lived in northern Greece when she was young.

ACTIVITY 8

Complete the sentences with the right form of **είμαι** in the simple past tense.

1. **A:** Αλέκα, πού _____ χθες το βράδυ;
   B: _____ στο σινεμά με τον Λάκη. Γιατί ρωτάς;
   A: Ποιος άλλος _____ μαζί σας;
   B: Κανένας. Μόνοι μας _____ .
2. Η νοσοκόμα και η αδελφή της δεν _____ στο πάρτι.

 Now do activities 9 and 10 on the recording.

Ήταν υπέροχα

ACTIVITY 11 is on the recording.

ACTIVITY 12 Correct the errors about Dialogue 3.

1 Η παρέα πήγε εκδρομή στη θάλασσα το Σάββατο.
2 Μαγειρέψανε και πήρανε φαγητά μαζί τους.
3 Φάγανε πατάτες και ήπιαν πορτοκαλάδες και ρετσίνα.

DIALOGUE 3

○ Πώς περάσατε την περασμένη Κυριακή;

■ Α, ήταν υπέροχα. Όλο το απόγευμα κάναμε μπάνια και βόλτες με τη βάρκα. Μετά στρώσαμε να φάμε.

○ Άκουσα ότι ψήσατε φρέσκο ψάρι στην άμμο.

■ Θαύμα ήταν. Ο Βασίλης με την Αλέκα ετοιμάσανε τα κάρβουνα, και οι άλλοι οργανώσαμε τα υπόλοιπα – ντοματούλες, τυράκι, ψωμάκι, ελιές - απλά πράγματα ...

▼ Αλλά φάγαμε σαν πασάδες ... Ήπιαμε μπίρες ...

■ Το φεγγάρι – πανσέληνος – ήταν μπροστά μας, η θάλασσα καθρέφτης ...

▼ Τραγουδήσαμε, χορέψαμε, ξαπλώσαμε ...

○ Αχ, κατάλαβα - και ζήλεψα!

▼ Σου είπαμε νά 'ρθεις, αλλά δεν ήθελες. ... Γιατί;

○ Ε, ήξερα ότι πέρσι εκεί που πήγαμε ήτανε χάλια ...

▼ Αμάν, πάλι γκρινιάρα - πέρσι εσύ είχες τα χάλια σου. Φέτος έχασες. Για να δούμε του χρόνου!

VOCABULARY	
στρώνω	spread, lay
ψήνω	bake, roast, grill
η άμμος	sand
ετοιμάζω	prepare
το κάρβουνο	coal
το υπόλοιπο	remainder, rest
σαν πασάδες	like royalty
το φεγγάρι	moon
η πανσέληνος	full moon
ο καθρέφτης	mirror
ξαπλώνω	lie down, stretch out
σου είπαμε νά 'ρθεις	we told you to come
χάλια	awful, a mess
η γκρινιάρα	grumbler, nagger

✓ The question *Πώς περάσατε;* to ask how something went

Πώς περάσατε; is useful for asking people how something went. It can be translated in a variety of ways.

Πώς περάσατε στην Αμερική; How did it go in America?
Πώς περάσατε την Πρωτοχρονιά; How did you spend the New Year?
Πώς περάσανε στο σπίτι σας; How did they enjoy (the time at) your home?

✓ The pronoun *ο άλλος* ('the other')

ο άλλος changes form like αυτός and ποιος (see page 226).

	masculine	feminine	neuter
singular	ο άλλος	η άλλη	το άλλο
plural	οι άλλοι	οι άλλες	τα άλλα

Εμείς μαγειρέψαμε το ψάρι – **οι άλλοι** ετοιμάσανε τη σαλάτα. We cooked the fish – the others prepared the salad.

✓ Another use of the simple past

The simple past is also used in certain expressions to give the impression that you have just realized something. Although the simple past is used, the sense is the present.

Α, κατάλαβα! Ah, I understand!
Ζήλεψα! I'm jealous!   **Άργησα!** I'm late!
Note   **πέρσι** last year   **φέτος** this year   **του χρόνου** next year

---

ACTIVITY 13

Translate the following sentences into Greek.

1 They laid the table.
2 They ate delicious things.
3 They stretched out on the sand.
4 I baked the potatoes.
5 The others did the rest.
6 We saw the full moon above the trees.
7 The water was like a mirror.

ACTIVITY 14

Complete the sentences using either **όταν** or **πότε**.

1 Δεν αγοράζω αυγά _____ δεν ξέρω από πού είναι.
2 Δεν ξέρω _____ θα πάμε στο χωριό.

🎧 Now do activities 15 and 16 on the recording.

A folktale

Ενα παραμύθι

Homer is just one landmark in a long and venerable
tradition of Greek storytelling. As elsewhere, traditional
stories start and end conventionally: **Μία φορά και έναν
καιρό ...** – 'Once upon a time' and **Και ζήσανε καλά και
εμείς καλύτερα.** 'And they lived happily ever after'
(literally: 'they lived well, and we better'). Below is an
excerpt from the opening paragraphs of a well-known
traditional tale, which is reminiscent of the King Lear
predicament. Enjoy reading it and see if you can answer
the questions that follow.

ΣΑΝ ΤΟ ΑΛΑΤΙ

Μία φορά και έναν καιρό ήταν ένας βασιλιάς και είχε τρεις
κόρες. Μία μέρα ήθελε να φύγει για τον πόλεμο και κάλεσε
τις θυγατέρες του να τις χαιρετίσει και να δει πόσο τον
αγαπάνε. Η πρώτη τον φίλησε και του είπε, 'Σαν τα μάτια
μου'. Η δεύτερη του είπε, 'Σαν τη ζωή μου'. Η τρίτη του
απάντησε, 'Σαν το αλάτι'.

Όταν άκουσε ο βασιλιάς πως η μικρότερη κόρη του τον
αγαπάει τόσο λίγο, θύμωσε και, πριν φύγει, της είπε να
πάρει δρόμο από το παλάτι.

Εκείνη η κακομοίρα άρχισε να γυρίζει από 'δώ και από 'κεί
και πουθενά δεν έλεγε την ιστορία της. ... Μία μέρα
έφτασε σ' ένα άλλο βασίλειο και ζήτησε λίγη δουλειά μέσα
στο παλάτι. ... Από κουβέντα σε κουβέντα καταλάβανε ότι
είναι βασιλοπούλα και το είπανε στο βασιλόπουλο. Πήγε
εκείνος και την είδε ... της μίλησε και, να μην τα
πολυλογούμε, την αγάπησε και την πήρε γυναίκα του.

The tale goes on to describe the wedding, introduce the guests and stage the reconciliation scene – illustrating the moral of the story.

ACTIVITY 17

In the story, find the Greek for the following words.

1 king
2 kingdom
3 prince
4 princess
5 palace
6 daughter (2 *options*)
7 unfortunate one
8 chat/conversation

ACTIVITY 18

Underline all the verbs in the text and give their present tense form (in the first person). Can you work out the meaning of those that are unfamiliar from their context?

ACTIVITY 19

Which daughter loved the king
a as she loved her eyes
b as she loved salt
c as she loved life itself

ΝΟΜΙΣΜΑΤΑ
COINS

Η Βαγγελιώ λέει του Περικλή για την περιπέτειά τους στην Κεφαλλονιά.

η περιπέτεια	adventure
όπως σου είπα	as I told you
τα αγριόχορτα	weeds
η αστυνομία	police
αξίζουν τίποτα;	are they worth anything?
ο αστυνόμος	policeman
χρυσός/ή/ό	gold

ACTIVITY 20

Listen to the story and answer the questions.

1 Τι έκανε ο Πέτρος πριν φύγει;
2 Στην Κεφαλλονιά, πού βρήκανε τα νομίσματα;
3 Πού τα πήρανε τα νομίσματα πρώτα;
4 Μετά, πού τα πήγαν τα νομίσματα;
5 Αξίζουνε πολλά αυτά τα νομίσματα;
6 Τι έχει το αυτοκίνητο;
7 Ποιος πληρώνει για να μάθει η Σοφία να οδηγεί;

ACTIVITY 21

Find the Greek expressions in the story that mean the following.

1 so soon?
2 taking the opportunity
3 as I said to you
4 unseen by anyone
5 Are they worth anything?

ACTIVITY 22

Read the following summary of the Cephalonian incident. There are two factual errors – what are they?

One afternoon as Vangelio and the rest were taking a walk along the beach they came across some coins lying among the weeds. The coins looked ancient, but even Craig, an archaeology student, could not be sure about their date or value. They couldn't tell either how long the coins had been lying there. They decided to take them to the museum, where they learnt that the coins were indeed rather old and gold. They then reported the find to the police.

STORY TRANSCRIPT

Pericles	Έφυγε ο Πέτρος; Τόσο γρήγορα;
Vangelio	Δεν ήτανε να μείνει πολύ – λίγες μέρες. Με την ευκαιρία αγόρασε κάτι πράγματα που ήθελε.
Pericles	Καλά έκανε. Τώρα, πες μου για την περιπέτεια στην Κεφαλλονιά.
Vangelio	Όπως σου είπα, ένα απόγευμα κάναμε μια βόλτα στα χωράφια, και να, εκεί μπροστά μας, είδαμε τα νομίσματα.
Pericles	Έτσι, ε; Ήταν στα αγριόχορτα χρόνια και χρόνια χωρίς να τα δεί άνθρωπος ... ;
Vangelio	Αυτό δεν το ξέρουμε. Τα παιδιά τα πήραν στην αστυνομία.
Pericles	Ο Κραίηγκ που είναι αρχαιολόγος τα κοίταξε καλά; Αξίζουν τίποτα;
Vangelio	Μαζί με έναν αστυνομικό τα πήγανε στο μουσείο και μάθανε πως είναι αρκετά παλιά – χρυσά ...
	...
Lakis	Βαγγελιώ! Πού έβαλες πάλι το αυτοκίνητο;
Vangelio	Γιατί; Τι έχει;
Lakis	Πάει ο καθρέφτης!
Vangelio	Αχ, Σοφία! Για την άδειά σου πόσα πλήρωσα, και έχω να πληρώσω!

Test

Now it's time to test your progress in Unit 11.

1 Give the past tense of the following verbs:

1 κάνω	4 παίζω	7 τρώω	9 μιλάω
2 μένω	5 δουλεύω	8 πίνω	10 γράφω
3 φεύγω	6 ακούω		

10

2 What is the Greek for the following nouns?
Example: field – **το χωράφι**

1 literature	4 pensioner	7 life	9 sand
2 exhibition	5 policeman	8 coal	10 gold
3 museum	6 nurse		

10

3 Complete the text with the words in the box.

> ξέρανε   βγήκανε   πήγαν   μπόρεσαν   άρεσε

Σταφύλια στ'αμπέλια
Grapes in the vineyards

Φέτος το καλοκαίρι τα δύο εγγόνια της Άννας από την
Γερμανία (1) _____ στο χωριό για πρώτη φορά.
Η ζωή εκεί τους (2) _____ πολύ. Δεν
(3) _____ πολλά ελληνικά αλλά (4) _____
εύκολα να παίξουν με τα άλλα παιδιά. Οι διακοπές δεν
ήταν μόνο παιχνίδι - για μία εβδομάδα όλοι
(5) _____ στα αμπέλια να βοηθήσουν με τα
σταφύλια.

5

4 Complete the sentences with the correct past tense form
of the verbs in brackets.

1 Τα παιδιά _____ τα κάρβουνα. (ετοιμάζω)
2 Λέλα, _____ το μάθημά σου; (γράφω)
3 Προχές πήγα στην βιβλιοθήκη και _____ τις
  ξένες εφημερίδες. (διαβάζω)
4 Τι σου _____ ο γιατρός; (λέω)
5 Πότε _____ να φύγει ο πατέρας σου; (θέλω)

6 Όχι, εγώ δεν το _____ αυτό. (ξέρω)

7 Τι _____ στα μαγαζιά σήμερα, Νικολέτα;
(ψωνίζω)

8 Παππού, _____ τα κλειδιά σου; (παίρνω)

9 Η Άννα _____ όταν είδε το σπίτι της Βίκης.
(ζηλεύω)

10 _____ στις έντεκα η ώρα σήμερα. (ξυπνάω)

| | 10 |

5 Match 1–4 with the appropriate response from a–d.

1 Ήταν έτοιμος ο Λάκης;   a Πολύ. Να πάτε!
2 Πώς περάσατε;   b Γύρισαν όλο τον κόσμο.
3 Πού ταξιδέψανε;   c Υπέροχα!
4 Σας άρεσε το έργο;   d Όχι, άργησε.

| | 4 |

6 Read the card and then decide whether the following
statements are true or false.

1 Lulu and her companion arrived two days ago.   T / F
2 When they arrived they went immediately
to the Louvre to see the Venus de Milo.   T / F
3 They didn't like the Pompidou Centre.   T / F
4 They went into Notre Dame.   T / F
5 This morning they had breakfast at the top
of the Eiffel Tower.   T / F
6 Lulu will see Aphrodite tomorrow.   T / F

Γειά σου Αφροδίτη

Χαιρετίσματα από το Παρίσι! Βρήκαμε μια καλή
ευκαιρία και ήρθαμε για δύο μέρες. Όταν φτάσαμε χθες,
πήγαμε στο Λούβρο και είδαμε καταπληκτικά πράγματα
- αλλά όχι την Αφροδίτη της Μήλου. Έπρεπε να ήσουν
κι εσύ μαζί μας! Το Κέντρο Πομπιντού ήταν απίθανο. Το
βραδάκι φάγαμε σε ένα ταβερνάκι κοντά στη Νότρ-Νταμ.
Σήμερα το πρωί, καφέ και κρουασάν στο ξενοδοχείο,
και μετά ανεβήκαμε στον πύργο του Άιφελ - πο-πο!
Λοιπόν, έφυγα. Η πτήση μας είναι στις δέκα απόψε. Θα
τα πούμε από κοντά αύριο!

Φιλάκια, Λουλού

| | 6 |

TOTAL SCORE | 45 |

If you scored less than 38 go through the dialogues and
the Language Building sections again, before
completing the summary on page 166.

Summary 11

 Now try this final test summarizing the main points covered in this unit. You can check your answers on the recording.

How would you:
1 ask a friend if he liked the exhibition?
2 ask him where he was last night?
3 ask him if his grandfather was a teacher?
4 say you weren't able to help him?
5 ask a friend if she saw Helen on Sunday?
6 say 'we bought three books at the exhibition'?
7 say they prepared the table for their breakfast?
8 say 'we danced on the sand'?
9 say you didn't want to drink ouzo, but you drank a lot of wine?

REVISION

To consolidate the simple past, try talking about things you've done recently – what you cooked yesterday, where you went last week, who you saw/spoke to this morning, what you read or watched on television last night, and so on. Think about what other people have done too, to practise different forms of the verbs. Coming up with as many different situations as you can will not only help the verb forms stick in your memory, it's also a very effective way to review vocabulary.

The things we used to do
Τι κάναμε

OBJECTIVES

In this unit you'll learn how to:

✓ talk about the things you like to do

✓ talk about things you used to do

And cover the following grammar and language:

✓ **μ'αρέσει να** ('I like to', 'I like ...-ing')

✓ the imperfect tense

LEARNING GREEK 12

Everybody has different motivations and priorities in learning a language, but certainly the common aim is to communicate with others. You don't have to be a hundred per cent correct in order to make yourself understood. Similarly you don't have to understand everything you hear in order to grasp the content of a message. So it may be better to concentrate on developing accuracy in writing: this is the place to consolidate sentence structure, verb endings, and gender and number agreements. Why not start writing a diary in Greek? Just a paragraph a day will help develop your fluency. When you write you have time to think about details and get them right. A more accurate grasp of grammar here will feed through into your spoken language.

Now start the recording for Unit 12.

12.1 I like working in the garden

Μ'αρέσει να δουλεύω στον κήπο

ACTIVITY 1 is on the recording.

ACTIVITY 2

Correct the statements which are false.

1 Ο κήπος δεν έχει πολλά λουλούδια.	T / F
2 Το μεσημέρι φάγανε φασολάκια από τον κήπο.	T / F
3 Η γυναίκα του κυρίου δεν τον βοηθάει.	T / F
4 Η κυρία θα φτιάξει καφέ.	T / F

DIALOGUE 1

○ Όταν έχω καιρό, μ'αρέσει να δουλεύω στον κήπο.

■ Ο κήπος σας είναι πολύ όμορφος – γεμάτος λουλούδια.

○ Ναι, φέτος έβαλα μερικά καινούργια τριαντάφυλλα, και πίσω φύτεψα μια λεμονιά.

■ Έχετε καθόλου λαχανικά;

○ Αμέ. Ντομάτες, κολοκυθάκια, φασολάκια ... Το μεσημέρι φάγαμε ένα καρπούζι – μέλι! – από τον κήπο μας.

■ Πο-πό μια γαρδένια, εκεί δίπλα στο βασιλικό! Πολλή δουλειά νομίζω έχει ο κήπος. Ποιος σας βοηθάει; ...

○ Της γυναίκας μου της αρέσει να ποτίζει κάθε πρωί.

■ Και 'μένα μ'αρέσει. Δυστυχώς, έχω μόνο μπαλκόνι.

○ Καθίστε εδώ, θα πιούμε καφεδάκι.

■ Σας αρέσει να παίζετε τάβλι, βλέπω.

VOCABULARY	
όμορφος/η/ο	lovely, beautiful, handsome
γεμάτος/η/ο	full
το τριαντάφυλλο	rose
φυτεύω	plant
η λεμονιά	lemon tree
τα λαχανικά	vegetables
αμέ	of course [*colloquial*]
το καρπούζι	watermelon
το μέλι	honey
η γαρδένια	gardenia
ο βασιλικός	basil
ποτίζω	water

✓ μ'αρέσει να ... ('I like to', 'I like ...-ing')

You are already familiar with the construction μ'αρέσει ('I like') used with nouns. To say what you like *doing*, you use μ'αρέσει να plus a verb. This verb is in the present tense and is in the same person as the person who 'likes'.

Μ'αρέσει να βγαίνω με τους φίλους μου. I like to go out with my friends.

Της αρέσει να μιλάει ελληνικά. She likes speaking Greek.

Δεν τους αρέσει να τρώνε αργά. They don't like eating late.

μ'αρέσει with a subject	*μ'αρέσει with a verb*
Μ'αρέσει η δουλειά.	Μ'αρέσει να δουλεύω.
Σ'αρέσει το ψάρι.	Σ'αρέσει να ψαρεύεις (to fish/fishing).
Του αρέσει ο περίπατος. (a walk)	Της αρέσει να περπατάει (to walk/walking).
Μας αρέσει το φαγητό.	Μας αρέσει να τρώμε.
Σας αρέσει το κρασί.	Σας αρέσει να πίνετε.
Τους αρέσουν οι γιορτές.	Τους αρέσει να γιορτάζουνε. (to celebrate)

ACTIVITY 3

A Write out the sentences in full using the right form of μ'αρέσει.

Example: Η Αννα/ξυπνάω/νωρίς
Της Άννας της αρέσει να ξυπνάει νωρίς.

1 ταξιδεύω/με το πλοίο. (me)
2 τρώω/φρούτα/κάθε μέρα. (her)
3 δεν παίζω/τάβλι. (them)
4 ψαρεύω/στη θάλασσα με τη βάρκα. (us)
5 δεν καθαρίζω/τα παπούτσια του. (him)
6 Η Μπέμπα/δεν βοηθάω/τον αδελφό της.
7 Ο Λάκης/δεν πληρώνω/λογαριασμούς του.
8 Γιατί/φεύγω/στις εφτά κάθε πρωί; (you informal)
9 Πότε/διαβάζω/την εφημερίδα; (you informal)
10 Πώς/μαγειρεύω/τα αυγά; (you formal)

B Write down five things that you like/do not like doing. Write down five things that various people you know like/do not like doing.

🔊 Now do activities 4 and 5 on the recording.

Βοηθούσαμε τους γονείς μας

ACTIVITY 6 is on the recording.

ACTIVITY 7

1 Πώς πήγαινε ο παππούς στο σχολείο;
2 Τι δεν είχανε το χειμώνα;
3 Τι παίζανε το χειμώνα;
4 Ποιον μήνα περιμέναμε;
5 Ποια ταινία δείχνει η τηλεόραση;

DIALOGUE 2

○ Παππού, πες μας τι κάνατε όταν ήσασταν μικρά.

■ Δεν υπήρχε τηλεόραση τότε, και έτσι ήμασταν πάντα έξω, και παίζαμε με τους φίλους μας.

○ Δεν πηγαίνατε στο σχολείο;

■ Πηγαίναμε στο σχολείο – με τα πόδια, μάλιστα – και όταν γυρίζαμε βοηθούσαμε τους γονείς μας με τις δουλειές.

○ Τι δουλειές, παππού;

■ Απ' όλες. Εμένα μου άρεσε να φέρνω το νερό.

○ Κρυώνατε πολύ;

■ Ε, τον χειμώνα έκανε κρύο, παιδί μου, και δεν είχαμε κεντρική θέρμανση ...

○ Και παίζατε χιονοπόλεμο και μετά ψήνατε κάστανα στα κάρβουνα στο τζάκι!

■ Ακριβώς. Αλλά περιμέναμε το Μάρτιο ...

○ Ναι, ναι, την άνοιξη γέμιζε ο ουρανός αετούς.

▼ Άννα, έλα, έχει τη Χιονάτη στην τηλεόραση.

VOCABULARY

μάλιστα	in fact [*also* yes – *emphatic*]
οι γονείς	parents
φέρνω	bring
κρυώνω	am cold
ο χιονοπόλεμος	snow(ball) fight
το κάστανο	chestnut
το τζάκι	fireplace
γεμίζω	fill
ο ουρανός	sky
ο αετός	kite
η Χιονάτη	Snow White

✓ The imperfect tense

The imperfect tense is used to describe a continuing, repeated, or habitual action in the past.

> Παίζαμε στο χιόνι. We used to play in the snow.

It is also used to describe an ongoing action that was interrupted.

> Ο Γιάννης διάβαζε την εφημερίδα όταν άκουσε την πόρτα .
> Yannis was reading the paper when he heard the door.

For *Group 1 verbs*, the imperfect is formed using the first stem (the one used for the present tense) + the endings for the simple past. If necessary (i.e. if the imperfect form has less than 3 syllables), the past augment is added.

> Έτρεχα δέκα χλμ κάθε μέρα. I used to run 10 km every day.
> [*imperfect*]
> Έτρεξα δέκα χλμ χθές. I ran 10 km yesterday. [*simple past*]

Note the distinction in usage between the imperfect (ongoing or continuous action) and the simple past (one-off or completed action).

> Έτρεχα στο πάρκο όταν είδα τον Λουκά. **I was running** in the park when I saw Louka.

Note that the simple past and the imperfect have the same form in verbs with the same first and second stems. These include θέλω – ήθελα, κάνω – έκανα, περιμένω – περίμενα, ξέρω – ήξερα. The context will help you distinguish between (for example) Τι κάνατε; 'What did you do?' (simple past) and 'What were you doing?' (imperfect).

ACTIVITY 8

A Write down the imperfect and the simple past (first person) of the following verbs in Greek: do, eat, play, water, want, clean, rest, write, arrive

B Write the following sentences in Greek.
  1 A: What were you doing in the kitchen?
     B: I was eating honey.
  2 A: Where did you use to play when you were young?
     B: We played in the garden, in the park, in the street, everywhere.
  3 A: Who was cleaning the house this morning?
     B: It wasn't Kosta. He was cooking in the kitchen.
  4 A: When did we use to arrive home in the evenings?
     B: When it was time (for us) to eat.

🎧 Now do activities 9 and 10 on the recording.

We were thirsty

Διψούσαμε

🔊 **ACTIVITY 11** is on the recording.

ACTIVITY 12

1 Πού ήταν τα παιδιά;
2 Τι ήπιαν τα παιδιά;
3 Τι λένε τα παιδιά για το δάσος;
4 Πώς τους βρήκε η μαμά τους;
5 Τι θέλει να κάνει ο γιατρός;

DIALOGUE 3

○ Περπατούσαμε γύρω-γύρω και δεν ξέραμε πού ήμαστε.
■ Τι κάνατε όταν σας βρήκε η μητέρα σας;
▼ Πίναμε νερό από το ποτάμι.
■ Διψούσατε, ε;
○ Ναι, και ήταν αργά, και πεινούσαμε.
■ Τι φάγατε;
▼ Δεν φάγαμε τίποτα.
○ Μόνο λίγα φρούτα που ήταν στο δάσος.
■ Τι φρούτα ακριβώς;
▼ Δεν ξέρουμε … Ήταν σκοτεινό το δάσος.
■ Έκανε κρύο;
○ Ναι, κρυώναμε πολύ και εγώ δεν φορούσα παλτό.
■ Τι κάνατε για να περάσει η ώρα;
▼ Μιλούσαμε και γελούσαμε και λέγαμε παραμύθια.
○ Και τότε μας άκουσε η Μαμά!
■ Ωραία. Ελάτε τώρα στο ιατρείο να σας εξετάσω λιγάκι.

VOCABULARY	
γύρω-γύρω	round and round
περπατάω	walk
το ποτάμι	river
διψώ	be thirsty
πεινώ	be hungry
το δάσος	wood, forest
σκοτεινός/ή/ό	dark
κρυώνω	feel cold, get cold
το παλτό	coat
γελώ	laugh
λέω παραμύθια	tell stories

✓ The imperfect: Group 2 verbs

Group 2 verbs (those ending in -άω – or -ώ, e.g. μιλάω) form the imperfect tense slightly differently: like Group 1 verbs, the first stem and the simple past endings are used, but -ούσ- is inserted between the stem and endings.

βοηθ(ά)ω – help

βοηθούσα	βοηθούσαμε
βοηθούσες	βοηθούσατε
βοηθούσε	βοηθούσαν(ε)

ζω – live

ζούσα	ζούσαμε
ζούσες	ζούσατε
ζούσε	ζούσαν(ε)

Note that with these verbs stress does not fall on the third last syllable: instead the stress always falls on -ούσ- .

✓ *γύρω-γύρω*

Greek often uses this form of doubling: σιγά-σιγά ('slowly'), γρήγορα-γρήγορα ('quickly'), καλά-καλά ('well'), and so on.

ACTIVITY 13

Use the imperfect to answer the following questions.

Example: Τι πουλούσες στο μαγαζί σου; (ρούχα)
Πουλούσα ρούχα.

1 Ποια γλώσσα μιλούσατε στον Καναδά; (αγγλικά και γαλλικά)
2 Τι ψήνατε την Πρωτοχρονιά; (Βασιλόπιτα)
3 Πού περπατούσατε προχθές; (στα βουνά)
4 Πού ζούσανε πριν πάνε στην Πάτρα; (Κόρινθο)
5 Οδηγούσατε όταν ήσασταν στη Νέα Υόρκη; (Ναι)
6 Δεν μπορούσες να βοηθήσεις τον αδελφό σου λιγάκι; (Όχι)

🎧 Now do activities 14 and 15 on the recording.

Το περιβάλλον

The rapid depletion of natural woodland in Greece, not least by the forest fires that seem to flare up without warning, has prompted a wide-ranging educational programme from the Department of the Environment, Land Use and Public Works. Below is an edited extract from the introduction to one of their school publications, *Ένα δένδρο μεγαλώνει μαζί μου* (*A tree grows up with me*). Read it through, see how much of it you can understand and then try activity 16.

Δύο λόγια για το δάσος

Το δάσος είναι ένα πλούσιο και πολυσύνθετο οικολογικό σύστημα και παίζει κύριο ρόλο στην οικολογική ισορροπία του περιβάλλοντος. Είναι μια πηγή ζωής για όλους μας.

Για πολλούς αιώνες οι άνθρωποι έκοβαν τα δάση για να ανοίξουν χωράφια για καλλιέργειες. Νομίζαν ότι υπήρχαν πάρα πολλά δένδρα και ότι πάντοτε θα υπάρχουν για κυνήγι, για ψυχαγωγία και για ό,τι άλλο θέλανε.

Για κάποιους, το δάσος ήταν σκοτεινό εμπόδιο στην πρόοδό τους. Βάζανε φωτιά στα δάση χωρίς σκέψη, κυρίως για οικονομικούς λόγους. Ποτέ δεν αφήνανε μικρά δένδρα στην θέση των μεγάλων, για να μεγαλώσει πάλι το δάσος με τον καιρό, έστω και μόνο του. Οι άνθρωποι έβλεπαν τα δάση σαν μια πηγή πετρελαίου, και μάλιστα μία πετρελαιοπηγή που την πίνανε και μετά την αφήνανε.

ACTIVITY 16

A Find the Greek words for the following. They appear in the order listed.

1 rich
2 complex
3 ecological balance
4 environment
5 source, well
6 centuries
7 crops
8 always
9 hunt
10 obstacle
11 without thought
12 progress
13 fire
14 even if
15 oil well

B According to the extract,

1 How important is a forest in maintaining ecological balance?
2 Why had people been cutting down forests over the centuries?
3 What method did people who did not value the forest use to clear the land?
4 What point is made about replanting policy in the past?
5 What was the attitude of people to this source of wealth?

ΟΔΗΓΟΥΣΕ ΑΝΑΠΟΔΑ
HE WAS DRIVING ON THE WRONG SIDE OF THE ROAD

Ο Λάκης λέει της Κυρίας Κατίνας τα νέα άπο το Εδιμβούργο.

τι έπαθε το παιδί;	what happened to the child?
ησυχάζω	calm down
χτυπάω	hit, (am) hurt
στρίβω	turn
Πάναγιά μου	good grief
ανάποδα	on the wrong side, wrong way round, upside down, inside out, backwards

ACTIVITY 17

Listen to the story and answer the questions which follow.

1 Τι ήταν το πρώτο πράγμα που έκανε ο Πέτρος στο αεροδρόμιο;
2 Γιατί;
3 Τι έγινε στο φανάρι;
4 Χτύπησε σοβαρά ο Πέτρος;
5 Τι ακριβώς έπαθε ο Πέτρος;
6 Σε ποιο νοσοκομείο πήγε;
7 Ποιο ήταν το πρόβλημα;

ACTIVITY 18

Listen to the story again carefully, to find out which four points in this summary of events are inaccurate.

Lakis is telling Katina what happened to Petros when he arrived in Edinburgh. She gets a little upset as she anticipates the story unfolding. Petros arrived safely, then hired a car to go to Stirling on an errand. It was early in the morning and, coming out of the airport, he was hit by another car as he was leaving the parking area. Petros was driving on the wrong side of the road – he had forgotten that people drive on the left-hand side in Britain. He went to hospital briefly, so that the doctors could see to the cut on his eye. He was laughing all the way there.

Lakis	Άκουσες για τον Πέτρο;
Katina	Πού, στο Εδιμβούργο; Έφτασε καλά;
Lakis	Μία χαρά έφτασε, αλλά στο αεροδρόμιο νοίκιασε ένα αυτοκίνητο για να πάει σε μια δουλειά στο Στέρλιγκ, και ...
Katina	Αμάν, τι έπαθε το παιδί;
Lakis	Ησύχασε Κατίνα – τίποτα σοβαρό.
Katina	Πες μου — τι έγινε; Χτύπησε;
Lakis	Ήταν αργά, και εκεί που έστριβε στο πρώτο φανάρι, τον χτύπησε ένας άλλος.
Katina	Πάναγιά μου!
Lakis	Οδηγούσε ανάποδα. Ξέχασε ότι οδηγούν στα αριστερά στην Βρετανία ...
Katina	Και τώρα; Μπήκε στο νοσοκομείο; Τι λένε οι γιατροί; Θα πάει η Βαγγελιώ να τον δει;
Lakis	Τίποτα, σου λέω. Λίγο έκοψε το μάτι του. Ευτυχώς. Γελούσε, μάλιστα, όταν μας το είπε.
Katina	Μα γιατί οδηγούν ανάποδα οι ξένοι;

Now it's time to test your progress in Unit 12.

1 Give the past and the imperfect tense of the following verbs

	Simple Past	Imperfect
1 γεμίζω		
2 κρυώνω		
3 τρέχω		
4 πεινώ		
5 πίνω		
6 διψώ		
7 βοηθώ		
8 φέρνω		

16

2 Answer the following questions in Greek using full sentences. The pictures are your cues.

When you were young - Όταν ήσουν μικρός:

1 What did you use to drink?

2 How did you use to go to school?

3 What did you like to play?

4 What music did you like to listen to?

4

3 Complete the sentences using the imperfect tense of the verb in brackets.

1 Ο πατέρας μας _____ πολύ. (δουλεύω)
2 Δεν _____ τίποτα, αλλά τώρα … ! (ξεχνάω)
3 Η οικογένεια _____ σε ένα όμορφο νησί. (ζω)
4 _____ έναν μεγάλο κήπο, γεμάτο λεμονιές. (έχω)

4

4 Complete these sentences expressing likes and dislikes using the verb in brackets.

1 Σ'αρέσει να _____ νωρίς; (ξυπνάω)

2 Του αρέσει να _____ παραμύθια. (λέω)

3 Της αρέσει να _____ βόλτα. (πηγαίνω)

4 Δεν μ'αρέσει να _____ τηλεόραση. Προτιμώ
να _____ ραδιόφωνο. (βλέπω, ακούω)

5 Της Μαργαρίτας της αρέσει να _____ στα
βουνά. (περπατάω)

6

---

5 Complete the text using the words in the box.

> έκανε κρύο   ταβέρνα   περίμενε   κάρβουνα   βόλτα
> όμορφο   περπατούσαμε   ουρανός   βράδυ   φεγγάρι

Προχθές το (1) _____ πήγαμε μία
(2) _____ στη Βούλα. Τι (3) _____ μέρος!
Βλέπαμε το (4) _____ μπροστά μας, και ακούγαμε
τη θάλασσα. Ο (5) _____ ήταν γεμάτος αστέρια.
(6) _____ γιατί είναι χειμώνας, αλλά εμείς είχαμε
κέφι. (7) _____ και γελούσαμε μέχρι να
φτάσουμε στην (8) _____ όπου μας
(9) _____ ένα δωμάτιο ζεστό, με
(10) _____ στο τζάκι.

10

---

6 Can you find the following 13 words in Greek hidden in
the grid?

basil, chestnut, gardenia, lettuce, watermelon,
vegetables, honey, wood (× 2), coat, fireplace, bird, full

Ρ	Ψ	Ε	Σ	Υ	Π	Ο	Υ	Λ	Ι
Κ	Α	Ρ	Π	Ο	Υ	Ζ	Ι	Φ	Ι
Ο	Π	Α	Τ	Μ	Δ	Α	Σ	Ο	Σ
Γ	Α	Ρ	Δ	Ε	Ν	Ι	Α	Μ	Κ
Ε	Δ	Ζ	Η	Λ	Θ	Κ	Λ	Ε	Α
Μ	Β	Α	Σ	Ι	Λ	Ι	Κ	Ο	Σ
Α	Μ	Α	Ρ	Ο	Υ	Λ	Ι	Ω	Τ
Τ	Γ	Λ	Α	Χ	Α	Ν	Ι	Κ	Α
Ο	Χ	Τ	Ζ	Α	Κ	Ι	Χ	Β	Ν
Σ	Π	Α	Λ	Τ	Ο	Ξ	Υ	Λ	Ο

13

TOTAL SCORE **53**

If you scored less than 45 go through the dialogues and the
Language building sections again, before completing the
Summary on page 180.

Summary 12

Now try this final test summarizing the main points covered in this unit. You can check your answers on the recording.

How would you:
1 say you like to drink ouzo in the evening?
2 say 'we don't like driving in the city'?
3 say they like to walk in the woods?
4 say you were cutting the bread when Yannis arrived?
5 say 'he was wearing a black coat when we saw him'?
6 say 'we were very thirsty'?
7 say the sky was dark and it was cold?
8 say 'our parents used to play tennis with their friends'?
9 say he used to tell us stories?

REVISION

Think about your own past – what you used to do at school, on holiday, at home. How many of these things can you express in Greek?

Go over all of your vocabulary thoroughly. Check your memory as well as your spelling. Once you've revised all the words you have recorded, make a game of it. For example, see how many items around you you can name in three minutes – write them down. Give yourself a general knowledge quiz: draw a grid and insert categories in each column – countries, people, flora and fauna, clothes, foodstuffs, jobs and professions, verbs, adjectives, and so on. Then choose a random letter in the alphabet at a time and see how many of the columns you can fill each round.

Health

Υγεία

OBJECTIVES

In this unit you'll learn how to:

✓ talk about your health

✓ recommend a course of action

✓ fill in a form by supplying personal details

And cover the following grammar and language:

✓ passive-form verbs

✓ **(ο) καλύτερος** ('better'/'best') and **(ο) χειρότερος** ('worse', 'worst')

✓ **να** to give advice

LEARNING GREEK 13

You may have decided that you would like to broaden the scope of your exposure to Greek. Published Greek material is not that widely available outside Greece, but a visit or phone call to one of the Greek bookshops in major cities will alert you to what can be found at the more elementary level. If you have a Greek Orthodox church nearby, take a look at what they offer: calendars are staples, and would be a good start – each year they include all sorts of useful and readable information. Next time you visit Greece, pick up some magazines to look through (alternatively, ask a friend to send or bring one or two back): advertisements provide concise, familiar, and topical items, but you may also enjoy working on a short article of interest. The national airline magazine at the moment provides a useful service to language learners, by printing its features in both English and Greek.

Now start the recording for Unit 13.

13.1 I don't feel well

Δεν αισθάνομαι καλά

ACTIVITY 1 is on the recording.

ACTIVITY 2

Correct the statements which are false.

1 Ο Νίκος έχει πόνο στο στομάχι.	T / F
2 Ο Νίκος θέλει να πάει στο φαρμακείο.	T / F
3 Το θερμόμετρο λέει 39 βαθμούς.	T / F
4 Η Άννα θα του φέρει ένα τσάι.	T / F
5 Οι δύο είναι στο γραφείο.	T / F

DIALOGUE 1

○ Αχ, δεν αισθάνομαι καλά.

■ Τι έχεις;

○ Από το πρωί έχω πονοκέφαλο, και τώρα πονάει το στομάχι μου. Αισθάνομαι κουρασμένος.

■ Για να δω αν έχεις πυρετό.

○ Ναι. Φέρε το θερμόμετρο.

■ Φφ ... 39 βαθμούς. Πονάει ο λαιμός σου;

○ Α-Α-αχ! Όλα πονάνε. Θέλω τη μαμά μου ...

■ Καλά. Πήγαινε να ξαπλώσεις. Νομίζω ότι έχεις γρίπη.

○ Υπάρχει κανένα φάρμακο; Κανένα χάπι; Κανένα σιρόπι;

■ Πήγαινε στο κρεβάτι σου, σου λέω, και έρχομαι. Θα σου φέρω μια ασπιρίνη και βλέπουμε.

VOCABULARY

ο πόνος	pain
αισθάνομαι	feel
ο πονοκέφαλος	headache
πονάω	hurt, ache
το στομάχι	stomach
κουρασμένος/η/ο	tired
ο πυρετός	temperature, fever
το θερμόμετρο	thermometer
ο λαιμός	neck, throat
η γρίπη	flu
το φάρμακο	medicine
το χάπι	pill
το σιρόπι	syrup
έρχομαι	come

✅ Passive-form verbs

There are a number of common verbs in Greek which, though active
in meaning, follow the patterns of a passive verb. Passive-form verbs
have the ending -μαι in the dictionary entry.

This course focuses on two main types of passive-form verb: those
ending in *-ομαι* and those ending in *-αμαι*.

έρχομαι – come		κοιμάμαι – sleep	
έρχομαι	*ερχόμαστε*	**κοιμάμαι**	**κοιμόμαστε**
έρχεσαι	*ερχόσαστε*	**κοιμάσαι**	**κοιμάστε**
έρχεται	*έρχονται*	**κοιμάται**	**κοιμούνται**

Other useful passive-form verbs ending in -ομαι: **κάθομαι** ('sit'),
φαίνομαι ('seem', 'appear'), **σκέπτομαι** ('think'), **αισθάνομαι** ('feel').

Other useful passive-form verbs ending in -αμαι: **θυμάμαι** ('remember'),
λυπάμαι ('regret'), **φοβάμαι** (fear', 'am afraid of').

✅ Parts of the body

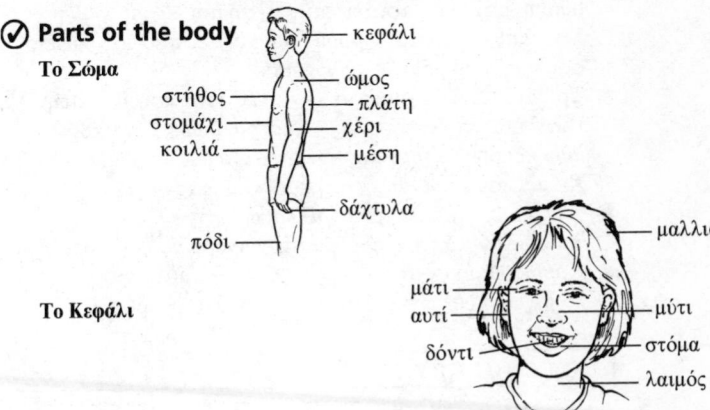

Το Σώμα

κεφάλι

ώμος

στήθος
στομάχι
κοιλιά

πλάτη
χέρι
μέση

δάχτυλα

πόδι

Το Κεφάλι

μαλλιά

μάτι
αυτί
δόντι

μύτι
στόμα
λαιμός

ACTIVITY 3

For 1–5 find the appropriate response from a–e.

1 Η δασκάλα δεν αισθάνεται
   καλά.

2 Πονάει το πόδι μου.

3 Τι κάνει ο παππούς;

4 Φαίνεσαι κουρασμένη.

5 Πού έβαλες τα χάπια μου;

a Δεν είμαι πολύ καλά.

b Κοιμάται.

c Γιατί, τι έχει;

d Δεν θυμάμαι.

e Βγάλε το παπούτσι
   σου, να δω.

 Now do activities 4 and 5 on the recording.

Are you ill?

Είσαι άρρωστη;

ACTIVITY 6 is on the recording.

ACTIVITY 7

1 Τι κάνει όλη μέρα η Ρούλα;
2 Τι χρειάζεται η Ρούλα;
3 Τι έχει σήμερα η Ρούλα;
4 Πού θα πάει ο Δημήτρης αύριο;
5 Τι υπάρχει στο συρτάρι;

DIALOGUE 2

○ Ρούλα, δεν φαίνεσαι καλά. Είσαι άρρωστη; Τι έχεις;

■ Πονάνε τα μάτια μου. Κάθομαι όλη μέρα μπροστά στην οθόνη, και τώρα πονάει και η μέση μου.

○ Μην κάθεσαι όλη την ώρα. Να φεύγεις από το γραφείο σου και να περπατάς κάθε τόσο.

■ Το κάνω! Σηκώνομαι και πηγαίνω στην κουζίνα, στην τουαλέτα, στο μπαλκόνι ... Σήμερα, όμως, δεν μπορώ να πάω πουθενά. Ούτε στο κρεβάτι. Πονάω!

○ Χρειάζεσαι μια καλύτερη καρέκλα ...

■ Καλά λες. Πρέπει να την αλλάξω αυτή.

○ Θα πάω αύριο το απόγευμα στην αγορά να δω τι υπάρχει.

■ Χρειάζομαι και σταγόνες να βάλω στα μάτια μου.

○ Νομίζω ότι έχω ένα μπουκαλάκι στο συρτάρι μου.

VOCABULARY	
άρρωστος/η/ο	ill, sick
η οθόνη	screen
η μέση	[here] back
το γραφείο	desk, office
κάθε τόσο	every so often
σηκώνομαι	get up
πουθενά	nowhere
ούτε	not even
χρειάζομαι	need
καλύτερος/η/ο	better
η καρέκλα	chair
αλλάξω	change
σταγόνα	drop
το συρτάρι	drawer

✓ Talking about your health

Τι έχεις; What's the matter?	Δεν είμαι καλά. I'm not well.
Δεν αισθάνομαι καλά. I don't feel well.	Είμαι άρρωστος. I'm ill.
Έχω πονοκέφαλο/βήχα.	I have a headache/cough.
Έχω κρυολόγημα.	I have a cold.
Πονάει το κεφάλι/η κοιλιά/το χέρι/ο λαιμός μου.	My head/belly/hand/throat hurts.

✓ (ο) καλύτερος ('better'/'best') and (ο) χειρότερος ('worse'/ 'worst')

the adjectives καλός ('good') and κακός ('bad') have irregular comparative and superlative forms.

καλός/ή/ό   καλύτερος/η/ο   better   ο καλύτερος/η/ο   best
κακός/ιά/ό   χειρότερος/η/ο   worse   ο χειρότερος/η/ο   worst

> Τα αγγλικά μήλα είναι **καλύτερα** από τα γαλλικά. English apples are better than French.

Note that the *adverb* 'better' is **καλύτερα**, and the adverb 'worse' is **χειρότερα**:

> Είσαι καλύτερα σήμερα; Are you better today?
> Αισθάνομαι χειρότερα. I feel worse.

✓ Making a recommendation

When making a recommendation, **να** is used to convey 'should':

να is followed by a verb using either the first stem (to recommend a regularly repeated action) or the second (to recommend a one-off action) + **present tense endings**.

> Να **διαβάζετε** λίγα ελληνικά κάθε μέρα. You should read/study a little Greek every day. [*first stem*]
> Να **διαβάσετε** λίγα ελληνικά απόψε. You should read/study some Greek this evening. [*second stem*]

μη(ν) is added to this construction to express a prohibition. Note the word order.

> Να μην **πίνεις** τόσο καφέ. You shouldn't/mustn't drink so much coffee. (*first stem – in general*)
> Να μην **πιεις** τόσο καφέ. You mustn't drink so much coffee. (*second stem – at this particular time*)

ACTIVITY 8

Using **να**

1. Advise someone to take an aspirin (now).
2. Advise someone against eating so much bread (every day).

(🔊) Now do activities 9 and 10 on the recording.

Είσαστε ασφαλισμένος;

ACTIVITY 11 is on the recording.

ACTIVITY 12

Supply the following information.

1 the man's name, surname and date of birth
2 who he is insured with
3 his marital status

DIALOGUE 3

○ Καλησπέρα σας. Θα ήθελα να γραφτώ στο ιατρείο σας.

■ Μάλιστα. Όνομα και επώνυμο παρακαλώ.

○ Λέγομαι Φίλιππος Δασκαλάκης.

■ Ημερομηνία γεννήσεως;

○ 5 Απριλίου 1971.

■ Η διεύθυνσή σας ποια είναι, παρακαλώ.

○ Μένω στη Νεάπολη - Βουλγαροκτόνου 14.

■ Είσαστε ασφαλισμένος;

○ Ορίστε το βιβλιάριό μου.

■ Ένα λεπτό. Είσαστε παντρεμένος ή ελεύθερος;

○ Παντρεμένος, με δυό παιδιά.

■ Λοιπόν. Συμπληρώσετε τα στοιχεία σας στήν κάρτα. Μη ξεχάσετε: πού εργάζεστε και την υπογραφή σας.

VOCABULARY

(εγ)γράφομαι	register, sign up
το όνομα και επώνυμο	first name and surname
λέγομαι	am called
ημερομηνία γεννήσεως	date of birth
η διεύθυνση	address
ασφαλισμένος/η/ο	insured
το βιβλιάριο	booklet
παντρεμένος/η/ο	married
ελεύθερος/η/ο	single
συμπληρώνω	fill in, complete
στοιχεία	particulars, facts
εργάζομαι	work
η υπογραφή	signature

✓ λέγομαι ('am called')

λέγομαι is a passive verb: it takes the same endings as the passive-form verbs ending in -ομαι – see page 232 and page 237.

λέγομαι	I am called	λεγόμαστε	we are called
λέγεσαι	you are called	λέγεστε	you are called
λέγεται	he, she, it is called	λέγονται	they are called

Πώς λέγεστε; What are you called? Λέγομαι Νίκος. I'm called Nick.
Πώς λέγεται αυτό στα ελληνικά; What is this called in Greek?

You can also use the following constructions as alternatives to λέγομαι:

Πώς είναι το επώνυμό σας; What is your surname?
Το όνομά μου είναι ... My name is ...
Πώς το λένε αυτό στα ελληνικά; What do they call this in Greek?

✓ εργάζομαι ('work')

εργάζομαι ('work') is another passive-form verb, often used instead of δουλεύω. The noun is η εργασία.

Τι εργασία κάνετε; What work do you do?
Πού εργάζεστε; Where do you work?
Εργάζομαι σε γραφείο/σχολείο/κατάστημα/εργοστάσιο. I work in an office/a school/a department store/a factory.

✓ Addresses

Addresses in Greek are written street name, followed by the number. In larger towns, area name might precede the town/city. The post code (ο ταχυδρομικός κώδικας) comes before the town/city name.

Η διεύθυνσή μου είναι ... My address is ...
Σεφέρη 22
Νέο Ψυχικό
11467 Αθήνα

ACTIVITY 13

Fill in the form with your own particulars.

1	ΟΝΟΜΑ	_____
2	ΕΠΩΝΥΜΟ	_____
3	ΗΜΕΡΟΜΗΝΙΑ ΓΕΝΝΗΣΗΣ	_____
4	ΔΙΕΥΘΥΝΣΗ	_____
5	ΤΗΛΕΦΩΝΟ	_____
6	ΥΠΟΓΡΑΦΗ	_____

Now do activities 14 and 15 on the recording.

Ενδεχόμενος καύσωνας

The Greek Ministry of Health (**Το Υπουργείο Υγείας**) regularly issues notices advising people on the best thing to do in times of crisis, such as an earthquake or a heatwave. Here is an edited selection of the sorts of advice provided in the public notice *Οδηγίες για προφύλαξη από ενδεχόμενο καύσωνα* (*Guidelines for protection against a possible heatwave*). Read it through, then try activity 16.

ΟΔΗΓΙΕΣ ΓΙΑ ΠΡΟΦΥΛΑΞΗ ΑΠΟ ΕΝΔΕΧΟΜΕΝΟ ΚΑΥΣΩΝΑ

1 Μένετε σε σκιά σε δροσερό μέρος.
2 Μη βγαίνετε έξω στον καυτό ήλιο, αν δεν είναι ανάγκη.
3 Βάζετε ελαφρά και ανοιχτόχρωμα ρούχα με ανοιχτό λαιμό.
4 Πίνετε συχνά δροσερό ή κρύο νερό με λίγο αλάτι – όσο βάζετε σε μια σαλάτα σας. Αποφεύγετε τη ζάχαρη και τα οινοπνευματούχα.
5 Μην τρώτε πολύ.
6 Στο σπίτι μέσα, μη μένετε ξαπλωμένοι – να περπατάτε λιγάκι. Αν είναι ζεστός ο αέρας, βάζετε μια κρύα πετσέτα στην πλάτη και στους ώμους σας. Η κίνηση βοηθάει την εξάτμιση και φέρνει δροσιά.
7 Να κάνετε συχνά ντους με δροσερό νερό.
8 Μιλήστε με το γιατρό σας για τα φάρμακα που παίρνετε.
9 Μην ξεχνάτε τα μωρά – και αυτά θέλουν ελαφρά ρούχα. Επίσης, μην αφήνετε τους ηλικιωμένους μόνους στο σπίτι – ίσως να χρειάζονται βοήθεια.
10 Η θάλασσα είναι μεγάλη βοήθεια στον καύσωνα, αλλά για δροσιά, όχι άσκηση. Μη ξεχνάτε το καπέλο και τα γυαλιά ηλίου: συχνά μέσα και έξω από το νερό, και να κάθεστε στη σκιά όχι κάτω από τον καυτό ήλιο.

ACTIVITY 16

Match the English translations a–j with the appropriate piece of advice (1–10) from the text above.

a Speak to your doctor about any medication you're on.
b Don't eat too much.
c At home, don't remain lying down – walk a little. If the wind is hot, put a cold towel on your back and shoulders. Moving about then encourages evaporation and cools you down.
d Shower frequently in cool water.
e Don't forget infants – they also need light clothes. Don't leave the elderly alone at home either – they might need help.
f Don't go outside into the blazing sun if it's not essential.
g Stay in the shade, in a cool place.
h The sea is a great boon during a heatwave, but for cooling down, not exercise. Don't forget a hat and sunglasses. Go in and out of the water often, and sit in the shade, not under the blazing sun.
i Wear open-necked clothes, light in weight and colour.
j Drink cool or cold water regularly, adding a little salt – as much as you would put in a salad. Avoid sugar and alcoholic drinks.

ACTIVITY 17

Translate the following into Greek sentences. You might need to use some of the new vocabulary introduced in the article above. (A dictionary might also be helpful.)

1 I like the shade.
2 She found a cool place.
3 We avoid the blazing sun.
4 It's not essential.
5 There was no movement at all.
6 During a heatwave, don't forget the elderly.
7 Bring your towel.
8 Drink cool water with a little salt.

13.5 Στο περίπτερο

 ΓΡΑΜΜΑ ΑΠΟ ΤΗ ΣΟΦΙΑ
LETTER FROM SOPHIA

Πέρασε ένας χρόνος. Η Σοφία έχει τελειώσει το σχολείο.
Φέτος το καλοκαίρι είναι στη Σκοτία με τον Πέτρο. Η
Κατίνα περνάει από το περίπτερο να μάθει τι γίνεται.

και ... και	both ... and
η ξενιτιά	foreign parts
συστήνω	introduce
η παράσταση	performance
μόλις	just [*time*]
πάλι	again
η επικοινωνία	communication
επιτέλους	at last
ο πρίγκιπας	prince
η σκοτσέζικη φουστανέλα	kilt

ACTIVITY 18

Listen to the story and answer the following questions.

1 Τι γίνεται στο Εδιμβούργο τον Αύγουστο;
2 Πότε σηκώνεται η Σοφία;
3 Τι είναι το e-mail;
4 Τι έμαθε ο Θανάσης από την Σοφία;
5 Τι αγόρασε η Σοφία;

ACTIVITY 19

Listen to the story again, then decide which of the
following is *wrong* in each case.

1 Vangelio has had (a) a telephone call (b) an e-mail
  (c) a card from Sophia
2 Sophia's holiday job in Edinburgh is (a) helping out at a
  theatre (b) preparing actors' clothes for a performance
  (c) waking the actors up early in the morning
3 Thanasis explains to Kiria Katina that e-mail (a) means
  electronic communication (b) has instantaneous delivery
  (c) has reached Scotland at last
4 We find out that Sophia (a) is learning to understand
  Scottish (b) has met the Prince of Wales (c) has bought a
  kilt

STORY TRANSCRIPT

Katina	Πήρες κανένα νέο από την κόρη σου, Βαγγελιώ;
Vangelio	Αμέ. Και τηλεφώνημα και κάρτα.
Katina	Τι λέει; Της αρέσει η ξενιτιά;
Vangelio	Πολύ ωραίο το βρίσκει το Εδιμβούργο. Το ξέρεις ότι εργάζεται;
Katina	Μπα! Τι εργασία βρήκε;
Vangelio	Τον Αύγουστο έχει η πόλη μεγάλο φεστιβάλ. Ο Κραίηγκ της σύστησε κάτι ηθοποιούς και τώρα βοηθάει μερικές ώρες την ημέρα σε ένα θέατρο.
Katina	Τι κάνει; Κάθεται και πουλάει εισιτήρια;
Vangelio	Όχι καλέ. Σηκώνεται πρωί-πρωί και ετοιμάζει τα ρούχα για την πρώτη παράσταση.
Thanasis	Κυρία Βαγγελιώ. Μόλις πήρα ένα e-mail από τη Σοφία.
Katina	Τί είναι πάλι αυτό το πράγμα, το e-mail;
Thanasis	Ηλεκτρονική επικοινωνία, κυριά Κατίνα. Η Σοφία λέει ότι επιτέλους άρχισε να καταλαβαίνει τα σκοτσέζικα.
Vangelio	Εμένα μου έγραψε ότι αγόρασε σκοτσέζικη φουστανέλα στην οδό του πρίγκιπα.

Now it's time to test your progress in Unit 13.

1 What is the Greek for the following passive-form verbs?

1	I feel	5	I seem	9	I work
2	I sit	6	I'm coming	10	I think
3	I remember	7	I need		
4	I sleep	8	I get up		

10

2 Τι έχουνε;

8

3 Supply the appropriate question for each response.

1 _____

Δεν αισθάνομαι καλά.

2 _____

Τρεις Μαρτίου 1972.

3 _____

Μοναστηρίου 45, Πειραιάς.

4 _____

Κουρουνιώτης, Αλέξανδρος Κουρουνιώτης.

5

4 Complete the sentences with the correct form of the verb in brackets.

1 Η Ελένη δεν _____ καλά. _____ το στομάχι της. (φαίνομαι, πονάω)

2 Εγώ _____ εδώ στο μπαλκόνι και σε _____ . (κάθομαι, σκέφτομαι)

3 Πρέπει να _____ τα φάρμακά μου. Δεν _____ να παίρνω τόσα χάπια. (αλλάζω, χρειάζομαι)

4 Ο Πάνος _____ άρρωστος χθες και δεν _____ στη δουλειά. (είμαι, πάω)

5 Οι γονείς μου _____ στις εξίμισι κάθε μέρα
και _____ στο τραπέζι στις εφτά. (σηκώνομαι,
κάθομαι)

10

5 Complete the text using the words in the box.

> πουθενά αμέσως και μόλις άλλο
> ούτε πάνω κανένα και ούτε

(1) _____ γύρισε ο Γιάννης στο σπίτι ήξερε ότι
δεν ήταν καλά. Μάλλον χειρότερα από χθες. Είχε
(2) _____ τρομερό πονοκέφαλο (3) _____
άσχημο βήχα. Ήθελε να πάρει (4) _____ χάπι,
αλλά δεν τα έβρισκε (5) _____ , (6) _____
στο μπάνιο, (7) _____ στην κουζίνα. Άνοιξε το
συρτάρι του γραφείου του και είδε ένα σιρόπι. Για το
λαιμό μου, σκέφτηκε. Πήρε το μπουκαλάκι και εκεί που
το άνοιγε, έπεσε από τα χέρια του, και (8) _____
στην οθόνη ... Αχ, δεν μπορώ (9) _____ είπε, και
πήρε τηλέφωνο (10) _____ στον γιατρό.

10

6 Write three brief diary entries. Say how you feel today,
what exercise you did, what hurts, does not hurt.
(This is a relatively free exercise. 1 mark per sentence in
each category. A bonus mark for any additional sentence.
Deduct half a mark for each error.)

Σάββατο 15 Αυγούστου

_____

_____

_____

5

TOTAL SCORE **48**

If you scored less than 40 go through the dialogues and the
Language Building sections again, before completing the
summary on page 194.

Summary 13

 Now try this final test summarizing the main points covered in this unit. You can check your answers on the recording.

How would you:
1 ask an acquaintance how she feels?
2 say your back aches?
3 ask a friend if he's ill?
4 advise a friend to take an aspirin and go to bed?
5 say 'Maria is coming to see us'?
6 ask someone you've just met his surname?
7 ask where Haris works?
8 say you get up early every day?
9 ask someone you know what he needs?

REVISION

To consolidate the passive-form verbs, try thinking up sentences to use them. For example: Your friend is sitting by the window, I remember the terrible fever that you had, You look better this evening, and so on.

Practise saying what's wrong with you, making sure you know the vocabulary you're likely to need if you have to go into a chemist or to the doctor when you're in Greece. Look up any parts of the body not included in this unit that you think you might want to use.

Which was the best?

Ποιο ήταν το καλύτερο;

OBJECTIVES

In this unit you'll learn how to:

- ✓ make comparisons
- ✓ express an opinion
- ✓ talk about money

And cover the following grammar and language:

- ✓ the comparative
- ✓ the superlative
- ✓ **περισσότερος** ('more') and **λιγότερος** ('less', 'fewer')
- ✓ more on numbers
- ✓ **είτε ... ή** ('either ... or')
- ✓ the possessive pronoun: **δικός μου** ('mine', 'my own'), etc.
- ✓ **ποιανού** ('whose')

LEARNING GREEK 14

If you use a computer, you might find it rewarding to explore what is available in Greek on the Internet. Use any search engine to help you locate material. It is straightforward, for example, to access Greek newspapers. Most systems now have integrated support for other languages, so that you can easily install Greek fonts and the necessary keyboard drivers on your computer by downloading the multilanguage support module using your WWW browser.

Useful sites include: **www.culture.gr**, the Greek Ministry of Culture site. **www.robby.gr**, a Hellenic Search Engine, and **www.thea.gr**, which gives a wide-ranging list of sites.

Now start the recording for Unit 14

Ο Σωτήρης είναι πιο ψηλός από τον Ανδρέα

ACTIVITY 1 is on the recording.

ACTIVITY 2

To whom does each of the following adjectives refer?

ψηλός ήρεμος πρακτικός δυνατός   νευρικός
ξανθός έξυπνος σοβαρός μελαχρινός

DIALOGUE 1

○ Ποιος από τους δύο θα είναι ο καλύτερος;
■ Για να δούμε. Ο Σωτήρης είναι πιο ψηλός απο τον Ανδρέα, αλλά ο Ανδρέας είναι πιο δυνατός.
○ Ποιος είναι πιο έξυπνος;
■ Να σου πω. Ο Σωτήρης έχει μαθηματικό μυαλό, ενώ τον Ανδρέα τον ενδιαφέρουν πιο πρακτικά πράγματα.
○ Καλά καλά, δεν ζητάμε επιστήμονα. Θέλουμε κάποιον που θα θυμάται τον ρόλο του.
■ Χρειαζόμαστε κάποιον ήρεμο. Ο Σωτήρης είναι νευρικός.
○ Κάνεις λάθος. Είναι σοβαρότερος από τον Ανδρέα.
■ Χμ ... Δεν γίνεται να τους κρατήσουμε και τους δυό;
○ Το έργο θέλει μόνον έναν Ίκαρο ...
■ Εντάξει. Πώς τον θέλουμε, ξανθό ή μελαχρινό;

VOCABULARY

ψηλός/ή/ό	tall
δυνατός/ή/ό	strong
έξυπνος/η/ο	clever
το μυαλό	mind, brain
ενδιαφέρω	interest
ζητώ	seek, ask for
ο επιστήμονας	scientist
ο ρόλος	role
ήρεμος/η/ο	calm
νευρικός/ή/ό	moody, temperamental
σοβαρός/ή/ό	serious
κρατάω	keep, hold
ξανθός/ια/ο	blond
μελαχρινός/ή/ό	dark-haired, dark-skinned

✓ The comparative

The comparative of adjectives is formed in one of two ways:

1 **πιο** + adjective + **από**

Ο Δημήτρης είναι **πιο μεγάλος από** τον Τάσο. Dimitris is older/bigger than Tasos.

2 the ending **-ότερος/-ότερη/-ότερο** is added to the adjective stem + **από**

Ο παππούς είναι **ψηλότερος** από τον πατέρα. Grandad is taller than father.

The only variants covered in this course are **καλός – καλύτερος/η/ο** ('better') and **μεγάλος – μεγαλύτερος/η/ο** ('bigger', 'older').

Ο Δημήτρης είναι **μεγαλύτερος** από τον Τάσο. Dimitris is older/bigger than Tasos.

Like other adjectives, comparatives agree with the nouns they refer to.

Η Έλλη είναι **πιο μικρή από** την Αναστασία. Ellie is younger/smaller than Anastasia.

Η Έλλη είναι **μικρότερη από** την Αναστασία. Ellie is younger/smaller than Anastasia.

Most comparatives can be formed using **πιο** or the **-τερος** ending. However, **πιο** tends to be used with words of three syllables or more and with adjectives that are 'newer' to the language.

✓ The superlative

The superlative is formed by adding the definite article before the comparative form of the adjective **πιο μεγάλος** or **μεγαλύτερος**, etc.

Ο Γιώργος είναι **ο πιο δυνατός**. Yorgos is the strongest.

Η Λιλή είναι **η μικρότερη**. Lili is the smallest/youngest.

Ο Λάκης ειναι **το πιο σοβαρό** παιδί στην τάξη. Lakis is the most serious boy in the class.

ACTIVITY 3

Complete the sentences with the correct comparative form.

1 Η Λέλα θα παίξει _____ ρόλο από την Κούλα. (σοβαρός)

2 Ποιος είναι _____ ; Ο Νίκος ή ο Γιάννης; (ψηλός)

3 'Γενικά, οι γυναίκες είναι _____ από τους ανδρες.' (πρακτικός)

🎧 Now do activities 4 and 5 on the recording.

It serves us right!

Καλά να πάθουμε!

ACTIVITY 6 is on the recording.

ACTIVITY 7

1 When did the woman buy her new fridge?
2 Which of the two fridges did she buy?
3 Why didn't they buy the more expensive one?
4 What does the friend say about his fridge?

DIALOGUE 2

○ Το ψυγείο μας δεν λειτουργεί σωστά. Πρέπει να αγοράσουμε καινούριο.

■ Χάλασε τόσο γρήγορα; Το πήρατε πέρσι!

○ Διαλέξαμε το φτηνότερο από τα δύο που μας άρεσαν και τώρα έληξε η εγγύησή του. Καλά να πάθουμε!

■ Τι έχει η συσκευή;

○ Δεν μπορούμε να ρυθμίσουμε τη θερμοκρασία – είτε τρέχουνε τα νερά, ή είναι πιό κρύο απ' ότι πρέπει.

■ Τι κρίμα. Πόσο πιο ακριβό ήταν το άλλο:

○ Α, δεν θυμάμαι. Όχι πολύ. Εγώ ήθελα το ιταλικό, αλλά ο Κώστας δεν ήθελε να ξοδέψει πολλά λεφτά.

■ Εμείς έχουμε γαλλικό – δέκα χρόνια, χωρίς βλάβη.

○ Το πλυντήριό μας είναι γερμανικό. Ξέρεις τι οικονομικό που είναι στην κατανάλωση νερού και ηλεκρισμού …

■ Αξίζει να πληρώσεις λίγο περισσότερα, για να είσαι σίγουρος.

VOCABULARY

το ψυγείο	fridge
λειτουργώ	function, work
χαλ(α)ώ	break down, go wrong
διαλέγω	choose
λήγω	expire
η συσκευή;	appliance
ρυθμίζω	regulate, adjust
τι κρίμα	what a pity
ξοδεύω	spend
η βλάβη	breakdown, fault
το πλυντήριο	washing machine
η κατανάλωση	consumption
ο ηλεκρισμός	electricity

✓ περισσότερος ('more') and λιγότερος ('less', 'fewer')

περισσότερος/η/ο ('more') and λιγότερος/η/ο ('less', 'fewer') agree with the nouns they refer to.

> Η Μαίρη παίρνει λιγότερη ζάχαρη. Mary takes less sugar.

περισσότερες λίρες	η λίρα – pound (*feminine*)
λιγότερες δραχμές	η δραχμή – drachma (*feminine*)
περισσότερα δολάρια/ευρώ	το δολάριο – dollar (*neuter*)
	το ευρώ – euro (*neuter*)

When περισσότερος or λιγότερος are used to refer to amounts of money in general, they agree with the plural noun λεφτά or χρήματα ('money'), even when the noun is not stated.

> Πλήρωσα περισσότερα απ' ότι ήθελα. I paid more than I wanted to.

As with all adjectives, to form the superlative the article is added.

> Η αδελφή του πήρε το περισσότερο. His sister took/got the most.
> Ποιος έχει τα λιγότερα προβλήματα; Who has the fewest problems?

✓ More on numbers

Note the plural of 1000 – χίλια (*masculine*) / χίλιες (*feminine*) – is χιλιάδες.

> μερικές χιλιάδες δραχμές – a few thousand drachmas

χιλιάδες does not change form no matter what it is describing.
χιλιάδες άνθρωποι – thousands of people

✓ είτε ... ή ('either ... or') and ούτε ... ούτε ('neither ... nor')

> Διάλεξε είτε το ένα ή το άλλο – δεν πειράζει. Choose either the one or the other – it doesn't matter.
> Δεν μ'αρέσει ούτε το ποδόσφαιρο ούτε το μπάσκετ. I like neither football nor basketball.

ACTIVITY 8

Make sentences in Greek with the appropriate form of περισσότερος and λιγότερος.

Example: Η Έλλη/ έχει/πολλά παπούτσια/Η Άννα
Η Έλλη έχει περισσότερα παπούτσια από την Άννα.

1 το κουτί/έχει/πολλά χρήματα/η τσάντα
2 το μπουκάλι/έχει/πολύ λάδι/το ποτήρι
3 Ο Σταμάτης/έχει/λίγες μπίρες/Ο Γρηγόρης
4 Το Σνόουντον/έχει/λίγο χιόνι/ο Όλυμπος

Now do activities 9 and 10 on the recording.

14.3 In my opinion

Κατά τη γνώμη μου

ACTIVITY 11 is on the recording.

ACTIVITY 12

Correct the sentences which are false.

1 Ο Αλέκος είναι αρχιτέκτονας.	T / F
2 Ο Μπιλ Γκέϊτς είναι διάσημος.	T / F
3 Ο Ελ Γκρέκο είναι καλλιτέχνης του σήμερα.	T / F

DIALOGUE 3

○ Έλα να κάνουμε ερωτήσεις ο ένας στον άλλον.

■ Ωραία, αρχίζεις εσύ. Ρώτα!

○ Ποιος είναι μεγαλύτερος, ο Ειρηνικός ή ο Ατλαντικός;

■ Ο Ειρηνικός, βέβαια. Ρωτάω εγώ. Ποιο είναι το ψηλότερο, ο πύργος του Άιφελ ή το Έμπαϊερ Στέϊτ;

○ Ούτε το ένα, ούτε το άλλο. Σήμερα είναι το Πετρόνας στην Μαλασία, αύριο ποιος ξέρει ποιο θα είναι.

■ Έξυπνε! Αρχιτέκτονας να σπουδάσεις για να λέμε το δικό σου κτίριο.

○ Ποιος είναι ο πιο πλούσιος επιχειρηματίας σήμερα;

■ Πρέπει να είναι ο Μπιλ Γκέϊτς. Πες τώρα, ποιος είναι ο πιο έξυπνος επιστήμονας του εικοστού αιώνα;

○ Κατά τη γνώμη μου, ο Αϊνστάιν. Ίσως κάνω και λάθος.

■ Δική σου σειρά να ρωτήσεις.

○ Ποιος είναι ο πιο γνωστός έλληνας καλλιτέχνης;

■ Ιστορικά, ο Ελ Γκρέκο νομίζω. Αλλά τώρα πρέπει να πούμε και για γνωστές γυναίκες!

VOCABULARY

το κτίριο	building
πλούσιος/α/ο	rich
ο επιχειρηματίας	businessman
του εικοστού αιώνα	of the twentieth century
η γνώμη	opinion
η σειρά	turn, queue, line
γνωστός/ή/ό	well-known
ο καλλιτέχνης	artist
ιστορικά	historically

LANGUAGE BUILDING

✅ The possessive pronoun δικός / δική / δικό μου ...

To emphasize possession, the form δικός / δική / δικό is used with the relevant genitive form of the pronoun (μου / σου / του / μας / σας / τους). It is translated 'my/your own', etc. or 'mine, yours', etc.

δικός (like an adjective) agrees with the noun it refers to and the pronoun reflects the possessor.

> **Το διαβατήριο είναι δικό μου.** The passport is mine.
> **Οι κάρτες είναι δικές της.** The cards are hers.

δικός occurs with or without the article ο / η / το as required.

> **Αυτή είναι η δική μου γνώμη.** That is my (own) opinion.
> **Η γνώμη είναι δική μου.** The opinion is mine.

singular	masculine	feminine	neuter
nom.	ο δικός μου	η δική μου	το δικό μου
acc.	τον δικό μου	τη δική μου	το δικό μου
gen.	του δικού μου	της δικής μου	του δικού μου

plural	masculine	feminine	neuter
nom.	οι δικοί μου	οι δικές μου	τα δικά μου
acc.	τους δικούς μου	τις δικές μου	τα δικά μου
gen.	των δικών μου	των δικών μου	των δικών μου

The forms δικός (etc.) του / της / μας / σας / τους ('yours' / 'his' / 'hers' / 'ours' / 'yours' / 'theirs') work in the same way.

✅ ποιανού ... ; ('whose ... ?')

> **Ποιανού** είναι τα φάρμακα; Whose are the medicines?
> Είναι δικά του. They're his.
> **Ποιανού** είναι οι γραβάτες; Whose are the ties?
> Είναι δικές μας. They're ours.

ACTIVITY 13

Use the prompts to ask whose each thing is and then reply using the appropriate form of **δικός μου**.

Example: Τα τριαντάφυλλα / μας
> *Ποιανού είναι τα τριαντάφυλλα; Τα τριαντάφυλλα είναι δικά μας.*

1 Το πλυντήριο / του   3 Οι εγκυκλοπαίδειές / τους
2 Η έκθεση / της   4 Ο καθρέφτης / μας

🎧 Now do activities 14 and 15 on the recording.

Electronic world

Ηλεκτρονικός κόσμος

ACTIVITY 16

Read the following piece of publicity and answer the
following questions.

1 What time of year is it?
2 What adjectives does the advertiser use to describe his
  'gifts'?
3 What does he say about the selection on offer?
4 What does he say about his prices?
5 What does he claim about bargains?

> Φέτος γιορτάστε τα Χριστούγεννα ηλεκτρονικά!
> Πάρτε ένα πρωτότυπο δώρο από τη μεγαλύτερη
> ποικιλία σε computer.
> Βρείτε τα πιο απίθανα δώρα στις καλύτερες τιμές.
> Έχουμε τις περισσότερες ευκαιρίες.

ACTIVITY 17

Study the illustrations and then answer the questions.

Ο Ηλεκτρονικός Υπολογιστής σας

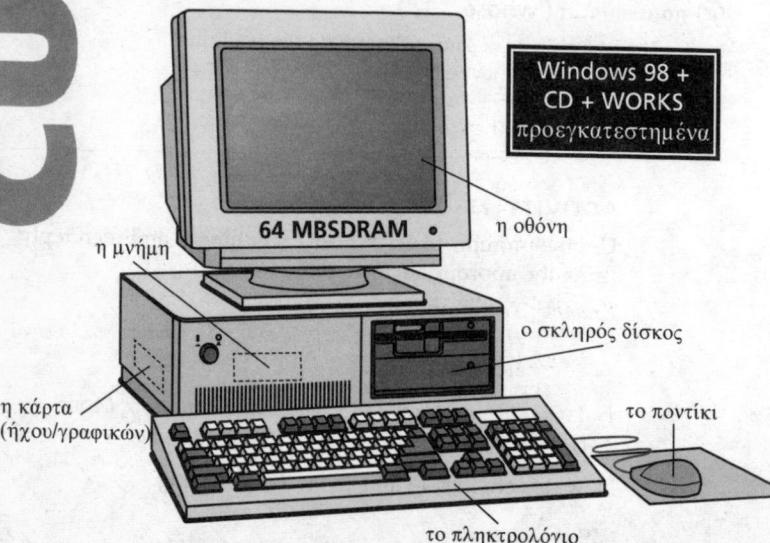

Windows 98 +
CD + WORKS
προεγκατεστημένα

64 MBSDRAM •   η οθόνη

η μνήμη

ο σκληρός δίσκος

η κάρτα
(ήχου/γραφικών)

το ποντίκι

το πληκτρολόγιο

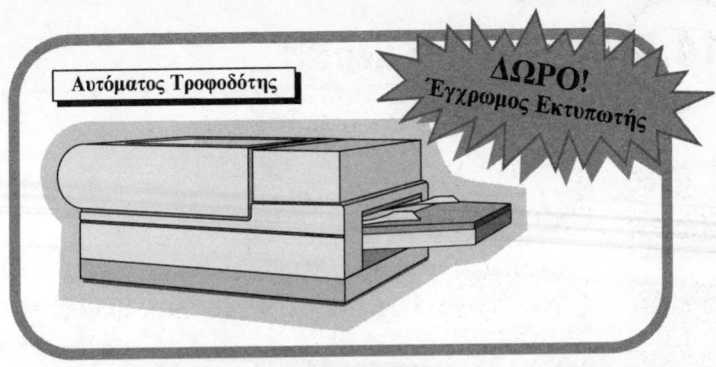

τιμή 1350€ + ΦΠΑ = 1593€
ή 395€ και 170€ Χ 8 μήνες = 1755€
δώρο: έγχρωμος εκτυπωτής

Προσφέρουμε!

*1 χρόνο εγγύηση
*δωρεάν σύνδεση και επίδειξη λειτουργίας
 στον χώρο σας

1 What is the Greek for:
  a hard disk?
  b keyboard?
  c screen?
  d mouse?
2 Is the cash price inclusive or exclusive of sales tax?
3 What are the alternative terms of payment?
4 What is your bonus if you buy this model?
5 Besides free connection and tuition in your own
  home/business, what is also offered if you buy this
  machine?

ΘΑ ΕΙΜΑΣΤΕ ΠΕΡΔΙΚΙΑ!
WE'LL BE AS FIT AS FIDDLES!

Περάσανε πέντε χρόνια. Μερικά πράγματα αλλάξανε,
άλλα μένουν τα ίδια. Το περίπτερο συνεχίζει στα χέρια της
Βαγγελιώς.

συστήνω	recommend, introduce
αν επιτρέπεται	if you don't mind (my asking)
να σου πω την αλήθεια	to tell you the truth
επιτυχημένος επιχειρηματίας	successful businessman
οι Βρυξέλλες	Brussels
χαλάω κόσμο	stir things up, cause a sensation
το χρυσό μου	my darling
ο νονός	godfather
η έρευνα	research
ο θησαυρός	wealth (here: of information)
σ'αυτά τα θέματα	in these matters
ο/η κουμπάρος/α	*used as a term of address amongst close friends [literally, best man/woman]*
όχι δα	certainly not
το σαράβαλο	wreck
η ανανέωση	renewal, change
το περδίκι	(young) partridge

ACTIVITY 18

Listen to the story and answer the following questions.

1 Ποιος το πλήρωσε το καινούργιο ψυγείο;
2 Πού δουλεύει τώρα ο Πέτρος;
3 Τι μαθαίνουμε για το παιδάκι;
4 Πού πάει ο Θανάσης, και γιατί;
5 Ποιος είναι ο άνδρας της Σοφίας;
6 Τι θέλει ο Περικλής;

ACTIVITY 19

Listen to the story again and write down what you learn
about Thanasis.

STORY TRANSCRIPT

Pericles	Καινούργιο ψυγείο, Βαγγελιώ;
Vangelio	Από τα καλύτερα, Περικλή μου. Μου το σύστησε ο Κραίηγκ. Διάλεξε κάτι να πιείς.
Pericles	Πόσα το πληρώσατε, αν επιτρέπεται;
Vangelio	Να σου πω την αλήθεια, δεν ξέρω. Μας το έκανε δώρο ο Πέτρος.
Pericles	Επιτυχημένος επιχειρηματίας ο γιος σας, ε; Μπράβο.
Vangelio	Μόνο που δεν τον βλέπουμε πολύ, τώρα που εργάζεται στις Βρυξέλλες ...
Pericles	Καλώς τα παιδιά! Τι κάνεις παλικαράκο μου ξανθό; Μεγαλώνεις; Χαλάς κόσμο;
Vangelio	Έλα 'δω, χρυσό μου - το πιο έξυπνο, όμορφο παιδί της γειτονιάς μας! Πού είναι ο μπαμπάς σου; Πάει με το νονό με το αεροπλάνο να σου φέρει παιχνίδια;
Pericles	Α, πήγε και ο Θανάσης στην Βοστόνη;
Sophia	Ναι, πάνε να δούνε κάτι καινούργιες ηλεκτρονικές συσκευές που μπορεί να βοηθήσουν τον Κραίηγκ με τις αρχαιολογικές έρευνές του. Ο Θανάσης είναι θησαυρός σ'αυτά τα θέματα ...
Pericles	Θέλω να κοιτάξει το δικό μου το σύστημα – δεν λειτουργεί καλά πια.
Vangelio	Σαν και μας, κουμπάρε! Σαράβαλα! Όλα θέλουν αντικατάσταση!
Pericles	Όχι δα σαράβαλα, κουμπάρα – μία ανανέωση και θα είμαστε περδίκια!

Test

Now it's time to test your progress in Unit 14.

1 Make comparisons in the form **είναι πιο + adjective + από**, using the prompts

   Example: ΟΠαππούς/ο πρωθυπουργός (older)
   Ο Παππούς είναι πιο μεγάλος από τον πρωθυπουργό.

   1 οι Πυραμίδες/ο Παρθενώνας (old)
   2 ο Σωτήρης/ο Ανδρέας (serious)
   3 η Αλίκη/η Μαρινέλα (blond)
   4 το σκόρδο/ο μαϊντανός (strong)
   5 ένα ποδήλατο/ένας υπολογιστής (expensive)
   6 η Αγγλία/η Αυστραλία (big)
   7 το Μίνι/η Τζάγκουαρ (expensive)
   8 η φίλη μου/η φίλη σου (beautiful)
   9 ο Σέιξπηρ/ο Όμηρος (good)
   10 το Έβερεστ/ο Όλυμπος (high)

   `20`

2 Supply the opposites.

   1 μεγαλύτερος   4 νευρικός
   2 φτωχός   5 μελαχρινή
   3 περισσότερα   6 κόντος

   `6`

3 Label the diagram in Greek.

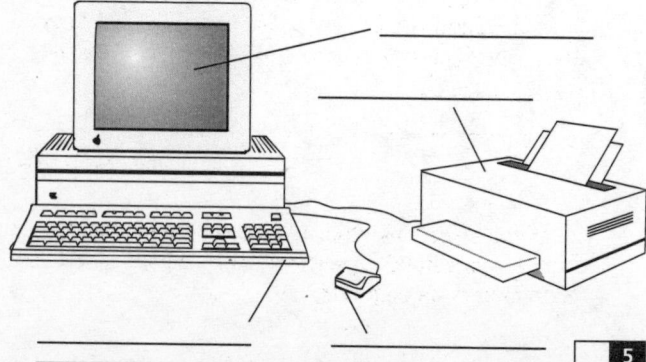

   `5`

4 Say whose each item is as in the example.

η Χριστίνα	ο Πάνος	η μαθήτρια	οι τουρίστες
Τα παπούτσια είναι δικά της.	Η γραβάτα	Η τσάντα	Οι γάτες

3

5 How would you do the following in Greek?

1 Ask which of the two women is blonder.
2 Ask a friend if he paid more for the new watch.
3 Ask which is the highest mountain in the world.
4 Ask whose glasses these are.
5 Ask a friend if it's her turn.

10

6 Complete the text using the appropriate tense of the verb in brackets.

Την περασμένη εβδομάδα ήθελα να (1 διαλέγω) _____ ένα καινούριο ραδιόφωνο. Δεν ήθελα να (2 ξοδεύω) _____ ούτε πολλά, ούτε πολύ λίγα λεφτά. (3 παω) _____ στο κατάστημα και (4 αγοράζω) _____ ένα αρκετά καλό γιαπωνέζικο σύστημα. Όταν (5 γυρίζω) _____ σπίτι, (6 βλέπω) _____ ότι δεν (7 λειτουργώ) _____ καλά. Δεν μπορούσα να (8 ρυθμίζω) _____ τους σταθμούς σωστά. Ευτυχώς, υπάρχει εγγύηση που δεν (9 λήγω) _____ ακόμα και δεν χρειάζεται να ανησυχώ. Αύριο (10 το αλλάζω) _____ .

10

TOTAL SCORE 54

If you scored less than 45 go through the dialogues and the Language Building sections again, before completing the summary on page 208

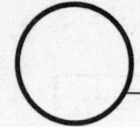

Summary 14

Now try this final test summarizing the main points covered in this unit. You can check your answers on the recording.

How would you:
1 ask who is more famous, Melina Mercouri or Sappho?
2 say 'we're looking for someone more practical'?
3 ask which computer is the best?
4 say your mobile is faulty?
5 say 'our car isn't working properly'?
6 ask whose suitcase this is? Say it's yours?
7 say your uncle was a rich businessman?
8 say it serves you right!?

REVISION

Congratulations on completing the course! After giving yourself a (well-deserved) break to allow things to sink in, you may want to revise those areas you found particularly difficult before doing the final review section. Going over points this time around, you will realize that you have acquired a solid basis on which you can continue to build. With an overview of the grammar and vocabulary of the course fresh in your mind, things you might not have understood properly before are likely to fall into place. To maintain or even build on your skills, try to keep up the habit of doing some Greek regularly – at least once a week. You might consider joining a class. What about seeking out local Greek people to speak to? Are you planning a(nother) trip to Greece or Cyprus? In the meantime, Γειά σας και στο καλό!

Review 4

VOCABULARY

1 Sort the words below into the four named categories.

αγριόχορτο αλάτι άρρωστες αρχιτέκτονας
βασιλοπούλα γεμάτο διαλέγω διάσημες
διευθυντής δυνατοί εγγόνι έκθεση έξυπνος
εργάτης έρχομαι επιχειρηματίας ζηλεύουμε
ήσυχη κάθομαι καθρέφτης κάρβουνο
κρυώνουμε λειτουργούν νοσοκόμα ξαπλώνει
ξένοι ξυπνάω οδοντίατρος παιχνίδι πληρώνεις
πόλεμος σκοτεινό σταφύλι συνταξιούχος
συσκευή φτωχό φύτεψα

| 1 Nouns referring to people |
| 2 Nouns referring to things |
| 3 Adjectives |
| 4 Verbs |

2 Match the expressions 1–6 with the appropriate translation from a–f.

1 Κατά τη γνώμη μου   a What's this called?
2 Καλά να πάθεις!   b What a pity!
3 Χάλασε κόσμο.   c Is it worth it?
4 Πώς λέγεται αυτό;.   d Serves you right!
5 Τι κρίμα!   e In my opinion
6 Αξίζει;   f He made a fuss.

GRAMMAR AND USAGE

3 Complete the sentences with the past tense of the verbs in brackets.

1 Ο Νίκος _____ την Μαρίνα στο ζαχαροπλαστείο. (περιμένω)

2 Πόσες χιλιάδες δραχμές _____ στην τσάντα σου εχθές; (έχω)

3 _____ την εφημερίδα σήμερα το πρωί; (διαβάζω)

4 Ποιος _____ μαζί σου στο σινεμά την
   Κυριακή; (είμαι)

5 Πόσους δίσκους _____ τα παιδιά από τον
   κατάλογο; (διαλέγω)

6 Της _____ της Θέκλας η εγκυκλοπαίδεια που
   _____ για τα γενέθλιά της; (αρέσει, παίρνω)

7 Τι σου _____ οι γιατροί; (λέω)

8 Η γάτα _____ ψάρι, αλλά δεν είχαμε. (θέλω)

9 _____ την έκθεση στο Ζάππειο; (βλέπω)

10 Ο αδελφός μου _____ ένα ωραίο ταξίδι
   πέρσι - _____ όλη την Ευρώπη. (κάνω, γυρίζω)

4 Complete the sentences with the correct form of the
  verbs in brackets.

1 Ο άνδρας μου δεν _____ καλά. (αισθάνομαι)

2 Ο παππούς και η γιαγιά _____ νωρίς κάθε
  βράδυ. (κοιμάμαι)

3 A: Πού _____ κορίτσια;
   B: Και οι δύο _____ στο βιβλιοπωλείο του
      θείου μου. (εργάζομαι)

4 Εγώ δεν _____ κάθε μέρα στο γραφείο. Είμαι
  εδώ μόνον τρεις φορές την εβδομάδα. (έρχομαι)

5 Η Μυρτώ δεν _____ πριν μιλήσει. (σκέφτομαι)

5 Give the Greek for what each person likes doing:

Example: Της Ελένης της αρέσει να μαγειρεύει.

1 Τα παιδιά

2 Εγώ

3 Ο Παύλος

4 Η Ράνια

6 Say what the following used to do, using the verb in
  brackets.

Example: Βοηθούσε την μητέρα στην κουζίνα.

1 (πάω)   3 (τρώω)

2 (παίζω)   4 (λέω)

7 Complete the sentences with the correct form of the adjective.

1 Η γάτα μας είναι _____ από τον σκύλο. (ήρεμος)

2 Οι διευθυντές είναι πολύ _____ με τη δουλειά σας. (ευχαριστημένος)

3 Μπαμπά, δεν μου έδωσες αρκετά λεφτά. Θέλω _____ .(πολλά)

4 Ο Τάκης είναι _____ αλλά ο Λάκης ειναι _____ από τον Χιούγκο – ποιον προτιμάς; (δυνατός, πρακτικός)

5 Η Ελένη είναι _____ από την Ειρήνη στα μαθηματικά. (καλός)

LISTENING

8 Listen to the advertisement for a range of towels and answer the questions which follow.

1 What sizes are available and what are the towels made of?

2 What does the advertisement say about the colours and designs?

3 What use does it suggest for the towels?

4 Who will the towels suit?

5 What does the advertisement claim about the prices?

6 Can you pay by credit card?

7 How much are
   (i) the large towels?
   (ii) the kitchen towels?

8 How long do the bargain prices last? (give dates)

9 Listen to Kiria Katina telling her friend about Sophia's toddler, then answer the following questions.

1 Τι χρώμα ειναι τα μαλλιά και τα μάτια του παιδιού;

2 Από πού πήρε το όνομά του, το παιδάκι;

3 Πότε είναι τα γενέθλια του μικρου Μανολάκη;

4 Τι του αρέσει να κάνει;

5 Τι του αρέσει να τρώει;

6 Τι πρέπει να τρώει, αντί για γλυκά;

7 Τι έφαγε στις κυρίας Κατίνας;

8 Τι κάνει κάθε απόγευμα;

9 Πόσες γλώσσες ξέρει το παιδί;

10 You've just come back from a trip to Athens and your
friend wants to know about it. Prepare your answers
then join in the dialogue on the recording. Try to do it
without using your notes.

Man Πώς περάσατε στην Αθήνα, λοιπόν;
You Say 'not bad at all!' Say you stayed at a small but
excellent hotel in Plaka.

Man Τι είδατε;
You Say many things. On the first day, of course, you
went to the Acropolis. It was something else!

You Say that now you have to see the marbles in
London.

Man Φάγατε νόστιμο ελληνικό φαγητό;
You Say that you found a taverna which served the
most delicious mezedes.

Man Τι κάνατε τα βράδια;
You Say one night you saw an ancient tragedy.

11 You're on the phone to the doctor's surgery. Prepare
your answers then join in the dialogue on the
recording. Try to do it without using your notes.

Receptionist Ορίστε, λέγετε
You Greet her, give your name, and say you'd
like to make an appointment.

Receptionist Ευχαρίστως. Ποιο είναι το πρόβλημα;
You Say that your son is not feeling very well.

Receptionist Τι ακριβώς έχει;
You Say you're not sure, but his stomach hurts
and he has a temperature.

Receptionist Ο Γιατρός μπορεί να σας δει στις δυόμισι
– σας κάνει;
You Say fine, you'll be there at half past two.

Answers

Unit 1

1 μαμά, ταξί, σινεμά, σαλάτα, λεμονάδα, ταραμοσαλάτα, αεροπλάνο, γιαούρτι, πρόβλημα, τηλέφωνο

2 ΜΠΙΡΑ, ΓΚΑΡΑΖ, ΤΖΑΤΖΙΚΙ, ΣΑΝΤΟΥΙΤΣ, ΝΤΟΜΑΤΑ, ΤΡΕΝΟ, ΟΥΖΟ, ΜΠΑΣΚΕΤ-ΜΠΩΛ, ΜΠΑΡ
Bill, Barbara, Betty, Donald, Delia, Gary, Wellington, Charles, Chipperfields, Jamaica

6 1 meeting; 2 parting; 3 meeting; 4 parting

7 1 c, 2 a, 3 d, 4 b

12 Α παρακαλώ, εντάξει, ευχαριστώ, καλή όρεξη, Β 1 γειά σας, 2 ευχαριστώ, 3 καλή όρεξη

13 *masculine*: ο μεζές, ο μουσακάς, ο καφές
feminine η τυρόπιτα, η ρετσίνα, η λεμονάδα
neuter: το τζατζίκι, το γιαούρτι, το κρασί, το τσάι, το ούζο, το σουβλάκι
το τζατζίκι – tzatziki, ο μεζές – meze (snack), η τυρόπιτα – cheese pie, το γιαούρτι – yoghurt, ο μουσακάς – moussaka, η ρετσίνα – retsina, το κρασί – wine, ο καφές – coffee, το τσάι – tea, η λεμονάδα – lemonade, το ούζο – ouzo, το σουβλάκι – souvlaki

14 1 Μία τυρόπιτα και μία μπίρα, παρακαλώ. 2 Ένα τσάι και έναν καφέ, παρακαλώ.

17 1 Yes, they serve beer. 2 No, they serve both hot and cold foods. 3 They have taramosalata, squid, and tzatziki. 4 They have tomato, lettuce, and Greek salad.

18 *Suggestions for Fiona: to eat* – καρπούζι, σταφύλια, *to drink* – πορτοκαλάδα, λεμονάδα, κόκα κόλα
Suggestions for Donald: starter – καλαμαράκια, *main course* – κοτόπουλο, σουβλάκι, *salad* – χωριάτικη, *to drink* – κρασί, μπίρα

19 1 F: They say 'good morning'. 2 T; 3 F: He says 'excuse me' – Συγγνώμη. 4 T; 5 F: She is offered a coffee. 6 F: A distant voice hails the taxi.

20 1 b, 2 c, 3 e, 4 a, 5 d

Test

1 1 d, 2 b, 3 g, 4 h, 5 e, 6 c, 7 a, 8 f

2 1 d, 2 c, 3 e, 4 b, 5 a, 6 f

3 ένα, μια, ένα, ένα, ένα, μια

4 1 ο, 2 η, 3 το, 4 το, 5 ο, 6 η, 7 το, 8 η

5 1 ΤΑΞΙ, 2 ΚΑΛΗΜΕΡΑ, 3 ΣΟΥΒΛΑΚΙ, 4 ΕΝΤΑΞΕΙ, 5 ΠΑΡΑΚΑΛΩ, 6 μπαμπάς,

7 χαίρετε, 8 ευχαριστώ, 9 τζατζίκι

6 1 Τί κάνεις; 2 Μία σαλάτα και μιά κόκα κόλα, παρακαλώ. 3 Ένα σουβλάκι και μία μπίρα, παρακαλώ. 4 Αντίο, στο καλό. 5 Καλησπέρα σας, τί κάνετε; 6 Καλημέρα σας/Χαίρετε . . . καλά ευχαριστώ. 7 Ευχαριστώ για το κρασί. 8 Μάλιστα.

Unit 2

2 1 F: The taverna is not mentioned – they drive past the church. 2 F: It's 2–3 minutes away. 3 F: No, but there's one in the town centre.

3 1 Η εκκλησία είναι εκεί. 2 Το ξενοδοχείο δεν είναι μακριά. 3 Πού είναι η τράπεζα; 4 Δεν είναι εδώ. 5 Πού είναι το βιβλιοπωλείο;

9 1 C, 2 A, 3 E, 4 D, 5 B

13 1 Pedhion tou Areos is on the *right*. 2 They reach the corner – *Patision* Street – and turn *left*. 3 It's *not* far.

14 1d 2c 3e 4a 5b

15 1 δέκα, 2 οχτώ, 3 εφτά, 4 εννιά

18 1 d, 2 b

19 1 F: Pericles says it's nearby. 2 T, 3 F: His friend's name is Petros. 4 F: He has a friend in Edinburgh. 5 F: It's three side-streets down, on the corner. 6 T

20 1 a, 2 b, 3 b, 4 b

Test

1 1 g, 2 c, 3 e, 4 a, 5 i, 6 h, 7 j, 8 b, 9 d, 10 f

2 F: 1, 10 M: 3, 6

3 1 B, 2 C, 3 A

4 1 είναι, 2 Είσαστε, 3 είναι, 4 είμαι, 5 είναι

5 1 Μήπως, 2 νά το, 3 Δυστυχώς, 4 Συγγνώμη, 5 μέχρι

6 1 Το, στην, 2 Η, στη 3 η, 4 στο, 5 –

7 1 Πού είναι η τράπεζα, παρακαλώ; 2 Υπάρχει ταχυδρομείο εδώ κοντά; 3 Μήπως ξέρετε που είναι το Ξενοδοχείο Βαρβάρα; 4 Θα πάρετε το πρώτο στενό δεξιά. 5 Υπάρχει (μια) τράπεζα δίπλα. 6 Θα πάτε αριστερά.

Unit 3

2 1 b, 2 b, 3 b, 4 c

3 θέλ-, έχ-, δουλεύ-
θέλω, θέλεις, θέλει, θέλουμε, θέλετε, θέλουνε

έχω, έχεις, έχει, έχουμε, έχετε, έχουνε
δουλεύω, δουλεύεις, δουλεύει, δουλεύουμε,
δουλεύετε, δουλεύουνε

7 1 F: She's English. 2 F: She says she's *not*
from that far away. 3 T, 4 F: She's
studying ancient Greek and philosophy.
5 F: He lives in Athens.

8 1 Είμαι Άγγλος. 2 Είναι Ελληνίδα. 3 Ξέρω
γαλλικά. 4 Ο Καναδάς είναι μακριά. 5 Δεν
ξέρει ελληνικά. 6 Μένεις στην Ιρλανδία;

12 1 more than 20 years, 2 She knows only
a little. 3 ancient; 4 12 years, 5 in
Birmingham, Athens, and Salonika

13 1 δεκαεφτά, 2 δεκαεννέα, 3 δεκαέξι,
4 δεκαοχτώ, 5 είκοσι, 6 έντεκα, 7 δεκατρία

17 1D 2E 3F 4A 5C 6B
1 Cynthia Harrod-Eagles, 2 Roddy Doyle,
3 Yiannis Ritsos, 4 Ruth Rendel, 5 Martin
Amis, 6 Margaret Atwood

18 1 He is Vangelio's son and Craig's friend.
2 from a letter, 3 economics, 4
archaeology, 5 coca cola, lemonade, ice-
cream, 6 two to three months

19 1 d, 2 b, 3 a, 4 c

Test

1 1 Πώς σε λένε; 2 Από πού είσαι; 3 Είσαι
Γερμανός; 4 Τί δουλειά κάνεις; 5 Πού
δουλεύεις;

2 Είσαστε Αγγλίδα; Όχι, είμαι Αμερικανίδα.
Από πού είσαστε; Από το Σικάγο. Πόσον
καιρό μένετε στο Μαντσέστερ; Δέκα
χρόνια.

3 1 Με, 2 από, 3 Τώρα, 4 εδώ, 5 στην, 6 σε,
7 λίγα

4 1 Ελλάδα, 2 Γερμανός, 3 Ιρλανδέζα,
4 Ιταλός, 5 Γαλλίδα, 6 αγγλικά

5 1 μένουν(ε), 2 είναι, 3 ξέρει, 4 δουλεύετε,
5 σπουδάζει, 6 είναι

6 δώδεκα, δεκαπέντε, δεκαεφτά, δεκαοχτώ,
είκοσι

7 Sample answer: Είμαι στην Σκοτία.
Δουλεύω σε γραφείο εδώ για δυο μήνες.
Μένω στο ξενοδοχείο Τσαρλζ. Ξέρω λίγα
ελληνικά!

Review 1

1 *things to eat*: παγωτό, γιαούρτι, τζατζίκι,
ταραμοσαλάτα
things to drink: κρασί, μπίρα, ούζο
places in town: βιβλιοπωλείο, πλατεία,
ταχυδρομείο, εκκλησία, τράπεζα, φούρνος,
περίπτερο
people: άνδρας, φίλος, γιος, Γαλλίδα
jobs/professions: φοιτήτρια, δικηγόρος

2 ο – Άγγλος, αρχαιολόγος
η – τυρόπιτα, Ιταλίδα, θάλασσα, μαμά,
ντομάτα
το – ξενοδοχείο, πανεπιστήμιο, καφενείο,
λάδι, ταξί

3 1 B, 2 E, 3 A, 4 C, 5 D

4 1 f, 2 d, 3 h, 4 j, 5 g, 6 i, 7 a, 8 c, 9 b,
10 e

5 1 i, 2 h, 3 d, 4 a, 5 f, 6 c, 7 j, 8 g, 9 b,
10 e

6 1 είναι, 2 μένουνε, 3 θέλω, 4 ξέρεις,
5 ξέρουμε, 6 σπουδάζει, 7 δουλεύεις

7 a στην, b από, c σε, d στο, e στο

8 1 Πόπη Χρίστου (Poppy Christou),
2 Κεφαλλονιά (Cephalonia), 3 Αθήνα –
κοντά στο κέντρο (Athens – near the
centre), 4 δεκαεφτά χρόνια (17 years),
5 Είναι γιατρός και δουλεύει σε ένα
νοσοκομείο. (She's a doctor and she
works in a hospital.) 6 Ναι, ξέρει κάλα
αγγλικά, λίγα γαλλικά και λίγα γερμανικά.
(Yes, she knows English well, a little
French, and a little German.)

9 1 στο πάρκο (not στο σταθμό), 2
δεκαπέντε χρόνια (not δεκα χρόνια), 3 τον
Καναδά (not την Κρήτη), 4 το φαρμακείο
(not το ταχυδρομείο)

Unit 4

2 1 a double room (with two beds), 2 two
days, 3 on the first floor, 4 the price
includes a shower; no dinner, but
breakfast, 5 yes

3 1 οι πλατείες, 2 τα λεμόνια, 3 οι Ιταλοί,
4 οι φίλες, 5 τα δωμάτια, 6 οι δικηγόροι,
7 οι τράπεζες, 8 τα διαβατήρια, 9 οι
τουαλέτες, 10 τα μπάνια, 11 τα κομπιούτερ

7 1b 2a 3a

11 1 Fourth, 2 in the car, 3 8.00pm onwards

12 1 έντεκα και είκοσι, 2 δέκα η ώρα, 3 τρεις
παρά είκοσι πέντε, 4 δύο παρά δέκα,
5 πέντε παρά πέντε, 6 οχτώ και τέταρτο

15A 1 The second (said to be suitable for
two people), as it is a studio flat
(γκαρσονιέρα), and would thus have
cooking facilities and its own bathroom.
The first offers a choice of two rooms, a
single and a double. The bathroom
apparently serves both.
2 1 is near the centre of town, 2 is
beside the station and opposite the
cinema.
3 The first is conveniently located. It
might be noisy. However, it's on the 5th
floor, with access by lift, so the traffic
might not be a problem. The second has
a garden, and hot water is included in
the offer. Its location could be seen both
as an advantage and a disadvantage.

16 1 F: κοντά στη σχολή, 2 T, 3 F: όχι τώρα –
την Κυριακή, 4 F: όχι πεύκα, αλλά
λεμονιές, πορτοκαλιές και ελιές, 5 T

17 1 It has a superb view – you can see all
of Athens from up there. 2 on Sunday,
3 Έλα μαζί μας! 'Come with us!' 4 She
says it's in the countryside; they swim in
the sea; the house has a garden with
lemon, orange, and olive trees. 5 She
tells him it doesn't matter – he can work
again on Monday.

Test

1 1 h, 2 e, 3 f, 4 c, 5 j, 6 a, 7 g, 8 b, 9 i,
   10 d
2 1 οι υπογραφές, 2 τα διαβατήρια, 3 οι
   κήποι, 4 οι τουαλέτες, 5 οι βαλίτσες, 6 τα
   γεύματα, 7 τα αυτοκίνητα, 8 τα κλειδιά,
   9 οι ελιές, 10 τα κινητά
3 ΔΕΥΤΕΡΑ, ΤΡΙΤΗ, ΤΕΤΑΡΤΗ,
   ΠΕΜΠΤΗ, ΠΑΡΑΣΚΕΥΗ, ΣΑΒΒΑΤΟ,
   ΚΥΡΙΑΚΗ
4 1 τρεις και είκοσι; 2 δώδεκα παρά δέκα;
   3 μεσάνυχτα; 4 οχτώ παρά πέντε;
   5 έντεκα και μισή; 6 εφτά και τέταρτο
5 1 εμπρός, 2 κλείσω, 3 δίκλινο, 4 με,
   5 χωρίς, 6 υπάρχει, 7 όροφο, 8 θέα,
   9 σερβίρετε, 10 βραδινό
6 1 το μπαλκονάκι, 2 το κρεβατάκι, 3 το
   δωματιάκι, 4 η κορούλα, 5 η βολτίτσα, 6 η
   δροσούλα

Unit 5

2 1 b, 2 a, 3 b
3 1 κόκκινη, 2 μεγάλο, 3 καλούς
7 1 T, 2 F: the black costs 35,000, the blue
   28,000. 3 F: He takes a 42.
8 1 πουλάει, 2 τρώνε, 3 μιλάμε, 4 πάνε
12 1 2 packets, 2 2 bottles 3 a kilo, 4 a few
   5 a quarter kilo
13 1 ένα κουτί σπίρτα, 2 ένα πακέτο
   καραμέλες, 3 ένα μπουκάλι ουίσκυ, 4 ένα
   ποτήρι πορτοκαλάδα
16 1 virgin olive oil – παρθένο ελαιόλαδο, a
   free tin of olives, 2 half-price – μισή τιμή,
   3 no, fresh – φρέσκο, €1.70 a kilo,
   4 strawberry and peach – φράουλα,
   ροδάκινο, buy two, get one free,
   5 butter, yogurt, milk – βούτυρο,
   γιαούρτι, γάλα. 6 a μόνο, b δώρο,
   c στραγγιστό, d μακράς διαρκείας
17 1 no, 2 a pen, 3 no, 4 an English one,
   5 chocolates, 6 she wraps it, 7 to the
   theatre, 8 It makes no difference which
   she takes.

Test

1 1 καλά, 2 ένα μικρό, 3 τα ωραία,
   4 νόστιμο, 5 φρέσκα, 6 ξένες, 7 τους
   μεγάλους
2 a εννιακόσια ενενήντα εννιά;
   b πεντακόσιες χιλιάδες; c διακόσια
   σαράντα; d εκατόν εξήντα; e είκοσι
   εφτά χιλιάδες
3 1 πακέτο, 2 κιλό, 3 μάτσο ντομάτες,
   κρεμμύδια, 4 μπουκάλι
4 1 τρώει, 2 πουλάει, 3 μιλάνε, 4 λες,
   5 υπάρχουν
5 1b 2a 3c
6 1 Πουλάω, 2 φρέσκα, 3 Μου δίνετε,
   4 γλυκό, 5 μέλι, 6 δώστε μου, 7 μικρό,
   8 Τίποτ'άλλο; 9 όλα μαζί, 10 Ορίστε

Unit 6

2 1 με το αεροπλάνο – by plane, 2 την
   Παρασκευή το πρωί – Friday morning, 3 η
   πρώτη πτήση – the first flight, 4 κατα τις
   έντεκα και τέταρτο – 11:15, 5 είκοσι τρεις
   χιλιάδες δραχμές το ένα – 23,000 each
3 1 Το τρένο φτάνει στις τεσσερισήμισι,
   2 Το καράβι φεύγει στις μια και τέταρτο,
   3 Πάω στην αγορα με τα πόδια κάθε Τρίτη.
7 1 Poseidon Beach, 2 a little further, 3 by
   taxi, 4 Hydra
8 1 εκείνο, 2 αυτούς τούς
12 1 F: They are leaving tomorrow. 2 F She
   complains that he drives too fast – in
   general.
13 1 Η μητέρα μου οδηγεί προσεχτικά.
   2 Ησύχασε, αυτά τα εισιτήρια είναι δωρεάν.
16 wheel – τροχός, steering wheel – τιμόνι,
   headlight – προβολέας, brake – φρένο
17 1 c, 2 e, 3 b, 4 a, 5 d
18 1 three, 2 Lakis, Pericles, Thanasis, 3 a
   car, a taxi, a scooter, 4 The brakes don't
   work. 5 The corner is dangerous. 6 He
   has two tickets for a concert …

Test

1 1 a, 2 c, 3 e, 4 d, 5 b
2 1 b, 2 d, 3 e, 4 c, 5 a
3 1 αυτό, εκείνο 2 αυτές, εκείνη 3 εκείνους
   4 εκείνα
4 1 πολλά 2 πολλή 3 πολύ 4 πολλές
5 1 Τι ώρα φεύγει το τρένο για το Βόλο;
   2 Από πού φεύγει; 3 Πότε φτάνει το
   λεωφορείο από τη Θεσσαλονίκη;
   4 Υπάρχει καθυστέρηση; 5 Δεν έχω
   πολλές αποσκευές
6 1 b, 2 d, 3 a, 4 c, 5 e
7 1 d, 2 e, 3 b, 4 a, 5 c

Unit 7

2 1 30 November, 2 a scarf, 3 a cognac,
   4 time passes very quickly
3 1 στις εφτά Ιανουαρίου, 2 στις είκοσι
   πέντε Νοεμβρίου, 3 το Σεπτέμβριο, 4 την
   πρώτη Μαΐου
7 1 F: They're going to the 'lunar park'
   (amusement park) at 5 o'clock. 2 F: Dad
   sees five balloons. 3 F: It's a bicycle. 4 T
8 1 των γυναικών, 2 του Γιάννη, 3 της
   Μαρίας
12 1 b, 2 b, 3 b, 4 a
13 1 b τα κλειδιά του c το βιβλίο του, 2 d το
   καπέλο της, e τα πέδιλά της, 3 f τα
   μπαλόνια τους, g τα ποδήλατά τους
16 1 a wine festival – γιορτή κρασιού,
   2 15–23 September, every evening – κάθε
   απόγευμα, 3 at the Paphos municipal
   park/public gardens – στο Δημοτικό Κύπο
   Πάφου, 4 all Cyprus wines – όλα τα
   κρασιά τις Κύπρου, 5 snacks: the list

includes many traditional Cypriot
delicacies: σουβλάκια – kebabs,
λουκάνικα παστουρμά – spiced garlic beef
sausages, σαλάτες – salads, λούντσα –
marinaded smoked pork, κεφτεδάκια –
meatballs, ντολμαδάκια – wrapped vine
leaves, χαλούμι – a type of cheese, ελιές
– olives, πιτάκια – little pies, σουτζούκι –
a sweet made of nuts rolled in wine-
must, 6 traditional music, dances,
theatre, shadow puppets (named after
the main character, Karagiozis) –
παραδοσιακή μουσική, χοροί, θέατρο,
Καραγκιόζης,
7 the Municipality of Limasol and the
Cyprus Tourist Organization – Δήμος
Λεμεσού, Τουριστικός Οργανισμός
Κύπρου 8 Drink Wine for a Long Life!
Πίνε Κρασί Να'χεις Ζωή

17 1 Δοκιμάστε τα όλα! 2 Χορέψτε,
τραγουδήστε, διασκεδάστε! 3 Φάτε
σουτζούκι! 4 Ελάτε να γιορτάσετε μαζί
μας.

18 1 on Sunday, 2 what the child is to be
called, 3 the child's grandmother,
4 Monique, 5 Katina, 6 a Greek name

Test

1 1 δεκατέσσερις Φεβρουαρίου, 2 τριάντα
μία Αυγούστου, 3 τέσσερις Ιουλίου
2 1 παίζει 2 γιορτάζει 3 βαφτίζουν
4 μαθαίνουν 5 αρχίζουν
3 1 Να η παρέα. 2 Είναι η επέτειός μας. 3 το
τέλος του χρόνου, 4 Έχω ένα δωράκι για
τη γιαγιά μου. 5 Πού είναι το σπίτι του
γιατρού;
4 1 c, 2 e, 3 a, 4 d, 5 f, 6 b
5 1 του Ολυμπιακού, 2 των παιδιών, 3 του
παππού, 4 της μαμάς και του μπαμπά, 5 του
φίλου μου
6 1 c, 2 a, 3 b, 4 e, 5 d

Review 2

1 1 τρίκλινο, 2 γιαγιά, 3 διαβατήριο,
4 φοράει, 5 θάλασσα, 6 λαϊκή, 7 έτοιμος,
8 πτήση, 9 κουτί, 10 κινητό
2 1 b, 2 e, 3 d, 4 a, 5 c
3 1 οδηγώ, 2 πουλάει, 3 φοράει, 4 τυλίγετε,
5 σερβίρουμε, 6 παίζουνε, 7 νοικιάζω,
8 μαθαίνω
4 1 για, στις, 2 Τον, στα, 3 στις, 4 Από, για,
5 στην, Την
5 1 κόκκινα μπαλόνια, 2 πολλούς φίλους,
3 πόσα κλειδιά, 4 τρεις πράσινες πιπεριές,
5 ωραία δέντρα
6 1 Ο Μιχάλης, 2 την Τρίτη, 3 τρία,
4 ποδόσφαιρο, 5 πέντε χιλιάδες το ένα,
6 στις οχτώ η ώρα, 7 Πλατεία Βικτωρίας,
8 4573291
7 1 παστίτσιο (a pasta dish), 2 it takes a
long time to make – παίρνει πολύ ώρα,
3 shortly – τώρα – σε λίγο, 4 to the street
market – στη λαϊκή, 5 two packets of

macaroni and a kilo of good cheese –
δύο πακέτα μακαρόνια και ένα κιλό καλό
τυρί, 6 some beers – μέρικες μπίρες,
7 fresh bread and flowers – ψωμί φρέσκο
και λουλούδια

Unit 8

2 1 F: At first she wants neither fish nor
meat. 2 T, 3 T
3 1 Μ'αρέσουν οι μαύρες γάτες. 2 Δεν του
αρέσουν τα μεγάλα ζώα. 3 Δεν τους
αρέσουν ούτε τα αυτοκίνητα, ούτε τα
λεωφορεία – προτιμούν τα ταξί. 4 Μας
αρέσουν τα ιταλικά παπούτσια. 5 Σ'αρέσει
το ποδήλατο της Ελένης;
7 1 the Berlin Philharmonic, 2 a comedy,
3 Agamemnon, 4 *Buena Vista (Social
Club)*
8 1 μ'αρέσουν, 2 της αρέσουν, 3 Μας
αρέσουν
9 1 απίθανο, 2 καινούριες,
13 1 c, 2 c, 3 b, 4 a
14 1 Ποια, 2 Ποιες, 3 Ποια 4 Ποιους ...
αυτούς, 5 Ποια
17 1a *Little Foxes*, 1b Saturday and Sunday,
1c students, 2a singing (chosen arias),
2b Donizetti, Bellini, Rossini and others,
2c Ελπίδα – Hope, a support society for
carriers of the AIDS-virus, 3a Patision
240, 3b Gwyneth Paltrow, Robert de
Niro, Anne Bankcroft, 3c probably not –
it has air-conditioning
19 1 at the village – the family were there
with a friend of Peter (her brother, who
is studying in Edinburgh), 2 Pix Lax,
3 terrific, 4 very much so, 5 Craig,
6 bouzouki and ouzo in a taverna
20 Thanasis suggests that all visitors *know
about* Greek music is bouzouki and ouzo
at a taverna.

Test

1 1 c, 2 a, 3 b, 4 d
2 1 φράουλες, 2 μπακαλιάρος, 3 φριχτό,
4 φάβα, 5 κάτι άλλο
3 1 c, 2 a, 3 b
4 1 λέει ότι, 2 άσε τους, 3 ούτε ... ούτε,
4 ποιος ... αυτός, 5 άλλη φορά
5 1 piano, guitar, bouzouki, 2 children
from the age of four learn to play music
easily, quickly, and correctly, 3 book a
place, 4 Monday, Wednesday, Saturday,
5 prices please: starting from 3000
drachmas an hour

Unit 9

2 1 Στο Βανκούβερ, 2 η αδελφή του, 3 τρεις
εβδομάδες, 4 στον Ειρηνικό Ωκεανό
6 1 F: Ο Λάκης λέει ότι θα πάρει ένα μήλο

μαζί του. (Η Κ. Πόπη λέει ότι θα θέλει σοκολάτα στο δρόμο.) 2 F: Η Κ. Πόπη λέει ότι έκανε κόπο. 3 F: Η Κ.Πόπη λέει ότι από αύριο μπορεί να κάνει δίαιτα ο Αλέκος. 4 F: Η Κ. Πόπη λέει ότι αύριο, ούτε χόρτα. 5 T

7 1 Μή γυρίσεις με ταξί! 2 Διάβασε το βιβλίο σου. 3 Πλήρωσε το λογαριασμό, παρακαλώ. 4 Γράψε ένα γράμμα στη γιαγιά. 5 Περιμένετε εδώ. 6 Μή φύγεις! 7 Πάρε ό,τι θέλεις! 8 Μή μιλάς αγγλικά!

11 1 b, 2 b, 3 a, 4 c

12 1 στην Αμεξάνδρεια, Αίγυπτο, 2 φθινόπωρο, 3 όχι πολλή – η θερμοκρασία είναι στους 32 βαθμούς, 4 την επόμενη Κυριακή

15 1 today (Sunday 23 May) and tomorrow (Monday 24 May), 2 north, 3 northern Aegean, 4 a 17–34 degrees (Athens is in Attica) b 12–30 degrees c 15–35 degrees, 5 in almost all of the rest of the country, 6 the sea will be good (i.e. calm) for trips throughout the Mediterranean

17 1 στο σπίτι, 2 φτιάχνουν γλυκά, 3 αύριο 4 στην Κεφαλλονιά, 5 ο Πέτρος, η Σοφία, η Βαγγελιώ, οΚραίηνγκ, ο Θανάσης, 6 μαζί τους στην Κεφαλλονιά

18 1 Petros is coming home (unexpectedly) for a few days. 2 Sophia, 3 She will see a turtle or two (the implication is that she doesn't have the chance to get away very often). 4 While everyone's away, who will help him at the kiosk 5 in the Ionian

Test

1 1 θα φύγει, 2 θα πληρώσω, 3 θα δούμε, 4 θα μας περιμένει, 5 Θα ρωτήσω

2 1 a η δίαιτα, b η θερμίδα, c τα βραστά χόρτα, 2 a παλιός, b έτοιμος, c ελεύθερος, 3 a αύριο, b απόψε, c μετά, 4 a θα τρέξω, b θα μιλήσω, c θα γράψω, 5 a το παλτό, b το γάντι, c η τσέπη

3 1 Διάβασε 2 τηλεφώνησε 3 φύγε 4 περίμενε 5 Μην

4 1 c ΩΚΕΑΝΟΣ, 2 d ΓΥΜΝΑΣΤΙΚΗ, 3 e ΧΕΛΩΝΑ, 4 a ΔΙΑΚΟΠΕΣ, 5 b ΠΟΡΤΟΦΟΛΙ

5 1 ό,τι 2 ότι 3 ό,τι 4 ότι 5 ό,τι

6 1 Θα κάνει ζέστη αύριο. 2 Η θερμοκρασία θα είναι στους 40 βαθμούς 3 Κάνει κρύο σήμερα. 4 Πάρε την ομπρέλα σου - βρέχει. 5 Φυσάει. Ο καιρός δεν είναι πολύ καλός. Πού είναι ο ήλιος;

7 1 πληρώσω 2 δουλέψω 3 θέλω 4 διαβάσω 5 φορέσω

Unit 10

2 1 F: στον Πειραιά, 2 F: μερικές εβδομάδες, 3 F: μόνο δύο-τρεις λέξεις, 4 T, 5 T

3 1 Η Λιλίκα δεν θέλει να πιεί πορτοκαλάδα. 2 Θέλω να αγοράσω καινούριο σπίτι του χρόνου. 3 Ο Τάκης θέλει να φάει έξω με

την παρέα του. 4 Τα παιδιά θέλουν να παίξουν ποδόσφαιρο το απόγευμα. 5 Ο Μάνος θέλει να φύγει με την πρώτη πτήση αύριο.

7 1 Το διαμέρισμα είναι στον πρώτο όροφο. 2 Μπαίνουνε από το χωλ. 3 Υπάρχει κεντρική θέρμανση. 4 Το ενοίκιο είναι 140,000 το μήνα, χωρίς τα κοινόχρηστα.

8 1 Η Αννα μπορεί να μαγειρέψει μεξικάνικο φαγητό. 3 Εμείς δεν μπορούμε να γράψουμε κινέζικα γράμματα. 4 Οι φοιτητές μπορούν να νοικιάσουν ένα αυτοκίνητο. 5 Ο γιατρός δεν μπορεί να δει τον Κώστα σήμερα.

12 1 F: Πρέπει, αλλά δεν μπορεί. 2 T, 3 F: Είναι μακριά. 4 F: Μιλάει για το πάρκιν. 5 F: Θέλει να πάει στον οδοντίατρο, να του καθαρίσει τα δόντια.

13 1 Πρέπει να πας στο μπακάλη. 2 Πρέπει να κλείσεις ραντεβού. 3 Πρέπει να πας με το αεροπλάνο. 4 Πρέπει να ανοίξεις το παράθυρο. 5 Πρέπει να την βοηθήσεις. 6 Δεν πρέπει να κάνεις δίαιτα.

17 ο δρόμος, 2 βράδυ, 3 γαλανός, 4 λεμονιά, 5 γειτονιά

18 1 Sometimes there's a friend, company; sometimes all there is is clouds. 2 Narrow streets are suggestive of a poorer community. 3 The sky will turn blue, a lemon tree will blossom. (Spring will come, emotional gloom will disperse!)

19 1 Στη Βουλιαγμένη. 2 Πρέπει να διαβάσει. 3 Την ερχόμενη εβδομάδα. 4 Με την άδεια οδηγήσεως. 5 Θέλει αυτοκίνητο. 6 Θέλει να πάει στην Αγγλία. 7 Οτι μπορεί να δει όλα τα πανεπιστήμια στο Internet.

20 A 1 d, 2 e, 3 a, 4 b, 5 c
    B 1 Sophia, 2 Thanasis, 3 Sophia, 4 Thanasis, 5 Sophia

Test

1 θα/να 1 διαφημίσω, 2 πληρώσω, 3 φορέσω, 4 μιλήσω, 5 μείνω, 6 φάω, 7 δω, 8 πω, 9 μάθω, 10 ακούσω

2 1 h, 2 f, 3 i, 4 j, 5 l, 6 d, 7 k, 8 e, 9 a, 10 b, 11 g, 12 c

3 1 βοηθήσει, 2 μάθουν, 3 τρέξει, 4 γιορτάσει, 5 παίξουν

4 1 μου, 2 του, 3 τους, 4 μας, 5 της

5 1 medicine in Thessaloniki, 2 in England, 3 She wants to work in a hospital there to see how they do things. 4 with friends in a flat in London, 5 She knows quite a lot of English but she doesn't speak it very well. 6 how to drive on the left hand side of the road, 7 She might go on some trips. 8 go out every night, 9 a paediatrician

Review 3

1 ρούχα: παλτό, παπούτσια, γυαλιά, παντελόνι, κασκόλ

φαγώσιμα: αρνάκι, κοτόπουλο, χόρτα,
κουραμπιέδες, καλαμαράκι
επαγγέλματα: οδοντίατρος,
ποδοσφαιριστής, καθηγητής, συγγραφέας,
δασκάλα
ψυχαγωγία: τραγούδι, ταινία, θέατρο,
μπουζούκι, ορχήστρα
στέγαση: διαμέρισμα, κρεβατοκάμαρα,
κουζίνα, σαλόνι, γκαρσονιέρα

2 1 c, 2 a, 3 c, 4 d, 5 b

3 1 d, 2b, 3 a, 4 c, 5 e

4 1 σ'αρέσουν, 2 Σας αρέσει, 3 σ'αρέσουν,
4 τους αρέσει, 5 μ'αρέσει

5 1 δει, 2 τελειώσω, 3 ξυπνήσει, 4 πάς,
5 διαβάσει

6 1 καθάρισε, 2 κλείσε, 3 φέρε, 4 δώσε,
5 ζητήστε

7 1 Σπουδαίος, 2 Απαίσιο, 3 έτοιμη,
4 καινούριο, 5 δερμάτινα, 6 κόκκινα,
7 φοβερός, 8 άσχημο

8 1 Σε ένα εξαιρετικό ξενοδοχείο στο Σαν
Τροπέ. 2 Κάνουν ηλιοθεραπεία, παίζουνε
μπήτς βόλεϊ και το απόγευμα θα πάνε σε
θεραπευτικά λουτρά. 3 Βλέπει τον
Κουέντιν Ταραντίνο. 4 Αύριο θα κάνουνε
ένα ταξιδάκι με το κότερο μέχρι το Σαν
Ρέμο. 5 Θα πρέπει να κάνει δίαιτα και
πολλή γυμναστική. 6 στις εντεκάμισι το
πρωΐ, 7 Τα γενέθλια της μαμάς.

9 1 ένα παλτό – coat (not bathing suit),
2 Ποιο – which one (not what colour),
3 τα χρώματα – colours (not sizes),
4 πράσινο – green (not yellow),
5 Μπορείτε – you can (not do you want
to), 6 το καφετί – the brown (not
the orange), 7 βάλω – put on (not wear),
8 σαράντα – 40 (not 30), 9 τριάντα εφτά –
37 (not 27), 10 το άλλο – the other
(not the black)

Unit 11

2 1 F: από την Αυστραλία, 2 F: έφυγε νωρίς,
3 Τ, 4 Τ

3 1 είπε, 2 έπαιξαν, 3 ήθελε, 4 ήξερα,
5 έφυγες, 6 έκανε, 7 είδες

7 1 σε ένα νησί, 2 ήταν ναυτικός,
3 διευθηντής του σχολείου

8 1 Α: ήσουν, Β: Ήμουν, Α: ήταν,
Β: ήμασταν, 3 ήταν,

12 1 την περασμένη Κυριακή, 2 ψήσανε ψάρι
στην άμμο, 3 δεν φάγανε πατάτες, φάγανε
ντομάτες και άλλους μεζέδες, και ήπιανε
μπίρες

13 1 Στρώσανε το τραπέζι. 2 Φάγανε νόστιμα
πράγματα. 3 Ξαπλώσανε στην άμμο 4 Εγώ
έψησα τις πατάτες. 5 Οι άλλοι κάνανε τα
υπόλοιπα. 6 Είδαμε την πανσέληνο πάνω
από τα δέντρα. 7 Το νερό ήταν σαν
καθρέφτης.

14 1 όταν, 2 πότε

17 1 βασιλιάς, 2 βασίλειο, 3 βασιλόπουλο,

4 βασιλοπούλα, 5 παλάτι, 6
κόρη/θυγατέρα, 7 η κακομοίρα, 8 κουβέντα

18 para. 1 1 ήταν: είναι, 2 είχε: έχω, 3 ήθελε:
θέλω, 4 να φύγει: φεύγω, 5 κάλεσε: καλώ
(invite), 6 να χαιρετίσει: χαιρετώ (greet)
7 να δει: βλέπω, 8 αγαπάνε: αγαπάω,
9 φίλησε: φιλώ (kiss), 10 είπε: λέω,
11 είπε: λέω, 12 απάντησε: απαντάω

para 2 13 άκουσε: ακούω, 14 αγαπάει:
αγαπάω, 15 θύμωσε: θυμώνω (be angry),
16 πριν φύγει: φεύγω, 17 να πάρει: παίρνω
(take)

para 3 18 άρχισε: αρχίζω (start), 19 να
γυρίζει: γυρίζω (turn), 20 έλεγε: λέω,
21 είπανε: λέω, 22 έφτασε: φτάνω (reach,
arrive at), 23 ζήτησε: ζητάω (ask for,
request), 24 καταλάβανε: καταλαβαίνω,
25 πήγε: πάω, 26 είδε: βλέπω, 27 μίλησε:
μιλάω, 28 πολυλογούμε: πολυλογώ (talk a
lot), 29 αγάπησε: αγαπάω, 30 πύρε: παίρνω

19 (a) the first, (b) the third, (c) the second

20 1 Αγόρασε λίγα πράγματα που ήθελε.
2 στα αγριόχορτα σε ένα χωράφι, 3 στην
αστυνομία, 4 στο μουσείο, 5 Πρέπει να
αξίζουν αρκετά – είναι χρυσά και αρκετά
παλιά. 6 κάτι έχει ο καθρέφτης, 7 η
Βαγγελιώ, η μητέρα της

21 1 Τόσο γρήγορα; 2 με την ευκαιρία,
3 όπως σου είπα, 4 χωρίς να τα δει
άνθρωπος, 5 Αξίζουν τίποτα.

22 1 They were walking across the fields.
2 First they went to the police and then,
accompanied by a policeman, to the
museum.

Test

1 1 έκανα, 2 έμεινα, 3 έφυγα, 4 έπαιξα,
5 δούλεψα, 6 άκουσα, 7 έφαγα, 8 ήπια,
9 μίλησα, 10 έγραψα

2 1 η λογοτεχνία, 2 η έκθεση, 3 το μουσείο,
4 ο συνταξιούχος, 5 ο αστυνομικός, 6 η
νοσοκόμα, 7 η ζωή, 8 το κάρβουνο, 9 η
άμμος, 10 το χρυσό

3 1 πήγαν, 2 άρεσε, 3 ξέρανε, 4 μπορέσαν,
5 βγήκανε

4 1 ετοιμάσανε, 2 έγραψες, 3 διάβασα,
4 είπε, 5 ήθελε, 6 ήξερα, 7 ψώνισες,
8 πήρες, 9 ζήλεψε, 10 Ξύπνησα

5 1 d, 2 c, 3 b, 4a

6 1F: They're staying two days; they
arrived yesterday 2 F: They went to the
Louvre but didn't see the Venus de Milo.
3 F: They thought it was great. 4 F: They
ate in a restaurant near Notre Dame.
5 F: They had breakfast at the hotel.
6 Τ

Unit 12

2 1F: Είναι γεμάτος λουλούδια. 2 F: Φάγανε
καρπούζι από τον κήπο. 3 F: Ποτίζει.
4 F: Ο κύριος θα φτιάξει καφέ.

3A 1 Μ'αρέσει να ταξιδεύω με το πλοίο. 2 Της αρέσει να τρώει φρούτα κάθε μέρα. 3 Δεν τους αρέσει να παίζουν τάβλι. 4 Μας αρέσει να ψαρεύουμε στη θάλασσα με τη βάρκα. 5 Δεν του αρέσει να καθαρίζει τα παπούτσια του. 6 Της Μπέμπας δεν της αρέσει να βοηθάει τον αδελφό της. 7 Του Λάκη δεν του αρέσει να πληρώνει τους λογαριασμούς του. 8 Γιατί σ'αρέσει να φεύγεις στις εφτά κάθε πρωί; 9 Πότε σ'αρέσει να διαβάζεις την εφημερίδα; 10 Πώς σας αρέσει να μαγειρεύετε τα αυγά;

7 1 με τα πόδια, 2 κεντρική θέρμανση, 3 παίζανε χιονοπόλεμο, 4 τον Μάρτιο, 5 την Χιονάτη

8A 1 έκανα – έκανα, 2 έτρωγα – έφαγα, 3 έπαιζα – έπαιξα, 4 ποτίζα – πότισα, 5 ήθελα – ήθελα, 6 καθαρίζα – καθάρισα, 7 ξάπλωνα – ξάπλωσα, 8 έγραφα –έγραψα, 9 έφτανα – έφτασα

8B 1 Α: Τι έκανες στην κουζίνα; 1Β: Έτρωγα μέλι. 2Α: Πού έπαιζες όταν ήσουν μικρός; 2Β: Παίζαμε στον κήπο, στο πάρκο, στο δρόμο, παντού. 3Α: Ποιός καθάριζε το σπίτι σήμερα το πρωί; 3Β: Δεν ήταν ο Κώστας. Αυτός μαγείρευε στην κουζίνα. 4Α: Πότε φτάναμε σπίτι τα βράδια; 4Β: Όταν ήταν ώρα (για) να φάμε.

12 1 Στο δάσος 2 Νερό από το ποτάμι 3 Ότι ήταν σκοτεινό και έκανε κρύο 4 Τους άκουσε 5 Να τους εξετάσει

13 1 Στον Καναδά μιλούσαμε αγγλικά και γαλλικά. 2 Την Πρωτοχρονιά ψήναμε βασιλόπιτα. 3 Προχθές περπατούσαμε στα βουνά. 4 Πριν την Πάτρα ζούσανε στην Κόρινθο. 5 Ναι, οδηγούσαμε στην Νέα Γόρκη. 6 Όχι, δεν μπορούσα να βοηθήσω τον αδελφό μου.

16A 1 πλούσιο, 2 πολυσύνθετο, 3 οικολογική ισορροπία, 4 περιβάλλον, 5 πηγή, 6 αιώνες, 7 καλλιέργειες, 8 πάντοτε, 9 κυνήγι, 10 εμπόδιο, 11 χωρίς σκέψη, 12 πρόοδο, 13 φωτιά, 14 έστω και, 15 πετρελαιοπηγή

16B 1 It plays a major role – Παίζει κύριο ρόλο. 2 to open up fields for cultivation – για να ανοίξουν χωράφια για καλλιέργειες, 3 They used to set fire to forests thoughtlessly – Βάζανε φωτιά στα δάση χωρίς σκέψη. 4 that young trees were never left in the place of those removed (even untended) to allow natural regeneration – ποτέ δεν αφήνανε μικρά δένδρα στην θέση των μεγάλων, για να μεγαλώσει πάλι το δάσος με τον καιρό, έστω και μόνο του. 5 It was like a(n oil) well that they would drink dry, then move on – ήταν σαν μια πετρελαιοπηγή που την πίναιε και μετά την αφήναιε.

17 1 Νοίκιασε ένα αυτοκίνητο. 2 για να πάει στο Στέρλιγκ, 3 Ένα άλλο αυτοκίνητο τον χτύπησε. 4 όχι, 5 Έκοψε λίγο το μάτι του. 6 Δεν πήγε στο νοσοκομείο, 7 Ξέχασε ότι οδηγούν στα αριστερά στην Βρεταινία.

18 1 It was late. 2 He was hit as he was turning at the first traffic lights. 3 Katina assumes he went to hospital: Lakis assures her that it was nothing – a small cut on the eye. 4 He was laughing when he told his parents about the incident.

Test

1 1 γεμίζω – γέμισα – γέμιζα 2 κρυώνω – κρύωσα – κρύωνα, 3 τρέχω – έτρεξα – έτρεχα, 4 πεινώ – πείνασα – πεινούσα, 5 πίνω – ήπια – έπινα, 6 διψώ – δίψασα – διψούσα, 7 βοηθώ – βοήθησα– βοηθούσα, 8 φέρνω – έφερα – έφερνα

2 1 Έπινα πολύ γάλα. 2 Πήγαινα στο σχολείο με το ποδήλατο. 3 Έπαιζα ποδόσφαιρο. 4 Μ'άρεσε να ακούω κλασική μουσική.

3 1 δούλευε, 2 ξεχνούσε, 3 ζούσε, 4 Είχαμε

4 1 ξυπνάς, 2 λέει, 3 πηγαίνει, 4 βλέπω, ακούω 5 περπατάει

5 1 βράδυ, 2 βόλτα, 3 όμορφο, 4 φεγγάρι, 5 ουρανός, 6 κρύωνε, 7 περπατούσαμε, 8 ταβέρνα, 9 περίμενε, 10 κάρβουνα

6 *Horizontal:* ΠΟΥΛΙ, ΚΑΡΠΟΥΖΙ, ΔΑΣΟΣ, ΓΑΡΔΕΝΙΑ, ΒΑΣΙΛΙΚΟΣ, ΜΑΡΟΥΛΙ, ΛΑΧΑΝΙΚΑ, ΤΖΑΚΙ, ΠΑΛΤΟ, ΞΥΛΟ
Vertical: ΓΕΜΑΤΟΣ, ΜΕΛΙ, ΚΑΣΤΑΝΟ

Unit 13

2 1 Τ, 2 F: θέλει φάρμακο. 3 Τ, 4 F: μια ασπιρίνη, 5 F: Είναι στο σπίτι.

3 1 c, 2 e, 3 b, 4 a, 5d

7 1 Κάθεται μπροστά στην οθόνη. 2 μια καινούρια καρέκλα, 3 πονάει, 4 στην αγορά, 5 ένα μπουκάλι σταγόνες,

8 1 Να πάρεις μια ασπιρίνη. 2 Να μην τρως τόσο ψωμί.

12 1 Philip Daskalakis, 2 5 April 1971, 3 Married

16 1 g, 2 f, 3 i, 4 j, 5 b, 6 c, 7 d, 8 a, 9 e, 10 h

17 1 Μ'αρέσει η σκιά. 2 Βρήκε ένα δροσερό μέρος. 3 Αποφεύγουμε τον καυτό ήλιο. 4 Δεν είναι ανάγκη. 5 Δεν υπήρχε καθόλου κίνηση. 6 Στον καύσωνα, μην ξεχνάτε τους ηλικιωμένους. 7 Φέρε την πετσέτα σου. 8 Πίνετε δροσερό νερό με λίγο αλάτι.

18 1 ένα μεγάλο φεστιβάλ, 2 πρωί-πρωί, 3 ηλεκτρονική επικοινωνία, 4 ότι η Σοφία άρχισε να καταλαβαίνει τα σκοτσέζικα, 5 μία σκοτσέζικη φουστανέλα.

19 1 b (Thanasis has had an e-mail from Sophia), 2 c (Sophia herself gets up early to get things ready), 3 c,4 b (She bought her kilt on Princes Street)

219

Test

1 1 αισθάνομαι, 2 κάθομαι, 3 θυμάμαι,
4 κοιμάμαι, 5 φαίνομαι, 6 έρχομαι,
7 χρειάζομαι, 8 σηκώνομαι, 9 εργάζομαι,
10 σκέφτομαι

2 1 Πονάει το δόντι του. 2 Πονάει το
στομάχι της 3 Έχει πυρετό. 3 Πονάει η
πλάτη της .

3 1 Τι έχεις; 2 Ποιά είναι η ημερομηνία
γεννήσεώς σας; 3 Ποιά είναι η διεύθυνσή
σας; 4 Πως λέγεστε;

4 1 φαίνεται, πονάει, 2 κάθομαι, σκέφτομαι,
3 αλλάξω, χρειάζεται, 4 ήταν, πήγε,
5 σηκώνονται, κάθονται

5 1 Μόλις, 2 και, 3 και, 4 κανένα, 5 πουθενά,
6 ούτε, 7 ούτε, 8 πάνω, 9 άλλο, 10 αμέσως

6 Possible answers
How you feel: Σήμερα αισθάνομαι
χάλια/πολύ άσχημα /Δεν είμαι καθόλου
καλά. Αισθάνομαι καλύτερα/εντάξει/μιά
χαρά. Αισθάνομαι υπέροχα.
What exercise you did: Έτρεξα
5 χιλιόμετρα/έπαιξα τένις/έκανα
γυμναστική/πήγα βόλτα με τα πόδια/με το
ποδήλατο/περπάτησα στα βουνα/έκανα
μάθημα αερόμπικ.
What hurts: Πονάει το
στομάχι/χέρι/αυτί/δόντι/πόδι (etc.) μου.
Έχω πονοκέφαλο/πυρετό/γρίπη/βήχα. Δεν
είμαι άρρωστος – τίποτα δεν πονάει!

Unit 14

2 Α: Σωτήρης: ψηλός, έξυπνος, σοβαρός,
Β: Ανδρέας: δυνατός, έξυπνος, ήρεμος,
πρακτικός. Ούτε ο Σωτήρης, ούτε ο
Ανδρέας είναι νευρικός. Δεν ξέρουμε
ποιος είναι ξανθός και ποιος είναι
μελαχρινός.

3 1 πιο σοβαρό / σοβαρότερο, 2 πιο ψηλός /
ψηλότερος, 3 πιο πρακτικές

7 1 last year, 2 the cheaper of the two,
3 Kosta didn't want to spend so much,
4 it's been going for ten years without
any problems

8 1 Το κουτί έχει περισσότερα χρήματα από
την τσάντα. 2 Το μπουκάλι έχει
περισσότερο λάδι από το ποτήρι. 3 Ο
Σταμάτης εχει λιγότερες μπίρες από τον
Γρηγόρη. 4 Το Σνόουντον έχει λιγότερο
χιόνι από τον Όλυμπο.

12 1 F: Η Χριστίνα του λέει να σπουδάσει
αρχιτέκτονας. 2 Τ, 3 F: ιστορικά, ο πιο
γνωστός, όχι ο πιο γνωστός της εποχής
μας.

13 1 Ποιανού είναι το πλυντήριο; Είναι δικό
του. 2 Ποιανού είναι η έκθεση; Είναι δική
της. 3 Ποιανού είναι οι εγκυκλοπαίδειες;
Είναι δικές τους. 4 Ποιανού είναι ο
καθρέφτης; Είναι δικός μας.

16 1 Christmas, 2 original (πρωτότυπο δώρο)

and incredible/fantastic (απίθανα δώρα),
3 It is the greatest (η μεγαλύτερη
ποικιλία). 4 They are the best (Οι
καλύτερες τιμές). 5 He has the most (τις
περισσότερες).

17 1a ο σκληρός δίσκος, b το πληκτρολόγιο,
c η οθόνη, d το ποντίκι, 2 exclusive: ΦΠΑ
– sales tax – is added to the first
amount given, 3. €395 downpayment
with eight further monthly payments at
€170, 4 a free printer (which has an
automatic feeder), 5 a one-year
guarantee

18 1 ο Πέτρος, 2 στις Βρυξέλλες, 3 Είναι
ξανθό, έξυπνο και όμορφο. 4 στην Βοστόνη
για να βοηθήσει τον Κραίηγκ με κάτι
ηλεκτρονικές συσκευές, 5 ο Κραίηγκ,
6 την βοήθεια του Θανάση

19 Thanasis remains good friends with
Sophia and all her family. He is young
Manolaki's godfather. He has a brilliant
career in computers and is at the moment
in Boston with Craig, where they are
exploring new technological equipment
which will be useful to Craig's
archaeological research. Pericles can't
wait for Thanasis to get back, so that he
can take a look at Pericles' failing system.

Test

1 1 Οι Πυραμίδες είναι πιό παλιές από τον
Παρθενώνα. 2 Ο Σωτήρης είναι πιό
σοβαρός απο τον Ανδρέα. 3 Η Αλίκη είναι
πιό ξανθιά από την Μαρινέλλα. 4 Το
σκόρδο είναι πιό δυνατό από το μαϊντανό.
5 Το κομπιούτερ είναι πιό ακριβό από το
ποδήλατο. 6 Η Αυστραλία είναι πιο
μεγάλη από την Αγγλία. 7 Η Τζάγκουαρ
είναι πιό ακριβή από το Μίνι. 8 Η φίλη
μου είναι πιό όμορφη από την φίλη σου.
9 Ο Όμηρος είναι πιό καλός από τον
Σέξπηρ (or vice-versa). 10 Το Έβερεστ
είναι πιό ψηλό από τον Όλυμπο.

2 1 μικρότερος, 2 πλούσιος, 3 λιγότερα,
4 ήρεμος, 5 ξανθιά, 6 ψηλός

3 1 οθόνη 2 πληκτρολόγιο 3 ποντίκι
4 εκτυπωτής

4 ο Πάνος: η γραβάτα είναι δική του
η μαθήτρια: η τσάντα είναι δική της
οι τουρίστες: οι γάτες είναι δικές τους

5 1 Ποια από τις δύο είναι πιό ξανθιά;
2 Πλήρωσες περισσότερα για το καινούριο
ρολόι; 3 Ποιο είναι το ψηλότερο βουνό
του κόσμου; 4 Ποιανού γυαλιά είναι αυτά;
5 Είναι η σειρά σου;

6 1 διαλέξω, 2 ξοδέψω, 3 Πήγα, 4 αγόρασα,
5 γύρισα, 6 είδα, 7 λειτουργούσε,
8 ρυθμίσω, 9 έληξε, 10 θα το αλλάξω

Review 4

1 Nouns referring to people: αρχιτέκτονας,
βασιλοπούλα, εγγόνι, εργάτης, διευθυντής,
επιχειρηματίας, νοσοκόμα, οδοντίατρος,

συνταξιούχος

Nouns referring to things: αγριόχορτο, αλάτι, έκθεση, καθρέφτης, κάρβουνο, παιχνίδι, πόλεμος, σταφύλι, συσκευή

Adjectives: άρρωστες, γεμάτο, διάσημες, δυνατοί, έξυπνος, ήσυχη, ξένοι*, σκοτεινό, φτωχό

Verbs: διαλέγω, έρχομαι, ζηλεύουμε, κάθομαι, κρυώνουμε, λειτουργούν, ξαπλώνει, ξυπνάω, πληρώνεις, φύτεψα

* ξένοι could also be a noun referring to people

2 1 e, 2 d, 3 f, 4 a, 5 b, 6 c

3 1 περίμενε, 2 είχες, 3 διάβασες, 4 ήταν, 5 διάλεξαν, 6 άρεσε, πήρε, 7 είπαν, 8 ήθελε, 9 είδες, 10 έκανε, γύρισε

4 1 αισθάνεται, 2 κοιμούνται, 3A εργάζεστε, 3B εργαζόμαστε, 4 έρχομαι, 5 σκέφτεται

5 1 Τους αρέσει να κολυμπάνε/να κάνουν μπάνιο. 2 Μ'αρέσει να ψαρεύω. 3 3 Του Παύλου του αρέσει να τρώει παγωτό. 4 Της Ράνιας της αρέσει να διαβάζει.

6 1 Πηγαίναμε στο σχολείο με τα πόδια. 2 Παίζανε στο χωράφι. 3 Τρώγανε μπροστά στο τζάκι. 4 Έλεγε παραμύθια/ιστορίες.

7 1 πιό ήρεμη, 2 ευχαριστημένοι, 3 περισσότερα, 4 δυνατότερος, πιο πρακτικός, 5 καλύτερη

8 1 all sizes – υπάρχουν απ'όλα τα μεγέθη, 100% cotton – εκατό τοις εκατό βαμβακερές, 2 superb colours and designs – υπέροχα χρώματα και σχέδια, 3 for bathing at home, in the swimming-pool, in the sea – για μπάνιο – στο σπίτι, στην πισίνα, στη θάλασσα, 4 towels for all the family – for tall people and short, slim, and stout – Πετσέτες για όλη την οικογένεια – ψηλούς και κοντούς, λεπτούς και χοντρούς, 5 bargain prices (we have the best prices in Greece) – τιμές ευκαιρίας (έχουμε τις καλύτερες τιμές στην Ελλάδα), 6 yes (pay cash or by credit card) – πληρώστε τοις μετρητοίς* ή με πιστωτική κάρτα, 7 (i) large from 12,000 drachmas – μεγάλες από 12.000 δραχμές, (ii) for the kitchen: 3 for 1000 drachmas – για κουζίνα: τρεις για 1000 δραχμές, 8 two weeks: from 3–17 May – από 3 Μαΐου μέχρι 17 Μαΐου. [* τοις μετρητοίς - old grammatical form]

9 1 τα μαλλιά ξανθά, τα μάτια μαύρα, 2 από τον παππού, 3 τον Ιούνιο, 4 του αρέσει να πηγαίνει βόλτες παντού – στο πάρκο, στη θάλασσα, στα μαγαζιά, 5 σοκολάτες, 6 φρούτα, 7 πατατάκια και αυγό, 8 κοιμάται λιγάκι, 9 δύο

Grammar summary

Nouns

Greek nouns vary in form depending on number (singular or plural), gender and case.

Gender
Nouns are either masculine, feminine or neuter.

masculine	singular	plural
ending in	-ος	-οι
	ο Άγγλος	οι Άγγλοι
ending in	-ας	-ες
	ο Έλληνας	οι Έλληνες
ending in	-ης	-ες
	ο χάρτης	οι χάρτες

feminine	singular	plural
ending in	-α	-ες
	η γυναίκα	οι γυναίκες
ending in	-η	-ες
	η τιμή	οι τιμές

neuter	singular	plural
ending in	-ι	-ια
	το παιδί	τα παιδιά
ending in	-ο	-α
	το ξενοδοχείο	τα ξενοδοχεία
ending in	-μα	-ματα
	το πρόβλημα	τα προβλήματα

Case

The *nominative* case is used for the *subject* of a sentence:
Ο άνδρας ξέρει την τιμή. *The man* knows the price.
The *accusative* case is used for the *object* of a sentence.
Ο άνδρας ξέρει **την τιμή**. The man knows *the price*.
The *genitive* case shows *possession*.
the woman's shoe – το παπούτσι **της γυναίκας**
The following charts cover the noun groups used in this course.

1 Masculine in -ος/-οι

sg. nominative	ο	φίλος	άνθρωπος
accusative	τον	φίλο	άνθρωπο
genitive	του	φίλου	ανθρώπου
pl. nominative	οι	φίλοι	άνθρωποι
accusative	τους	φίλους	ανθρώπους
genitive	των	φίλων	ανθρώπων

2 Masculine in -ας/-ες

sg.			
nominative	ο	αγώνας	άνδρας
accusative	τον	αγώνα	άνδρα
genitive	του	αγώνα	άνδρα
pl.			
nominative	οι	αγώνες	άνδρες
accusative	τους	αγώνες	άνδρες
genitive	των	αγώνων	ανδρών

3 Masculine in -ης/-ες

sg.			
nominative	ο	καθηγητής	χάρτης
accusative	τον	καθηγητή	χάρτη
genitive	του	καθηγητή	χάρτη
pl.			
nominative	οι	καθηγητές	χάρτες
accusative	τους	καθηγητές	χάρτες
genitive	των	καθηγητών	χαρτών

4 Feminine in -α/-ες

sg.			
nominative	η	εφημερίδα	γυναίκα
accusative	την	εφημερίδα	γυναίκα
genitive	της	εφημερίδας	γυναίκας
pl.			
nominative	οι	εφημερίδες	γυναίκες
accusative	τις	εφημερίδες	γυναίκες
genitive	των	εφημερίδων	γυναικών

5 Feminine in -η/-ες

sg.			pl.		
nominative	η	βιβλιοθήκη	οι	βιβλιοθήκες
accusative	την	βιβλιοθήκη	τις	βιβλιοθήκες
genitive	της	βιβλιοθήκης	των	βιβλιοθηκών

6 Feminine in -η/-εις

sg.			pl.		
nominative	η	πόλη	οι	πόλεις
accusative	την	πόλη	τις	πόλεις
genitive	της	πόλης	των	πόλεων

7 Neuter in -ι/-ια

sg.			pl.		
nominative	το	τραπέζι	τα	τραπέζια
accusative	το	τραπέζι	τα	τραπέζια
genitive	του	τραπεζιού	των	τραπεζιών

8 Neuter in -ο/-α

sg.			pl.		
nominative	το	διαβατήριο	τα	διαβατήρια
accusative	το	διαβατήριο	τα	διαβατήρια
genitive	του	διαβατηρίου	των	διαβατηρίων

9 Neuter in -μα/-ματα

sg.			pl.		
nominative	το	πρόβλημα	τα	προβλήματα
accusative	το	πρόβλημα	τα	προβλήματα
genitive	του	προβλήματος	των	προβλημάτων

Some nouns are irregular, eg. η οδός which is masculine in form but is a feminine noun - η - and is qualified by adjectives in the feminine: η κύρια οδός - the main street.

The definite and indefinite articles

The Greek for the definite article 'the' is ο with a masculine noun, η with a feminine noun, and το with a neuter noun. Articles change to suit the case and number of the noun. For the form of the definite article in all cases, see the noun charts on pp. 222-3.

The Greek for the indefinite article 'a' is ένας with a masculine noun, μια with a feminine noun, and ένα with a neuter noun.

	masculine	*feminine*	*neuter*
nominative	ένας	μια	ένα
accusative	ένα(ν)	μια	ένα
genitive	ενός	μιας	ενός

The definite article is used more frequently in Greek than in English. It is used:
– with proper names: Ο Τάκης, Η Λέλα, Η Αγγλία, Το Βέλγιο
– when referring to nouns even in a general way:
   Μ'αρέσει η μουσική. I like music.
   Μ'αρέσουν οι φράουλες. I like strawberries.

Greek does not use the indefinite article before names of occupations:
   Είμαι φοιτήτρια. I'm a student.

Adjectives

Agreement
Adjectives agree in number, gender and case with the noun they qualify.

Adjectives covered in this course follow one of the following patterns.
ending in -ος/-η/-ο

		masculine	*feminine*	*neuter*
sg.	*nominative*	άσχημος	άσχημη	άσχημο
	accusative	άσχημο	άσχημη	άσχημο
	genitive	άσχημου	άσχημης	άσχημου
pl.	*nominative*	άσχημοι	άσχημες	άσχημα
	accusative	άσχημους	άσχημες	άσχημα
	genitive	άσχημων	άσχημων	άσχημων

ending in *-ος/-α/-ο*

		masculine	*feminine*	*neuter*
sg.	*nominative*	ωραίος	ωραία	ωραίο
	accusative	ωραίο	ωραία	ωραίο
	genitive	ωραίου	ωραίας	ωραίου

pl. nominative	ωραίοι	ωραίες	ωραία
accusative	ωραίους	ωραίες	ωραία
genitive	ωραίων	ωραίων	ωραίων

The adjective πολύς / πολλή / πολύ is irregular.

	masculine	feminine	neuter
sg. nominative	πολύς	πολλή	πολύ
accusative	πολύ	πολλή	πολύ
genitive	πολύ	πολλής	πολύ
pl. nominative	πολλοί	πολλές	πολλά
accusative	πολλούς	πολλές	πολλά
genitive	πολλών	πολλών	πολλών

Comparatives

To make a comparison between two things you use *the construction* πιο + adjective + από:

Το ούζο είναι πιο ακριβό από την ρετσίνα. Ouzo is more expensive than retsina.

or the *comparative form* of the adjective, which is made up of the adjective stem + -ότερος/-ότερη/-ότερο or -ύτερος/-ύτερη/-ύτερο

Η Νίκη είναι ψηλότερη από την Βιολέτα. Nicky is taller than Violet.

To say 'as ... as', you use τόσο + adjective + όσο:

Ο πατέρας του δεν ήταν τόσο πλούσιος όσο ο Ροκεφέλερ. His father was not as rich as Rockefeller.

Superlatives

The superlative in Greek is formed by putting the relevant definite article – ο/ η/το /οι/οι/τα – in front of the comparative form.

ο πιο κοντός άνδρας στο δωμάτιο – the shortest man in the room
Διάλεξε το ακριβότερο αυτοκίνητο της έκθεσης. She chose the most expensive car in the exhibition.

Irregular comparatives and superlatives

καλός/ή/ό – good   καλύτερος/η/ο – better
ο/η/το καλύτερος/η/ο – best

κακός/ιά or -ή/ό – bad   χειρότερος/η/ο – worse
ο/η/το χειρότερος/η/ο – worst

πολύς – much, many   περισσότερος/η/ο – more
ο/η/το περισσότερος/η/ο – the most
λίγος little, few   λιγότερος/η/ο – less/fewer
ο/η/το λιγότερος/η/ο – the least

Ποιος θέλει περισσότερο αλάτι; Who wants more salt?
Είσαστε οι καλύτεροι μαθητές του σχολείου. You're **the best** pupils in the school.*

In comparisons like this*, Greek usually uses the *genitive*:
ο καλύτερος ηθοποιός του κόσμου – the best actor in the world   **225**

Question forms

ποιος	who	ποιανού	whose
ποιο	which	πόσο	how much

Ποιος είναι αυτός; Who is that?
Ποιανού είναι αυτό; Whose is that?
Πόσο είναι αυτό; How much is that?
Ποιο χρώμα θέλετε; Which colour do you want?

Note that when these question words are used as adjectives, they change to match the number, gender, and case of the questioned.

ποιος

		masculine	feminine	neuter
sg.	nominative	ποιος	ποια	ποιο
	accusative	ποιον	ποια	ποιο
	genitive	ποιανού	ποιανής	ποιανού
pl.	nominative	ποιοι	ποιες	ποια
	accusative	ποιους	ποιες	ποια
	genitive	ποιανών	ποιανών	ποιανών

πόσος/η/ο ('how much, how many') changes like a standard adjective.

Pronouns

As the *subject* of the sentence (*nominative*)

I	εγώ	we	εμείς
you	εσύ	you	εσείς
he, she, it	αυτός, αυτή, αυτό	they	αυτοί

As the person is understood in the verb ending, the pronoun is used for emphasis or to ask a question.

Εμείς θέλουμε κοτόπουλο. **Εσείς**; We want chicken. And you?

Notes

1 The εσύ form is used when speaking to a child or someone you know well. (informal form).

2 The εσείς form is used when speaking to a person you don't know well or to a group of people (including children). (formal/polite form)

As the *object* of the sentence (*accusative/genitive*)

direct object (accusative)		indirect object and possessive (genitive)	
με	μας	μου	μας
σε	σας	σου	σας
τον/την/το	τους/τις/τα	του/της/του	τους

The indirect object pronoun is used when the object is indirectly affected by the action of the verb: often a preposition is used or understood after the verb. Verbs taking an indirect object include δίνω, ('give'), στέλνω ('send'), λέω ('say'), γράφω ('write'), απαντ(ά)ω ('reply'), τηλεφων(ά)ω ('telephone'), φέρνω ('bring').

Της δίνω ένα δώρο. I give her a gift / I give a gift to her.

The position of direct and indirect object pronouns

Both direct and indirect object pronouns come *before* the verb:

Τον καταλαβαίνετε; Do you understand him?

Του στείλανε ένα ωραίο βιβλίο. They sent him a nice book.

When there are two pronouns, the indirect comes before direct.

Θα μου το δώσει. He'll give it to me.

However, when the verb is in the imperative, the pronoun comes after the verb. Here, when there are two object pronouns, the indirect can come *before* or *after* the direct.

Δώσε μου τον κατάλογο. Give me the menu.

Φέρε μου το! / Φέρε το μου! Bring it to me!

There is a strong form of the object pronoun, used for emphasis.

me	εμένα	we	εμάς
you	εσένα	you	εσάς
him, her, it	αυτόν/αυτή(ν)/αυτό	them	αυτούς/αυτές/αυτά

Αυτόν θα τον δουμε στην Αθήνα, αυτούς στον Πειραιά. We'll see *him* in Athens, *them* in Piraeus.

Possessive pronouns

The possessive pronoun is the same as indirect object pronoun: see the chart on page 95. The possessive pronoun comes *after* the noun.

το αυτοκίνητό μου* – my car

ο φίλος του – his friend

η γάτα τους – their cat

*Note that words stressed on the third last syllable are given a second stress when they are followed by one of these pronouns.

To say 'mine', 'yours', 'his', 'hers', etc., the article + the adjective δικός + the possessive pronoun is used. Each pronoun follows the pattern of 'mine':

'mine'

ο δικός μου	η δική μου	το δικό μου
το δικό μου	τη δική μου	το δικό μου
του δικού μου	της δικής μου	του δικού μου
οι δικοί μου	οι δικές μου	τα δικά μου
τους δικούς μου	τις δικές μου	τα δικά μου
των δικών μου	των δικών μου	των δικών μου

δικός agrees with the number, gender and case of the noun referred to, and the pronoun refers to the possessor.

Ο σκύλος είναι δικός του. The dog is his.

Τα παπούτσια δεν είναι δικά σου. The shoes are not yours.

227

Demonstrative pronouns/adjectives

Demonstrative pronouns include: αυτός/ή/ό - this/that, τούτος/η/ο - this/this one, εκείνος/η/ο - that/that one, τόσος/η/ο - so much/many, τέτοιος/α/ο - such. These pronouns follow the pattern of adjectives (as indicated) – see page 224.

Θέλω τούτο το μήλο, όχι εκείνο. I want this apple, not that one.

Note the word pattern is pronoun/adjective + article + noun:

αυτές οι καρέκλες – these chairs

εκείνα τα καρπούζια – those watermelons

Prepositions

- στο(ν)/στη(ν)/στο to say 'to' / 'in' / 'at' / 'on' a country/place
This form is a combination of σε + the relevant article, το(ν) / τη(ν) / το, matching the gender, number, and case of the related noun. Most prepositions are followed by the *accusative* case.

Η αδελφή μου πήγε **στην** Ιταλία. My sister went **to** Italy. (Italy, η Ιταλία, is feminine.)

Ο Γιάννης δεν είναι **στο** σπίτι. John is not **at** home. (Home, το σπίτι, is neuter.)

Είμαστε **στις** Βρυξέλλες. We're **in** Brussels. (Brussels, οι Βρυξέλλες, is feminine plural.)

- με το(ν)/τη(ν)/το+ *means of transport*
με ('with'), is used to introduce means of transport: με το αυτοκίνητο ('by car'), see page 77 for further examples.

- Prepositions showing things in relation to each other
The most common combinations are the following, using σε (as discussed above) and από ('from').

Note that there is no 'σ' (σε) in front of the article when you have από.

preposition + στο(ν)/στη(ν)/στο		*preposition* + από το(ν)/τη(ν)/το	
κοντά στο*	near	μακριά από το**	far from
δίπλα στο	next to/beside	πίσω από το	behind
μπροστά στο	in front of	απέναντι από το	opposite
μέσα στο	inside	πάνω από το	above
		κάτω από το	below/under
		έξω από το	outside

* στο(ν)/στη(ν)/στο/στους/στις/στα depending on the number and gender of the noun that follows

** το(ν)/τη(ν)/το/τους/τις/τα depending on the number and gender of the noun that follows

Adverbs

Many adverbs (often derived from adjectives) end in -α or -ως. Adverbs in -α are mostly adverbs of manner, e.g. γλυκά ('sweetly'), δυνατά - ('strongly', 'loudly'), σωστά - ('correctly'). Adverbs of frequency include ταχτικά ('regularly'), and συχνά ('often'). Adverbs ending in -ως are often derived from learned adjectives. Examples include αμέσως ('immediately'), τελείως ('completely'), ακριβώς ('exactly'), δυστυχώς ('unfortunately'), ευτυχώς ('fortunately').

Verbs

There are 2 kinds of regular verbs in Greek – Group 1 and Group 2 (a and b). *Group 1* consists of all verbs which are not stressed on the last syllable, such as κάνω ('do') and δουλεύω ('work'). *Group 2* consists of all verbs that end in -άω, or -ώ, such as μιλάω ('speak', 'talk'), αγαπάω ('love'), and οδηγώ ('drive').

In addition to Group 1 and Group 2, there are a few *irregular* verbs.

Greek verbs are made up of a *stem + endings*. They normally have two (or sometimes three) different stems. The ending tells you who is doing the action.

1 Group 1 verbs

	present endings	past endings	with θα/να (future/subjunctive): 2nd stem + present endings
I	-ω	-α	2nd stem + -ω
you (*singular*)	-εις	-ες	2nd stem + -εις
he/she/it	-ει	-ε	2nd stem + -ει
we	-ουμε	-αμε	2nd stem + -ουμε
you (*plural*)	-ετε	-ατε	2nd stem + -ετε
they	-ουν(ε)	-ανε	2nd stem + -ουν(ε)

Group 1 can be further subdivided into two categories. Note that A and B show general patterns – there are exceptions

A Group 1 verbs which do not change stem.
e.g. κάνω (do), θέλω (want), and ξέρω (know).

	present	past	with θα/να (fut./subj.): 2nd stem + pres. endings
I	κάνω	έκανα	κάνω
you (*singular*)	κάνεις	έκανες	κάνεις
he/she/it	κάνει	έκανε	κάνει
we	κάνουμε	κάναμε	κάνουμε
you (*plural*)	κάνετε	κάνατε	κάνετε
they	κάνουν(ε)	κάναν(ε)	κάνουν(ε)

B Group 1 verbs which follow certain patterns in the stem

(i) ζ>σ: ζ at the end of the first stem becomes σ at the end of the second e.g. αγοράζω – θα αγοράσω (buy), διαβάζω – θα διαβάσω (read), γυρίζω – θα γυρίσω (return)

αγοράζω – buy

229

	present	past	with θα/να (fut./subj.): 2nd stem + pres. endings
I	αγοράζω	αγόρασα	αγοράσω
you (*singular*)	αγοράζεις	αγόρασες	αγοράσεις
he/she/it	αγοράζει	αγόρασε	αγοράσει
we	αγοράζουμε	αγοράσαμε	αγοράσουμε
you (*plural*)	αγοράζετε	αγοράσατε	αγοράσετε
they	αγοράζουν(ε)	αγοράσαν(ε)	αγοράσουν(ε)

(ii) ν>σ: ν at the end of the first stem becomes σ at the end of the second, e.g. φτάνω – θα φτάσω (arrive), κλείνω – θα κλείσω (close), πληρώνω – θα πληρώσω (pay)

φτάνω – arrive

	present	past	with θα/να (fut./subj.): 2nd stem + pres. endings
I	φτάνω	έφτασα	φτάσω
you (*singular*)	φτάνεις	έφτασες	φτάσεις ...

(iii) φ/ευ >ψ: φ or ευ at the end of the first stem becomes ψ at the end of the second e.g. γράφω – θα γράψω (pay), χορεύω – θα χορέψω (dance), μαγειρεύω – θα μαγειρέψω (cook)

φ >ψ γράφω – write

	present	past	with θα/να (fut./subj.): 2nd stem + pres. endings
I	γράφω	έγραψα	γράψω
you (*singular*)	γράφεις	έγραψες	γράψεις ...

(iv) γ/ζ/χ >ξ: γ, sometimes ζ, or χ at the end of the first stem becomes ξ at the end of the second, e.g. ανοίγω – θα ανοίξω (open), παίζω – θα παίξω (play), τρέχω – θα τρέξω (run)

γ>ξ ανοίγω – open

	present	past	with θα/να (fut./subj.): 2nd stem + pres. endings
I	ανοίγω	άνοιξα	ανοίξω
you (*singular*)	ανοίγεις	άνοιξες	ανοίξεις ...

2 Group 2 verbs

Group 2a: verbs stressed on the last syllable, ending in -(ά)ω

	present endings	past endings	with θα/να (fut./subj.): 2nd stem + pres. endings
I	(α)ώ	-α	2nd stem + -ω
you (*singular*)	-άς	-ες	2nd stem + -εις
he/she/it	-άει	-ε	2nd stem + -ει
we	-άμε	-αμε	2nd stem + -ουμε
you (*plural*)	-άτε	-ατε	2nd stem + -ετε
they	-άν(ε)	-αν(ε)	2nd stem + -ουν(ε)

Group 2a verbs can be subdivided into categories that follow certain patterns in the past tense:

(i) stem + -ησ- e.g. μιλ(ά)ω – θα μιλήσω (speak)

μιλάω/μιλώ – speak

	present	past	with θα/να (fut./subj.): 2nd stem + pres. endings
I	μιλ(ά)ω	μίλησα	μιλήσω
you (*singular*)	μιλάς	μίλησες	μιλήσεις
he/she/it	μιλάει	μίλησε	μιλήσει
we	μιλάμε	μιλήσαμε	μιλήσουμε
you (*plural*)	μιλάτε	μιλήσατε	μιλήσετε
they	μιλάν(ε)	μίλησαν(ε)	μιλήσουν(ε)

(ii) stem + -ασ- e.g. περν(ά)ω – θα περάσω (pass)

περν(ά)ω/περνώ – pass

	present	past	with θα/να (fut./subj.): 2nd stem + pres. endings
I	περν(ά)ω	πέρασα	περάσω
you (*singular*)	περνάς	πέρασες	περάσεις ...

(iii) stem + -εσ- e.g. φορ(ά)ω – θα φορέσω (wear)

φοράω/φορώ – wear

	present	past	with θα/να (fut./subj.): 2nd stem + pres. endings
I	φορ(ά)ω	φόρεσα	φορέσω
you (*singular*)	φοράς	φόρεσες	φορέσεις ...

Group 2b: verbs stressed in the last syllable, which do **not** have the optional -(α)- as part of the ending in the present tense. e.g. οδηγώ (drive), καλώ (invite).

	present endings	past endings	with θα/να (fut./subj.): 2nd stem + pres. endings
I	οδηγώ	οδήγησα	οδηγήσω
you (*singular*)	οδηγείς	οδήγησες	οδηγήσεις
he/she/it	οδηγεί	οδήγησε	οδηγήσει
we	οδηγούμε	οδηγήσαμε	οδηγήσουμε
you (*plural*)	οδηγείτε	οδηγήσατε	οδηγήσετε
they	οδηγούν(ε)	οδήγησαν(ε)	οδηγήσουν(ε)

3 Irregular verbs

τρώω – έφαγα – **θα φαω** (eat)

	present	past	with θα/να (fut./subj.): 2nd stem + pres. endings
I	τρώω	έφαγα	φάω
you (*singular*)	τρως	έφαγες	φας
he/she/it	τρώει	έφαγε	φάει
we	τρώμε	φάγαμε	φάμε
you (*plural*)	τρώτε	φάγατε	φάτε
they	τρών(ε)	φάγαν(ε)	φάν(ε)

πίνω – ήπια – θα πιώ (drink)

	present	past	with θα/να (fut./subj.): 2nd stem + pres. endings
I	πίνω	ήπια	πιω
you (*singular*)	πίνεις	ήπιες	πιεις
he/she/it	πίνει	ήπιε	πιει
we	πίνουμε	ήπιαμε	πιούμε
you (*plural*)	πίνετε	ήπιατε	πιείτε
they	πίνουν(ε)	ήπιαν(ε)	πιούν(ε)

λέω – είπα – θα πω (say)

	present	past	with θα/να (fut./subj.): 2nd stem + pres. endings
I	λέω	είπα	πω
you (*singular*)	λες	είπες	πεις
he/she/it	λέει	είπε	πει
we	λέμε	είπαμε	πούμε
you (*plural*)	λέτε	είπατε	πείτε
they	λέν(ε)	είπαν(ε)	πουν(ε)

Note also:
βλέπω – είδα – θα δω (see, watch)
δίνω – έδωσα – θα δώσω (give)
φεύγω – έφυγα – θα φύγω (leave)

είμαι – am

	present	past	with θα/να (fut./subj.):
I	είμαι	ήμουν(α)	είμαι
you (*singular*)	είσαι	ήσουν(α)	είσαι
he/she/it	είναι	ήταν(ε)	είναι
we	είμαστε	ήμασταν	είμαστε
you (*plural*)	είσαστε/είστε	ήσασταν	είστε/είσαστε
they	είναι	ήταν(ε)	είναι

υπάρχω – am/exist (there is)

	present	imperfect	past
I	υπάρχω	υπήρχα	υπήρξα
you (*singular*)	υπάρχεις	υπήρχες	υπήρξες
he/she/it	υπάρχει	υπήρχε	υπήρξε
we	υπάρχουμε	υπήρχαμε	υπήρξαμε
you (*plural*)	υπάρχετε	υπήρχατε	υπήρξατε
they	υπάρχουν(ε)	υπήρχαν(ε)	υπήρξαν(ε)

With υπάρχω, for future and subjunctive uses, the stem used depends on the context.

Passive-form verbs (present tense)

έρχομαι – come

I	έρχομαι	we	ερχόμαστε
you (*singular*)	έρχεσαι	you (*plural*)	έρχόσαστε
he/she/it	έρχεται	they	έρχονται

There is a slight variation for verbs ending in -αμαι, e.g. θυμάμαι (remember), κοιμάμαι (sleep), λυπάμαι (be sorry, regret).

κοιμάμαι – sleep

I	κοιμάμαι	we	κοιμόμαστε
you (*singular*)	κοιμάσαι	you (*plural*)	κοιμάστε
he/she/it	κοιμάται	they	κοιμούνται

Tenses

The present tense
Greek has only one form for the present tense, so δουλεύω is the equivalent of both 'I work' and 'I am working'.

The future
In Greek, the future simple is formed with θα + second stem stem + present endings, and the future continuous with θα + first stem + the present endings.

θα μαγειρέψω – I'll cook	θα μαγειρεύω – I'll be cooking
θα μιλήσω – I'll speak	θα μιλάω – I'll be speaking
θα φάω – I'll eat	θα τρώω – I'll be eating

The imperfect tense
The imperfect tense is used

1 to describe something which used to happen frequently or regularly in the past:
    Χόρευα **κάθε** Σάββατο. I used to dance every Saturday.

2 to describe what was happening or what the situation was when something else happened:
    Έβλεπα τηλεόραση όταν έφτασε. I was watching television when she arrived.

To form the imperfect tense:
– for Group 1 verbs, use the first stem together with the past endings. Add the augment where necessary.

I	έκανα	έτρεχα	we	κάναμε	τρέχαμε
you	έκανες	έτρεχες	you (*pl*)	κάνατε	τρέχατε
/she/it	έκανε	έτρεχε	they	έκαναν(ε)	έτρεχαν(ε)

– for Group 2 verbs, use the first stem + -ούσ- + past endings

I	μιλούσα	οδηγούσα	we	μιλούσαμε	οδηγούσαμε
you (*s*)	μιλούσες	οδηγούσες	you (*pl*)	μιλούσατε	οδηγούσατε
he/she/it	μιλούσε	οδηγούσε	they	μιλούσαν(ε)	οδηγούσαν(ε)

– the imperfect of irregular verbs uses the same principle: first stem + past endings (with augment where necessary). Notice also the γ used to separate/add fluidity to two independent, consecutive vowel sounds.

I	έτρωγα	έπινα	έλεγα	έβλεπα
you (*singular*)	έτρωγες	έπινες	έλεγες	έβλεπες ...

The negative

To give the negative of any verb, place δεν in front of it.

Δεν ξέρω. I don't know.

The imperative

The imperative is used to give orders or instructions. It is formed using the second stem + -ε when speaking to a child or a close friend, and second stem + -(ε)τε for formal situations and when addressing more than one person.

δούλεψε – (you singular) work! δουλέψτε– (you plural) work!

The negative imperative is formed using μη(ν) with the standard second person present tense of the verb.

μη δουλεύεις – don't work (you singular)
μη δουλεύετε – don't work (you plural)

The subjunctive

The subjunctive is used to show an action or state as something not (yet) fulfilled – i.e. to express a wish, a desire, an expectation, a hope, an obligation, and so on. It is most often used in constructions with να. Examples of the subjunctive include Θέλω να ... (φύγω). I want to ... (leave). /Πρέπει να ... (φύγω). I must ... (leave)./ Ίσως να ... (φύγω). Perhaps I'll ... (leave). See Units 10, 13.

Numbers

See pages 21, 35, 53 and 65 for lists of numbers.

When numbers are used with nouns, they agree with the thing(s) being described, e.g. drachmas (feminine) or dollars (neuter).

Verb list

This is a list of all verbs shown in the course. Only present and past tense is shown for the regular verbs. Remember that the future is formed using the past stem (perfective) + the present tense endings. (Those marked * are second conjugation: stressed in the last syllable; add -ασ-, -ησ-, or -εσ- to form the second stem; use second conjugation endings.)

Present tense	Past tense	
*αγαπ(α)ώ	αγάπησα	love
αγοράζω	αγόρασα	buy
ακούω	άκουσα	hear, listen to
αλλάζω	άλλαξα	change
ανοίγω	άνοιξα	open
αξίζω	άξιζα	am worth it
απαντ(ά)ω	απάντησα	answer
*αργώ	άργησα	delay, am late
αρχίζω	άρχισα	start, begin
αφήνω	άφησα	leave, leave alone, allow
βάζω	έβαλα	put, put on
βαφτίζω	βάφτισα	baptize, christen
*βοηθ(α)ώ	βοήθησα	help

βρέχω	έβρεξα	wet
*γελ(α)ώ	γέλασα	laugh
γεμίζω	γέμισα	fill
γιορτάζω	γιόρτασα	celebrate
*γλεντ(α)ώ	γλέντησα	make merry, have fun
γνωρίζω	γνώρισα	recognize, know
γράφω	έγραψα	write
γυρίζω	γύρισα	return, turn
δείχνω	έδειξα	show
διαβάζω	διάβασα	read
διαλέγω	διάλεξα	choose
διαφημίζω	διαφήμισα	advertise
διψ(α)ώ	δίψασα	am thirsty
δουλεύω	δούλεψα	work
ενδιαφέρω	ενδιέφερα	interest
εξετάζω	εξέτασα	examine
ετοιμάζω	ετοίμασα	prepare
ζηλεύω	ζήλεψα	am jealous
*ζητ(α)ώ	ζήτησα	ask for, look for
*ζω	έζησα	live
ησυχάζω	ησύχασα	calm down, relax
θέλω	ήθελα	want
θύμωνω	θύμωσα	get angry
καθαρίζω	καθάρισα	clean
*καλώ	κάλεσα	invite
κάνω	έκανα	do, make
καταλαβαίνω	κατάλαβα	understand
κλείνω	έκλεισα	close, book, reserve
κόβω	έκοψα	chop, cut
κοιτάζω	κοίταξα	see (to), look at
*κρατ(α)ώ	κράτησα	keep, hold
κρύβω	έκρυψα	hide
κρυώνω	κρύωσα	am cold
λειτουργώ	λειτούργησα	function, work
λήγω	έληξα	expire
μαγειρεύω	μαγείρεψα	cook
μαθαίνω	έμαθα	learn
μεγαλώνω	μεγάλωσα	raise, grow up
*μιλ(α)ώ	μίλησα	speak
*μπορώ	μπόρεσα	can, am able to
νοικιάζω	νοίκιασα	rent, hire
νομίζω	νόμισα	think, presume
ξαναλέω	ξαναείπα	repeat
ξαπλώνω	ξάπλωσα	lie down, stretch out
ξέρω	ήξερα	know
*ξεχν(α)ώ	ξέχασα	forget
ξοδεύω	ξόδεψα	spend

*ξυπν(α)ώ	ξύπνησα	wake (up)
*οδηγώ	οδήγησα	drive
οργανώνω	οργάνωσα	organize
παθαίνω	έπαθα	suffer, undergo
παίζω	έπαιξα	play
*πάω	πήγα	go
*πειν(α)ώ	πείνασα	am hungry
περιμένω	περίμενα	wait, wait for, expect
*περν(α)ώ	πέρασα	pass
*περπατ(α)ώ	περπάτησα	walk
*πετ(α)ώ	πέταξα	fly, throw away
πέφτω	έπεσα	fall
πληρώνω	πλήρωσα	pay
*πον(α)ώ	πόνεσα	hurt, ache
ποτίζω	πότισα	water
*πουλ(α)ώ	πούλησα	sell
*προτιμ(α)ώ	προτίμησα	prefer
ρυθμίζω	ρύθμισα	regulate, adjust
*ρωτ(α)ώ	ρώτησα	ask
σερβίρω	σερβίρισα	serve
σπουδάζω	σπούδασα	study, educate
*σταματ(α)ώ	σταμάτησα	stop
στρίβω	έστριψα	turn
στρώνω	έστρωσα	spread, lay
συμπληρώνω	συμπλήρωσα	fill in, complete
συνεχίζω	συνέχισα	continue
συστήνω	σύστησα	recommend, introduce
ταξιδεύω	ταξίδεψα	travel
τελειώνω	τελείωσα	finish, end
*τηλεφων(α)ώ	τηλεφώνησα	telephone
τρέχω	έτρεξα	speed, run
τυλίγω	τύλιξα	wrap
υπάρχω	υπήρξα	exist, am there
φέρνω	έφερα	bring
*φιλ(α)ώ	φίλησα	kiss
*φορ(α)ώ	φόρεσα	wear
φτάνω	έφτασα	arrive
φτιάχνω	έφτιαξα	make, prepare
*φυσ(ά)ω	φύσηξα	blow
φυτεύω	φύτεψα	plant
χαιρετ(α)ώ	χαιρέτησα	greet
*χαλ(α)ώ	χάλασα	break down, go wrong, spoil,
χάνω	έχασα	lose
χιονίζει	χιόνισε	snow (impersonal)
χορεύω	χόρεψα	dance
*χτυπ(α)ώ	χτύπησα	hit, (be) hurt
ψήνω	έψησα	bake, roast, grill

Irregular verbs

There are not that many irregular verbs in Greek. The following are the most frequently used and are covered in this course.

present	past	subjunctive (with θα/να)	
βγαίνω	βγήκα	βγω	go/get out
βλέπω	είδα	δω	see, watch
δίνω	έδωσα	δώσω	give
έχω	είχα	έχω	have
λέω	είπα	πω	say, tell
μένω	έμεινα	μείνω	stay, live
μπαίνω	μπήκα	μπω	go/get in
πάιρνω	πήρα	πάρω	get/take
πηγαίνω/πάω	πήγα	πάω	go
πίνω	ήπια	πιώ	drink
στέλνω	έστειλα	στείλω	send
τρώω	έφαγα	φάω	eat
φεύγω	έφυγα	φύγω	leave

Passive form

(found in the present tense only in this course)

αισθάνομαι	feel	κοιμάμαι	sleep
βιάζομαι	am in a hurry	λέγομαι	am called
γίνομαι	become, happen	λυπάμαι	be sorry, regret
δέχομαι	receive, accept	σηκώνομαι	get up, rise
εγγράφομαι	register, sign up	σκέπτομαι	think, reflect on
επιτρέπεται	it is allowed	φαίνομαι	seem, appear
εργάζομαι	work	φοβάμαι	fear, be afraid of
έρχομαι	come	χαίρομαι	enjoy, delight in
κάθομαι	sit	χρειάζομαι	need

Vocabulary

A

	αγαπ(ά)ω	love
η	Αγγλία	England
	αγγλικά	English (language)
η	αγορά	shopping centre, market
	αγοράζω	buy
το	άγχος	strain, pressure
ο	αγώνας	struggle
η	άδεια	permission, licence, leave
η	αδελφή	sister
ο	αέρας	air, wind
το	αεροπλάνο	aeroplane
ο	αετός	kite
	αισθάνομαι	feel
ο	αιώνας	century
	ακόμα	yet, still
	ακούω	hear, listen to
	ακριβός/ή/ό	expensive
	ακριβώς	exactly
το	αλάτι	salt
η	αλήθεια	truth
	αλήθεια	really
	αλλά	but
	αλλάζω	change
	αλλιώς	otherwise
	άλλος	other, next
	αμάν	good grief
	αμέ	of course [colloquial]
η	Αμερική	America
η	άμμος	sand
το	αμπραγιάζ	clutch
	αν	if
η	ανανέωση	renewal, change
	ανάποδα	wrong way round, upside down, inside out, backwards
ο	αναπτήρας	lighter
η	ανατολή	east
ο	άνδρας	man, husband
η	άνεση	convenience
	άνετος/η/ο	comfortable
ο	άνθρωπος	person
	ανοίγω	open
η	άνοιξη	spring
	ανοιχτός/ή/ό	open
η	αντικατάσταση	replacement
	αντίο	bye
	αξίζει	it's worth it
	απαγορεύεται	it is forbidden
	απαίσιος/ια/ο	horrible
	απαντ(ά)ω	answer

	απέναντι	opposite, across the road
	απίθανος/η/ο	fantastic
	απλός/ή/ό	simple
	από	from
οι	αποσκευές	luggage
το	αποχωρητήριο	toilet
	απόψε	tonight, this evening
	αργά	slowly, late
	αργότερα	later (on)
	αργώ	delay, be late
	αριστερά	(on the) left
	(μ')αρέσει/αρέσουνε	(I) like
	αρκετά	enough, quite
	αρκετός/ή/ό	enough, quite a number
το	αρνάκι	lamb
	άρρωστος/η/ο	ill, sick
	αρχίζω	start, begin
	αρχαίος/α/ο	ancient
το	ασανσέρ	lift, elevator
το	αστέρι	star
η	αστυνομία	police
ο	αστυνόμος	policeman
	ασφαλισμένος/η/ο	insured
	άσχημος/η/ο	ugly, bad
το	άτομο	person
το	ατύχημα	accident
το	αυγό	egg
η	αυλή	yard, courtyard
	αύριο	tomorrow
το	αυτί	ear
το	αυτοκίνητο	car
	αυτός/ή/ό	this, this one
	αφήνω	leave, leave alone, allow

B

	βάζω	put (on)
η	βαλίτσα	suitcase
ο	βασιλιάς	king
ο	βασιλικός	basil
	βγαίνω	go out, get out
	βέβαια, βεβαίως	certainly
η	βενζίνη	petrol, gas
το	βενζινάδικο	garage [for petrol], gas station
η	βέσπα	scooter
ο	βήχας	cough
το	βιβλίο	book
το	βιβλιοπωλείο	bookshop
το	βιβλιάριο	booklet
η	βιτρίνα	shop window
η	βλάβη	breakdown, fault

	βλέπω	see, watch
	βοηθ(ά)ω	help
η	βόλτα	stroll, ride
ο	βορράς	north
το	βουνό	mountain
το	βραδινό	evening meal, dinner
το	βράδυ	(late) evening
	βραστός/ή/ό	boiled
	βρε	expression of exasperation, usually precedes the name of the person addressed
	βρέχει	it's raining
η	βροχή	rain

Γ

	γαλάζιος/ια/ιο	blue
η	Γαλλία	France
το	γάντι	glove
η	γάτα	cat
	γεια σου/σας	hello, bye
η	γειτονιά	neighbourhood
	γελ(ά)ώ	laugh
	γεμάτος/η/ο	full
	γεμίζω	fill
	γεμιστός/η/ο	stuffed, filled
τα	γενέθλια	birthday
η	Γερμανία	Germany
το	γεύμα	meal
	για	for
η	γιαγιά	granny, grandma
	γιατί	why, because
ο	γιατρός/η γιατρός	doctor
το	γιαούρτι	yogurt
ο	γιος	son
	γιορτάζω	celebrate
η	γκαρσονιέρα	studio flat
ο	γκρινιάρης/η γκρινιάρα	nag, grumbler
	γλεντ(ά)ω	have fun
	γλυκός/ιά/ό	sweet
η	γλώσσα	language, tongue
η	γνώμη	opinion
	γνωρίζω	recognize, know
	γνωστός/ή/ό	well-known
οι	γονείς	parents
το	γούστο	(sense of) fun, taste
η	γραβάτα	tie
το	γράμμα	letter
ο/η	γραμματέας	secretary
το	γραφείο	office, desk
	γράφω	write
	γρήγορα	quickly, fast
η	γρίπη	flu
τα	γυαλιά (του ηλίου)	(sun)glasses
η	γυμναστική	(physical) exercise
η	γυναίκα	woman, wife
	γυρίζω	return
	γύρω	around
η	γωνία	corner

Δ

ο	δάσκαλος/η δασκάλα δασκάλα	teacher *(m/f)*
το	δάσος	wood, forest
το	δάχτυλο	finger, toe
	δείχνω	show
	δεν	(do) not [*used to make verbs negative*]
	δεν (με) πειράζει	it doesn't matter, I don't mind
το	δέντρο	tree
	δεξιά	(on the) right
	δέκα	ten
	δερμάτινος/η/ο	leather
	Δεσποινίς	Miss
η	Δευτέρα	Monday
	δεύτερος/η/ο	second
	δηλαδή	in other words, that is to say
	διαβάζω	read
το	διαβατήριο	passport
οι	διακοπές	holidays, vacation
	διαλέγω	choose
το	διαμέρισμα	flat, apartment
	διάσημος/η/ο	famous
	διαφημίζω	advertise
η	διεύθυνση	address
ο	διευθυντής	manager
το	δίκλινο	double room (with two beds)
ο	δικηγόρος/ η δικηγόρος	lawyer
	δικός/ή/ό μου	my, mine, my own
	διπλός/ή/ό	double
	δίνω	give
	δίπλα	next door, beside, next to
	διψ(α)ώ	am thirsty
	δοκιμάζω	try, try on
το	δόντι	tooth
η	δουλειά	work
	δουλεύω	work
η	δραχμή	drachma
η	δροσιά	cool(ness)
	δύο	two
	δυνατός/ή/ό	strong
η	δύση	west
	δύσκολος/η/ο	difficult
	δυστυχώς	unfortunately
το	δωμάτιο	room
το	δώρο	gift

Ε

η	εβδομάδα	week
το	εγγόνι	grandchild
	(εγ)γράφομαι	register, sign up
	εγώ	I
	εδώ	here
το	έθιμο	custom, practice
	είμαι	am
το	εισιτήριο	ticket

η	είσοδος	entrance
	είτε ... ή	either ... or
	εκεί	there [preposition]
	εκείνος/η/ο	that [adjective]
η	έκθεση	exhibition, display
η	εκκλησία	church
οι	εκπτώσεις	sales
ο	εκτυπωτής	printer
	ελεύθερος/η/ο	single, free
η	Ελλάδα	Greece
	ελληνικά	Greek (language)
	εμείς	we
	εμπρός	*phrase used on answering telephone*
	ένα	one
	ένας/μια/ένα (*m/f/n*)	a, an
	ενδιαφέρω	interest
	εννιά	nine
	εντάξει	all right, OK
	εξαιρετικός/ή/ό	exceptional, excellent, outstanding
	εξαρτάται	it depends
η	εξέταση	examination
	έξι	six
η	έξοδος	exit
το	εξωτερικό	abroad
η	εξοχή	countryside, outdoors
	έξυπνος/η/ο	clever
	έξω	outside, out
η	επέτειος	anniversary
	επικίνδυνος/η/ο	dangerous
η	επικοινωνία	communication
ο	επιστήμονας	scientist
η	επιστροφή	return, round-trip
	επιτέλους	at last
	επιτρέπεται	it is allowed
	επιτυχημένος/η/ο	successful
ο/η	επιχειρηματίας	businessman/ businesswoman
	επόμενος/η/ο	the following, next
η	εποχή	time, period, age, season
το	επώνυμο	surname
	εργάζομαι	work
το	έργο	film, movie; work of art, completed job
το	εργοστάσιο	factory
	έρχομαι	come
η	έρευνα	research
	εσείς	you [*formal or pl.l*]
	εσύ	you [*informal or sg.*]
	ετοιμάζω	prepare
	έτοιμος/η/ο	ready
	έτσι	like that, so
	ευθεία	straight
η	ευκαιρία	opportunity
το	ευρώ	euro
η	Ευρώπη	Europe
	ευτυχισμένος/η/ο	happy
	ευχαριστώ	thank you
η	εφημερίδα	newspaper
	εφτά	seven

	(ε)χθές	yesterday
	έχω	have
	έχω κρυολόγημα	have a cold

Ζ

το	ζαχαροπλαστείο	cake shop, confectioner's
η	ζέστη	heat
	ζεστός/ή/ό	hot
	ζηλεύω	am jealous
	ζητώ	ask for, look for
	ζω	live
η	ζωή	life
η	ζώνη	belt
το	ζώο	animal

Η

	ή	or
ο/η	ηθοποιός	actor, actress
ο	ηλεκτρικός	underground, subway
ο	ηλεκτρισμός	electricity
η	ηλιοθεραπεία	sunbathing
η	ημερομηνία	date
η	ημερομηνία γεννήσεως	date of birth
	ήρεμος/η/ο	calm
	ησυχάζω	calm down, relax
	ήσυχος/η/ο	quiet

Θ

η	θάλασσα	sea
	θαυμάσιος/α/ο	wonderful
η	θέα	view
το	θέατρο	theatre
	θέλω	want
η	θερμίδα	calorie
η	θερμοκρασία	temperature
η	θέση	place, position, seat
	θυμάμαι	remember
	θυμώνω	be/get angry

Ι

το	ιατρείο	surgery, consulting rooms, doctor's office
	ίσια	straight
	ίσως	maybe, perhaps

Κ

	και	and
	και ... και	both ... and
	καθαρίζω	clean
το	καθαριστήριο	dry cleaner's
	κάθε	every
ο	καθηγητής/η καθηγήτρια	professor, lecturer (*m/f*)
	καθόλου	none, not at all
	κάθομαι	sit
ο	καθρέφτης	mirror
η	καθυστέρηση	delay
	καινούριος/α/ο	new

ο καιρός	time, weather
καλά	fine
το καλαμαράκι	baby squid
καλή όρεξη	enjoy your meal
καλημέρα	good morning
καληνύχτα	goodnight
καλησπέρα	good evening, good afternoon
ο καλλιτέχνης	artist
το καλοκαίρι	summer
καλός/ή/ό	good
καλύτερα	better
(ο) καλύτερος/η/ο	(the) best
καλώ	invite
κάνω	do, make
το καράβι	boat
το κάρβουνο	coal
η καρδιά	heart
η καρέκλα	chair
το καρπούζι	watermelon
η κάρτα	card
το κασκόλ	scarf
το κάστανο	chestnut
κατά	towards, at about
καταλαβαίνω	understand
ο κατάλογος	menu
καταπληκτικός/ή/ό	amazing, fantastic
το κατάστημα	department store
κάτω	down
το καφενείο	café
καφετής/ιά/ί	brown
η κεντρική θέρμανση	central heating
το κέντρο	town centre, city centre
το κερί	candle
το κεφάλι	head
οι κεφτέδες	meatballs
ο κήπος	garden
το κιλό	kilo
ο κιμάς	mince, ground meat
ο κίνδυνος	danger
το κινητό	mobile (phone), cell phone
κίτρινος/η/ο	yellow
κλείνω	close; book, reserve
κλειστός/ή/ό	closed
το κλειδί	key
το κλίμα	climate
το κλουβί	cage
κόβω	chop, cut
η κοιλιά	belly (lower abdomen)
κοιμάμαι	sleep, am asleep
τα κοινόχρηστα	communal charges
κοιτάζω	see (to), look at
το κολοκυθάκι	courgette, baby marrow, zucchini
το κομμάτι	piece
κοντά	near, nearby
ο κόπος	effort, hard work
η κόρη	daughter
το κορίτσι	girl
ο κόσμος	people, world

το κοτόπουλο	chicken
κουβεντιάζω	chat, discuss
το κουδούνι	bell
η κουζίνα	kitchen
κουρασμένος/η/ο	tired
το κουτί	box
το κρασί	wine
κρατ(α)ώ	keep, hold
το κρέας	meat
το κρεβάτι	bed
η κρεβατοκάμαρα	bedroom
το κρεμμύδι	onion
η Κρήτη	Crete
το κρύο	cold
κρύος/α/ο	cold
κρυώνω	be cold
το κτίριο	building
το κυνήγι	hunt
η Κύπρος	Cyprus
η Κυριακή	Sunday
η κυρία	lady, Mrs
ο κύριος	gentleman, Mr

Λ

το λάδι	oil
η λαϊκή	street market
ο λαιμός	neck, throat
το λάστιχο	tyre, rubber
τα λαχανικά	vegetables
λέγετε	*phrase used on answering telephone*
λέγομαι	am called
λειτουργώ	function, work
η λέξη	word
το λεπτό	minute
λέω	say, tell
το λεωφορείο	bus
η λεωφόρος	avenue
λήγω	expire
η λιακάδα	sunshine, fine weather
λίγος/η/ο	little, few
(ο) λιγότερος/η/ο	less, (the least, the fewest)
το λιμάνι	harbour
το λίτρο	litre
ο λογαριασμός	bill, check; account
η λογοτεχνία	literature
λοιπόν	so, well, therefore
το λουκούμι	delicious; Turkish delight
το λουλούδι	flower
το λούνα παρκ	amusement park
λυπάμαι	regret

Μ

μα	but
μαγειρεύω	cook
το μαγιό	bathing suit, swimsuit
μαζί	with
μαθαίνω	learn

το	μάθημα	lesson
ο	μαθητής/η μαθήτρια	pupil, scholar (m/f)
ο	μαϊντανός	parsley
	μακριά	far
	μάλιστα	of course, certainly, in fact
τα	μαλλιά	hair
η	μαμά	mum, mom
το	μαντήλι	handkerchief
το	μαρούλι	lettuce
το	μάτι	eye
το	μάτσο	bunch
	μαύρος/η/ο	black
	μεγάλος/η/ο	big, large
	μεγαλώνω	raise, grow up
ο	μεζές	snack
	μεθαύριο	the day after tomorrow
	μελαχρινός/ή/ό	dark-haired
το	μέλι	honey
η	μελιτζάνα	aubergine, eggplant
	μένω	stay, live
η	μέρα	day
η	μεριά	place, side
	μερικά	some, a few
το	μέρος	part, place
	μέσα	inside, in
τα	μεσάνυχτα	midnight
η	μέση	waist, lower back; the middle
το	μεσημέρι	midday
το	μεσημεριανό	lunch
	με συγχωρείτε	excuse me
	μετά	after, afterwards
	μέχρι	as far as, until
	μη(ν)	no [used to make words other than verbs negative]
	μηδέν	zero, nothing
το	μήλο	apple
ο	μήνας	month
η	μητέρα	mother
ο	μηχανικός	mechanic
	μικρός/ή/ό	small
το	μικρό όνομα	first name
	μια χαρά	just fine
	μιλ(α)ώ	speak
	μισός/ή/ό	half
η	μόδα	fashion
	μόλις	just [time]
	μόνο	only
το	μονόκλινο	single room
	μονός/ή/ό	single
η	μοτοσυκλέτα	motorbike, motorcycle
το	μουσείο	museum
ο	μουσικός	musician
	μπαίνω	go, get in
ο	μπακάλης	grocer
ο	μπακαλιάρος	cod, haddock
το	μπαλόνι	balloon
ο	μπαμπάς	dad

το	μπάνιο	bath
το	μπαρμπούνι	red mullet
η	μπίρα	beer
	μπλε	blue
	μπορώ	can, be able to
το	μπουζί	spark-plug
το	μπουκάλι	bottle
	μπράβο	well done
το	μυαλό	mind, brain
η	μύτη	nose
το	μωρό	baby

N

	να	to, for, (so) that
ο	ναυτικός	sailor
τα	νέα	news
το	νερό	water
	νευρικός/ή/ό	moody, temperamental
το	νησί	island
	νοικιάζω	rent, hire
	νομίζω	think, presume
το	νόμισμα	coin, currency
ο	νονός/η νονά	godfather/godmother
ο	νοσοκόμος/η νοσοκόμα	nurse (m/f)
το	νοσοκομείο	hospital
	νόστιμος/η/ο	tasty, delicious
ο	νότος	south
το	νούμερο	size [clothes, shoes], number
η	ντομάτα	tomato
το	ντουζ	shower
η	νύχτα	night

Ξ

	ξαναλέω	repeat
	ξανθός/ή/ό	blond
	ξαπλώνω	lie down, stretch out
	ξένος/η/ο	foreign
ο	ξένος/η ξένη	foreigner (m/f)
το	ξενοδοχείο	hotel
	ξέρω	know
	ξεχν(α)ώ	forget
ο	ξιφίας	swordfish
	ξοδέυω	spend
το	ξύλο	wood
	ξυπν(α)ώ	wake (up)

Ο

	οδηγώ	drive
ο	οδοντίατρος	dentist
η	οδός	street
η	οικογένεια	family
	οικογενειακός/ή/ό	family
τα	οικονομικά	economics
η	οθόνη	screen
	όλος/η/ο	all, everything
η	ομάδα	team
	όμορφος/η/ο	lovely, beautiful, handsome
η	ομπρέλα	umbrella

το	όνομα	name
	όποτε	whenever
η	όπισθεν	reverse
	οργανώνω	organize
	ορίστε	may I help you?, here you are
ο	όροφος	floor [level]
	ότι	that [conjunction]
	ό,τι	whatever
η	Ουαλία	Wales
η	ουρά	tail
ο	ουρανός	sky
	ούτε	not even
	ούτε ... ούτε	neither ... nor
	οχτώ	eight

Π

ο	πάγος	ice
το	παγωτό	ice-cream
	παίζω	play
το	παιδί	child
η	παιδική χαρά	playground
	παίρνω	get, take
το	παιχνίδι	game
το	πακέτο	packet, pack(age)
	πάλι	again
	παλιός/ιά/ιό	old
το	παλτό	coat
	Παναγιά μου!	good grief!
το	πανεπιστήμιο	university
το	παντελόνι	trousers, pants
	πάντοτε	always
	παντρεμένος/η/ο	married
	πάνω	up
ο	παππούς	grandad, grandfather
το	παπούτσι	shoe
το	παράθυρο	window
	παρακαλώ	please
το	παραμύθι	story
η	Παρασκευή	Friday
η	παράσταση	performance
η	παρέα	company, group of friends, gang
το	παρ-μπριζ	windscreen
ο	πατέρας	father
	πάω	go
το	πέδιλο	sandal
	πειν(α)ώ	am hungry
η	Πέμπτη	Thursday
	πέντε	five
το	περιβάλλον	environment
	περιμένω	wait (for), expect
	περίπου	about, approximately
το	περίπτερο	kiosk
ο	περισσότερος	the most
	περν(α)ώ	pass
	περπατ(α)ώ	walk
	πετ(α)ώ	fly
	πηγαίνω	go
	πίνω	drink
η	πιπεριά	pepper [vegetable]
η	πλατεία	(town/city) square

η	πλάτη	back
το	πληκτρολόγιο	keyboard
οι	πληροφορίες	information
	πληρώνω	pay
το	πλοίο	ship
	πλούσιος/ια/ιο	rich
το	πλυντήριο	washing machine
το	ποδήλατο	bicycle
το	πόδι	leg, foot
ο	ποδοσφαιριστής	footballer, soccer player
	ποιανού/ής	whose
η	ποικιλία	selection, assortment
	ποιος/α/ο	who, which
ο	πόλεμος	war
η	πόλη	city
	πολύ	very
	πολύς/πολλή/πολύ	much, many, a lot
	πον(α)ώ	hurt, be in pain, ache
ο	πονοκέφαλος	headache
ο	πόνος	pain
η	πόρτα	door
η	πορτοκαλάδα	orange juice
το	πορτοφόλι	wallet, purse
	πόσος/η/ο	how much, how many
το	ποτάμι	river
	πότε;	when?
	ποτέ	never
το	ποτήρι	glass
	πού	where
	πουθενά	somewhere, anywhere, nowhere
το	πουκάμισο	shirt
	πουλ(α)ώ	sell
το	πουλί	bird
το	πούλμαν	coach, bus
το	πράγμα	thing
το	πρακτορείο	ticket office
	πρέπει	must, have to
ο	πρίγκηπας	prince
ο	προβολέας	headlight
	προς	towards
	προσεκτικά	carefully
	προτιμ(α)ώ	prefer
	προχθές	the day before yesterday
	πρωθυπουργός	prime minister
το	πρωί	morning
το	πρωινό	breakfast
	πρώτος/η/ο	first
η	πτήση	flight
ο	πυρετός	temperature, fever
ο	πωλητής/η	salesman/
	πωλήτρια	saleswoman

Ρ

το	ραντεβού	appointment
τα	ρέστα	(small) change
το	ροδάκινο	peach
το	ρολόι	watch, clock
το	ρούχο	item of clothing

243

το	ρύζι	rice
	ρυθμίζω	regulate, adjust
	ρωτ(α)ώ	ask

Σ

το	Σάββατο	Saturday
το	Σαββατοκύριακο	weekend
το	σακ βουαγιάζ	travel bag
η	σαλάτα	salad
το	σαλόνι	living room, lounge
	σαν	like
το	σανδάλι	sandal
η	σειρά	turn; queue, line
ο	σεισμός	earthquake
	σερβίρω	serve
	σηκώνομαι	get up, rise
	σήμερα	today
το	σιρόπι	syrup
	σκέπτομαι	think, reflect on
ο	σκληρός δίσκος	hard disk
το	σκόρδο	garlic
	σκοτεινός/ή/ό	dark
η	Σκοτία	Scotland
	σοβαρός	serious
η	σούπα	soup
το	σουπερμάρκετ	supermarket
το	σπίτι	home, house
	σπουδάζω	study
	σπουδαίος/α/ο	superb, excellent
η	σταγόνα	drop
ο	σταθμός	station
	σταματ(α)ώ	stop
	στέλνω	send
το	στενό	side-street
το	στήθος	chest
το	στιλό	pen
το	στιφάδο	casserole
	στο/ στη/ στο	at (m/f/n)
	στο καλό	take care
τα	στοιχεία	particulars, facts
το	στόμα	mouth
το	στομάχι	stomach
	στρίβω	turn
	στρώνω	spread, lay
	συγγνώμη	excuse me
ο/η	συγγραφέας	writer
	συμπληρώνω	fill in, complete
το	συνάλλαγμα	foreign exchange
η	συναυλία	concert
	συνέχεια	continuously
	συνεχίζω	continue
το	σύννεφο	cloud
ο/η	συνταξιούχος	pensioner, senior citizen (m/f)
το	συρτάρι	drawer
η	συσκευή	appliance
	συστήνω	recommend, introduce
	συχνά	often
το	σχολείο	school
το	σώμα	body
	σωστά	correctly

Τ

το	τάβλι	backgammon
η	ταινία	film, tape
η	ταλαιπωρία	bother, trouble, hardship
το	ταξιδιωτικό γραφείο	travel agency
η	ταυτότητα	identity (ID card)
	ταυτόχρονα	simultaneously
η	ταχύτητα	gear, speed
	ταχτικά	regularly
το	ταχυδρομείο	post office
	τελειώνω	finish, end
	τελευταίος/α/ο	last, latest
το	τέλος	end
το	τελωνείο	customs office
	τέσσερα	four
η	Τετάρτη	Wednesday
το	τέταρτο	quarter
το	τζάκι	fireplace
η	τηλεόραση	television
το	τηλέφωνο	telephone (number)
	τηλεφωνώ	telephone
	τι;	what?
	τι γίνεται;	what's happening?, what's up?
	τι έχεις;	what's the matter?
	τι κρίμα	what a pity
	τι ώρα είναι;	what time is it?
η	τιμή	price, value, honour
το	τιμόνι	steering wheel
	τίποτ' άλλο;	anything else?
	τόσος/η/ο	so much, so many
	τότε	then
	τώρα	now
η	τουαλέτα	toilet
η	τούρτα	(birthday) cake
το	τραγούδι	song
η	τράπεζα	bank
η	τραπεζαρία	dining room
το	τρένο	train
	τρέχω	speed, run
	τρία	three
το	τριαντάφυλλο	rose
η	Τρίτη	Tuesday
	τρίτος/η/ο	third
ο	τροχός	wheel
	τρώω	eat
η	τσάντα	bag
η	τσέπη	pocket
	τυλίγω	wrap
το	τυρί	cheese

Υ

η	υγεία	health
τα	υλικά	materials, ingredients
	υπάρχει/ υπάρχουν	there is/there are
	υπέροχος/η/ο	wonderful, excellent
το	υπνοδωμάτιο	bedroom
η	υπογραφή	signature
το	υπόλοιπο	remainder, rest

Φ

η	φάβα	pea purée
το	φαγητό	food
	φαίνομαι	seem, appear
τα	φανάρια	traffic lights
το	φαρμακείο	chemist's, pharmacy, drugstore
το	φάρμακο	medicine
το	φεγγάρι	moon
	φέρνω	bring
το	φεριμπότ	ferry
	φέτος	this year
	φεύγω	leave
το	φθινόπωρο	autumn, fall
ο	φίλος/η φίλη	friend
	φιλώ	kiss
το	φλυτζάνι	cup
	φοβερός/ή/ό	awful, awesome
ο	φοιτητής /η φοιτήτρια	student (m/f)
η	φορά	time
	φορ(α)ώ	wear
ο	φούρνος	bakery
η	φράουλα	strawberry
το	φρένο	brake
	φρέσκος/ια/ο	fresh
	φριχτός/ή/ό	terrible
	φτάνω	arrive
	φτηνός/ή/ό	cheap
	φτιά(χ)νω	make, prepare
	φυσάει	it's windy
	φυτεύω	plant
	φωτεινός/ή/ό	bright, sunny
η	φωτιά	fire
ο	φωτογράφος	photographer

Χ

	χαίρετε	hello, goodbye
	χαιρετώ	greet
	χαλ(α)ώ	break down, go wrong, spoil, mess, s/th awful
το	χάλι	
	χάνω	lose
το	χάπι	pill
ο	χάρτης	map
το	χαρτί	paper
ο	χαρτοφύλακας	briefcase
ο	χειμώνας	winter
(ο)	χειρότερος/η/ο	worse, (the worst)
το	χέρι	hand, arm
	χίλια	thousand
το	χιλιόμετρο	kilometre
το	χιόνι	snow
	χιονίζω	snow
	χορεύω	dance
τα	χόρτα	greens
ο	χορτοφάγος	vegetarian
	χρειάζομαι	need
ο	χρόνος	year
	χρυσός/ή/ό	gold
το	χρώμα	colour
το	χταπόδι	octopus
	χτυπ(α)ώ	hit, (am) hurt
η	χώρα	country
το	χωράφι	field
το	χωριό	village
	χωρίς	without

Ψ

το	ψάρι	fish
	ψηλός/ή/ό	tall
	ψήνω	bake, roast, grill
το	ψυγείο	fridge

Ω

ο	ώμος	shoulder
η	ώρα	time, hour
	ωραίος/α/ο	nice, good, beautiful

Glossary of grammatical terms

Accusative: The case used for the direct object of a verb and after most prepositions, such as από, με, χωρίς.

Adjective: A word used to give information about a noun.

η **πράσινη** γραβάτα – the green tie

Adverb: A word used to give information about a verb, adjective or another adverb. In Greek, many adverbs end in -ως or -α

τρέχει **γρήγορα** – he runs quickly

Agree: To match another word in number (singular or plural), gender (masculine, feminine or neuter).

Augment: The vowel added to the beginning of the stem to give a verb in the past tense a third syllable.

βλέπω – έβλεπα   ξέρω – ήξερα
τρώω – έφαγα   λέω – είπα

Case: The grammatically required form of a noun, adjective, or pronoun. Modern Greek has 3 cases: nominative, accusative, and genitive.

Comparative: The form of an adjective or adverb used to express higher or lower degree. See also *Superlative*.

Η Αλίκη είναι **μικρότερη** από την αδελφή της. Alice is younger than her sister.

Definite article: In English, the definite article is 'the'. In Greek, the definite articles are ο, η, το, and the plural forms οι, τα

Direct object: The noun, pronoun, or phrase directly affected by the action of the verb, and expressed in the accusative.

Η Ελένη αγαπάει **τον Γιάννη**. Helen loves John.

Ending: A letter or letters added to the stem of the verb to show the tense, person, and number; also the changes that affect nouns and adjectives, to show number and gender and case.

έδωσά – I gave
τα λουλούδι**α** – the flowers

Feminine: See *Gender*.

Future tense: The form of a verb used to express what will happen.

Gender: In Greek, all nouns have a gender – masculine, feminine or neuter. It is grammatical, not biological. Gender is reflected in the form of the article used (ο/η/το; ένας/μια/ένα). Gender also affects the form of accompanying words such as adjectives, etc.

Genitive: The case used to indicate possession, to show the indirect object of a verb, after some prepositions, and in a number of other constructions.

Η αδελφή **της** Ελένης – Helen's sister

Imperative: The form of a verb used to express orders, instructions, or suggestions.

Imperfect tense: The form of a verb used to express a continuous or habitual action in the past.

Indefinite article: In English, the indefinite articles are 'a' and 'an'. In Greek they are ένας, μια, ένα.

Ένας φίλος σου. A friend of yours.

Indirect object: The noun, pronoun, or phrase indirectly affected by the action of the verb. It takes the genitive case.

Δώσε **μου** το αλάτι. Give me the salt.

Έστειλε μια κάρτα **στην οικογένεια της**. She sent a card to her family.

Intonation: The pattern of sounds made in a sentence as the speaker's voice rises and falls.

Irregular verb: A verb that has atypical stem changes. Many common verbs such as τρώω (I eat), and λέω (I say), are irregular.

Masculine: See *Gender*.

Neuter: See *Gender*.

Nominative: The case used for the grammatical subject of a sentence. In the singular, the dictionary form of nouns, personal pronouns, adjectives.

Noun: A word that identifies a person, thing, place, or concept.

Number: Indicates whether a noun or pronoun is singular or plural. Number is one of the factors determining the form of accompanying words.

singular:	ένας σκύλος	– a dog
	μια γάτα	– a cat
plural:	δύο σκύλοι	– two dogs
	δύο γάτες	– two cats

Object: See *Direct object*, *Indirect object*.

Passive-form verb: A verb which follows the patterns of a passive verb, but is active in meaning, such as έρχομαι and θυμάμαι.

Person: A category used to distinguish between the 'I'/'we' (first person), 'you' (second person), and 'he'/'she'/'it'/'they' (third person) forms of the verb.

Μιλάω. (1st p. sing.)

Εσείς φεύγετε. (2nd p. pl.)

Possessive forms: Adjectives and pronouns used to show belonging.

Το αυτοκίνητο μου. My car.

Αυτό είναι δικό σου. This is yours.

Preposition: A word (e.g. για, με, etc.) or phrase (e.g. μακριά από, δίπλα στο, etc.) used before a noun or pronoun to relate it to another part of the sentence.

Τα κλειδιά είναι κάτω από το τραπέζι. The keys are under the table.

Present tense: The form of a verb used to express something happening or in existence now, or as a habitual occurrence.

Pronoun: A word used to stand for a noun. Pronouns may refer to things or concepts ('it', 'them'), or people ('I', 'you', 'she', 'him'), and may be indefinite ('someone').

Κάποιος το έστειλε αυτό χθες. Someone sent this yesterday.

Regular verb: A verb that follows the common set patterns.

Simple Past Tense: The form of a verb used to relate completed actions in the past.

Stem: The part of a verb to which endings showing tense, number, and person are added.

καταλαβαίνω   καταλαβαίνεις

Stress: the syllable in a word which is given the strongest emphasis.

πότε – when   ποτέ – never

Subject: The noun, pronoun, or phrase that performs the action indicated by the verb.

Η μητέρα μου θέλει καφέ. My mother wants coffee.

Subjunctive: The subjunctive is used to show an action or state as something not (yet) fulfilled, such as a wish, a hope, or an obligation.

Superlative: The form of an adjective or adverb used to express the highest or lowest degree of comparison. See also *Comparative*.

Η Ελένη ήταν η πιο όμορφη γυναίκα του κόσμου. Helen was the most beautiful woman in the world.

Syllable: A unit of pronunciation which forms either the whole or part of a word.

Tense: The form of a verb which indicates **when** the action takes place.

Verb: A word or phrase used to express an action or a state.

Δουλεύει. He/she is working.

Δεν είμαι καλά. I am not well.

247

Index

In addition to the Language Building pages listed below, see also the relevant section of the Grammar Summary.

adjectives 63, 95
  demonstrative 79
  πολύς/πολλή/πολύ 79
  possessive form 201
  comparatives + superlatives 197
adverbs 81
articles: definite + indefinite 7
alphabet 2,3
είτε ... ή 199
forms of address 5
gender 7
genitive case 93
imperative 81, 125
μ'αρέσει 109
μ'αρέσει + να 169
 να + subjunctive 137–141, 169
  να for recommendations 185
  for wishes 91
  to point, show 91
nationalities 33
negatives 3, 95, 125
numbers
  1 – 10   21
  11 – 20   35
  21 – 100   53
  200+/1000s   65
ότι/ό,τι 111, 125
ούτε ... ούτε 109
plurals 49
prepositions 19, 77
pronouns
  demonstrative 79
  direct object 139

indirect object 109, 139
interrogative 113
possessive 95, 201
word order 139
quantities 67
questions
  Γιατί; Why? 81
  Κάθε πότε; – How often 78
  Ποιανού – Whose? 201
  Ποιός είναι αυτός; Who is this/that? 113
  Πόσον καιρό; – How long? 35
  Πόσο; – How much? 51, 67
  Πόσον χρονών; – How old? 93
  Πότε; – When? 157
  Πού; – Where? 17
  Τι; – What? 31
stress 5
time 53
  days 51
  months 91
verbs
  I am – είμαι, there is – υπάρχει 17
  I was 157
  future 123
  passive form 183
  present – regular
    1st conjugation 31
    2nd conjugation 65
  past 155, 157
  imperfect 171, 173
  irregular verbs 123, 155

W9-CFJ-114

TIME WARPER:

Fated

PEGGY MARTINEZ

THIS book is a work of fiction. Names, characters, places and incidents are the product of the author's imagination or are used fictitiously. Any resemblance to actual persons, living or dead, business establishments, events or locales is entirely coincidental.

Fated
ISBN: 978-1-63422-117-7
Copyright ©2015 Peggy Martinez
All rights reserved.
Cover Design by: Marya Heiman
Interior Format by: Courtney Nuckels
Editing by: Chelsea Brimmer

For more information about our content disclosure, please utilize the QR code above with your smart phone or visit us at

www.cleanteenpublishing.com.

Prologue

Today I woke up a hundred years younger. That's a hard thing to accomplish since I'm only eighteen years old. I'd like to think that if I fudge up and accidently come across one of my ancestors I won't somehow screw up the time stream and... then what? Would I ever be born? Would I wake up one day in this century and just cease to exist? Sheesh... that would probably top my worst-days-ever list.

I should probably back up and begin my story from yesterday... or would it still be considered *yesterday* when my yesterday takes place a hundred years from now?

See? So confusing!

So let me start over from the beginning, from the day I woke up a normal teenager and went to bed a... *time warper.*

CHAPTER One

M INTON'S USED BOOKSTORE WAS NEW, AND FROM the street, I could tell it was just my kind of place. A low glow came from the inside, casting light on the shelves and shelves of used books, random antique paintings, and knickknacks. As I pushed through the door, a small bell chimed above me—a real bell, not one of those digital ones most stores have now. I inhaled deeply, pulling in the faint scent of old paper and spices through my nostrils. Nothing could beat the smell of old books.

"Can I help you?" The voice came from a headless cashier sitting behind the counter, his face buried in a *Star Wars* novel.

"Umm, no thank you, I'm just going to browse a bit," I said to the cover of the book.

"Cool. Let me know if you need anything," the guy behind the counter called after me.

I'd already moved down an aisle, lost in a booklover's euphoria. I quickly realized the used bookstore was a genuine treasure trove of old books—not just used ones, but also books that were decades old, some of them even older. I came across a particularly beautiful copy of *Jane Eyre*, and after a long inner debate, I left it on the shelf with a soft sigh. I *did* have several copies of it, after all, not

3

to mention the three different DVD versions of the movie I'd also collected.

I walked back to the front of the store and headed toward the only glass case in the shop. There were several lovely pieces—some in gaudy art deco, some more delicate and closer to my taste—but nothing that I couldn't live without. I was just about to turn and head for the door when something in the far corner of the case caught my eye.

A gray stone pendant, half covered in black satin, claimed my attention. I glanced up and found the cashier still ensconced in his place behind the cash register, totally engrossed in a galactic adventure of epic proportions. I kind of hated to interrupt him.

"Is there any way I can see something from this case?" I asked into the silence.

The cashier held up a finger as he finished the paragraph he was reading. When he placed a bookmark in his book and set it down, I was pleased to discover the dude did, in fact, have a head. He reached over, grabbed a set of keys, and moved to stand near the glass case. His black-rimmed glasses were large and should have been dorky, but his blue eyes shone from behind them. Taking into account how well put together his clothing was and the way his hair was meticulously done, I was sure he wore those glasses to complete his *look*. Nerdy was the new cool.

"Which piece did you want to see?" he asked.

"That one in the corner," I said, pointing to the pendant. I could feel anticipation building inside of me. I couldn't wait to hold the beautiful stone in my hand.

He pulled the pendant out of the cabinet, and I was pleased to see it was attached to a long, silver chain. He set it on top of the counter, and I marveled at how lovely it was. The light gray stone was about the size of a quarter and shaped like a teardrop. An intricate pattern of thin silver wire wrapped around the top of the stone, forming a loop for the chain to hang through. It was beautifully crafted. I reached out and picked it up, running my thumb along its smooth surface. My pulse fluttered wildly, and I could have sworn the stone warmed to my touch. Frowning down at the pendant in my hand for a moment, I set it back down.

The clerk picked the necklace up and opened the back of the cabinet, preparing to put it away. It didn't feel right; I knew I couldn't leave without it. I wanted that pendant more than anything. It was meant for me—I was sure of it—even if I didn't understand it.

What an odd thing to think.

But it didn't matter how odd the thought was; I still wanted the pendant.

"No. I want it," I said quickly.

The clerk glanced up at me, his eyes searching mine. "You didn't even ask how much it is," he answered.

The truth was, I didn't care how much it was. It was mine, and I was going to buy it. Luckily for me, it didn't cost much.

I walked out of the bookstore with my impromptu purchase and smiled to myself, feeling happier than I had in a long time. I pulled the necklace out of its small, white box as I walked past the glass window of the store, staring at my reflection. My red hair was blowing softly in the breeze, my cheeks were lightly flushed, and my brown eyes were brighter than normal. I clasped the chain about my neck, and as soon as the stone lay against my skin, I felt… *right*. But how could that be? How could a piece of jewelry make me feel whole?

Nearby, a streetlamp flickered on, rousing me from my confusing thoughts and feelings. I looked around and frowned; I was out later than I'd planned. Hitching my messenger bag higher up on my shoulder, I walked quickly in the direction of my apartment building in the falling darkness.

I'd walked home alone many times over the last few weeks, but this time was different. There was more than a shadow moving in my peripheral vision, and something other than the nippy breeze was tickling the fine hairs at the base of my neck. An icy dread settled into my heart, and a shiver shook my body as if a cold, clammy finger had caressed my spine.

I picked up my pace, still distracted by the necklace that hung about my neck and all my confusing thoughts. I turned a corner and promptly collided with someone. Grabbing my messenger bag with both hands, I prepared myself to whack the crap out of the assailant, when I realized the perpetrator was a little old lady who stood nearly three inches shorter than my own five-and-a-half feet. The poor woman had no idea how close she'd come to being squashed like a roach.

"Whoa," I said breathlessly. "I'm so sorry—I didn't see you. I hope I didn't hurt you."

I put a hand over my heart and berated myself for being such a girl. I'd almost assaulted an old lady, for God's sake.

The old woman still hadn't spoken, and when her eerie, translucent blue eyes searched mine, I took a step back. Those eyes were odd—a little creepy, even. The corner of the old woman's mouth twitched just a bit, and I absently wondered if she'd heard my thoughts. If it were at all possible, *this* old lady could accomplish it. I shivered involuntarily and rolled my eyes at my own stupidity.

"Okie dokie then." I shrugged. "If you're okay, I'm okay."

Still, she said nothing, and that was my cue to move along. I'd had enough *weird* for one night.

"Well, I'll see you 'round, then," I said, edging around her to go home.

As I passed her, the aged woman latched onto my arm and pulled me to an abrupt halt. The air around us immediately crackled to life, charged with some strange energy. My hair began to float around my face as if someone had chafed a big balloon all over my head. Her eyes glowed brightly, lighting up her wrinkled face.

I wanted to jerk my arm free, to turn away from her and run, but I found myself unable to do either. Caught in some kind of energy bubble, I couldn't regain control of myself. It was a horrifying feeling of helplessness, and deep down, I recognized that something was happening in that moment that would change my life forever... whether I wanted it to or not.

She gave a slight nod, as if she'd made up her mind about something, and closed her eyes. For a brief moment, I thought that everything would be okay—she'd let me go, and all would be right in my little world. But then she spoke, and everything changed.

Words tumbled from her mouth, a rough-sounding brogue of some ancient dialect I'd never heard before. I didn't know how I knew it was an ancient language, but there it was. The words were powerful. Terrifying. And even though the language she spoke was foreign to my ears, the meaning of her words echoed in my mind, searing themselves within my soul.

Blessed of Amerach, cursed by time's fate.

Rise up. Warrior. Priestess. Embrace the powers that await.

My pounding heart echoed loudly in my ears along with the words she spoke, causing my head to grow fuzzy. The laws of time and gravity seemed all but suspended, and in that moment, nothing existed outside of our bubble.

A brilliant light exploded all around us, and I felt a searing pain bite into the sensitive skin behind my left ear, tearing a gasp from my throat. Suddenly, I was on my hands and knees on the sidewalk, my heart racing out of control. I glanced up quickly to where the woman had been standing, but she was nowhere to be seen. Trying to gain control over the fear I felt, I squeezed my eyes shut and focused on getting my trembling legs to cooperate. A few minutes later, I pushed myself off the pavement. My ears popped as I stumbled to my feet, reeling from everything that had just happened.

Opening my eyes, I glanced around the neighborhood, expecting to find wreckage from the explosion I'd just felt, but everything looked perfectly normal. I wiped the sweat off my forehead with the palm of my hand and squeezed my eyes shut again, trying to piece everything together. None of it made sense, and the harder I tried to rationalize everything, the larger my headache grew.

I brushed my hands off on my jeans and reached up with trembling fingers to touch the side of my neck. There was nothing there to explain the burning pain I'd felt only a few moments earlier. Grabbing my messenger bag off the ground, I headed to my apartment building on shaky legs.

What had just happened to me? Was I losing my mind?

When I finally made it home, I kicked my shoes off and plopped down on my sofa to try and wrap my pounding head around everything that had just taken place. I rubbed behind my ear where I'd felt the burning sensation earlier and shook my head.

What the hell?

I tried to remember the old woman's features—anything about her, really—but found I couldn't capture any details except her eerie, pale blue eyes. Everything was a blur, a fast-fading memory. Maybe I *was* going insane. What was I supposed to do? Call the police? And... what? Report an attack that I had no witnesses to? Tell them there had been an explosion, or that some freaky old lady had burned me... even though I had no burn marks? I was pretty sure that wouldn't go well.

With a weary sigh, I heaved myself off the couch and headed to the bathroom. A hot shower sounded like a good idea. I stayed in the shower a long time, thinking through all the things that had happened to me that evening, trying to sort it all out in my mind and come up with a reasonable explanation. Nothing came to me. Zilch. Nada.

When my skin had endured entirely too much hot water, I dried off and slipped a nightgown on before sitting on my bed. I stared at the pendant that I'd bought that evening as it sat on my dresser. The more I thought about it, the more I became convinced it was another weird part of my day. I'd never felt so strongly about anything as I had when I bought the pendant. It was almost as if I couldn't have left it even if I'd wanted to.

Frowning, I walked over and picked up the stone, feeling better as soon as I touched it. Clasping the necklace about my neck, I sighed deeply. My thoughts calmed as soon as it lay against my skin. I decided, as I slid into bed and turned out the lamp, that I could think everything through the next morning. Maybe by then, everything would make more sense. Maybe I would be able to figure out what had happened to me. Or maybe just pretending like nothing had ever happened would be a better plan. Maybe.

As I drifted off to sleep, my mind still swirled around what I should do. Vivid dreaming was not a part of my plan, but then again, nightmares rarely were.

I ran through the fog-laced forest, aware that I was being chased by someone who meant to kill me. I knew if I were caught I would die—my predator could taste my fear, and he liked it. I knew without a doubt my death was what the predator desired above all else. It growled, and the sound raised the hairs on my arms, pushing me to move even quicker. My bare feet flew over the uneven ground, and branches reached out their arms to snag and tear the hem of my gown, leaving fresh cuts along my pale legs.

And still, I ran.

Somewhere close by, I could hear the tick-tock of a clock—a soft reminder that time was running out. It kept pace with the frantic beating of my heart.

I turned my head just a fraction—just the slightest of movements, really—but the motion cost me dearly. I rebounded off an invisible barrier and landed on the forest floor in a heap. Scrambling to get my feet under me and flee into the night once again, I moved as quickly as possible, but I

wasn't quick enough. I stood on tired legs, trying to move, but I was ensnared in some sort of invisible trap. No sound would come from my screaming lips. The trap pulsed. Pulsed again. And then it began constricting tighter and tighter around me.

I gasped, trying to pull in a much-needed breath of air into my lungs, but nothing happened. My head spun as my oxygen was cut off. I became frantic—my lungs were burning, my vision was dimming, and still, the invisible cocoon tightened around me. The more I pushed, the more I struggled, the more the invisible trap squeezed the life out of me.

Before long, I welcomed the darkness.

CHAPTER Two

JOLTING AWAKE FROM THE NIGHTMARE, I coughed and gulped air into my raw, oxygen-deprived lungs. Sweat beaded on my forehead as a wave of nausea threatened to empty my stomach. *I need a drink of water,* I thought, my brain still groggy.

A light breeze ruffled a strand of hair into my face, chilling my sweat-dampened skin. *Wait, a breeze?*

Reluctantly, I cracked my eyelids open and realized I was sitting outside on the ground between two brick walls, in what appeared to be an alleyway. I squeezed my eyes shut again and counted to ten. When I reopened them, my surroundings were the same and I was just as mystified. It was early morning, and I was still dressed in my nightgown. I jumped up, only to be rewarded with the ground tilting precariously beneath me. How in the *crap* had I gotten outside?

My heart nearly exploded out of my chest, and my legs began shaking violently. Taking several deep breaths, I peered around to take in my new surroundings. I was standing in a filthy alley with discarded rubbish everywhere and laundry hanging between the buildings. A panic attack was building in my chest, and I'd have given anything for a brown paper bag right about then. The opening of the alley was several feet away, so I gathered what energy and bravado I had and walked toward the street ahead of me.

Just before I stepped onto the sidewalk, another peculiarity hit me. I wasn't sure how I knew, but deep down I could tell this street was the same street I lived on... even though it was completely different. I had lived on Palmetto Street for the past three months, but where was the cute little Internet café on the corner? Where were all the cars that were usually parked in front of the buildings? What was a horse-drawn carriage doing on the street?

My mind raced, trying to come up with a reason for everything that was happening, some kind of logical explanation. How could this be explained? I was either still dreaming, or I had entered an alternate reality where I was a flippin' crazy person. I doubted I was in an alternate reality, and a quick slap to my own face proved I wasn't still dreaming. So what, exactly, had happened?

My mind snagged on the memory of the old lady from the previous evening, and a huge rock of uncertainty settled in my stomach. What was it she had said? "Cursed by time's fate"? Yeah, that was it. But surely, it couldn't mean... that was just impossible.

I was pretty sure I wasn't in Kansas anymore. No, a tornado hadn't landed me in a different place, but perhaps that dream had. Everything seemed to have changed after I bumped into the little old woman. One thing I was certain of was that blowing off everything that had happened the previous night had been a huge mistake. Remembering the encounter more fully, I reached up to touch the skin behind my ear and gasped when I felt tiny, raised welts there.

Oh. My. God.

My knees threatened to buckle, so I grabbed onto the brick wall to keep myself from falling into a heap and crying like a baby. I slapped myself again for good measure, just to clear my thoughts.

What the crap am I going to do now?

Glancing down at my torn, dirty nightgown, I noticed fresh scratches on my legs. I took another deep breath and tried not to freak out. Instead of visions of sugarplums dancing through my head, I had visions of a mental institution pounding inside my skull. In order to be sure my fears were real, I had to find someone to talk to… or maybe a newspaper to read.

My eyes adjusted slowly to the early morning darkness, and I stifled a groan. How would I be able to approach anyone looking like a street urchin? I attempted to smooth my hair into some semblance of order; I could only imagine how bad it looked.

Just then, I spotted a young boy, no older than seven or eight years old. He was across the street, whistling as he walked down the sidewalk. Before I could talk myself out of it, I ran over to talk to him. As I got closer, he took in my appearance, and his eyes widened. I didn't blame him—I probably looked as disturbed as I felt.

"Excuse me, can I ask you a question?"

His eyes scanned the area for escape routes. Smart kid.

"My mum says not to be speakin' to anyone I don't know, Miss."

"Ah, well, my name is Sage. If you tell me your name, then we'll know a little about each other, and we won't really be strangers anymore, now will we?"

I pasted a smile on my face that was sincere and warm, and his shoulders relaxed a fraction—I guessed a young woman in a dirty nightgown didn't rate high on the threat meter.

"My name's Jax, Miss," he said shyly.

"Nice to meet you, Jax," I replied, letting the gratitude I felt seep into my voice. "Jax, could you tell me the date, please?"

"It's Sunday, September twenty-third," he stated matter-of-factly.

"Okay… but what year is it?" I asked.

Jax looked at me, his face scrunched up as if there were a puzzle in my words somewhere he couldn't figure out. "The year is 1904, Miss."

Uh, 1904?

"Dear Lord," I murmured. My mind immediately rejected what the little boy had told me; it was just too impossible to comprehend. But, instead of screaming out the fears and frustrations building up inside of myself, I tucked them all away to revisit later. Right now, I had to focus on my immediate problem—getting help.

Jax started to edge around me, no doubt anxious to get away from the crazy woman.

"Thank you," I whispered.

He looked back at the last moment and said, "If you'll be needing help, Miss, sometimes they have room at Howell Home on Franklin Street. The mistress there isn't overly friendly, but she'll help you if she can."

I smiled and thanked him. He scurried off, leaving me alone in a city starting to wake up, and with the dawning realization that I had somehow landed myself in a different time.

I glanced down at my nightgown once again and cringed. Being dressed as I was could land me in a whole heap of trouble no matter what year it was. I took off down the street as quickly as possible, my heart pounding and my head spinning. Surely, I didn't believe I was in a different time. Maybe this was all an elaborate hoax, or maybe some super awesome cosplaying convention had moved into the city while I was sleeping, and Jax had been a part of that. I nodded my head at my own conclusions. That could totally be it.

I will not freak out, I will not freak out, I will not freak out.

I quietly repeated the mantra to myself, praying it would help me keep my composure and come up with a believable story… just in case I needed one. I walked briskly in what I hoped was the right direction. If I remembered correctly, Franklin Street was only a couple of blocks away. I kept to the dark shadows of buildings, hoping no one would see me and ask questions I didn't have answers to.

A nasty worm of uneasiness wiggled itself into my heart as I walked. Several times, I had to stop myself from looking over my shoulder and checking to see if anyone were following me. I was definitely on the road to becoming certifiably schizo. I guessed freaky old ladies, terrifying dreams, and a little time travel would do that to a girl. My heart, traitor that it was, tripled its already-frantic beat, and I picked up my pace accordingly. Turning a corner, I found myself at a dead end. A tall, wooden fence that didn't exist in my time blocked off one end of the alley.

A low, menacing laugh echoed from somewhere behind me, causing the fine hairs on the nape of my neck to stand on end. I swung around to face whatever was coming, but there wasn't anyone nearby. I squinted, trying to see my surroundings through the dark and foggy morning.

Without any warning, a gust of wind whipped my hair into my face as something flew past me, nearly knocking me off my feet. I sucked in a hissing breath and grabbed my arm. My fingers came away smeared in blood from a throbbing gash. Another raspy chuckle, closer this time, emanated from within the fog-shrouded darkness.

The next blow came much faster and harder. I cried out as I was slammed into a brick wall, face first, and cut again. This time, the gash was on my thigh, deeper than the first, and it hurt like a mother. I scrambled to my knees and tried to shake off the black spots dancing at the edge of my vision.

"Tsk-tsk, such determination for one so young," a husky female voice purred close to my ear.

My right hook caught her on the side of the head, and she went sprawling to the ground not too far away from me. Obviously, she hadn't expected "one so young" to pack a nasty punch. Her look of astonishment was almost comical, but I didn't take the time to appreciate the tiny victory. I scrambled to my feet and sprinted toward the alley opening. Whatever drugs this woman was on that made her so quick and sure of herself also made her super dangerous, and I could only hope I would be able to get away if I ran for my life. Unfortunately, my assailant was very fast, very strong, and at the moment… very pissed off.

She hit me from behind like a human wrecking ball,

and I went down just as hard. I spit out blood and gravel as I struggled to get free from her grasp—all in vain. Before I could blink, I was unceremoniously flipped over and straddled.

The woman sitting on my middle, wearing a black silk dress, was the most beautiful woman I had ever seen. The perfection of her silky, blonde hair and pouty, rose-colored lips were only marred by her freakish red eyes, which were currently filled with an inhuman rage. She slapped me with such force that my head snapped back and my vision dimmed dangerously. My only lucid thought was that unconsciousness would have been a welcome relief.

"I could have made this relatively quick, but you made me break a nail."

The pout in her voice caught me off guard. *Who is this woman?*

"Now I shall enjoy your terror as I kill you nice… and… slow…" she said, dragging each word out.

I focused on her face, willing myself to stay conscious long enough to give her the one-fingered salute. I wasn't going to let her see my fear, even though I could feel it paralyzing me. But then I caught a glimpse of her teeth— or what should have been her teeth—and my terror quadrupled. Two long fangs extended a good inch below the natural line of her teeth. Two wickedly sharp fangs that didn't belong in any normal human's mouth. The fear felt before was nothing compared to what I experienced in that moment. My heart thumped so hard I was sure it was going to explode from my chest.

That would probably make her very happy indeed, I thought vaguely.

A terrible grin spread over the woman's lovely face,

and her fangs flashed as she lunged for the vein thumping wildly at my neck.

I opened my mouth to let out the bloodcurdling scream building in my throat when I felt the air around me stretch and shift. The air felt flexible, almost pliable. My fingers tingled and twitched, aching to bend the air to my will, though what that meant, I had no idea. The entire sensation was foreign to me.

I glanced up at the vampire on top of me, her fangs only inches from my neck and her face frozen in shock. As I jerked back, the rubberized air around me snapped back into my body. I grunted and tried to dodge the impending attack. Unfortunately, whatever miniscule advantage I'd had the second before had ended. The woman snapped out of her frozen state and plunged her razor-sharp teeth into my neck. I didn't even have time to scream.

The next thing I knew, I felt the monster being jerked off me. A screeching sound, so shrill I was sure my eardrums would puncture, pierced the fading darkness. The silence that followed was profound. I couldn't summon the strength to open my eyes, and my body felt weightless as someone lifted me off the concrete.

I vaguely recalled being supported by strong arms as I threw up next to a building. A jolting movement once again brought me back to the brink of consciousness. I cracked my eyelids open and moaned. A masculine voice shushed me, telling me in a soothing voice reserved for frightened children that everything would be okay. I must have giggled because I heard the same voice ask me, "Have I said something funny, Miss?"

Miss. Everyone was calling me "Miss" now.

Everything is so far from okay, I mused. *Freaky old*

ladies, vampires, and time travel... Oh my!

I giggled again and looked up into a pair of lovely green eyes focused on me in concern. At least, if I were going to die, it would be in the arms of a beautiful man. I reached out to touch the mystery guy's face and noticed my hand was caked in blood, dirt, and God knows what else. This time, I let the darkness claim me, and I didn't fight it one iota.

CHAPTER Three

WHY, OH WHY, WOULDN'T THE POUNDING IN MY head cease? The inside of my mouth felt like sandpaper, and my eyes weren't doing much better—I'd been trying to pry them open unsuccessfully for several minutes. When they did finally crack open, I blinked in surprise. I was in a plain but clean room that held a wardrobe, a washstand, a dresser, and a full-length mirror. A single chair and bedside table were near my small bed, and I was covered with a lovely, handmade blue-and-white granny-square quilt.

I found myself dressed in a clean, white-cotton nightgown, and my neck and arm were bandaged. My lip felt busted, and I was pretty sure I didn't want to see how I looked. I groaned out loud as the memories of my attack came back to me. Closing my eyes tightly, I tried to staunch the flow of events that came rushing back like an unwelcome storm. Had I really been cursed, traveled through time, *and* been attacked by a vampire? If my injuries were any indication, then yes, it was all very real.

I blinked rapidly to keep the tears at bay. I couldn't have a breakdown just yet—I didn't even know where I was.

What am I going to do? Can I ever get back to my own

time? Is it even possible?

The door creaked open, and I hastily wiped my eyes. A young woman in a crisp white shirt and long blue skirt came in carrying a tray. Her shoes squeaked on the well-polished, wooden floor, and the contents of the tray she carried rattled precariously.

"Ah, you're finally awake." She settled a hand over her heart. "You had us just about worried to death, showing up here all bloodied and then sleeping close to two days straight," she said as she set the tray on the bedside table.

"Two full days?" I gasped. "It's been that long?"

"It has. And poor Travis has been worrying himself sick, wondering if you'd be all right." She wrinkled her nose—which was set on a lovely face sprinkled lightly with freckles—as if she'd smelled something rotten. Her hair was light brown and piled high on her head in a loose bun. She may have seemed a little mousy at first glance, but her intelligent gray eyes made her very lovely indeed.

"Travis? Who's Travis, and exactly where am I?"

The woman poured a cup of tea as she answered me. "Travis is an instructor at the home, and he's the one who carried you all the way here after you were attacked. As to the where we are; well, you are now an unofficial resident of Howell Home." She smiled brightly in my direction like it was the best news she had shared with anyone in long while.

Okay, so Travis was the green-eyed mystery man. *Oh God, I hope I didn't call him beautiful out loud when I was semi-conscious.* And what the heck was Howell Home?

"Sugar or milk in your tea?" my new companion asked.

"Just sugar, please."

Although, I'd have preferred a nice, strong latté right

about then. Screw that, a bottle of Jack.

"And you are?" I asked her.

"Oh. My name's Phoebe." She smiled shyly and held the cup of tea out to me.

"Nice to meet you. My name's Sage. Sage Hannigan," I told her as I took the delicate teacup.

"Very pleased to meet you, Miss Hannigan. I'm going to go and fetch you something to eat and let Mrs. Howell know you're finally awake. I'm sure she has a good many questions for you."

I'm sure she does, I thought. My stomach knotted in apprehension.

No sooner had I finished my cup of tea, than a small whirlwind of a woman blew into the room. I didn't know what I'd expected the owner of Howell Home to look like, but this petite, blonde-haired woman with piercing blue eyes was definitely not it. She couldn't have been more than twenty-five or twenty-six years old, although it was hard to tell with those small spectacles perched on her nose.

"Please close your mouth," she snapped. "It's impolite to have your mouth flapping open, imitating a fish out of water."

My mouth closed with an audible snap, and I bit back a smart-assed retort. Instead, I fixed a scowl on my face and crossed my arms, hoping I came off as nonchalant and tough. I was pretty sure lying in bed, wearing ruffles, and sporting bandages ruined the effect, though. I sighed.

"Phoebe told me your name is Sage Hannigan," she

commented.

I nodded my head.

"And may I presume, Miss Hannigan, that you have no idea what you are or what is going on?" she asked with a delicately raised brow.

"What I *am*? What do you mean 'what I am'?" I asked in utter confusion.

"It's just as I thought," she murmured to herself. "With everything else that's going on, I get someone who doesn't even know her own powers." She scowled at the ceiling.

"*Hello!* Remember me? Could you please tell me what the hell you're talking about?"

"Watch your language and your tone, Sage. You are a warper, and it seems you have no idea what that even means," she chided. "Oh well! All in due course. I'll have Phoebe come up with your lunch and some suitable clothing. Then, we'll have a nice long chat in the library." She held up a hand to silence my protests.

"You will feel much more clearheaded after you get some food in your system and freshen up a bit." She paused, and when I didn't object, she continued, "Once you are ready, I'll try and answer all the questions you have."

I reluctantly agreed. I mean, what else was I going to do, click my heels three times and say, 'There's no place like home'?

When Phoebe returned, and after I had devoured a lunch of chicken soup and freshly baked bread, the fun began.

Phoebe helped me dress in the clothing appropriate for the time period. I couldn't help but wonder how in the world women walked around all day in a corset—it was a freaking torture device! After refusing to let her tighten the stays any more for fear of cracking a rib, I dressed in clothing I was *definitely* not used to. The blouse was an antique cream color, high-necked, with pretty lace trim, and it had very full sleeves that gathered just above the elbow and then tightly followed my forearms. The dark green skirt was full and flowed all the way to my ankles.

Phoebe changed my bandages to smaller ones that couldn't be seen under my new clothing, and I tucked my necklace under my blouse, inexplicably pleased with its familiar warmth on my skin. Phoebe wanted to put my hair up into a bun, but I pled a headache and she opted to braid it down my back instead. I stepped in front of the full-length mirror to see if I looked as foolish as I felt. My eyes widened. If it weren't for the cut lip and scrapes on my cheek, I'd have looked quite respectable.

I snorted at my reflection. *Respectable, my ass!*

"All right, Phoebe, let's do this!" I squared my shoulders and headed out to talk with the woman who knew what was going on, and who I hoped would give me some answers.

A gentleman I'd not seen before was sitting with Mrs. Howell and Travis in front of a large fireplace in the library. When I was finally noticed, Travis and the other gentleman stood as I made my way over to the trio.

I plastered a smile on my face. *No need to be hostile*, I told myself. *Not yet, anyway.*

"Sage, this is Travis Connely, whom you've inadvertently met."

He grasped my hand in a warm, firm handshake. I looked up into his now-familiar green eyes and smiled warmly at him. He had a handsome face with a slightly crooked nose, which only added to his rugged charm.

"Thank you so much, Mr. Connely. For saving my life, I mean."

He dipped his head slightly in an embarrassed gesture. "Oh, it was nothing, Miss Hannigan. You seemed to be holding your own against the vampire," he said with a grin.

Holding my own? Is he serious?

"I came around the corner just as you froze her mid-attack, and when I mentioned the scene to Dr. Blake, well, he knew immediately what you were."

"Speaking of Dr. Blake," added Mrs. Howell, "Sage, this is Dr. Aldwin Blake. He is an instructor here at Howell Home, and he is going to try and explain some things to you."

I turned to greet the doctor and barely caught a gasp before it left my throat. He was several inches taller than I and cut a very fine figure in a black coat. His hair, so black it almost seemed to have blue highlights, fell in thick waves haphazardly over his ears, almost covering one eye. The half-covered eye was primarily what had caused my reaction to him... mainly. His right eye, so pale blue it seemed more silver than blue, was covered in a milky film. I assumed he was blind in that eye.

A scar ran from his eyebrow to the top of his cheekbone on the same side of his face. It looked as if someone had cut him with the intent not only to maim his eye, but also to mar his good looks. The scar had the opposite effect, though; instead, it enhanced his fiercely good looks. His other eye, a perfect and brilliant cornflower-blue, was fixed on my face. Something like disappointment and resignation flickered there.

I realized belatedly that I'd been staring too long, so

I thrust my hand out and spoke softly. "Very nice to meet you, Dr. Blake. I'd appreciate any help you can give me with all that is going on."

He settled his marred features into an indifferent mask and grasped my hand in his. It was just as warm as Travis' hand had been, but his touch sent a shiver of delight up my arm.

"The pleasure is all mine," he replied in a clipped tone. When he pulled his hand from my grasp, his jaw clenched.

"Now that all the pleasantries have been made," Mrs. Howell intoned, "let's get down to the reason for our visit, shall we?"

I sat on a loveseat next to Travis while Mrs. Howell and Dr. Blake took the armchairs opposite us.

"Sage, as I mentioned before, we are all of the opinion that you are a warper. We hope to help you understand what that means and to assist with anything in our power."

I took a deep, steadying breath. "Okay, so what is a warper, and why do you think I am one? Does it have to do with time travel?" The last was barely a whisper for fear of being thought crazy.

My eyes rounded in shock when Mrs. Howell laughed loudly.

"Yes, of course it has to do with time travel, and so much more! Tell me," her eyes were wide with anticipation, "what year do you come from?"

Encouraged by her easy acceptance, I told her, "I live—or did—in the year 2004."

The silence was deafening.

I glanced down at the carpet, suddenly less sure of myself, and peeked at everyone from under my lashes. Their expressions ranged from amazement to astonishment and then to wariness from Dr. Blake.

"I'd love to tell you all about the twenty-first century," I said, "but could we do it later? I would appreciate it if you could explain the whole warper thing to me for now."

Mrs. Howell shook her head as if to clear it. "We certainly can." She motioned for Dr. Blake to take over the discussion.

Dr. Blake stood and asked questions as he paced in front of the fireplace. "Sage, what do you know about your family, your ancestry?"

I unclenched my teeth to answer. "I don't really know anything about my heritage. My mother and father were both killed in a car accident when I was five. I didn't have any other family, so I lived in several foster homes until my eighteenth birthday."

His features softened a bit, and I turned my face away to hide the emotions I felt well up.

"Did you happen to find an object recently that you were mysteriously attracted to or felt a magnetic draw toward?" he asked softly.

Involuntarily, my hand flew to my chest, where the stone pendant lay warm against my skin. He noticed the gesture, so I pulled out the necklace to show him. Mrs. Howell and Travis sucked in a loud breath, and Dr. Blake's eyes lit up.

"What is it?" I asked, hating how small my voice sounded.

"It's a piece of the ancient druid standing stones from Scotland. This stone, in particular, was said to be blessed by the druid priestess Amerach, giving its wearer special abilities."

"So, if I take it off, would I be sent back home?" I

wasn't able to mask the excitement in my voice.

"I'm afraid it's not that simple," Mrs. Howell answered.

"It never freaking is," I mumbled under my breath.

"It isn't the stone that made you a warper, Miss Hannigan," Dr. Blake replied. "You were already marked—or chosen, if you will—to be one. The necklace is just a talisman to help you tap into your abilities and to help a handler find you to activate your dormant mark and powers."

"My mark?" I asked. And then, like a puzzle, everything clicked into place. Not an old trinket, a *talisman*. Not a crazy old lady, a *handler*. Not a burn, a *mark*. Nausea overwhelmed me, and the room swayed a bit—or was that me? Warm hands were at my elbows, and as I looked into Dr. Blake's face, I felt myself calm. A moment later, Mrs. Howell put a glass of water in my hand, and I drank it gratefully.

"May I see it?" he asked softly.

He didn't need to explain. For some reason, I knew he was asking about the mark. I nodded and turned my head to look over my right shoulder. I felt the barest feather of a touch over the spot, and a delicious shiver danced up my spine. The heat radiating from his body made me want to lean into him; instead, I held myself rigid.

"Yes," he said briskly, turning to the others. "She has the white spiral-of-life tattoo, the mark of Amerach, behind her ear."

Clearly, he was not as affected by our proximity as I was. Mrs. Howell and Travis both came to exclaim over the mark I had yet to see for myself, and I started to squirm with everyone standing so close, studying me like a science experiment. Dr. Blake cleared his throat, and they shuffled off to take their seats once more.

"So, what else can you tell me?" I asked.

Dr. Blake gave me the condensed version of "Warper History 101." There were only a handful of instances recorded in history in which a warper had been chosen. It was a rare occurrence, a rare gift bestowed upon chosen young women of Celtic ancestry. All records indicated that the warper had no control over the actual time warp, and in every instance, there had been some impending crisis that only a time warper could address in order to prevent irreversible damage to the human and preternatural worlds.

Preternatural. I wondered exactly what kind of creatures existed in my newly realized world. I mean, here I was, discussing druid priestesses, time travel, and vampires. It wouldn't be too much of a leap to imagine the preternatural community consisted of a whole lot more. I shivered.

Oblivious to my inner turmoil, Dr. Blake continued his lesson.

"Warpers also have individual powers that vary from person to person. The powers must be honed to become effective in self-defense during combat."

It was too much to take in; my head spun with the flood of information.

"Do you have any books or anything that can tell me how I can get back to my own time? Or what would happen if I just chose not to be a warper?" Panic laced my voice, but I couldn't help it.

"Our books are very limited when it comes to warpers, but I'll study them more thoroughly to see if I can find anything about returning to your time. As for the other…

no one can force you to do anything; but not doing what you were destined to do won't get you home any faster. It may even be catastrophic to our time, sending out a ripple that distorts yours."

Sheesh, no pressure there! I rubbed my temples, trying to ease the mounting tension headache.

"Maybe we should all take a break before dinner," Travis suggested, his concerned eyes searching mine.

I smiled in thanks.

"We can all rest, freshen up, and meet for dinner in two hours. Sage, I'll send Phoebe up to help you later." Mrs. Howell ended the meeting as abruptly as it had begun.

Everyone left the library and headed in different directions, leaving me in the center of my own little tornado of emotions.

CHAPTER Four

After wandering around, lost in my thoughts, I realized I didn't know the way to my room. I groaned at my own stupidity. Howell Home was huge; I should have paid attention on the way down to the library. Looking around in dismay at all the identical doors, I spotted one next to a painting of a woman reading to a little girl that looked somewhat familiar.

I knocked softly on the door, but there was no reply. Cracking the door open just enough to stick my head into the room, I gave an uncontrolled squeal of delight and quickly pushed into the room, making my way through a small library while taking in its perfection. It was absolutely charming, and I could have happily died right then and there. There were hundreds of books lining the floor-to-ceiling shelves. A beautiful bay window, complete with a window seat covered in oversized decorative pillows, overlooked a quaint courtyard.

Two comfortable-looking armchairs were arranged in front of a small, cozy fireplace. A large writing desk sat in another corner of the room. The decor was on the masculine side, but it was warm and inviting. I walked over to the seating area and picked up a book someone had left on one of the chairs.

32

It was a slim book of poems by Edgar Allen Poe. I smiled and was setting it back down when a door I hadn't noticed jerked open. I jumped, accidentally dropping the book to the floor as Dr. Aldwin Blake walked in. He looked shocked to find me there.

What the heck? This is a library, right?

When I took in his appearance, I noticed he had shed his coat and tie, and a number of the top buttons of his shirt were undone.

My gaze was riveted to the several inches of skin exposed there. I felt my cheeks warm and then promptly felt foolish—I lived in the twenty-first century, where men and women could practically prance around nude if they wanted. And here I was, all hot and bothered over a little chest exposure.

That's when it dawned on me. Dr. Blake had just come through a connecting door, which probably connected to his bedroom. This was his freaking *personal* library.

Holy crap.

He was standing there, looking at me like I was losing my mind, when I finally found my voice. "God! I am such an idiot. I was looking for my room, which shouldn't have been too hard to find if I'd been paying attention, when I stumbled upon this library—your library, evidently. I was so charmed by it that I didn't stop to think it was a private library. I'm sorry. If I had known..."

My babbling died off as Dr. Blake stepped toward me, his proximity cutting off my train of thought. He stopped just in front of me and retrieved the book I had dropped.

"No apologies necessary, Miss Hannigan."

He smiled a crooked little grin, and I swear to God, I nearly melted into a puddle right there. I turned my eyes away from his gaze, afraid he'd be able to sense how he affected me. I was mortified. He was practically a stranger.

"Do you enjoy reading, Miss Hannigan?" he asked, his tone once again cool.

I nodded, not wanting to risk my inner pink-loving, teenage-babble-monster getting out again.

"Well, there are hundreds of excellent books here and in the downstairs library. Feel free to borrow any you'd like. Would you like me to show you to your room?"

I nodded again, feeling like an idiot.

When we arrived at my room, I turned to him, wanting to make up for my appalling behavior. And then, to my absolute dismay, I heard myself blurt out, "Are you blind in your right eye?"

His face showed shock and disbelief for a second before his features settled into a cold, detached mask. "Yes, Miss Hannigan, I am."

He barely whispered the response, but it cut me deeply all the same. With that, he turned on his heel and left me standing in my doorway, my hand placed over my treacherous mouth.

By the time I struggled out of the corset by myself—which took entirely too long and involved foul language—washed my face in a water basin, and finally lay down on my bed, I was unable to quiet the tornado of thoughts and emotions swirling around in my head. I still clung to the hope that I'd wake up safe and sound back in my apartment in 2004, and I'd laugh my butt off at the ridiculously elaborate dream I'd had. But, as much as I craved that, I was coming to the conclusion that my reality was much, much more complicated. Not only had I found out I'd time-traveled to a different year and that vampires were real, but I'd also found out I was chosen to wield powers and help fight the forces of evil. I was so in over my head, just hoping I could live up to all the expectations and do whatever it took to get back to my time. Still wide awake a little while later, I wasn't surprised to hear Phoebe knock at the door.

When she came in, her arms loaded with clothing, my mood darkened even further. Not only did I owe Mrs. Howell for taking me in—and now for all the clothing—but I also owed Dr. Blake an apology. I wasn't very good at owing people. I'd worked hard for everything I'd gotten in my old life; that fact was something I was very proud of.

As soon as I had turned eighteen, my parents' small trust fund was released to me, and I'd said *adios* to the hellhole of a foster home I'd lived in for the past year, choosing to rent myself a small apartment in Charleston. Furnishing it with odds and ends from various thrift stores had kept my bills to a minimum, and I'd started selling repurposed vintage clothing on the Internet recently, so the small amount I had left wouldn't dwindle down too far. I really hoped I'd see my little eclectic apartment again soon.

Phoebe helped me dress again, and even though I had to put the accursed corset back on, I couldn't help but smile at my reflection as I left for dinner. I thanked Phoebe and fiddled nervously with a strand of my hair as I headed out the door. I was just going around the corner when Dr. Blake's door swung open and he stepped out. Dear Lord, he looked yummy in his black evening clothes. He stopped mid-stride when he caught sight of me, and quite comically, his jaw dropped. He recovered quickly, and his gaze raked over me, assessing me and leaving my skin feeling uncomfortably warm all over.

My dress was made from a lovely, dark green satin; it had little capped sleeves and left most of my shoulders bare. The bodice was trimmed with tiny, black seed pearls. The entire dress was bustled in the back, and the fabric cascaded down to my feet. When he still hadn't said anything, only stared at me, I began to fidget and lose confidence.

"Is it horrible? Phoebe said it was perfectly acceptable for an evening meal, but I don't know the appropriate attire for dinner here." I self-consciously touched the back of my hair, which had been neatly arranged in a lovely loose knot on top of my head. A green satin and black-lace rose was pinned to the side. "Phoebe said the green dress brought out the auburn of my hair." I bit my lip.

"You look lovely," Dr. Blake said softly.

I released the nervous breath I hadn't realized I'd been holding as he turned to leave. Catching up to him quickly, I touched his arm to get his attention. He stopped so abruptly that I plowed into his back. It was like running into a small tree—a small, firmly muscled tree—and I rebounded off him at least a foot.

Dr. Blake turned lightning fast and grabbed my arms to steady me before I ended up ass-over-teakettle. As soon as I was steady, he jerked his hands off me as if I'd burned him. I didn't blame him, but it still hurt.

"Was there something you wanted, Miss Hannigan?"

Yes… for you to call me Sage.

I shook my head to clear it. "No… I mean, yes!"

"Well, which is it?" he asked impatiently.

I swallowed hard and met his cold gaze without flinching. Heat rushed to my face, and I frowned slightly.

There was something about him, other than his magnetic pull and handsome arrogance, which made me all giddy. I just couldn't put my finger on it.

"I want to apologize for earlier today." He started to cut me off, but I raised my hand and pinned him with the haughtiest stare I could muster. "What I meant to say was, I didn't mean to be so rude and pry into your personal business like that. I don't know what came over me. One moment I was opening my mouth to thank you, and the next moment, I was insulting you. It was inexcusable."

By the end of my little speech, I was looking at the ground and fiddling with my stone pendant. A large hand closed over mine, and I immediately stopped fiddling—hell, I think I stopped breathing. I looked up into his eyes and found they weren't quite as cold as usual.

"You're welcome," he said gently.

He let go of my hand and stepped away, much to my addled brain's disappointment. "If you'll walk with me, I'd be glad to show you to the dining room."

A huge grin split my face, and Dr. Blake looked slightly stunned for a second. I took the arm he offered and followed him to dinner.

CHAPTER Five

*T*HE WHOLE PLACE IS A FRONT! MY MIND SCREAMED AS I tried to digest everything I had just learned.

Howell Home was a front for the clandestine Cerberus Society. My head had started spinning as soon as Travis had dropped that bombshell on me. After my initial shock, though, I closed my mouth—since it had been very unattractively hanging open—and wondered why this news would surprise me. Considering the amount of knowledge the people here at Howell Home had about the preternatural world, it only made sense there was more to this place than met the eye.

To the outside world, Howell Home was a safe house that took in unfortunate young women and provided them the skills necessary to seek gainful employment. This would keep them off the streets, keep them from begging, or worse. I shivered to think of what "worse" could mean to women of this era. While Howell Home did, in fact, help women regularly, it did so only to keep eyes from prying into its real mission—to act as a base of operations for Cerberus. At the moment, the only residents were Mrs. Howell, Dr. Blake, Travis Connely, Phoebe, and now myself. There were also a few trusted servants in the Home's employ.

Cerberus, which evidently had been around for hundreds of years, studied, recorded, and tried to maintain a balance between the human and preternatural worlds. Its number-one mission was to keep all preternatural activities a secret from the human population. That included taking care of any problems that might threaten mortal lives or expose the preternatural community, which would no doubt cause mass panic. Imagine the Salem witch hunts multiplied by the population of the entire world and involving dozens of creatures that most humans had no idea existed, except in vague fairy tales and bedtime stories. I definitely saw the seriousness of the job these people were doing.

Travis was doing most of the talking over dinner, telling me all about Cerberus and what the society involved. He was of the opinion that a recent influx of vampire attacks was the reason I'd warped into their midst. Perhaps there was some kind of uprising going on... or something more sinister brewing. Their investigation into the attacks had not turned up anything to date, and the vampire leaders in the area kept assuring them it was the work of rogue vampires. However, Cerberus members weren't convinced.

As he took a breath to shovel in some of his roasted turkey, I asked, "So, what exactly are you suggesting I do since you are known in the preternatural community and your society can't come up with anything? What could *I* accomplish? I know I am here for a reason, but what are you getting at, exactly?"

Travis glanced over at Mrs. Howell and Dr. Blake. She gave a slight nod, and Dr. Blake scowled into his plate.

"We think perhaps some of the more powerful

vampires are hiding things from us. We happen to know that a particularly powerful and influential vampire named Soren is looking to employ a young lady. We thought, after you were trained properly, and if you could secure the position, that you'd be able to find out if anything is going on that we need to know about."

Holy shit! They want me to become a spy and infiltrate a powerful vampire's home?

I laid down my fork and glanced at Dr. Blake, who was looking at Travis like he could gladly throttle him. The feeling was mutual. I looked to Mrs. Howell and wondered why she wasn't the one playing spy, but understanding sparked quickly in the back of my mind. She couldn't because she was too well known in both the human and preternatural communities.

I stared down at my plate, no longer hungry. I knew this was one of the reasons I was here, but could I put myself in such a vulnerable position? Could I do it if it meant getting back to my own time and making sure it stayed the future that I remembered?

Yes; yes I could.

I looked up at Travis, who seemed to be holding his breath, awaiting my answer.

"I'll do it."

CHAPTER Six

THE NEXT MORNING, PHOEBE HELPED ME DRESS IN A corset, black skirt, white shirtwaist, and a little black-and-red vest with black velvet buttons marching up the front. A sheer black scarf tied around my neck gave it a touch of sass. While I didn't look bad, I really missed the comfort and simplicity of my jeans and T-shirts.

I was anxious to start the day, to get one step closer to my main goal—getting back home. *If* I ever got back home. I shook my head to dislodge that wayward thought.

"I will not think about that; it is not an option," I said fiercely to my reflection, but behind my eyes, I saw a smidge of uncertainty.

I went to meet Mrs. Howell in the library to discuss my daily schedule. When I arrived, she was sitting behind the desk with a pair of small glasses perched on the tip of her nose. She hardly glanced up from what she was writing but motioned me to take a seat.

"Have a seat, Miss Hannigan. I'll be finished with this letter in just a minute." After she sealed the letter and set it aside, Mrs. Howell took off her glasses and relaxed back into her chair. "We decided the best thing to do would be to give you a condensed course in all the areas we thought most important to you as a warper. After breakfast each morning, you will meet with Mr. Connely in the library to learn as much as possible about the preternatural community. You, Phoebe, and I will meet after that for lessons in etiquette and manners."

I must have snorted out loud, because she gave me an impressive teacher's glare.

"Miss Hannigan, in order for you to leave this house, much less mingle in polite society here in 1904, you will have to be able act like you belong in this time. Quite frankly, you will need extensive coaching to make that happen."

I knew she was right, but *man*, I was not looking forward to a daily dose of princess training.

"I understand," I mumbled.

"Good. After lunch each day, you will meet with Dr. Blake in the old ballroom to learn basic offensive and defensive techniques."

I swallowed almost audibly. "I'll be sparring with Dr. Blake?" Inwardly, I groaned.

Mrs. Howell raised her eyebrow to an impressive height—she must practice that look in the mirror.

"He'll be fine, I'm sure," I murmured hurriedly, my cheeks warm.

Fine, indeed. I covered my snort with a little cough. I'm pretty sure I hadn't fooled her, though.

"We'll start today after breakfast. Go ahead to the dining room, and I'll see you in a little while."

She smiled encouragingly at me, but I could read the we've-got-our-work-cut-out-for-us look all over her face.

After breakfast, I went to meet with Travis in the study to learn about the preternatural community. Since I was about to become intimately involved with vampires and other supernatural beings, I was willing to learn anything that would keep me alive. Maybe, in the process, I would find a way home. Travis seemed more than eager to teach me all that he could, so we got started with my new favorite subject, vampires.

We decided to skip all the history and origins of vampires and got right down to what was important: vampire strengths, vampire weaknesses, and how to defend against and exploit them, respectively. After an hour of researching vampires, I found they didn't have very many weak points. Unfortunately, they *did* have a whole lot of strong ones. I took a deep breath and blew a stray lock of hair out of my face.

"So," I said with my jaw set, "vampires are super strong, have very fast reflexes, and have excellent eyesight—especially at night. Their senses of smell and hearing are two of their greatest strengths. Is that right so far?"

Travis looked up at me, his lips thinned into a grimace, and nodded.

"Okay, then what, pray tell, could possibly be their weakness? Because from where I'm standing, it doesn't seem like they have any at all."

I seriously needed to punch something really flipping hard. Travis must have sensed my frustration and tendency toward violence, because he came around the desk with both hands up, trying to calm me.

"I know it seems that they are invincible, but they do have vulnerabilities. Let's talk about those for a little while before we end the class."

All I could manage was a nod.

"Okay, vampires have many strengths, as we have already pointed out. Let's start on the best ways to kill a vampire."

Finally! I perked up a little, ready to learn something useful.

"Fire is one of the best, and most permanent, ways to kill a vampire. Beheading and staking through the heart are also very effective. Staking can actually be tricky—you have to do it perfectly through the heart because if you miss the organ, you will just have one very angry vampire on your hands. Usually, if you stake a vampire, you want to do it during the day, when most of them rest. That's when they are weaker. Beheading, well... that will kill just about anything, won't it? You have to have a very sharp sword and a wicked swinging arm, though, because it is hard to cut through bone. And, well... let's not mention the mess."

He looked up at me and stopped, probably because I looked just as green as I felt. It was easier to think of vampires as mythological creatures, like those I had watched hundreds of times on television. I mean, I owned just about every classic vampire movie ever made. But to think about doing the things Travis was talking about to someone, some *thing*, like the blonde vampire woman who'd attacked me—something *real*—well, that was a whole other story. Swallowing nervously, I glanced at the clock and was very glad to see the end of "Vampires 101" for the day.

I hurried to the dining room to meet with Mrs. Howell and Phoebe, the whole time giving myself a little pep talk about taking one for the team. I would soon be mingling with deadly creatures as a spy, and here I was, dreading a little class on manners and the art of being feminine. After all, how bad could it be?

It could be very, very bad.

I spent the next hour being poked, stripped, and measured for appropriate garments. Standing up on a small stool in my white shift and corset, Mrs. Howell and a dressmaker circled me, taking notes on everything from my measurements to my skin tone, even my posture. I'd never in my life felt so ridiculously on display. Every time I fidgeted, Mrs. Howell sucked her teeth, clicking her tongue on the roof of her mouth, and the little French woman went into a tizzy. Feathers, ribbons, hats, and fabrics were passed around and draped over me, and all I could think of was getting the hell out of there and taking a jog to let out some pent-up energy. By the time it was all said and done, I couldn't even have told you the color or quantity of anything that was ordered—I had totally zoned out of the fiasco going on around me. The next thing I knew, it was time for me to get dressed once again and prepare for Dr. Blake's class. I'd never been more relieved.

After rapidly escaping the women's clutches, I arrived at my next class. I hesitated on the threshold of the old ballroom in the back of the mansion. I was more than ready to spar—I really *needed* to after the last hour—but I hoped the person with whom I was sparring wouldn't be a problem. Surely, I could shut my ridiculous attraction to Dr. Blake out of my mind and just concentrate on my training. Of course I could. I would. I nodded my head, answering myself.

"Are you going to stand there all afternoon, Miss Hannigan, or do you plan on joining me?"

I swear, the man had super-powered hearing. His back was to me when I entered; his arms were stretched above his head, loosening his muscles in preparation

45

for our upcoming fight. He had shed his jacket, and his untucked white shirt hung nearly to the knees of his soft, loose pants.

I frowned and looked down at my outfit. When I looked up again, he had turned to face me with a bored expression on his face.

"How am I supposed to do anything in this… this fluffy dress?" I asked, exasperated. "It will be impossible for me to maneuver. Why can't I wear pants like the ones you have on?"

"You can't go around wearing pants in this era, Miss Hannigan; you'd likely be jailed for indecent exposure."

I snorted, but Dr. Blake ignored me.

"You will have to train in the clothing you'd be wearing if you got into an altercation. You'll just have to work harder and have a few tricks up your sleeve to gain the upper hand. Now, are you ready to begin, or are you going to stand there and complain all day instead?" He crossed his arms and arched a brow.

Pompous ass.

"I'm ready, oh Great One," I answered, performing a mock bow. I thought I saw the corner of his lip twitch, but I couldn't be sure. Maybe my eye had twitched.

"All right, I thought we'd start off by seeing if we could get a demonstration of your powers today."

My eyes widened, and I began to shake my head.

"We cannot determine what you are capable of if we do not test you a little," he said slowly, as if he were talking to a child.

My temper flared, and before I could stop myself, I marched across the room and poked him directly in the chest. "You do *not* have to talk down to me." I enunciated each word with a jab of my finger. Standing toe-to-toe with him now, I added softly, "I have no idea how to tap into my powers or how to control them when I do."

His nostrils flared as if he were inhaling some new, exotic scent. "We'll figure out what triggered your powers during the vampire attack and go from there." Stepping back from me, he pulled out a huge mat and rolled it open across the floor.

Here we go, I thought.

"Tell me, what were you feeling when you were being attacked, right before your powers manifested?" Dr. Blake asked.

"Besides being scared shitless?" I muttered.

I immediately clapped my hand over my mouth. *Dang it! I really do need to work on my princess social skills.*

Dr. Blake's lip quirked up at one side. "Yes, besides that. What emotions were you feeling?"

I thought about it for a moment. "I was scared. I was also in shock at finding out about vampires. Then, my shock and fear turned into a red-hot fury. Fury that I was going to die before I'd fully lived, and that I'd die a victim."

I looked up and saw understanding in his eyes, and they seemed a little too knowing. I hadn't told him that my fury had also been for never having truly loved or been loved in return. His eyes were way too discerning for my taste. Wanting to break the uncomfortable tension I was feeling, I cleared my throat and looked away.

"All right. Anger I can work with, especially since you seem to have quite a temper."

My mouth flapped open with a retort balanced on the tip of my tongue, but I swallowed it back and shrugged, thinking, *Ah well, what the hell.* He was right.

His brows rose at my agreement with his assessment of my character. He gestured to the mat, and we both quickly took our positions. I felt ridiculous in my skirts, but I grudgingly accepted that I had to work with them while living in 1904. I took a pose I'd learned in self-defense classes as Dr. Blake began to circle me, preparing to attack.

Even though I knew I was perfectly safe, I still couldn't keep my fists from clenching and my heart from thumping irregularly. This was my ultimate fear—the fear of being a victim.

Dr. Blake lunged, and I quickly dodged to my left. My skirts got tangled a bit as I moved, but I still eluded his grasp, just barely. I cursed under my breath, and Dr. Blake began grinning devilishly.

Well, come on, then.

I made a come-get-some sign with my hand, displaying false cockiness to mask my nervousness. That was my first mistake. My second mistake was thinking Dr. Blake would take it easy on me, or that his blind eye would give me an edge. He plowed into me, taking me down so quickly my head spun. With both of my hands tightly pinned above my head in only one of his larger ones and both of my legs held completely immobile by his longer, stronger ones, we were lying chest-to-chest, both breathing hard. It would have been nice at any other time, but at that moment, I was just pissed about losing so quickly.

"Get off; you win, damn you!"

A hard glint flashed in his eye, and his words took on a cruel edge. "Why don't you make me?"

"I mean it. Get off! You're heavy," I ground out.

"Whatever are you going to do about it, Sage? You're female; you're weak and helpless. Pathetic, really. If I killed you, you would be getting what you deserved."

A red haze filled my vision... they were so similar, those words.

My terror soared beyond reasoning, and I began to struggle in earnest as the images I'd blocked from my mind so long ago slithered in. I never forgot the words he had spoken, or the mingled scent of his unwashed body, tobacco, and mint. The phantom smell swelled up around me so strongly I almost gagged. And then, the rage came, but this time a power came with it that I wish I'd had back on that hot July night when I had been only fifteen and so helpless.

I welcomed the power as it surrounded me like a pliable bubble. My left hand came free, and I became aware of Dr. Blake frozen above me, his face questioning. My shock almost made me drop the tentative grasp I had on the bendable power. Returning my focus to my current predicament, I wiggled my other hand free from Dr. Blake's grasp and rubbed my wrists. I could still feel the bubble of power surrounding me and pulsing from my body like an invisible membrane.

On a whim, I skimmed my fingers over the scar on Dr. Blake's face, lingering at the point where it began above his brow. I pushed back the hair that fell over his blind eye, unable to stop myself. He would never know. A slow breath escaped my lips as I pulled myself out from beneath his body. Standing up, I took a few steps back, feeling like I was on the outside of reality, looking in.

Such an odd sensation, I thought.

Reluctantly, I released my hold on the power and

felt it snap back into my body just as Dr. Blake made an 'oomph' sound, landing face-first on the mat, hands clutching air where my hands had once been.

"What the bloody hell?" He jumped up and swung around. His hand went to the scarred side of his face as if he felt the lingering sensation of my impulsive touch.

"Good God, Sage! That was amazing! One second I had you pinned, and the next, you were gone—vanished!" His boyish smile and enthusiasm was contagious, and I felt myself grinning in return.

I started to walk toward him when I realized my legs felt like Jell-O. Holy crap, was I exhausted!

Dr. Blake was by my side instantly, helping me into an armchair. I rested my head on the back of the chair and vaguely heard him say he was going to get tea. The next thing I knew, his hand was on my shoulder, gently shaking me awake.

"Here, Sage; have some tea and a muffin. The sugar will help you."

I sat up and did as I was told for once. Dr. Blake sat in an armchair close to mine and had a cup as well.

"You called me Sage," I remarked after I had, in a quite unladylike way, inhaled an entire muffin.

He looked a bit confused for a second, and then I saw a muscle twitch in his jaw as his mouth settled into a thin line.

"I am sorry, Miss Hannigan. I got excited when you did so well," he said, his tone once again arctic.

I sighed. *Geez, I screwed that up.*

"When I pinned you down—" he began, and I stiffened at the memory, "—the look on your face… Well, I almost stopped because it seemed too real to you," he said.

I looked him directly in the eye. "Yes, yes it was," I whispered.

Standing wearily, I walked to the doorway on shaky legs. "What happened..."

I trailed off, cleared my throat, and began again. "What happened was a long time ago, and I promised myself I'd never be helpless again. Please, don't waste energy feeling sorry for me."

"I don't," he replied, astonishing me. "I feel proud to know you. You are a very surprising woman, Miss Hannigan."

I looked over my shoulder at him, my eyes full of the gratitude I felt. "Thank you, Dr. Blake."

As I walked out the door, I called over my shoulder, "And, Doctor? Please call me Sage."

CHAPTER
Seven

THE NEXT DAY, I FOUND MYSELF WITH A LITTLE FREE time before I had to go to Mrs. Howell's class, so I went for a walk around the small courtyard and garden, glad to be outdoors after so many days of being cooped up inside. It was a beautiful day, and it seemed so peaceful and quiet compared to the city I was used to. Sure, there were noises of people bustling about and life flowing around me, but it was different—more muted. The air seemed a bit fresher, and life seemed a lot less rushed than in the twenty-first century.

I found a little stone bench in an alcove of the wall surrounding the courtyard. Taking a deep breath, I inhaled the rich, heady scent of the overhanging magnolia tree warming in the sunshine and sat on the bench, letting the warmth of the day seep into my own skin, too. My worries slowly faded into the back of my mind, and I relaxed for the first time in days. I guessed I'd have to be content with visiting this spot for the next few weeks to keep from going stir-crazy indoors since I wasn't going to be able to go out in public for a while—all part of the big plan. I sighed.

I was going to be training hard for the next few weeks to prepare myself for my warper duties. At the moment, I didn't feel powerful or destined to do anything but survive. No, most of the time I felt like myself, an eighteen-year-old girl—a little scared and a lot uncertain. I shook my head. Instead of being myself, here I was, in training to join members of a secret government society to save the future I held dear.

Cerberus' plan was quite simple, really. I would train and keep hidden so I could take on the persona of a young widow who needed employment to help make ends meet. Evidently, I was going to let it slip to the gossip mills that I was hunting for a husband. I grimaced at the thought of men courting me while I had so much going on, but they told me it would make my entire cover more believable. I also couldn't be tied to Mrs. Howell and the other Cerberus members, which meant I had to become a very convincing young woman from 1904. Once accomplished, I would wiggle myself into the employ and good graces of one of the oldest and most powerful vampires in the city.

Before my garden walk this morning, I'd had the good sense to finally ask Travis what kind of position Soren needed filled. Evidently, the vampire had a soft spot for pretty young women reading to him every night and attending public outings with him. I had thought Travis was joking, and I'd laughed so hard I had tears running down my face—until I realized he was serious. Then, I'd laughed even harder. I mean, seriously? A big, scary-ass vampire who liked to be read bedtime stories?

When Travis had reminded me of the danger of the situation, I quickly sobered. Soren might share my love of reading, but he was also strong enough to snap my neck with one hand if he thought he was being betrayed or spied on. I'd be "pretty safe," though—at least, that's what

Travis had said.

As safe as one can be while working for a monster, I'd thought.

I would have to watch my every step and word if I ever wanted to get back home… if I ever wanted to make it out of this mess alive.

A shadow fell over me. I snapped my head up and sprang to my feet. I must have been dozing because I hadn't heard anyone approach. My heart skipped a beat when I found myself staring into Dr. Blake's scarred face, and I'm pretty sure my fluttering heart had nothing to do with being startled.

"Miss Hannigan, it seems Mrs. Howell is on a rampage looking for you," he announced dryly.

Holy crap! What time was it?

He smirked. "From what I gathered, you missed your class with her, and she was muttering something about women from the future being ill-mannered, stubborn, and uncooperative."

I sat back down, biting back a groan. I hadn't meant to miss her wretched class. Much to my shock, Dr. Blake sat down on the bench beside me so closely I could smell his unique scent of musk, fresh herbs, and honey.

"Thank you, Dr. Blake. I didn't realize I'd been out here that long. I needed some time to think in the fresh air, but the sun relaxed me *too* much." I smiled over at him.

The wind blew faintly around us, ruffling strands of hair out of my loose braid and into my face. He reached over and tucked a strand behind my ear. I sucked in a breath as his fingers skimmed my cheek and behind my ear, over the mark of Amerach. I felt a fluttering deep in my stomach, and my breathing became shallow. Biting my lip, I looked into his face to see if I could decipher what I saw there.

The strangest string of emotions crossed his face, as if he were fighting within himself.

My heart was pounding erratically now, and I felt a little lightheaded. That's the only explanation I could come up with for what happened next—that I was dizzy and a bit delusional.

I felt slightly weightless, as if I could let go of reality and float away like a wayward balloon by looking into Dr. Blake's eyes. The air shimmered around him, kind of like the fumes in the air when you're pumping gas into your car. Everything became a bit hazy, but instead of becoming blurry, Dr. Blake's face came into sharper focus. His skin seemed to shine, almost glow, and his eyes were an even more brilliant blue than usual. His skin shimmered and looked sun-kissed. I wanted to press myself against him just to see if it would rub off on me.

His scent exploded in my nostrils as I inhaled, and I found myself wondering if a lick of his skin would taste like warm honey. I might have tested out my theory, since I had leaned completely into his personal space, if Dr. Blake hadn't jumped up with a look of horror on his face.

What the hell? I shook my head and swayed a little.

Dr. Blake cleared his throat and asked softly, "Sage, are you ill? You look a little pale."

"Yes, I think I am. Maybe I've been in the sun too long," I murmured as I reluctantly looked up at him. Everything seemed back to normal. I tilted my head left and right and then squinted at him to see if I could recreate what I had just experienced. Nope, and now I definitely felt like a moron. His eyes narrowed.

"Definitely too much heat," I replied, still a little uncertain.

He seemed relieved and let out a long breath. "Let's go inside, then, and find Mrs. Howell to let her know you just lost track of time."

He smiled and offered me his arm. I walked inside with him, the phantom scent of honey still teasing the back of my tongue.

CHAPTER Eight

L ATE THAT NIGHT, I TURNED OVER AND PUNCHED MY pillow for the twentieth time, trying to fluff it up and get more comfortable so I could actually sleep. It didn't work. I jumped out of bed, grabbed the candle on my nightstand, and headed out of my room. Maybe the library would have a book I could borrow. I hadn't read anything good in a long time.

When I got to the library, I stopped just outside, noticing the door slightly ajar and a light shining from inside. Maybe someone else couldn't sleep and had come to find a book as well. I hesitated a moment, wondering if I should retreat to my room, when I heard a hiccup and then a decidedly feminine giggle. Curiosity won out, and I pushed the door open a little so I could peek inside to see what was going on. I'm sure my jaw just about unhinged as I took in the scene before me. Mrs. Howell, dressed in her long, white nightgown with her lovely blonde hair hanging down almost to her waist, was sitting Indian-style on a rug in front of the fireplace. Beside her was a half-empty bottle of liquor, and in her hand was an almost-empty glass.

"Ah! Sage! Please, do come in and join me! I hate to be the only one having fun." She smiled crookedly and hiccupped at the same time.

I gave a little jump at being caught staring and looked around as if help would pop out of the woodwork to explain this bizarre scene. As I walked over to the party of one, I noticed how young she looked with her hair down and her eyeglasses missing.

"Is anything wrong, Mrs. Howell?" I asked. Something had to be wrong... I mean, this was a drunken version of Mary Poppins!

Her big, blue eyes looked up at me, shinning with too much liquor and amusement. "Why would anything be wrong? Everything is just... fine." She drew out the last word.

I sat down on the carpet next to her, moving the bottle a little out of the way.

"And please, call me Elaine. After all, I'm not that much older than you."

She smiled, and my only thought was, W*ow, if she smiled like that a little more often, men would be lined up at her doorstep!*

I smiled back, and for the first time in a long time, I actually felt like myself. Tension seeped out of my body. Yeah, she was well on her way to being good and toasted, but who was I to judge?

Elaine jumped to her knees, produced a second glass from nearby, and without much spilling, she poured a glassful and thrust it at me, sloshing some on her hands in the process. I started to say no, but then I noticed something I hadn't caught before—a telltale puffiness under her eyes that could only have come from crying—and I wondered what had caused her so much anguish that she'd cried late at night when no one could see.

"What the hell," I announced more to myself than to Elaine. "No one should have to drink alone." I threw back half the contents of the glass. The alcohol burned going down, but the aftertaste was a pleasant surprise.

The next thing I knew, the bottle was quite empty, and Elaine and I had gone from buzzed to three sheets to the wind. We talked about all kinds of things, and I was surprised to find out how much we had in common. It was easy to understand in that moment that no matter what era you were from, women were, deep-down, the same creatures. When I tried to explain technology, society, and rock 'n' roll to her, her expressions were so funny I laughed until my sides hurt. Vaguely, I recalled acting out and singing "You're the One That I Want!" from the movie *Grease*, and afterwards going into detail about the black-leather getup Olivia Newton John had worn. Her face was priceless—going from horrified to longing in quick succession—and I laughed so hard I got stomach cramps and hiccups.

We were both singing, "I Can't Get No Satisfaction," when I heard a gasp from Elaine. I looked in the direction she was staring to see Dr. Blake and Travis Connely standing just inside the library door. I stuttered to a stop, my heart plummeting to my toes. Dr. Blake had his arms crossed over his chest, his trademark scowl in place, and poor Travis was looking at us in absolute shock.

I slapped a hand over my mouth to keep from giggling at the whole ridiculous scene, but when I looked over at Elaine and saw her crying, I went from irritated and amused to pissed off in a second flat. Surely, she was entitled to a little fun, a little time to let go of everything and be irresponsible for once.

I jumped to my feet—wobbling only a bit, thank goodness—and opened my mouth to give someone a piece of my mind. Before I could say anything, I heard snorting next to me. I looked over at Elaine and realized she was laughing so hard she was snorting and crying as she held her stomach.

"Should… see… your… faces!" she gasped out through very unladylike snorts.

She flounced back onto the loveseat, and ignoring the wobbly room, I sat down beside her. When Elaine finally stopped laughing, her shoulders slumped as exhaustion took its place. She leaned over and put her head on my shoulder, her eyelids already drooping.

"I would love to have been born in your time, Sage," she said with a yawn. "Though, I never would have known the love of my life or have been given the purpose I now live with." She looked up at me through bloodshot eyes and frowned slightly. "You know, I guess I really wouldn't want to have been born in your time after all…" The last part of her sentence slurred as she dozed off on my shoulder.

She must have loved someone very deeply, I thought, slightly jealous. My eyes were closing against my will when Travis came into my line of vision.

"Let me take her to her room. She wouldn't want to be seen, and everyone will be waking up soon," he whispered, gazing at Elaine, who had begun to snore softly.

I nodded, and Travis gently gathered her into his arms and carried her out of the library. I knew I needed to get to my room, too. Unfortunately, my head was feeling foggy.

I tried to stand and felt like I'd stepped onto a Tilt-A-

Whirl. Dr. Blake was at my side in a blink.

"Shit, I forgot about him."

His eyebrow shot up into his hairline.

I groaned. "Did I say that out loud?"

His lip twitched into a gorgeous smirk of a smile. "I'm afraid you did. Let me help you into your room, Sage."

I sighed and tried to move my rubbery legs, when Dr. Blake scooped me up into his arms. I squeaked in alarm.

"Shush! You'll wake the whole house," he said close to my ear.

I suppressed a shudder. "Put me down! I'm not too drunk to walk, for crying out loud."

I felt more than heard a deep chuckle, probably because even though I was arguing, my body had gone limp in his arms. *Traitorous hormones!*

His body heat and the swaying as we ascended the staircase had me snuggling into him. I felt his arms stiffen, and that sobered me up just a little. Unfortunately, I was too drunk to let him brush me off so easily.

Dr. Blake carried me into my room and set the candle on my dresser. He carefully set me down on the edge of the bed and stepped back.

I stood up quickly and took his hand in mine—liquid courage and all that. His eyes narrowed, and he very nearly jerked my hand off as he snatched his from my grip. My eyes widened at the violent reaction, and he must have seen the hurt in my eyes before I looked away because his gaze softened a fraction.

"Go to bed, Sage; you'll be more yourself in the morning, once all the alcohol is out of your system."

I ignored him, put both my hands flat on his chest, and was gratified to hear him hiss in a breath. The sound made my bones liquefy.

Feeling a little brave, I slid my hands up his muscled chest and then around the back of his neck to dig my fingers into his thick, wavy hair. I stretched up on my tiptoes and leaned into the arch of his neck to inhale his addictive scent.

Just one little taste can't hurt, I thought as I licked the skin at the hollow of his neck. A moan escaped my lips, and I felt a shudder run through the length of his body.

Dr. Blake grabbed my arms, which I figured was to push me away, and I was disappointed. Instead, he held me at arm's length, studying my face in the candlelight, looking for something. What, I didn't know.

"You don't find me attractive, Dr. Blake? Am I not your type? Not ladylike enough?" I asked, meaning to come off nonchalant. But I heard my voice crack at the end and couldn't help but hate myself for it.

A growl of frustration erupted from his throat just before he pulled me to him and crushed his lips to mine.

Later, I would berate myself for not freezing that moment, to savor the beauty and passion of the kiss, but you could hardly think of those things when you were being kissed so thoroughly. Actually, I barely remembered my name right then.

He kissed me like a man starved, with a wild abandon that drove me insane. I had never been kissed so passionately, so completely that my head spun and my body went limp. When he broke the kiss, both of us were breathing heavily. I kissed his neck and leaned into him, our bodies flush again, and then I licked his pulse point. A delicious friction was building between us, and I rocked myself against him, needing to get as close as possible.

"Aldwin... you taste like wild honey, and it drives me crazy."

His entire body went rigid, and I could feel him start to pull away from me.

"What did I do?" I whispered.

His eyes were blue chips of ice, and his jaw was clenched so hard it looked like it was about to break. "Sage, this shouldn't have happened. I'm sorry." He gently moved me away from him.

I was still reeling from the kiss we'd shared and the electric current flowing around us. Stumbling backward, I sat on my bed, feeling rejected, and I couldn't bear to look at him. "Okay. If you would, please shut the door when you leave."

My voice came out quietly, but even I could hear the steel behind the words. I lay down and pulled the covers over myself.

"Sage..."

I stiffened, then heard him sigh heavily as he quietly left, shutting the door behind him.

I didn't cry. Survivors didn't cry.

That's what I kept telling myself.

CHAPTER Nine

I WAS AMAZED AT HOW QUICKLY THE WEEKS FLEW BY. My mornings were filled with classes, and my afternoons were filled with pushing myself to the limit as I practiced my combat and warper abilities. It was difficult to find the perfect balance between being a lady and a kick-butt warper.

While I still yearned for my jeans and tees, I found that I didn't loathe my skirts quite as much as I had originally. There was something empowering about knowing you'd have the upper hand in a fight because you would be underestimated and dismissed as a piece of fluff. What could I say? I liked to think of myself as a badass in a corset. Now, if only the corsets were leather...

Classes about the preternatural world with Travis were the easiest part of my day. My mind eventually began to accept all the things in my new world, the things that went bump in the night that I'd never believed in a few short weeks ago. Travis taught me the basics about vampires, shifters, werewolves, fae, and other creatures, and it wasn't long before I began learning how to spot them all. Some were easier than others because their eyes were a big giveaway.

Most newly made vampires' eyes, for instance, were ringed in bright red, while the older, more powerful vampires' eyes were ringed in gold or silver. Vampires were able to cast an appearance illusion while in society, making their eyes seem either normal to humans, or cause people to glance away and not make eye contact. The weaker, newly made vampires relied on charms made by witches to keep their illusions strong for longer periods of time.

Shifters' and werewolves' eyes had a distinct animal shape and often had dual- or tri-colored irises—brown with golden streaks or gold with black streaks. The eye shape and color were more pronounced close to a full moon or right before they were going to shift. Extreme emotions—such as anger, lust, or hate—would cause their eyes to start the shifting process.

Other preternatural creatures were harder to spot, with fae being one of the hardest because of their superior glamour skills. Travis hypothesized that because I was able to see the blonde vampire's red-ringed eyes, I would be immune to the illusions vampires used to hide their biggest giveaway. That was sure to come in handy.

The hardest class for me was Elaine's etiquette class. After eighteen years in a different era, it was a challenge to learn the proper way to sit, stand, walk, and eat. It was even harder not to fidget, snort, or curse under my breath. When we began learning dances, I felt relieved. Finally, there was something I was halfway decent at. Part of me loved unlocking more of my feminine side—dressing up, being treated like a lady. But mostly, I was dying to rock out to my iPod and dance around my apartment in boy shorts and a tank top while no one was watching. I pushed away my wild side, though. I had a job to do, and I was going to see it through.

Needless to say, by the time I got to my afternoon classes with Dr. Blake, I had so many pent-up frustrations

I'd take them out on him. For several days, we worked on controlling my warping abilities, since they would be a huge advantage in tough situations. We found out one day, with Travis's help, that I had been freezing my entire surroundings. With a lot of practice and concentration, I learned to focus my energy into freezing only my opponent and not everyone in the room, and that helped me conserve a lot of energy. I still became weak after using my powers, but not nearly as badly as I had before.

We also figured out my reflexes were becoming quicker since my abilities had been activated. And perk number three of having awesome warper abilities was that I could expend some of my energy into punching and kicking, making myself stronger. I became more of a threat and an asset. In all honesty, I was starting to enjoy the extra strength my powers gave to me.

Dr. Blake and I sparred daily, and I learned how to take an opponent down using just my hands and legs. My body had hurt for a solid week after the initial daily drilling, but eventually, it got used to the abuse I put it through. We never discussed what had happened in my room the night Elaine and I had had a little too much fun; we both were trying too hard to pretend it had never happened. If only it were that easy.

Being in close contact with Dr. Blake was a sort of sweet torture; he'd made it clear he wasn't interested in me like that, even though I was pretty sure he found me attractive. I'd noticed the way he looked at me when he thought I wasn't looking. I could only assume he didn't want to get involved with a student, or maybe he just wasn't interested in a relationship at all. I could deal with that as long as I got to punch things.

CHAPTER Ten

IN THE PAST THREE WEEKS, I HADN'T STEPPED FOOT outside of Howell Home or its stone-walled courtyard. I was used to jogging, shopping, and going out on a whim. True, I'd never had many friends and was too much of a loner, but sometimes, adult interaction was needed. I wasn't usually reckless or stupid, so there was no excuse for my next actions.

Walking around in the courtyard, making my rounds close to the stone wall late in the afternoon, I came across an iron gate hidden by overgrown vines. I cleared away as much of the overgrowth as possible to get a better look. There was an old, rusty handle, and I gave it a single, quick jerk to see if would open. With a loud, metallic screech, it swung open.

I glanced around quickly, thinking the whole city must have heard the racket I was making. When no sirens blared and no one came running to jerk me back within the perimeter, I hesitated only another second before squeezing through the opening and making my way to the main street in front of Howell Home. I kept looking over my shoulder nervously as I walked, feeling like a naughty child caught with her hand in a cookie jar. I hadn't been out and about in 1904 Charleston, so I felt a little conspicuous. But I wasn't a prisoner, and I wasn't a weakling, so I squared my shoulders and continued on.

A few moments later, I stopped dead in my tracks. Carriages went by on the street, and several men and women walked leisurely down the sidewalk. I felt the strangest sensation of disconnectedness, of being in 1904 but not belonging, like I was walking in a dream and at any moment I would morph back into my modern self. I gave a start at that thought and glanced down in alarm. My long, cream-colored walking dress was covered by a calf-length, cream-colored coat, trimmed with intricate black embroidery down the front edges and around the neckline. A single button at my waist closed the coat. On top of my dark auburn tresses, sitting a little off-kilter, was a straw hat trimmed in black roses, ribbon, and tulle. A huge, stupid grin split my face. I looked like any other lady taking an afternoon stroll! With a spring in my step and a whole lot more confidence, I continued on.

Charleston looked the same, and yet completely different. Some of the buildings were almost identical to those in my time. I walked several blocks, taking in the familiar sights and hoping I'd be able to see the city as I remembered it again someday. Eventually, I came upon a little street market and immediately wished I had a few coins in my pocket. My stomach rumbled, agreeing with me. I meandered through the tables and stalls, enthralled by all the people bartering and selling fresh food and other handmade items.

I was admiring a handmade silk scarf when I felt someone's eyes on me. While I scanned the crowd, I felt a small tug on my sleeve. I looked down into the face of a dirty little boy with adorable dimples.

"Excuse me, Miss. The gentleman asked me to give this to you."

I looked at the folded piece of paper like it was a viper. Who would be sending me a note? I didn't know anyone outside of Howell Home.

"He said he wouldn't pay me if you didn't take it, Miss."

The little boy's lip began to quiver, obviously concerned that I wasn't going to let him finish his job, so I smiled at the child and took the note.

He didn't waste any time once his mission was accomplished, running expertly through the throng of people at the market. Even though I walked quickly after him, I couldn't catch a glimpse of either him or his employer. Without lifting my skirts and causing a scene by flat-out running after the child, I had no chance to track him down with so many people milling about. I cursed under my breath, and then cursed some more at my immediate relapse into *unladylike* behavior.

It was getting late, and I wasn't sure how long I could be gone without being missed, so I shoved the note into my skirt pocket and headed back to my temporary home. Luckily, I made it back to Howell Home in pretty good time. I darted into the alley and squeezed through my hidden gate, running quickly to the back door and letting myself in. When I found no one waiting for me, I let out a shaky breath and headed to my room.

I was puzzling over the note in my pocket when I ran smack into Travis Connely. *Dang it, running into people is starting to get old.* I laughed nervously.

"Sorry, I wasn't paying attention to where I was going... again."

He fidgeted a bit, running his fingers through his hair,

and didn't quite look me in the eye. "No harm done, Sage. I hope you had a pleasant day?"

I cocked my head, searching his face for any accusations there. He seemed to be genuine, maybe a little more nervous and twitchy than normal, but I couldn't find any sign that he knew of my impromptu day out.

"Yes, it was lovely outside today. I'll see you at dinner, Travis. I'm on my way to freshen up, if you'll excuse me?"

"Of course," he said with a relieved breath and a tiny bow.

I didn't have time to think about his sketchy behavior; my hand curled around the note in my pocket, and I quickened my pace, ready to get to the privacy of my room to read it. My stomach churned. Whatever was written in the note… well, it couldn't be good.

When I got to my room, I bolted the door. My heart was pounding in my ears. Tossing my hat and jacket on a chair, I sat on the edge of my bed, pulled the note out of my pocket, unclenched the fist I had made around it, and smoothed it out on the coverlet. With trembling fingers, I unfolded the note to read its contents.

Dear Madame,
You cannot stop what has already been set into motion. I will kill you if I have to.

I was still puzzling over the note at dinner that night, barely noticing what I ate. Who could the sender have been? Only a handful of people knew of my existence, and that was what concerned me the most. It would mean that someone I had come to know, someone I trusted, was as fake as Tammy Faye Baker's eyelashes. I wondered if it were possible for some kind of preternatural creature, or maybe a witch, to have sensed or foreseen my time travel. I made a mental note to ask Travis the next day.

If I hadn't been so preoccupied with my own troubled thoughts, I might have noticed the tension in the dining room—the unusual silence might have tipped me off as well. Mrs. Howell's voice cut through my thoughts, startling me.

"How was your day, Sage? Uneventful?"

Her eyes pierced me to my seat, and her tone sent up a red warning flag. I glanced around the table, finally noticing the tension rolling off everyone. No one's gaze would meet mine.

I set my fork down and slowly returned her accusing gaze. "It was a pretty good day," I replied carefully.

"Was it now?" she asked, a little too sweetly. "Anything you wish to discuss with us?"

I narrowed my eyes at her. *Was she referring to my escape today, or was she alluding to the note I had received? Could she possibly know about that?* I kept my face impassive, not wanting to give anything away.

"Would you like to tell us what you were doing traipsing about the city by yourself today, putting our entire mission in jeopardy? Or would you prefer to pretend it never happened?"

Crap! My first instinct was to act like I had no idea what she was talking about, but it was clear that she was fully aware of my trip to the market, and I didn't feel like playing games.

"It seems to me you have already been informed of my trip to the market. There is nothing else to tell. I took a walk because I was feeling cooped up; I made a mistake in judgment."

Elaine slammed both palms down on the table so hard a glass of wine tipped over. I flinched, and Travis and Dr. Blake both seemed just as surprised. She stood up and leaned forward with both hands still on the table in front of her. Her eyes blazed in fury.

"You were cooped up? You made a *mistake*?" she shouted. "A mistake could get one of us killed. Maybe even *all* of us. Don't you care, Sage?"

Travis and Dr. Blake jumped out of their seats when I stood up. I could imagine what my face looked like with thoughts of throttling someone dancing in my head.

"I said I made a mistake, *Elaine*. So you can back off... *now*," I growled.

"You need to grow up, Sage. At this rate, you won't make it out of here alive."

With that parting shot, she exited the room, floating on a cloud of righteous fury.

My shoulders slumped in defeat.

"She didn't mean that," Travis said softly.

"Actually, I'm pretty sure she did," I muttered.

CHAPTER
Eleven

I JUST ABOUT HAD ENOUGH. EVERYONE WAS BEING polite—*that* wasn't the problem at all—but I would rather deal with people screaming at me and throwing things to show their anger. No, everyone was polite, in a detached sort of way. They were still talking to me, but only when strictly necessary. Classes were tolerable, but beyond frustrating. My jaw was sore from having clenched it for so long, trying to just get through another day of shunning. The worst part was knowing I deserved it, and they still didn't even know about the letter.

As I sat at the dinner table for three torturous days after my infamous excursion, listening to conversation flow around me, without me, I wanted to hurl my wineglass against the opposite wall and watch it shatter into a thousand pieces just to see everyone's reactions. I was pretty sure it wouldn't have earned me any brownie points, though. Instead, I dropped my fork onto my plate with a loud clang and stood up slowly from the table.

Everyone's attention was riveted on me. I leaned forward and rested my palms on the table, one on either side of my plate. Lowering my head, I took a deep breath, but my voice came out wobbly when I spoke.

"I'm sorry, okay? I know I've disappointed everyone. I know I screwed up, and I know you are all pretty pissed at

73

me right now, and I deserve that. I have no excuse, except that I was feeling restless and caged in. I never meant to put everything we have worked so hard for in jeopardy."

Unfortunately, a few tears had already escaped down my cheeks, and I could feel my emotions on the brink of a total breakdown. I swiped at my face quickly and made a beeline for the dining room doors. After I made it out, I gathered up my skirts and ran up the stairs two at a time, passing a scandalized maid in the process. By the time I'd made it to my room, Dr. Blake had caught up with me, and tears were flowing freely down my face.

"Go away!"

I ran into my room to slam the door, but he wedged his foot in the doorway. I looked up through my tears into a face filled with tenderness and concern. A sob escaped from somewhere deep inside me, and I began to cry in earnest. Dr. Blake pushed the door open, and I went to sit on the edge of my bed in defeat. I heard the click of the door shutting and then felt a dip in the bed behind me. I hated to be seen at such a weak moment and to feel so vulnerable.

Dr. Blake's steady fingers pulled the pins out of my hair, allowing it to fall in waves past my shoulders. He pressed a tender kiss to my temple and gently tugged me back onto the bed into his arms. I turned into his embrace with my face pressed into his white linen shirt. His arms felt strong and sure around me.

I cried like I had cried only one other time in my life. I cried for the unfairness of life, for the future I might never get to see again, and because I never asked to be burdened with so much. Dr. Blake held me in his arms all night, whispering nonsense to me and caressing my arms and back until I fell into a deep and dreamless sleep.

CHAPTER

Twelve

THE NEXT MORNING, I WOKE IN BED ALONE, THANK God. I was dreading facing everyone. I rarely cried, and I never broke down as I had done the night before. After I splashed my face with cool water and dressed, longing for my concealer and eye drops, I headed down to breakfast.

Standing in front of the double doors that led into the dining room, I took a deep breath and squared my shoulders, but I stifled a screech and spun around when I felt a light touch on my shoulder. Elaine stood there, sans the scowl she had worn for the past several days. I straightened my posture and raised my chin a smidge as I looked her directly in the eye.

"Sage, we are all very proud of you. You have come a long way in the past several weeks. You are a hard worker, a quick learner, and when most other young women would have broken down going through all the things you have, you tapped into an inner strength and moved on."

She took a deep breath and continued, "Please forgive me for reacting too harshly. I allowed the worry I felt when I realized you had put yourself in danger to color my actions." She looked down at her hands clasped in front of her.

I got the distinct impression it was almost as hard for her as it was for me to apologize to anyone. How could I not forgive someone who had helped me so much, someone who cared about me? I impulsively pulled her to me for a hug, and after a moment's surprise, she hugged me back.

"Of course I forgive you," I said fiercely. I gave her one last squeeze and then stepped back. Throwing her a quick grin, I entered the dining room for breakfast.

I dug into my food with gusto, and my heart felt lighter even though my stomach felt empty from missing most of the previous night's meal. When Dr. Blake entered, looking refreshed and charming, my heart gave a little flutter, and I couldn't help but smile when I remembered how gentle and sweet he'd been the night before.

He met my eyes briefly and gave me a little wink. It was a good thing I was already sitting down. Dang, that man was some major eye candy. I gave him a sassy grin in return and then finished my breakfast. Mrs. Howell informed everyone that instead of our regularly scheduled classes, we would all be meeting in the library to go over some things. I glanced at her, but her demeanor gave nothing away. I was pretty sure I wasn't in trouble again.

Travis, Dr. Blake, Phoebe, and I waited in the library for Elaine to arrive. I pretended to skim the pages of the book in my hand, but instead I studied my three companions. I couldn't imagine any of them sending me that blasted note, alerting preternaturals of my presence, or one of them being a traitor.

I looked at Dr. Blake and knew he could be moody and unpredictable. Lord knows he looked dangerous enough to be a bad guy. Surely, I would be able to tell, though. And after holding me gently through the night, I just couldn't imagine my intuition being that off when it came to him.

I glanced over at Travis and Phoebe, deep in conversation by the fireplace. Travis had saved my life and killed a vampire the day I met him. He seemed otherwise genuine and gentle, but sometimes I wondered about his enthusiasm for killing preternaturals. I also had to consider the fact that when I came home after getting the note, I ran into him acting suspiciously.

I narrowed my eyes at Phoebe, who was currently looking adoringly at Travis through her lashes as he spoke animatedly to her. I hadn't realized she had a thing for Travis, but any fool could see it right then. I was surprised I hadn't noticed before. Phoebe was pretty and quiet, and even though she was technically a servant, she was treated as an equal and a trusted member of the group. I didn't think she was a traitor. Not because she was a woman—I knew better than to make assumptions like that. I just didn't know all that much about Phoebe, and I thought it unlikely that she would betray a man she felt strongly for. I needed to learn a little more about her before I made any judgments, however.

I shook my head in frustration. Howell Home also staffed several other servants, and although they were considered trustworthy, they would all be at the top of my list to investigate. I might have to come clean to Elaine about the note. I really didn't want to mess up the relationship we had just mended, though. I bit my lip, thinking about the predicament I had gotten myself into. It was then that Elaine walked in with her normal whirlwind fashion and beckoned everyone to take a seat.

Once we got settled, she cleared her throat and addressed us all.

"For the past six weeks, we have all worked very hard together, day-in and day-out, to prepare Sage for her mission. Travis has assured me she has learned all he can teach her about preternaturals. I am convinced she will fill her role as a lady born to this era without flaw... even though she still has a tendency to curse most unladylike under her breath."

She said the last with a hint of amusement and affection in her voice, and I felt my eyes go a little misty.

"Dr. Blake has also assured me that she has a firm grasp on her abilities as a warper and has been one of his brightest pupils in matters of combat and knife handling."

My cheeks felt like they were on fire as I glanced quickly over at Dr. Blake. The blasted man grinned at me, probably loving how uncomfortable I was with all the praise.

"So," Mrs. Howell continued, "we are going to celebrate by attending a house party tonight. Our plan will be put into motion starting then."

Elaine was beaming at all of us, and I felt like I had been punched in the gut. So soon? Was I ready to do this already? Everyone was talking excitedly and shaking hands, oblivious to my inner turmoil. It seemed the demon of self-doubt had made camp right inside my chest.

Elaine walked over to me. "Sage, if you will meet me in my room, I have a few things to show you, and then we will take you to the townhouse we have procured for you."

I nodded, barely hearing her. She probably had some last-minute princess advice to impart. I caught my snort just in time.

"I'll meet you there as soon as I grab a breath of fresh air."

I caught her worried look just before she masked it. Placing a hand on her arm, I smiled. "Just in the courtyard, I promise. Don't worry."

I gave her a quick squeeze before making my way outside to sort out my thoughts and regain my composure.

CHAPTER
Thirteen

HALF AN HOUR LATER, I MADE MY WAY UP TO Elaine's room, a little less freaked out and a lot more calm. I knocked gently on the door and heard a muffled reply from within. I opened the door slowly, hoping it had been a *come in* reply. Her room was a pleasant surprise of colors and textures.

The drapes were a deep red, and a colorful rug had been placed in front of the fireplace. *She must have a thing for sitting in front of fireplaces,* I mused, remembering our girls' night not so very long ago. A single turquoise-blue chair sat in front of the window with a huge, fluffy pillow adorning it.

I couldn't tell what color her bedspread was because it was completely covered in clothing. It looked like her dresser had thrown up. She stood next to the bed, hands on her hips and a huge grin spread across her face.

"What's going on?" I asked. "Need help with some spring cleaning?" She couldn't have missed my smirk.

Her grin only got wider. "No… this is all for you."

My smirk quickly faded, and she laughed at my distress.

"What do you mean this is for me?" I asked, staring at the ungodly amount of frilly underthings and skirts hanging off her bed.

"Come on over, Sage. These were all specially made with your mission in mind."

Walking over to the bed, my doubts broadcast on my face for anyone to see, I spotted a corset and nearly cursed out loud. Luckily, all the foulness I wanted to spew stayed locked away in my happy little mind.

Elaine noticed my look and clucked her tongue at me. "Really, Sage, you should see your face. You shouldn't be so quick to judge."

I picked up a cream-colored corset and noticed a difference right away. It was made out of a buttery-soft, suede-like material, with tiny seed pearls stitched all around the neckline. It had one-inch straps and hooked up the front instead of tying in the back. The corset felt a lot lighter than the one I normally wore. I cocked my eyebrow in question at Elaine.

She smiled knowingly. "It doesn't have a bone or ivory core like most corsets. The inner is made with a material not yet available to the regular population. I have no idea what the material is, but it is lighter and much more flexible than a normal corset."

I held it to my chest, running my fingers over the soft fabric, and then I spied its twin in black. I had to stop myself from kissing her smack on the mouth. It was a thing of beauty. She laughed at my obvious enthusiasm over the black corset.

"These are absolutely amazing," I exclaimed in awe.

Elaine beamed at me. "I knew you'd love those. Now, here are several more items I think you will appreciate as well."

The next thing she showed me made me grin even

wider, if that were at all possible. Several pairs of garters were making me all fluttery inside. Who knew I could learn to love lingerie so much? Of course, I blamed it on the fact that these garters would not only hold up my stockings, but would also allow me to comfortably conceal a dagger in them.

I was shown several skirts made of lightweight materials, all with hidden pockets, and the right-side pocket slit open on the inside so I could have easier access to the dagger strapped to my garter. Man, this day was just getting better and better. I was feeling downright giddy with these amazing items.

Finally, Elaine showed me my new shoes. At first glance, I couldn't figure out what was special about them besides being pretty awesome looking. I picked up a pair that had a two-inch heel, were calf high and overlaid in black lace. The bottom had a nice tread, so I wouldn't be slipping. I looked inside and found a hidden slot sewn into the right-foot shoe—just perfect to conceal a dirk. Several were clearly meant to be for eveningwear, and the rest were for everyday wear. All of them were calf length—the perfect height—and they were all modified to hide a weapon. Shit kickers, Edwardian style. *Me likey.*

"Your townhouse has been modestly furnished, and several outfits and dresses have been sent there ahead of you," Elaine mentioned as I stood there, taking in everything.

I shook my head, feeling overwhelmed. "I don't know what to say…" My voice wavered.

Elaine took my hands in hers. "None of that, now. We are all very glad to help you; not only are we elated to assist a warper, but we have also grown very fond of you,

Sage."

I smiled at the woman who, under abnormal circumstances, had become one of my only friends. "Elaine, thank you… for everything," I said sincerely.

She cleared her throat. "Yes, well, I'll send these things over right away. Dr. Blake will be taking you to your new place; he has a few more things for you as well."

An unbidden picture of Dr. Aldwin Blake showing me women's undergarments had me laughing out loud, and Elaine looked at me as if I'd lost my mind. I waved a hand as I shook my head. "Sorry, just had a funny thought." She shook her head but didn't question me. Thank goodness.

"Well, get going! You have a lot to do before tonight's grand entrance." She smiled while she shooed me out the door and shut it firmly behind me. I stood outside her closed bedroom door a few moments before walking determinedly toward my uncertain future.

CHAPTER Fourteen

LESS THAN AN HOUR LATER, I FOUND MYSELF COVERED in a black, hooded cloak and being ushered quickly into a small, black carriage with Dr. Blake waiting inside. I tried to muster a smile.

"This all seems to be happening so quickly, and sometimes I still feel like it is a dream that I will wake up from at any moment."

The carriage lurched forward; I slumped back against the cushions and closed my eyes. I sat that way for a while, swaying gently in my seat while the carriage made its way down the street. I was startled when Dr. Blake spoke.

"Do you have someone waiting for you when you get back home, Sage? Is there some young man going insane without you right now?" The question was so out of the blue, and his eyes were searching my face so intently, that I just stared at him stupidly for several moments before I could form a reply.

"No, I don't," I whispered. "I don't have anyone missing me. Not a boyfriend, not a family member, not even a friend. Isn't that sad?" I sighed, feeling deflated. "I kept myself from having friends, didn't allow people to get too close to me. I regret that now, because if I don't make it back, no one will miss me. Selfish of me, isn't it?" I glanced at him, my emotions hanging heavy in the air.

"Not selfish at all," he said gently. "We all want to be remembered, to be loved, and to be missed when we are gone." He gazed back at me with intense eyes. "I'd miss you a hell of a lot if you were to warp back to your own time," he said slowly. "I hope our mission succeeds—I know it has to—but I hope you don't go back. I hope you end up stuck here with me."

My jaw dropped open.

"*That's* selfishness, and I don't regret it or apologize for it," he stated passionately.

I sat there for several moments, trying to gather my thoughts into some semblance of order as I searched his eyes, hoping I hadn't read too much into his words. I wanted to tell him that deep inside, I secretly hoped I wouldn't warp again, either; but just then, the carriage came to an abrupt halt. We sat there for a few more silent moments, waiting for the sign that all was clear for us to go inside. A thump on the roof from the driver told us we were good to go. Dr. Blake jumped down from the carriage and held his hand out to me. I put my hand into his much larger one and felt the current between us sizzle to life.

I looked into his handsome face and hesitantly reached over to trace his lips with my finger. I felt him suck in a breath. He reached up and pulled the hood of my cloak back over my head, took my hand, and brushed a light kiss over my knuckles before helping me down from the carriage. We walked quickly up the steps to my new townhouse while Dr. Blake stayed alert, looking around us and hoping our arrival hadn't been noted by anyone. We stepped inside as soon as the door opened, and both of us let out a relieved breath.

I pushed my hood back and checked out my new home. It was a modest-sized, two-story house with immaculate marble flooring in the foyer and a beautiful staircase that led to the second floor. Dr. Blake began showing me around the first floor. The first door to the left was a small, comfortable-looking sitting room, decorated in shades of cream and sea green; it would be perfect for hosting teatime conversations. The first door on the right opened into a larger sitting room that housed a small piano and was beautifully decorated with hand-carved, nineteenth-century mahogany furniture, upholstered in gorgeous wine-and-gold brocade.

I ran my hand lightly over the back of a lovely small settee and tried to imagine it in my apartment. I shook my head—nah, it definitely wouldn't fit in with my hodge-podge collection of thrift-store furniture finds.

The second door on the right led into a room that acted as an office and small library. I could see myself spending many nights curled up in the chair by the large fireplace, reading. I shook my head to clear the wishful vision. We looked around the rest of the first floor, including the small, pristine kitchen, before heading upstairs. The second floor boasted two small bedrooms and a larger master bedroom with an attached sitting room. I walked in and looked around the cozy room, complete with a large four-poster bed and small vanity covered in small bottles and pots. It would suit me well.

Dr. Blake cleared his throat from the doorway. "If you will permit me?"

I snorted and beckoned him to come on in.

"Mrs. Howell sent everything you will need ahead of

us. Of course, if you find that you are in need of something we haven't thought of, please don't hesitate to ask."

I walked over to the armoire and opened the doors only to gawk at the amount of stuff that was crammed inside. *Good God.*

"Did Mrs. Howell mention that I had a few things for you?"

I wondered briefly why he seemed so nervous. "She did," I said, my curiosity piqued.

He walked over to the bed and knelt down to retrieve a leather satchel beneath it. After he laid it gently on the bed, he crooked his finger for me to come closer. I raised my brow but went over anyway. Curiosity killed the cat and all that jazz.

He opened the satchel and took a long, wooden box out of it. When he withdrew a beautiful dirk from inside the case, my breath caught in my throat. It was probably the most beautiful weapon I had ever seen. I had handled several knives and swords while training with Dr. Blake, but this one—a sgian-dubh, if I remembered correctly— was astonishingly superior to anything I had trained with. The blade was perhaps eight inches in length, and the hilt was another four inches. The hilt was ebony with intricate Celtic knots carved into it. He handed it to me with a look of apprehension in his eyes, as if he were holding his breath for some reason.

I took it from him, my hand shaking slightly, and when I grasped the hilt in my hand, it fit as if it were a long-lost extension of my body, as if it had been made just for me. I ran my fingers lightly over the carvings, and then I noticed meticulously etched words down the length of the blade. Holding it closer to my face to read the words,

I realized they were in another language. *Ta mo chroi istigh ionat* was beautifully engraved into the blade. I looked up at my silent companion.

"It's Gaelic," he said softly.

I held the blade out from my body and gave a few flicks of my wrist, letting my hand get use to the feel of it, but it wasn't necessary. My hand had a mind of its own, and it felt as though it was meant to hold this dirk. I shook my head at the absurdity of my thoughts.

"It's beautiful," I said. "What does the engraving mean?"

Dr. Blake grinned and shook his head at me. "Oh no; you'll have to figure that one out on your own."

"Are you serious?" I squealed. "You've handed me the single most wonderful item I have ever received, and you won't tell me what it says on the blade?"

I saw the look of amusement and determination on his face and sighed. There would be no talking him into it.

"Well, I'm going to enjoy every moment I have this. It will be hard for me to give it back," I said as my fingers caressed the carvings on the hilt once more.

"It's yours, Sage. I had it made for you."

My eyes flew wide in surprise. *He had this made for me as a gift?* If I hadn't known better, I'd have sworn I saw a blush creep up his neck.

"I wanted to get you something special, something to show you how proud I am of all that you have accomplished. So, do you like it?"

I nodded and murmured, "It's perfect." No one had ever given me something so thoughtful. I threw myself into his arms. His shock only lasted a second before he relaxed and hugged me back… as if he had a choice.

I pulled back to look into his handsome, imperfect face. "Thank you, Aldwin." I got on my tiptoes and pressed my lips gently to his.

I wanted to tell him so much with that kiss, but I wasn't sure how he felt, or if I should be putting myself out there. My future—our future—was too uncertain. I pulled back, slightly breathless and more than a little dizzy, and chuckled under my breath at how this man affected me. Talk about kissing a girl senseless.

He drew away reluctantly to show me what else he had in his case of goodies.

There was a smaller, plainer version of my dirk. *It would be perfect for my garter holster*, I thought excitedly. The last item he withdrew from the case made me blink in surprise. What the heck was that doing in a case of weapons?

A unique cuff bracelet was the last item. The bracelet was probably three to four inches wide and had an antique silver finish. A butterfly topped the cuff, its wings spread from one side to the other, and several precious gemstones were encrusted in its wings. The center of the beautiful insect looked like the innards of a clock or watch. I realized that it *was* a watch when I heard a soft ticking. A strong feeling, almost like a premonition, swept over me and made my heart skip a beat. Things were about to change imminently, and I wasn't sure I wanted them to.

I frowned slightly. "It's lovely, but why is it with these?" I asked, motioning toward the weapons on the bed.

His eyes twinkled like a boy about to show off his favorite toy. He moved closer to me with the bracelet in his hand. "Look. See how the butterfly is raised a little off the base of the bracelet?" His breath fanned my cheek; I nodded my head in answer. "If you apply just the right amount of pressure…"

I heard a soft click as he pressed down on the center of the butterfly, and a jewel on the side of the bracelet, designed to look like the winding mechanism, popped free with a *snick*. Dr. Blake pulled the small jewel free of the bracelet and showed me the one-inch needle.

My eyebrows shot up. Clearly, I had no clue about this kind of James Bond stuff.

"The needle has been coated with a substance that will knock a grown man or preternatural out for hours. It can only be used once, so use it only if you absolutely have to."

He pressed the gemstone-studded pin into the bracelet and put the cuff on my arm. It, too, fit perfectly. I wasn't big on jewelry, but this was just unique enough to be my style and could come in very handy.

Just then, a knock came from the back entrance downstairs, making me jump.

Dr. Blake smirked and headed for the door. "That will be your household staff starting to arrive. I'll leave you to get acquainted with your new surroundings while I make sure everything gets underway for your big night tonight." He turned to go.

"Aldwin…" I started.

His shoulders tensed visibly.

"I mean, Dr. Blake…"

I wanted to pour my heart out to him and tell him how much he had come to mean to me, but all my uncertainties about the future and my feelings rushed to stop me. He had stopped and was looking at me, searching my face with his good eye. I dropped my gaze to the bracelet on my wrist.

"...Thank you for everything. You have become the one constant in my life, the one person I can trust. I hope we can continue to be friends."

He looked slightly pained at my words, and I wondered briefly if he had planned on distancing himself from me now that I was no longer his student. The thought sent a stab of pain straight to my chest.

He bowed ever so slightly and answered quickly, "Yes, of course. *Friends*." He turned back toward the door, and without looking back said, "Sage, call me Aldwin. We are to be *friends*, after all."

The word friends came out caustically, but before I could say anything in reply, he strode from the room and left me standing there, wondering how I had screwed up again.

CHAPTER
Fifteen

THE DAY FLEW BY QUICKLY AFTER THAT. I MET WITH the three people who would staff my small townhouse, all of whom were trustworthy in the eyes of Cerberus. The cook, Mrs. Weston, was a short, round woman with beady little brown eyes that I swear could see my deepest, darkest secrets inside. She freaked me out a bit, and I wouldn't have been surprised at all to learn that the woman was proficient in throwing hexes on unsuspecting mortals.

Zachary was to be my butler, but he was also acting as my driver and night security. He was a tall, thin man; and despite his impeccable clothing and softly spoken words, he scared the bejesus out of me. I could definitely see him playing the role of an assassin in some thriller movie. Luckily, the young woman who was to be my lady's maid, a pretty girl named Marie, was quite normal. Right then, the normal, dark-haired lady's maid had her lovely green eyes roaming slowly over Dr. Aldwin Blake's sexy body.

Great—three for three.

After making sure everyone was getting settled in, I hurried up the stairs to indulge in a bath before I had to get ready for my big night. Bubble baths were a luxury I would never again take for granted. I let out a groan of pleasure as I sank into the warm water that filled the old-fashioned claw-foot tub. I lathered up my hair and body with a silky, lemongrass-scented soap as I thought about the upcoming evening. It should be pretty uneventful—just talking, mingling, and dancing. I winced. I would rather be fighting vampires or doing... well, just about anything else. Talking and mingling weren't really my thing. Dancing I could handle... but small talk? Bleck! I soaked until the water cooled and my fingers raisined up, then wrapped a towel around myself and decided to try on my new, fancy underwear.

Once I donned the new garments, I stood in front of my full-length mirror, barely able to recognize myself. The cream-colored corset fit me like a second skin and accentuated my trim waist and modestly sized chest. I slid the small dagger into the sheath attached to my specially made garter and couldn't suppress the shiver of excitement that zinged through me.

I gave a couple of lunges and kicks to make sure the garter wouldn't slip and to see how well I could move in my new-and-improved corset. Actually, I just wanted to show off in front of the mirror. I grinned at my reflection, dressed head to toe in cream and lace. I looked like a hot lingerie model... if you could ignore the wicked-looking dagger strapped to my right thigh and the cocky smirk plastered on my face.

Marie came in and lifted the dress I had chosen for the night over my head, letting the silky fabric slide down my lace-clad body and buttoning up the back when everything was in place. I glanced back at the mirror after I was dressed to see the full effect of my ensemble. The dress was a deep lavender-colored silk that flowed gracefully down to my ankles, it gathered at the waist and fell open in the front to reveal a silver underskirt. The bodice had a sweetheart neckline, and hundreds of tiny, deep-plum-colored beads had been sewn into it. The same beading adorned the sleeves and formed an intricate pattern on the bottom of the silver underskirt. The dress was gorgeous, and I felt beautiful wearing it.

I slipped on a pair of cream-colored, suede shoes with a two-inch heel, and then slid my beloved sgian-dubh into the hidden slot of my right shoe. I turned left and right to see if anyone would be able to tell I was wearing two weapons, and much to my delight, they seemed invisible. Marie also fixed my unruly hair into a pretty updo for the evening, and I had to admit, once we were done, I did indeed look like a woman on a mission to find a husband. The purples in my gown looked lovely with both my complexion and my deep auburn hair.

I slid the clockwork butterfly cuff onto my wrist, grabbed the wrap that matched my gown, and headed downstairs. Pushing the churning in my stomach to the back of my mind, I focused on the task at hand—be a lady, play the part, and for God's sake don't make a fool of myself.

CHAPTER
Sixteen

FOR A SPLIT SECOND, AS I STEPPED OUT OF THE carriage in front of Mrs. Lillian Sebast's huge home, I imagined myself running away with my tail tucked between my legs. Instead, I gripped my fan and invitation tighter in my hand and sucked up my doubts and fears. I walked forward with the other dozen or so guests, making their way up the stairs of the brightly lit home.

I could hear laughing and music flowing from inside and swallowed the lump of fear sneaking its way up my throat. I was definitely not a socialite—heck, I could even be described as something of an introvert. I liked going out and doing things, but I didn't care to hang out or go to parties where there would be a crush of people. I always felt like I would be swallowed up in a sea of bodies, and I unfortunately tended to hyperventilate in tightly packed spaces.

I can do this, I have to do this, I thought and lifted my chin in determination. *I didn't work this long and hard to fail in the face of a little house party.*

When I reached the front door, I saw an older woman, elegantly dressed in brown silk, greeting everyone as they made their way inside. The doorman took my invitation and then announced me to the woman in the receiving line. She looked over at me, assessing me with a quick glance, and smiled warmly as I made my way closer to her.

"Ms. Hannigan, we are so glad you accepted our invitation tonight. When I heard that a young widow just out of mourning moved into the area, I just had to be the first to welcome you to Charleston."

I smiled graciously at her, even though I was pretty sure she had only wanted to be able to say she was the first person to have had me at her party. I would be great fodder for the gossip mill.

"Thank you so much, Mrs. Sebast. I am truly honored to have received an invitation to your elegant home."

She beamed at my compliment as I moved on into the ballroom of her veritable mansion.

I stood frozen in the doorway of the main room, taking in the sight before me. Never before had I seen anything so breathtaking. The room was lit by hundreds of candles; boughs of greenery and flowers draped the entryways; women were dressed in lovely gowns in dozens of colors; and gentlemen dressed in their finest talked in groups, flirted with young ladies, and danced with them in the center of the enormous room. It was a dizzying spectacle, and I couldn't drag my eyes away from the scene.

Someone bumped into my elbow as I stood there gaping like a goober and broke the spell I had been under. I took a deep breath, snapped open my fan, and strolled along the outer perimeter of the ballroom in an unhurried pace, even though my pulse was doing the opposite. Several heads turned my way discreetly, and many more eyes swiveled my way to try and get a glimpse of the newest addition to their little society party. I hated to be the center of attention normally, but it was my goal to see and be seen at this party, so I was pleased to have been noticed on any level.

I was standing at the refreshment table half an hour later with a glass of lemonade when Mrs. Sebast made her way over to me. She had a good-looking gentleman in tow and seemed way too pleased with herself. I braced myself.

"Ms. Hannigan. May I call you Sage, dear?"

I had just started to nod when she went on without waiting for my consent.

"I was just telling Mr. Michaels, here, what a lovely young lady you are and how you are new to town. He insisted on meeting you right away, so I brought him over to make introductions."

She smiled a Cheshire-cat smile, and Mr. Michaels held out his hand. I placed mine in his, and he kissed the back of it lightly, smiling up at me with a twinkle in his green eyes. I found myself a little charmed and smiled back.

"Very glad to meet you, Ms. Hannigan. Would you honor me with the next dance?"

I swallowed slowly and answered, "I'd be delighted to, Mr. Michaels."

This was it. I hoped my princess training was worth all the frustration I'd endured and I wouldn't disgrace Elaine or myself.

At first, I felt a little stiff while dancing, scared to death I'd make a mistake or trip over my gown... maybe even my partner's feet. Luckily, as the dance went on, I felt more relaxed and confident in my abilities. I felt light on my feet and didn't mind the company of the charming man I was dancing with. At the end, I made my way back to the side of the room, only to be asked by several other gentlemen if I'd save a dance for them. With partner after partner, I danced, laughed, flirted lightly, and kept a look out for Elaine and the others.

Feeling the room a little stuffy and myself a little overwhelmed, I picked up a glass of wine and made my way to a verandah that opened out to a small garden to get a breath of fresh air. A slight breeze, followed by a prickly, static-electric sensation on the back of my neck caused my footsteps to falter as a shadow fell over me. I looked over my shoulder and directly into the gold-rimmed eyes of my very first vampire encounter.

My eyes widened and my pulse rate picked up, even though I was trying my damnedest to keep it under control. The stone of Amerach warmed slightly as if to warn me to keep my wits about me; I didn't want to accidentally time-freeze anyone because of my intense fear.

The vampire stared at me with an uncomfortable scrutiny, and his gaze traveled slowly over the pulse point at my neck like a silken caress. I struggled not to turn and flee, even though my instincts were screaming for me to do just that. What seemed like hours but could have only been moments passed, and his gaze finally snapped back to mine.

He smiled like nothing out of the ordinary had just happened, and his smile alone could have been used as a weapon since its effect was pretty devastating to my equilibrium. The man, er, vampire, was drop-dead gorgeous. From his golden-ringed hazel eyes to his shoulder-length, deep brown hair, he was astonishingly handsome.

The vampire then spoke to me as if we were old friends. "May I have the pleasure of your company, or am

I intruding?" he asked in a slightly accented voice.

My, my, he is sure of himself, isn't he?

Men who thought they were God's gift put me on edge, and I felt my pulse slow as I filed this vampire under the same mental list under which I'd filed all other predators. He might be handsome and ooze sexual confidence, but he used and abused people, so he belonged on my shit list. I saw his eyes widen slightly as he probably realized my pulse had slowed and my eyes bore directly into his.

I was just about to cut him down with the sharp edge of my tongue when I realized what a mistake that would have been. I needed a foot in the door of the vampire community, and this vampire could perhaps help me accomplish that. I relaxed my unwittingly stiffened posture and attempted a small smile.

"I would be very happy to have such charming company," I said as genuinely as possible

I almost felt sorry for the poor bloodsucker—he looked a little confused at my mixed signals, but held out his arm anyway. I looped my arm under his and allowed him to stroll with me. Walking arm-in-arm and smelling his decidedly masculine scent, all while knowing what he was capable of, just about shot my already-fraying nerves.

The vampire seemed content to stare at me for the first several minutes during our walk, and my pulse fluttered wildly in my throat. I was getting extremely pissed off at my companion and his annoyingly odd behavior. I guess snapping at him had been inevitable. Finally, I came to an abrupt stop, and he almost bumped into me.

"Would you please stop staring? You are making me nervous," I hissed through gritted teeth. "I mean, really, can we talk about something… anything?" I looked over at his unusually beautiful eyes and tried to smooth out the scowl I could feel settling on my face.

His eyebrows rose at my outburst, but he didn't seem offended; quite the contrary, he seemed pleased that I had snapped his head off. "What would you like to discuss? The weather? The party decor? I am at your service." He gave a slight, mocking bow, as if he were being a gracious host.

I sighed. Why couldn't I have gotten an easier vampire to deal with? This guy was going to be hell on my nerves.

"Why don't you tell me something about yourself, since I don't know who you are or anything about you?" I said, trying to sound sincerely interested in him.

"I'd much rather talk about you," he replied in his silky voice.

Gah, that's it! He was *trying* to drive me insane.

"Okay, I will tell you something about myself if you promise to tell me something about yourself in return—tit for tat," I said, then grinned and fluttered my eyelashes a tiny bit to see if my womanly charms would work on him.

He chuckled under his breath, and the sound raised little goose bumps all over my exposed skin.

"All right, that sounds fair." He motioned for me to begin as he took a sip of his wine.

I pursed my lips and thought about what I'd reveal to my vampire companion. I'd have to come off genuine. I took a drink of my wine and turned to look at the silent vampire. "I don't have any family, or even friends really, and I don't like to admit how lonely I am sometimes."

Where the hell had that *come from?* I frowned into my glass before taking another sip.

If he'd been surprised by my admission, he didn't show

it. Instead, he looked at me until I felt like squirming, so I cleared my throat. "And you?" I asked softly.

"Ah, yes. Tit for tat, right?" He smiled like he was indulging me and took a long drink of his wine.

In the back of my mind, I wondered if he enjoyed wine or just drank it to keep up appearances.

"I have found myself loathing social gatherings such as this the past few years." His eyes darkened and his voice lowered as he spoke. "Until tonight, that is."

I covered my snort with a delicate cough, wondering how many times he'd used that line on unsuspecting victims. His eyes narrowed dangerously, making me wonder if he'd caught my inelegant snort.

"Well, don't we sound like a cheerful pair?" I teased, mostly to fill the awkward silence. I smiled widely at him and felt his arm stiffen under my hand. I started to remove my hand, wondering what I had done to make him put his guard up, when he became statue-still.

I sucked in a sharp breath, and my vision narrowed in on my vampire escort, teetering on the brink of freezing time. I didn't like to be surprised or not to know what was going on—it put me at a huge disadvantage, and I couldn't afford that.

The vampire's eyes dilated, and the gold ring around his irises became more pronounced. His glamour was slipping for some reason.

I cleared my throat and gently removed my hand from his arm, not wanting to make any sudden movements. He seemed to snap out of his trance as I rid myself of his arm, and his eyes mellowed out a bit.

"I'd better head back inside; it's getting late." My voice came out a little shaky. I could still feel the tension rolling off my companion, and it freaked me out.

"Yes, that would be good. Sorry to have kept you too long. I've enjoyed our time together."

I nodded my head since my tongue wasn't cooperating.

He reached for my hand, and I placed mine in his as etiquette dictated. His lips grazed the back of my hand, and my entire body stiffened at the sizzling contact. The vampire gazed up at me from under his lashes and grinned.

When he released me, I walked quickly to the verandah doors, hoping it wasn't too obvious that I was glad to get away from him.

My relief, however, didn't last long.

CHAPTER
Seventeen

I WAS CORNERED BY A RATHER OBNOXIOUS MAN WHO seemed to want to monopolize my attentions, when something across the room caught my eye. I don't know what it was, exactly, that drew my attention to the couple— they seemed normal enough, and certainly no one else noticed anything amiss. All I know is that I couldn't tear my eyes away from the young man and woman. My asshat companion was chattering on about something or another, so enraptured with himself that he didn't notice my inattention.

The young lady was extremely lovely and dressed in the height of fashion with thick, raven-black hair styled beautifully on top of her head. The gentleman was leaning in a bit too close to be proper, speaking softly in her ear. I was just about to dismiss the scene when I caught a glimpse of the young woman's eyes… ringed in red. I barely contained my gasp. I watched her give her gentleman friend a sultry look and then glide slowly out of the room. The man looked around quickly, gulped down the contents of his wineglass, and a few seconds later, followed the female vampire.

Holy crap! I wasn't supposed to be hunting vampires; I was supposed to be making a splash in society. What was

103

I supposed to do, though? Just ignore what was happening and... *what*? Hope someone else would intervene? It wasn't likely that any other lady in the room had a dagger strapped to her thigh or a sgian-dubh hidden under her silk skirts. Besides, I wasn't the type to leave things up to fate. It's a cruel bitch, and I wasn't waiting around for her to deal me any cards.

Making an excuse to my self-absorbed admirer, I made my way across the ballroom to find the female vampire. I walked quietly down a dimly lit hallway, trying to breathe deeply, center myself, and regulate my pulse. Reaching down, I pulled the dirk from my boot, hoping I wouldn't have to use it and yet feeling a thrill go through me at the thought of wielding it. The dirk felt right in my hand, and I once again marveled at the connectedness I felt with it.

I dropped my hand to my side, hoping that if I came upon a stray partygoer, my skirts would hide it. Pausing outside several doors, I tried to see if I could sense anything from within—I didn't want to give away the element of surprise. I walked a bit quicker then, hoping I wouldn't be too late to stop the vampire's midnight snack. A shuffling sound a few feet away and around a bend in the hallway grabbed my attention. I held my breath and tightened my grip on my dirk as I rounded the corner. My heart nearly leapt out of my chest in anticipation. A door leading outside stood slightly ajar. Swallowing my fear before it could choke me, I made my feet move forward so I could gently push the door open.

The full moon shone down on a scene straight out of someone's nightmares, maybe even my own. Like a cruel lover, the vampire had the man in a sadistic embrace, holding him tightly against the house's brick wall, her fangs dug into his neck. The blood pouring out of his wound contrasted starkly with the bright white of his shirt. The vampire made guttural sounds of pleasure deep in her throat as she took his blood and his life. The animalistic sounds snapped me out of my shock, and I cried out in fury as I lunged for her.

Lesson number one: A vampire in the middle of dinner probably won't appreciate being interrupted.

My anguished cry gave me away as I lunged and thrust my dirk toward her chest. My heart nearly stopped when I was swatted away like nothing more than a pesky fly. I scrambled off the ground, only to be backhanded back down again. I shook off the feeling of déjà vu and tried to tap into my newly acquired inner power; surely, all those combat classes hadn't been for nothing.

I sure as hell wasn't going down without a fight, and if I could, I'd make the parasitic bloodsucker pay for what she'd done. I felt a calm settle over me more intensely than I'd ever felt before as I slowly adjusted my grip on the sgian-dubh. My whole body felt alive as an intense vibration hummed through my veins. I wiped the blood from the corner of my mouth and called on my powers just enough to be standing directly in front of the vampire before she could blink.

The look on her face was priceless—her pupils completely dilated, and the red ring around her irises almost swallowed the color of her eyes whole.

Taking advantage of her bewilderment, I head-butted her directly on the bridge of her nose and felt a glow of satisfaction when I heard a crunching sound. By the look on the vampire's face and the blood pouring from her nose, I gathered she wasn't in her happy place. She kicked me in the stomach with such force it was nothing short of a miracle that I still had my spine intact as I went flying across the lawn.

"Who are you?" the vampire demanded. "*What* are you?" she amended in a hiss, her eyes narrowed dangerously at me as I slowly got to my feet and plastered a sneer on my face.

"Wouldn't you like to know, leech," I spat.

With the promise of murder in her eyes, the vampire bared her fangs and lunged just as I warped forward with my dirk ready. I hurtled to the right at the last possible nanosecond and put all my forward momentum, strength, and warper energy into a single swing of my dirk. I landed a few feet away and swung around just in time to see the vampire's head land at her feet. The vampire's body fell next to her severed head almost as an afterthought. I stood there in stunned silence, surveying the gruesome scene before me as if I were an outside spectator.

With my ears feeling like they had been stuffed with cotton and my breathing escaping in rugged gasps, I staggered over to the body of the male victim and dropped to my knees next to him, checking for a pulse on the unravaged side of his neck. He was dead. I had been too late.

I don't know how long I knelt there; it could have been minutes or hours. Who's to say? A sound close by had me on my feet and in a defense stance quicker than any normal human should have been able to move.

"Sage? Dear God, are you hurt?"

Some sane part of my brain registered the voice as someone I knew, so I lowered my dirk a fraction and focused on the person standing a few feet away from me. Elaine stood there, one hand on her chest, the other raised slightly, palm out, as if to appease a wild beast.

I looked around myself at the carnage down in the dirt and the blood splatters on my arms and dress. My hair had come undone and hung around my shoulders and in my face. I must have looked like an insane-asylum escapee. My body felt all wrong, so I sat back down on the ground next to the man I hadn't saved just as a single tear tracked down my cheek. Somewhere close by, I heard Elaine saying something, but I had no idea what it was. I couldn't bring myself to really care.

I swept my eyes over the back garden, feeling as though someone were watching me, but the only thing I could hear was my own raspy breathing. Aldwin and Travis then burst through the back door. Travis stopped just outside the door and surveyed the scene grimly as Aldwin walked over to me and held out a hand. I looked up into his understanding eyes and grasped his hand, allowing him to pull me off the ground and into his embrace. The daze I had found myself in melted away, and all the sounds around me came rushing back as if someone had flipped a switch and unmuted the world.

Aldwin threw a black-velvet, hooded cape over me, tied it under my chin, and grasped one of my arms to lead me across the lawn, avoiding the decapitated body of the vampire. Unfortunately, he couldn't shield me from remembering those now-sightless, red-rimmed eyes. After exchanging a few quiet words with the others, he quickly led me along the back of Mrs. Sebast's home.

The carriage was waiting on the side of the house with Zachary in the driver's seat. Aldwin nearly lifted me into the carriage, and before the night's events could sink in, we were entering the townhouse through the back door.

Not an hour later, I fell into bed, exhausted in both body and mind.

Aldwin had stood outside my bedroom silently as I'd allowed Marie to help me wash off and change into clean clothing before bed. I'd known that all I had to do was say the word and he would have held me and let me cry my eyes out on his shoulder. I'd almost gone to him, but I could barely stand myself at that moment. Truthfully, I hadn't wanted to be held, hadn't deserved to be comforted, and had wanted to be alone. Eventually, I'd come out of my washroom clean and dressed for bed after I'd dismissed Marie for the night. I couldn't bring myself to meet Aldwin's worried gaze, and when he'd started to speak to me, I cut him off with a quick slash of my hand.

I lay numbly in my bed, wide awake most of the night. I don't know if my lack of tears was because I was still in shock or because I had become heartless, but I would have given anything to cry. Instead, I just felt hollow.

CHAPTER
Eighteen

THE NEXT DAY, I HAD MY ALL-IMPORTANT INTERVIEW with the vampire, Soren, and my stomach churned at the thought of having to work in close contact with another vampire. I had been told that the majority of vampires were not as savage as the two I had dealt with, but I thought it more likely they only hid it better and didn't make a public spectacle of themselves. I had already formed a prejudice after two unpleasant associations with the preternatural beings, so it was going to be hard to remain objective in my dealings with them.

I dressed smartly in a white shirtwaist blouse that buttoned up the front and sported quite a bit of see-through lace at the modest, square neckline, and a dark brown skirt decorated with tiny, white pinstripes. I wore fashionable brown leather boots with my dirk stashed safely inside, along with a small, white velvet hat with a wide, brown ribbon and a tulle train hanging down the back. I'd vetoed some of the more atrocious hats that had feathers and such, but hats were a huge part of 1904 fashion, and I had to comply. A pair of white lace gloves and my butterfly cuff bracelet completed the ensemble.

I couldn't quite bring myself to eat much, so I munched on toast and had a glass of tea before Zachary brought the carriage around to take me to Soren's home.

I expected a short drive through town, but I didn't realize the vampire lived on the outskirts of the city, nor did I take into consideration that travel took longer than I was used to. At least an hour later, the carriage pulled up to a monstrosity of a home. Zachary opened the door to the carriage and helped me down. I thanked him and made sure he knew I wouldn't be too long. After I smoothed my skirts with only slightly shaking hands, felt for my thigh holster through my skirt for reassurance, and took several deep breaths, I strode up the steps to the front door.

I gave the doorknocker a few good raps and amused myself wondering if a bald hunchback or maybe a thin, deathly pale grim-reaper sort of person would answer the door. Much to my disappointment, a very average, if not stiff and formal, butler answered. I handed him the calling card Elaine had had made for me.

"Ms. Sage Hannigan. I have an appointment with Sir Soren Blackwell."

I raised my eyebrow and purposely left off the vampire part of his title, but I couldn't keep a tiny grin off my face when I thought of calling him Sir Soren Blackwell, Vampire Extraordinaire.

I was led into a sitting room to wait while Sir Soren was told of my arrival. I looked around the cheerful room decorated in shades of blue and rolled my eyes. This room was boring even for my taste, much less a vampire's. Where was the black, red, and skulls? Maybe he reserved those for his torture chamber. I was grinning at my own clever self when the butler returned to fetch me to my hopefully soon-to-be employer.

The butler preceded me into another sitting room,

this one a bit smaller and cozier. I scanned the room and noticed an adjoining door on the other wall, behind a large desk.

"Sir Blackwell will be with you momentarily."

He poured me a cup of tea, making it how I preferred, and left me grasping the china cup while sweat started to trickle down the small of my back. I put my teacup down, sat on the beautiful settee, and closed my eyes to get a handle on my fears and try to banish my self-doubts. I felt a little calmer after a few moments and opened my eyes, only to shriek like a little girl when I found myself looking up into the gaze of one Sir Soren Blackwell, vampire leader—who, unfortunately, had been my annoying mystery vampire companion from the party the previous night.

I narrowed my eyes at him, but his devastatingly sexy grin only grew wider.

"Ms. Hannigan, how very nice to meet you."

"Sir Blackwell, it seems I am at a disadvantage. I didn't realize who you were last night, and I see now that you knew the whole time who I was." I raised my eyebrow, daring him to deny it. Of course, he didn't.

I stood up and, before I could think, nearly stuck my foot down my own throat. "You knew I would be seeking your employment today, and you were just playing games. Did you even plan on interviewing me at all, or did you just want to see the look on my face when I realized who you were?" I could feel my blood pressure rising along with my anger.

"I wasn't playing games, Ms. Hannigan. I wanted to see the real you before you went on your best behavior for this interview, and I don't apologize for it."

When he put it that way, I felt like a teenage drama queen who was overreacting to the entire situation. The previous night must have affected my emotions more than I'd realized.

I took a deep breath and said, "I'm sorry. Of course, you were well within your rights to do so. I'm just a bit tired—I didn't sleep well last night." I put all the womanly charm I could muster into a smile as I gazed up at him through my lashes. I must admit, it felt pretty awesome when he sucked in a quick breath and his eyes dilated just slightly, accentuating the unnatural golden ring around his irises. "Can we start over?" I asked as I held out my hand to him.

"Who could deny such a beautiful young woman?" he murmured as he kissed the back of my hand. Even though I had my lace gloves on, I could still feel the unsettling way something fluttered deep in my stomach when his lips pressed against my hand. My heart was beating erratically, and I nearly snatched it from his grip. Luckily, I was able to restrain myself. He looked at me like he could devour me, and I shivered at the thought.

Frickin' vampire.

I cleared my throat and took a tiny step back, out of his personal space. He looked amused at my retreat but motioned for me to take the seat in front of his desk. Of course, instead of sitting behind the desk, he leaned on the corner of it only a foot from me. I tried really, really hard not to scowl at him.

"So, exactly what kind of position are you looking to fill, Sir Blackwell?" I asked, ready to get down to business.

He didn't answer right away, and when I realized the mistake in my word choice, it was too late. My cheeks warmed, and that, of course, ratcheted up my aggravation meter. I thrust out my chin and narrowed my eyes at him, channeling Elaine's teacher stare, daring him to mention my unintentional double entendre. The vampire wasn't that stupid, though—brownie points for him.

"I have a position that recently opened up, and I need to fill it as soon as possible. I'm a busy man, and I have some functions and other things that I cannot attend without a female escort. I would require you to attend parties, a few meetings, write letters for me, and indulge me in some harmless eccentricities."

I nearly snorted at that last, but reined myself in at the last second. Standing, I walked slowly over to a large window. "I don't understand why you have this position in the first place. You're a good-looking, wealthy man with many connections; why not just snap your finger so some young, beautiful girl will follow you around, doing all those things for free?"

Oh my God. Why did I just say that? He didn't seem offended or even surprised that I'd asked, though, so I didn't freak out just yet.

"I am all those things, and I could do just as you suggested—"

I rolled my eyes since he couldn't see my face.

"—but that would cause a whole other set of problems I have no desire to deal with."

I turned around to face the handsome vampire with a question on my face.

"Those young women would have marriage on their minds, and more than likely, so would their mothers. I don't want to deal with matchmakers and empty-headed young women gossiping about fashion and whatever else young women flitter on about." He grimaced at his train of thought, and I found myself grinning at the powerful vampire who was cringing at the thought of dating a debutante.

"I understand," I said after a moment, "but why would having me on your arm keep the matchmaking mothers away?"

He looked a little surprised at my question, and I wondered what I was missing.

"Surely, you are not so naïve?" he asked with an incredulous look on his handsome face. "Everyone will assume you are my mistress, darling."

My mouth popped open with a little 'O', and I wondered why Travis or Elaine hadn't warned me. Of course that was his plan. I should have realized...

I thought it over for a minute, but really, there was nothing to mull over for long. I didn't care what people thought of me normally, and I hoped to be long gone from 1904 soon, so I definitely didn't need to keep a pristine reputation here. Working so closely with him would give me ample opportunity to find out all I could about the supposedly rogue vampires.

I smiled across the room at my bloodsucking companion. "I'd be glad to be your pretend mistress, then. Should I call you Soren?"

The vampire walked across the room to stand only inches away from me. His power seemed to roll off him, making me realize in a blink who and what I was dealing with. Unfortunately, he seemed prone to dark mood swings at the most bizarre moments. I caught myself before I backed up a step to get away from the power radiating from him. I couldn't appear to be a weakling, cowering away from his stare at every turn. I stiffened my back and tilted my chin up to stare directly into his powerful eyes. Idly, I wondered how old he really was and how much he had seen in those years to make him seem so untouchable.

"Yes, Soren would seem right, wouldn't it? And I'll call you Sage, of course." He leaned in a bit closer, his eyes boring into mine, and his breath stirring the hairs around my temple. "It won't be so bad pretending to be lovers, will it?" he asked in a low, husky voice.

I swallowed and wet my lips with the tip of my tongue. His gaze followed the movement, and I'm pretty sure my heart rate would have tripped emergency alarms had I been hooked up to a hospital monitor.

"No, it won't be so bad," I honestly replied. "But, that's all it will be, correct? Just an understanding? A masquerade to keep your bachelorhood intact, so you can carry on with your nefarious deeds?" I was trying for a teasing tone, wanting him to take the bait and ease back on the powerful waves rolling off his body. I felt like those waves were battering my body against the rocky shore of a deserted beach somewhere.

He produced a devilish smile that did nothing to assuage my nervousness, and his eyes twinkled at the challenge.

I gulped.

"Having you on my arm will be a delight, I'm sure. I find myself looking forward to our... *conversations*."

His voice lowered to a rumble, causing the deep recesses of my stomach to quiver. His tone made it clear he had more in mind than mere conversations, but I wouldn't let his insinuations scare me off; I was getting exactly what I needed out of this deal. I felt ecstatic and wanted to jump up and down or dance a jig.

A moment of insanity seized me, and I decided to see how safe I'd be while working in close quarters with Soren. I'd never known that somewhere inside me was a little girl who liked to play with fire. Hell, this little girl evidently was a pyromaniac, just waiting for the right moment to add gasoline to the mix and pray she wouldn't get burned. Before I lost my nerve, I leaned my body slightly into his and wrapped my arms around his neck, burying my fingers into his hair.

"Seal the deal with a kiss?" I asked, my lips an inch away from his.

He seemed momentarily thrown off kilter but recovered amazingly fast as he gently rubbed his lips across mine; one caress, two caresses, three caresses. *Oh my.* Suddenly, his lips mashed against mine as he angled his head to gain better access; his arms encircled my waist, and he crushed me against his chest. I brought my hands down to his shoulders to steady myself against the tremors that threatened to wrack my body.

My mind screamed that this wasn't supposed to be happening just as my lips opened to allow his tongue access inside me. The rational part of my mind went completely silent as my pretend vampire lover kissed me like I was some foreign delicacy to savor. I ran my tongue over his bottom lip, and he answered in kind with a growl deep in his throat.

Somewhere between the growl and my aggressive response, something that neither of us expected happened. I felt my body tighten like it was getting ready to spring— or like I was about to warp—and a warm rush of power washed over me, leaving a tingly sensation all across my

body. I gasped, and Soren jerked away from me like I'd whipped out a stake and gone all Buffy on him.

Oh, shit.

CHAPTER
Nineteen

S OREN STARED AT ME FROM A FEW FEET AWAY WITH
a mix of wonder and rage. Let me tell you, being at the
receiving end of a vampire's powerful stare was not a fun
position to be in. My lips still felt tingly and swollen, and
my heartbeat was winning its own little race as I slipped
my hand into my pocket. My fingers didn't even graze the
hilt of my dirk before Soren had me pinned against the
top of his desk.

I only entertained warping for a split second before I
dismissed it as counterproductive; I'd already screwed up
my mission bad enough.

With his hands around my neck, he leaned down and
whispered harshly into my ear. "Who are you, and who
sent you?"

I opened my mouth with no idea what to say, when
he cut me off.

"And don't dare lie to me—I already know you are not
who you say you are after that little show of power."

My mind went blank momentarily. Had that been *my*
power? If it had been, I had never experienced it like that
before. I'd thought it had been his power washing over me.

The fingers of his left hand were digging into my
cheeks as he held me in place. I tried to think quickly, to

come up with some logical explanation for what had just happened that he would believe, but I was sure he'd see right through any crap I might feed him. So, I told him the truth.

I took as deep as a breath as I could and said, "I don't know what that power wave was... I thought it came from you. I am here to try and figure out what is going on with the rogue vampires at the behest of Cerberus." I met his stare with difficulty. His grip lessened just enough to allow me to breathe a bit easier.

"So, Cerberus must suspect me of being involved in, or at least aware of, what is going on in order to send in a *spy*." He nearly spat the word.

I didn't deny it when he looked at me for confirmation.

"That still doesn't explain you," he said thoughtfully. You're not a vampire or a werewolf, nor are you entirely human, as much as you'd like me to believe you are," he commented almost lazily to himself. "One more time. Who are you?" he asked.

I opened my mouth to deny it when he grabbed the edge of my skirt and jerked it up over my knees. My sense of self-preservation kicked into high gear, and I couldn't have stopped myself from warping if I'd tried. Even as inhumanly fast as I'd warped, Soren was just fast enough to grab the dirk from the thigh holster on my garter. I was across the room and against the far wall, breathing heavily, before I realized he had been going after my weapon and hadn't intended on sexually abusing me.

It was too late to take it back, though. His rage earlier was nothing compared to his shock just then. He looked at me with wide eyes, the golden ring around them glowing brightly. I looked at the ground, cursing myself for allowing my fears to rule me. Again. Straightening my skirt, I walked slowly over to the settee and sat down, feeling more tired than ever and feeling disappointed that I'd ruined my mission before it had even begun.

Soren came over to sit in the chair in front of me. He reached over slowly and handed me my dirk. I raised a brow in surprise.

"You're a warper," he said, his voice soft and a bit thoughtful.

I jerked back in surprise. How would he know?

He looked at me, guessing my thoughts. "When you've lived as long as I have, there isn't much you don't know about or at least have heard about," he said with a dismissive wave of his hand. He stroked the imaginary stubble at his chin and sighed. "Things are far worse than I imagined, then."

I snorted. "You could say that. I've been working on my powers and taking classes for weeks since I warped here, just to go undercover and blow it all in one hour with a damn kiss." I couldn't help myself; I was pissed at the whole situation, and I didn't see the need to pretend in front of him any longer. I dropped my head into my hands. "Now what the hell am I supposed to do?" I groaned.

If he was offended at my blunt language, he didn't say anything; actually, his next words were not even close to what I was expecting.

"We continue on with your mission just as planned," Soren stated, causing my mouth drop open.

"What do you mean? *You* were my mission—to figure out what was going on in your little vampire secret society that was big enough to cause a warper to warp from a hundred years away!" My voice had been steadily rising until I almost shouted the last part.

He didn't react to my outburst; he simply raised an eyebrow, and I entertained fantasies of throwing my dirk at him for a split second.

"I am not aware of what is going on except for the rise in rogue killings and a few other whispers in the vampire gossip mill. So, like I said, we will continue on as you planned and won't mention to Cerberus that I have been enlightened to these recent events."

I looked at him in astonishment. Was he proposing a partnership? Was it even possible? I felt a spark of hope in my chest.

"I want to figure out what is going on as much as you do, Sage. The killings make my way of life dangerous and unstable, not to mention what would happen if mass panic seized the city," he said sincerely.

I couldn't believe it. Not only would I still be able to investigate, but I'd also be able to do it with the help of one of the most powerful vampires in the U.S. Maybe that kiss hadn't been the stupidest thing I'd ever done, after all.

Standing up, I walked over to him and stuck my hand out. "How about we shake on it this time?" I said with a hint of sarcasm in my voice.

Amusement sparkled in his annoyingly gorgeous eyes as he took my hand in his.

"We'll start tomorrow," he said as he gripped my hand.

CHAPTER Twenty

O N THE DRIVE BACK TO THE TOWNHOUSE, I DEBATED telling the others about the day's outcome. I hated to lie to everyone, especially Aldwin, but I had a feeling that if they knew what had happened, they would pull the plug on the entire operation, and I couldn't allow that. I wouldn't be lying, exactly—more like an omission of the truth, and that was different… right? I couldn't afford to let anyone else call the shots when it came to my only hope at getting back home, and this would benefit Cerberus as well. I nodded my head at the brilliance of my logic. I was doing the right thing.

When I got back home, it was nearing dinnertime, and I felt exhausted. A stack of invitations and calling cards were on a small table when I entered the foyer. I flipped through the fancy cards, wondering how they would feel after tomorrow night when I showed up on the arm of one of the most eligible bachelors in town, who also happened to be known to keep mistresses. I smiled. At least it would be interesting.

Marie hurried to take my gloves and hat. "Mrs. Howell, Mr. Connely, and Dr. Blake are waiting to have dinner with you, Ms. Hannigan." She sounded a bit breathless.

Wow, that was quick. I guess they were anxious to

hear how it had gone. *This should be fun*, I thought, and swallowed nervously. I really did hate to lie, even if it was for their own good.

I entered the small sitting room, and chatter stopped abruptly as all eyes anxiously turned to me. I let a huge grin split my face, and in return Elaine let out a very unladylike *"Whoop!"* Travis stood there a bit stunned, while Aldwin came over to give my arm a squeeze and say, "Good job, Sage. We knew you could do it."

I blushed and looked away from his approving gaze; my heart felt a pain for being so deceitful. Travis came over, shook my hand, and offered his congratulations as I led everyone into my little dining room to talk and celebrate over dinner.

Dinner flew by quickly with everyone in high spirits at my supposed success, and we all laughed and toasted our good fortune. We were enjoying a dessert of fruit cobbler and ice cream when I asked the question that had been on my mind since earlier that day.

"Why didn't any of you tell me Soren would expect me to pretend to be his mistress as part of my employment with him? It would have been nice to have known ahead of time, so I wouldn't have been thrown off guard," I said with a little chuckle.

You could have heard a pin drop.

I looked around at my dinner companions, my fork poised halfway to my mouth. I lowered it and asked quietly, "What did I say?"

Elaine cleared her throat. "It's just that he never has before. His female companions just took care of things behind the scenes, so to speak, and went with him to secret meetings and such, so it was never necessary to have that kind of understanding or cover." She looked a bit bewildered at this turn of events and looked over at Aldwin. "Dr. Blake?" she asked.

I looked over at him and couldn't help but shiver when I saw his thunderous expression.

He laid down his fork and took a long drink of the wine he had served in celebration before speaking. "He either knows something is up and wants to keep an eye on you—"

If it were at all possible, his expression darkened even further.

"—or he is *interested* in you and wants to keep an eye on you. Either way, it's a complication."

He had no idea what the real complications were. I nearly laughed out loud at the ridiculousness of the whole situation. I looked over at Travis, who was scowling down into his plate, and since he hardly ever scowled, I figured I'd better try and salvage the situation.

"I don't think he was onto anything, Aldwin." *Unless you counted him pinning me to the top of his desk,* I thought absently. I must have had a bit too much wine—I'm pretty sure it wasn't a good time to giggle.

"And I very seriously doubt he has a crush on me. He is a very powerful vampire who could have any woman he wants. He wouldn't look twice at someone like me when he has so many choices," I said honestly.

Aldwin threw his hands in the air. "You have no idea of your aura, do you, Sage?" This came from Elaine, who had an incredulous look on her face that I couldn't fathom. "You draw people to yourself; you are beautiful and so very sure of who you are," she said.

It was my turn to look incredulously at her. Me?

Beautiful and sure of myself? I had never felt that way.

Elaine shook her head at the doubtful look on my face.

"Either way," I said, clearing my throat, "I don't think we are compromised, and we should continue on as planned." I took a long drink of my wine while everyone started loudly discussing the situation.

Suddenly, Travis stood up from the table, and we all stopped to stare at his abruptness.

"She's right. We should carry on as planned. Our dealings with the vampire have been above reproach." He cleared his throat and continued on, looking tired and irritated. "The mission is too important to back out of now."

I stood up as well, looking around the table at the people who had become my friends in the past few weeks. It suddenly hit me how much I was going to miss everyone if I got my wish to go back home. "I don't plan on backing out, and nothing short of locking me up would stop me from carrying on with the mission. And I dare anyone to try *that*," I said as I met each of their stares.

No one spoke for a moment.

"Good. Well, that settles that. I don't know about all of you, but I have had a long day, and I have to meet with Soren tomorrow, so I'd love to try and get some rest." I purposely ignored the daggers Aldwin was glaring at me and went around the table to embrace Elaine. "It's going to be fine," I whispered in her ear. I pulled back and gave her a small, encouraging smile.

She clucked like a worried hen. "I see you have your mind made up, so I won't argue. You do look tired, so try and get some sleep. Aldwin will stay here to secure the townhouse before heading back to Howell Home." She walked out of the dining room with Travis in tow, leaving me alone to face the wrath of one very pissed-off doctor.

"Aldwin, please don't. I just can't handle any more today." I walked over to him, but he wouldn't look at me, and his jaw was clenched so hard I thought it might shatter. I sighed, walked out of the dining room, and headed upstairs to my bedroom. I almost made it, too, but as I opened my bedroom door, I realized Aldwin was right on my heels. I didn't even bother to try and shut him out, I just left the door open and commenced with operation ignore the large, sexy, brooding doctor.

The door closed, but I knew he was in the room; I could feel him staring holes into the back of my head. Whatever. I *so* did not need any drama. I plucked the pins out of my hair, feeling a little stress seep away when it all came free. Pulling my shirt out of the waistband of my skirt, I turned to raise an eyebrow at my Peeping Tom, giving him a chance to leave.

He scowled even harder at me. "We need to discuss this, Sage," he growled, his fury barely contained.

"You may think we need to discuss this, but I don't *need* to do anything except go to bed," I snapped, my own irritation starting to stir. *Pompous, arrogant, overbearing, caveman!*

He crossed his arms defiantly.

Ah, well, two could play at that game. I unbuttoned the top button of my shirt, then the second, and then the third.

He stood, unmoved and unaffected.

Hardball, is it? I grinned; I did love a good challenge. My blouse was hanging open when I turned my back

126

to Aldwin. I slipped it slowly off my shoulders. Then, I reached behind me to unbutton my skirt, pausing long enough to give him another chance to leave. When I heard nothing, I continued. As the last button came free, I held my skirt up and wondered if I had enough guts to go on with my little challenge. Maybe I should just let him win and get it over with.

Nah, I wasn't a quitter, even if it meant embarrassing myself a little. I was bone tired, and I tended to do stupid things when I was exhausted. And obviously, I hadn't learned anything from my actions earlier in the day.

Mind made up, I dropped my skirt and stepped out of the bundle of fabric on the floor. I was now clad only in my cream corset, panties, thigh-high stockings held up by my garters, brown leather high-heeled boots, and two dirks. I turned around slowly, my cheeks flaming at my own brazenness.

When I saw the look in his eye, though, I knew it had been worth it. All his rage had melted away, and I found myself standing before a man who was starving... and I was the main course. He walked over to me, his movements graceful and predatory as he circled around me. I couldn't quite pull off a smirk or a snarky comment, not when he looked at me like that. I let a soft sigh escape my lips.

"Aldwin..."

He reached over and tucked a lock of hair over my shoulder, grazing the bare skin there. I nearly stopped breathing, and my corset felt way too tight as I sucked in a breath. He stepped even closer to me and lifted my chin gently with his hand, causing me to meet his eyes as he leaned in to kiss me. Just the promise of his kiss was enough to cause my knees to tremble in anticipation.

He had barely grazed my lips when I heard his breath hiss in through his teeth. I felt light-headed and confused. Why wasn't he kissing me senseless? Why was he *sniffing* my neck?

Before my mind could catch up with what was going on, he grabbed both my arms in a bruising grip and shook me once so hard my head snapped back.

His glacier-colored eyes filled with blue fire. "You *kissed* him?"

My eyes widened at the anger rolling off him. *How in the hell is he able to tell that?*

"What do you mean?" I asked, my mind scrambling to make sense at the turn of events.

"Don't play games with me, Sage," he said, his body starting to shake with barely restrained violence. "I can *smell* him all over you," he growled.

"What do you mean 'you can *smell* him on me'?" I asked, my anger rising. "Yes, he kissed me, all right? I was undercover and winging it all on my own out there. I'm just trying to survive in a world I don't understand yet, Aldwin," I ground out.

My arms were starting to hurt where he was still grabbing me; I'd probably have bruises by morning.

"Now, get your fucking hands off me," I said, so low and menacingly that I didn't even recognize the sound of my own voice.

That seemed to snap him out of his rage—he dropped his hands and stepped away from me, then he raked a hand through his hair and yanked on it in frustration.

"Get out," I said quietly, not looking at him.

"Sage…" he whispered.

I heard the regret in his voice, but at that moment it didn't matter. "I said get out, Aldwin."

Long after I heard the door close behind him, and long after I'd stripped down to dress in my soft cotton nightgown, I could still smell the heavy aroma of honey and spices lingering in my room. I banished it all from my mind; I was too tired to deal with so many weird things at once. The next day, I would have to deal with a brooding vampire and whatever other shit would be thrown in my path.

I slept straight through the night as if I hadn't a worry in the world.

CHAPTER
Twenty-one

THE NEXT DAY CAME TOO QUICKLY, AND I DIDN'T FEEL any better about the altercation with Aldwin the night before. Too many things didn't add up, and I couldn't for the life of me figure out what it all meant. I was obviously missing something, and as soon as I could put the energy and thought into it, I was going to figure out what it was.

I was picking at my lunch when Marie brought me a black card with Soren's name embossed in red on the front. On the inside, written in a bold, slashing hand, was the equivalent of a vampire summons.

I will pick you up at seven tonight. Please wear the gown I have provided.

Even though it wasn't signed, I knew who had sent it. *What gown?*

I looked up at Marie, who I'd just realized was still standing close by, and sure enough, she held a large, black box with a red velvet bow attached to the top. I scrunched up my nose. Great, next he'd be telling me what underwear to put on.

In the privacy of my own room, after writing a quick note to Elaine to tell her I'd be accompanying Soren out to a private dinner later, I stood at the foot of my bed, staring at the offending box. I contemplated ignoring his instructions altogether. I had several lovely gowns, and I didn't want him to think he was calling all the shots. That would have worked out well, had I not opened the box.

My curiosity got the best of me once again, and having opened the box, there was no possible way I was going to wear anything else. I caressed the silky fabric with a finger, and then gently lifted the sapphire-colored dress out of the box. It had very fine sleeves that would drape elegantly at the edge of my shoulders and across my breasts, leaving a lot of skin exposed. The bodice was finely ruched all the way down to the hips, and then the wispy fabric fell elegantly to the floor. It was breathtaking.

I bathed a few hours later and washed my hair with the lemongrass-scented soap I'd come to enjoy. Afterwards, I dressed quickly in my specialty underthings and slipped my dirks in their proper places. My hand caressed the engraving of my sgian-dubh, and I felt a pain in my chest at the thought of Aldwin and how we'd left things. He hadn't shown up at all that day, and I wouldn't get to talk to him until at least tomorrow.

I sighed and slipped into the dress Soren had given me. Marie came in, and her eyes widened when she took in my appearance. I hoped that was a good reaction. She buttoned me up and then expertly managed my hair into a loose bun on top of my head, shaping a few small, escaped curls around her finger to lie softly around my temples and on the back of my neck. Marie made my unruly, semi-curly hair look like it was purposely styled to look whimsical.

I heard voices downstairs, so I quickly grabbed my cuff bracelet and made my way down to begin my first night as the pretend mistress of Sir Soren Blackwell. As a result of some meditating and deep breathing I had done that afternoon, I felt calmer than usual. That's not to say I wasn't intimidated at the thought of being out at night with a vampire, investigating violent vampire crimes. Geez, I felt like I was in the middle of a bad horror film. I just had to remember not to go into any basements.

Soren met me at the foot of the stairs, wearing a fashionable black suit with a black waistcoat and a sapphire-blue neck cloth. His eyes seemed brighter than normal, and I wondered if he had dropped using his glamour a little, or if his mood affected his eyes. He didn't say anything, but he continued to stare at me like I was some intricate mystery to solve.

I stepped off the last stair, causing him to take a step back. He cleared his throat and offered me his arm. I took a deep breath and grasped it. Nodding to Zachary as he held the door open for us, I tried to give him a reassuring smile as we passed. Soren helped me into his fancy black carriage and seated himself right next to me. He tapped the top of the carriage, and we were off.

The silence was unsettling, not to mention the vampire sitting too close to me. I could hear my breathing and the clopping of the horse's hooves.

"I hope you don't think you have a right to tell me how to dress since I wore this tonight," I blurted. I looked over at my silent companion and raised my brow, pretty sure his nighttime vision was good enough to see it in the dark interior of the carriage.

"Of course not. You have to admit, it does look divine on you, though," he answered dismissively. "I need you to look the part tonight since we will be dining with a very particular group," he said in an annoyingly vague manner.

I relaxed slightly back into the plush cushions. "What kind of group? I need to know what I will be getting into."

"It will be a mixed group of important people from the preternatural community—a few leaders, some influential people, and their wives or lovers. Nothing to get nervous about. You will be with me, and no one is foolish enough to harm someone under my protection," he said, as though he dealt with this every day.

Oh wait, he probably *did* deal with this every day. Oh how I longed for the days when the most drama I ever saw was who was kissing whom on *The Bachelor*. I closed my eyes and wondered if my life would ever be so utterly safe and boring again. Somehow, I didn't think I'd like the answer to that.

We arrived at our destination a few minutes later, and I was glad to see that it looked like nothing nefarious was going on, just a normal house party. As Soren helped me out of the carriage, he whispered into my ear, "No matter what you see inside, please remember that most of these people are not human or are only partially human, so they don't abide by society's moral code."

I looked up into his very inhuman eyes and whispered back, "Why tell me this now and not earlier?"

"I just don't want you to be shocked, or I wouldn't have said anything at all," he murmured close to my ear.

"I am from a hundred years in the future, Soren. It would take a lot to shock me," I whispered back. My lips accidentally grazed his ear.

His body jerked almost imperceptibly as he stepped back to hand me all the way down from the steps of the carriage. I hooked my arm under his, and we strolled up to the front door like we had been together for years.

A beady-eyed little butler, whose eyes widened when he saw who was standing on his front step, answered the door. The butler jumped into gear very quickly, taking Soren's cane and hat, and I had to suppress a laugh at his fawning.

Soren frowned in my direction as if he knew what I was thinking. I cleared my throat and sobered. *This is a pretty serious situation, and I could possibly be the only human present.* Okay, that thought knocked the grin right off my face.

We were led into a very large sitting room filled with dinner guests. Several heads swung our way, and the eerie silence that followed made goose bumps pop up on my arms. Soren's hand came around to rest on the small of my back, bringing me closer to his side in a show of possession. A man, maybe an inch or two taller than me with not-quite-normal eyes and reddish-brown hair, walked up to us and extended his hand. Soren squeezed my waist in encouragement, and I put my hand into the gentleman's.

He bowed over my hand and kissed the back of it lightly, then spoke smoothly. "Any guest of Soren's is welcome in my home." There was a throaty, masculine rumbling in his voice that reminded me of a great cat purring.

My eyes widened in understanding. His eyes were a beautiful honey brown, but they definitely had a feline quality to them.

"Sage, this is Dwennon MacAllister."

"Pleased to meet you, Mr. MacAllister. I am honored to be invited into your lovely home." I plastered a smile on my face, hoping it came off as sincere. Truth was, I was already feeling a little out of my element, standing between a vampire and a shifter. I pushed all my doubts to the back of my mind and breathed in deeply through my nose.

I noticed a tall, runway-model-perfect woman approaching out of my peripheral vision, and the closer she came, the more confused I felt. I swear I could smell her skin, or maybe it was her perfume? If it was perfume, why did it remind me of Aldwin down to the warmed-honey notes? I narrowed my eyes as she joined our little group, and when she met my eyes, hers widened for a split second, probably wondering why I was giving her the stink eye.

Dwennon turned to the woman and introduced her as Milena. Milena and I exchanged the normal pleasantries, but it was evident to everyone that a little tension was going on. She cleared her throat and motioned toward a trio of women that were probably every man's fantasy come to life. They were standing by a far wall, drinking out of tall glasses.

Milena said in a silky voice, "The merleaders are getting anxious to begin, so the sooner we start, the better, Dwennon."

"Yes, of course; let us begin the meeting, then. If you'll excuse me, Sage, Soren." He smiled as he moved away with Milena at his side to address each group in the room.

I raised my brow at Soren when he kept his arm around me. "Merleaders?" I asked softly.

My brow furrowed as I gazed over at the three women, all dressed in soft shades of blue and green silk. Their eyes seemed a little larger than normal, but there was something compelling about them, something that made me want to walk across the room just to be closer to them.

Soren leaned in close to whisper, "Those are the

leaders of the merfolk."

I looked up into his eyes to see if he was joking with me, but I was pretty sure Soren didn't joke very often; and if he did, it wouldn't be about something like this. His brow, too, was creased in thought, and I had a sneaking suspicion that he hadn't known the merfolk would be at this little gathering.

I wrinkled my forehead in thought. From the little I had learned of merfolk from Travis, I knew that most of them never left the water, and the few who could only did so for hours at a time and very rarely. There were only a select few who had the ability to transform their fins into feet, and not without great difficulty and some sort of sacrifice.

My eyes were once again drawn to the ethereal trio— so beautiful and unearthly. I could smell the faint scent of the ocean and hear the call of the waves beckoning me before Soren pinched my arm, snapping me out of the merfolk's spell. I rubbed my arm and shook my head, making up my mind to steer clear of the compelling, Tim Burton version of *The Little Mermaid*.

I was trying not to look in the far corner of the room, where I was pretty sure a vampire was having an appetizer, but it was very hard not to see something when I desperately wanted to be sure the appetizer was okay. I made a slight movement, and Soren squeezed my side lightly just as I heard a soft moan coming from said appetizer. Sheesh. Mortified, I blushed and was relieved to hear Dwennon announce loudly that we would all discuss business over dinner. I was a little shocked that I was to be included in this meeting, but I guessed being with Soren was really going to pay off.

CHAPTER
Twenty-two

ONCE WE WERE SEATED AT THE LARGE DINING table, I took a look around myself and tried to catalog names and faces, along with species. There were Soren and I; Dwennon and a beautiful, petite, redheaded woman that Soren informed me was Dwennon's mate and second-in-command; the trio of merleaders; Milena, with a tall man just as runway-perfect as she was; and then another powerful vampire, along with his human female companion.

The only people I couldn't file away as either human or a specific preternatural species were Milena and her companion. Something was familiar about them, though, and I'd bet my ass they weren't entirely human. I made a mental note to ask Soren later. We were all served a first course of pumpkin soup, and then the meeting began.

"As some of you have noticed, tonight the merleaders have joined us for our monthly meeting. Normally, they only venture on land once or twice a year to check in with us and share their concerns. Livana got in touch with me a few days ago, though, and I thought you all should hear what she has to say in light of the recent issues we have been having." He motioned for the merleader, Livana, to speak.

I found myself leaning forward, enraptured with the singsong quality of the beautiful merwoman's voice. Another pinch from Soren brought me back to myself, shaking my head to dislodge her powerful pull. I kept my eyes averted from hers as she spoke, and it muted her allure just a little. She thanked Dwennon and everyone for having them here on short notice. Dwennon, Soren, the other vampire leader, and—much to my surprise—Milena all nodded in acknowledgement.

"We came to make you all aware that there has been an abnormal pattern of killings in my area, *seemingly* by merfolk." Her emphasis on the word *seemingly* implied she wasn't convinced her people were doing the killing. "Several bodies have been found in, or near, our area of water. We have hidden as many as possible, but several have been found; and although most people will believe it was accidental drowning, some will start to wonder why so many are happening at the same time. Also, it seems a rumor has spread locally of a mermaid sighting." She spat the last as if it were too disgraceful to even speak. "The occasional death could be attributed to us, but we have never been this reckless as a group." She gripped her glass of water and took a long drink when she was done speaking.

Soren's entire body had become rigid next to mine, and my mind raced at the implications. Dwennon looked over at Soren and raised his brow. Soren cleared his throat and confirmed what everyone already knew. "We have seen a large number of rogue vampire attacks in the city by young or newly made vampires. My investigation has led me in circles, and I cannot locate the source or reason behind the attacks. The leader of the southern vampire coven confirmed the same thing in his area." He glanced at the vampire sitting at the end of the table, who nodded in agreement.

Everyone was looking grim and tense when Dwennon took over again. "I'm afraid I don't have any good news to contribute to this meeting, either. We have had to hide several bodies over the last few weeks. They were found in the ghettos and in abandoned alleyways." A muscle ticked in his cheek as he struggled to keep his anger in check. His wife ran her hand down his arm, and he unclenched his jaw to continue. "All the bodies were torn apart from a were or shifter attack. We don't usually have rogues or lone shifters, so this has caused several packs to go into hiding or move out of the city entirely."

Everyone was quiet for a moment, thinking over all the information that had been presented. I was in my own little world, my mind racing to process all that I had learned, when a thought came to me. "Someone wants to frame the preternatural community," I whispered under my breath. *But why?*

Soren hissed, and I looked up just in time to see every eye in the room trained on me. Supernatural hearing. I was such an idiot. My hand itched to grasp the dirk through my gown, but Soren grabbed my hand, saving me from making that mistake again. I plastered an indifferent look on my face and set my jaw.

"What did you say, Sage?" Dwennon asked from his end of the table.

I turned to face him and repeated myself, slowly and loud enough that even the vampire's human companion could hear me. "I said, it seems to me that someone wants to frame the preternatural community since they are not trying to hide the fact that these are supernatural killings. Instead, they are *flaunting* the fact that they are. The only conclusion I can come to is that this person wants the world to know about you, and they want to expose your nasty side. They want the world to hate and fear you."

I held my breath, wondering how they would take my butting in and making assumptions.

"She's right. If we'd had this meeting a week or more ago, we might have come to the same conclusion ourselves and perhaps prevented some of these deaths." This came from Dwennon's mate, and I gave her a small smile in thanks.

"But who and why? That is what we need to find out before they do irreparable damage and we end up in a bloody war," Soren stated grimly from beside me.

I couldn't argue with that logic. Someone was trying awfully hard to cause panic and bring the preternatural community under suspicion.

"Another thing is that if this person is going through all this trouble, we can only guess they have something bigger planned, something to top anything we have seen so far," Soren added.

I shook my head. It made sense the more I thought about it. "Something huge is about to happen; this was all just a taste of what is coming," I said thoughtfully.

Something shifted in the room. I wasn't sure what, but I felt it just a second before everyone jumped to their feet. Damn, I was getting slow, and I was the one with the warper abilities.

Soren had me behind his back before I could process the movement. I heard a growl coming from the shifter's direction and a hiss coming from the vampire's direction.

Slowly, I reached down, pulled my sgian-dubh from its sheath at my ankle, and spoke very softly. "Soren, move."

He shook his head—just a slight movement, but I saw it, and it ticked me off. Last thing I needed was an overbearing vampire bodyguard. I took a breath and prayed that my voice came out steady.

"I am going to move in front of Soren to talk. On my word, I mean no harm. I have a dirk in my hand, but it is only for my own protection."

No one said anything, so I took it as a good sign. I moved as slowly as possible with all my muscles clenched in a fight-or-flight reflex. Moving around Soren, I stopped in front of the table full of preternatural creatures barely reining themselves in. Only Milena and her companion were seated at the table, watching the whole fiasco like it was some play going on for their amusement. I held out my hand, slowly set the sgian-dubh in front of me on the table, and then held up my hands in acquiescence.

"Who are you to know so much about us? If you were just a mistress of Soren's, you wouldn't know nearly as much as you do," Dwennon growled. His eyes elongated slightly as he spoke.

Damn, another strike out for me.

Soren put his hand on my arm, and I made an executive decision under pressure. "I'm a warper," I said softly.

Soren flinched, and Dwennon looked confused, as did the merleaders. Only Milena didn't look surprised; her brow only rose slightly at the admission.

Who the hell is she? I wondered again.

"A warper?" Dwennon asked.

Soren answered for me. "A warper blessed by the druid

priestess Amerach. She warped here from a hundred years in the future because of what is happening in our time." He sighed and sat down heavily in his chair.

I heard a chuckle come from our vampire friend at the other end of the table. "Soren, you have let the lust you feel for your pretty little mistress addle your wits."

Before Soren could reach his hand out to stop me, I let my warper power ooze out of its place inside me to encase everyone in the room. I picked up my dirk and walked over to the vampire with his sneer still frozen on his face. *It would be so easy to kill him*, I thought vaguely. My powers rushed warmly over me, and I brushed my hand out to caress the pliable bubble, wishing I could stay this way, safe inside my bubble of power.

When I let the bubble snap back into me, only a split second had passed for everyone else in the room, and I was holding the vampire in a death grip with my sgian-dubh pressed against his throat. His human companion screamed, and I rolled my eyes at her hysterics. Everyone seemed frozen in shock at my show of power, and I laughed out loud. I admit I sounded a bit hysterical, even to my own ears.

"I did warp here, vampire, and I can do without your smart-ass comments," I spat. "I'm here to help you all take care of this big mess. I didn't *make* the mess, but I don't have a choice—I have to help you clean it all up, or my ass will have to stay here permanently. And I like my own time very much," I hissed through my teeth.

"I didn't ask to be brought here; I didn't ask to have the pleasure of taking out one of your rogues the other night, either. I didn't ask to see her kill a man right in front of me, but here I am, and I deserve a little more respect," I snarled as I flung him away from me. The vampire swung around, and I immediately fell into a defensive stance, my dirk in the ready position.

He straightened his dinner jacket and looked at me like he saw me in an entirely new light. He bowed slightly at the waist and then looked up at me. "My apologies, Madame Warper, I am at your service."

He held out his hand to me, and I stood there, blinking stupidly at him for a second. I walked slowly over to him and let him grasp my hand; he brought it up to his lips and kissed it lightly.

"If anyone can help us, I'm pretty sure you would be the woman to do it." He smiled widely at me, flashing fangs, and I rolled my eyes at the vampire. *Figures.* I should have just threatened his life at the beginning of dinner. I looked around the table at all the preternaturals gaping at the show I'd just put on for them and lifted my brow.

Dwennon cleared his throat and said, "Well, that answers that."

I bent over and sheathed my dirk before I rejoined Soren.

"You are going to get yourself killed, pulling those kinds of stunts," he whispered loudly as I sat down, "but you looked bloody sexy doing it."

I blushed against my will.

Dwennon looked around the table at everyone. "We should all work together and put everything and everyone we have into finding the person responsible for this mess. I agree with Sage—this is building up to something huge, something that will make all these recent attacks look like child's play. We need to stop whatever it is before it happens. I trust you all feel the same way."

Everyone nodded their assent, and they all agreed to keep in close contact for the next week with any news.

Later that night, as I lay in bed thinking over everything that had happened that evening, I knew I'd have to come clean with Cerberus before they heard secondhand that a warper was in town. Everyone at dinner had agreed to keep my presence a secret so we would have a slight advantage, but I didn't know any of them well enough to trust their word, so I planned on coming clean the next day. It was the right decision, and it would take a load off my mind—and chest—to be able to be truthful with the only friends I had.

CHAPTER
Twenty-three

THE NEXT DAY, MY NERVES WERE BUNCHED UP AND on edge, ready to lash out on some poor, unsuspecting soul. I hadn't sparred in several days, and I could have used the distraction and release. I didn't want to tell Elaine and the others that I had let the cat out of the bag and lied to them, but I didn't want to deal with the aftermath of them finding out through the grapevine, either. If nothing else, the preternaturals and I could use the resources and contacts that Cerberus would be able to offer. The light lunch I'd eaten soured in my stomach at the thought of seeing Aldwin after our last encounter.

Travis was pacing in front of Howell Home when I arrived. "We got your note; I hope everything went well last night." His eyes searched my face for some clue as to why I'd called a meeting.

"I think it went well, but there are some things I need to discuss with everyone." I walked up the steps, and he swung the door open for me. We walked to the library together, and I couldn't shake the feeling he wanted to shake me to get some answers quicker. But his hands stayed clenched at his sides, and I almost felt bad for making him fret longer.

When we entered the library, Elaine and Phoebe

greeted me, and Aldwin kissed my hand without meeting my gaze. I quickly buried the deep disappointment I felt. Everyone took their places around the room and turned questioning eyes to me. I swallowed several times and nervously twirled my cuff bracelet around my wrist. I wasn't used to addressing this group—my only friends—and I hated the thought of disappointing them again.

"I'm just going to say what I came to say," I stated as I looked around the room, pleading silently for them to understand. I cleared my throat and blurted it all out. "Soren knows I'm a warper. The meeting last night consisted of several preternatural leaders, and I was in a position in which I felt it best to reveal myself to them."

I cringed at Phoebe's gasp, and I'm pretty sure I heard Aldwin swear under his breath. I looked up at Elaine, who only seemed stunned speechless, and Travis, who looked incredulous.

"Before you all jump to conclusions about how horribly I've handled this, let me tell you what I learned last night."

I told them about the merpeople, shifter, and vampire killings throughout the city over the last three months. Even Aldwin seemed genuinely startled that the issue was more widespread than anyone had realized. Elaine sucked in a breath when I mentioned the merleaders making the trip to be present at the meeting. I told them my theory about all the killings leading up to something larger, a grand finale. No one argued with me.

Everyone seemed subdued when we discussed our next course of action. It seemed the logical thing to do was to join the preternaturals and try to find a link that would lead us to whoever was the mastermind behind the killings. Aldwin came over to me and asked if I would mind his company back to the townhouse. I smiled tiredly up at him, grateful for a chance to talk. He left to tell Elaine that we were leaving, and I caught a glimpse of a pale Phoebe staring at Travis. He seemed angry and withdrawn into himself. I wondered if it was because all our planning had been for nothing, or if it was because they had been unaware of how large the problem really was. Before I could mull it over any more, Aldwin returned, and we left to go back to the townhouse.

After riding in an awkward silence for what seemed like forever, I realized we had passed the street the townhouse was on. I looked over at Aldwin, and he smiled at me shyly, looking like an adorably naughty boy.

"I wanted to take you somewhere today so you could just enjoy yourself and not have to worry about everything that is going on. I hope you don't mind."

I shook my head, unable to speak for fear of turning into a blubbering mess.

"Sage, if you don't want to go with me, I can take you back. I wouldn't force you," he said after a moment.

"No, I want to go. I just didn't expect you to do anything so sweet for me after the other night." I felt embarrassingly emotional that he had been thoughtful enough to plan a short little getaway.

"That was *my* fault. I overreacted, and I had no right to put my hands on you as I did; I don't know what came over me. 'I'm sorry' seems ridiculously inadequate."

I reached over and tenderly caressed the scarred side of his face. This man had no idea the hold he had over my heart. "Let's forget it ever happened and start fresh, okay?" My heart skipped a beat when he placed a gentle kiss into my palm.

I napped on Aldwin's shoulder, which completely embarrassed me, but he just tucked me closer to his side and told me to relax until we arrived. When the carriage finally came to a stop, I stepped out and gasped in pleasure. We were on one of the loveliest beaches I had ever seen. It was absolutely secluded; I could smell the salt water and hear the waves splashing onto the beautiful sandy shore. I turned and nearly knocked Aldwin over when I hugged him tightly around his neck. "Thank you," I whispered into his ear, my voice thick.

He grinned at my enthusiasm. "The look on your face is all the thanks I need."

Zachary handed a large basket and blanket down to Aldwin from the top of the carriage and clicked his tongue at the horses.

"He'll be back later to pick us up," Aldwin teased, waggling his brows.

I laughed out loud and felt amazingly free from the watchful eyes of the world. I only made it a few steps before I took off my shoes and stockings and unpinned my hair.

We ate lunch on a blanket in the sand and threw crumbs to the birds. Aldwin rolled his pant legs up, and we ran hand-in-hand along the beach, laughing like carefree children. He threw me over his shoulder and threatened to toss me into the ocean, laughing the whole time when I squealed and attempted to wiggle free.

At the end of the most wonderful day of my life, we lay in each other's arms, kissing tenderly and trying our best to ignore the fact that we needed to return to town. I glanced over at the gorgeous man on the blanket next to me, whose eyes were closed and expression was relaxed. I reached over to caress his face. When my hand feathered over the scar on his cheek, he grabbed my hand and leaned his face into my palm.

"Aldwin, what happened to your eye?" I asked softly.

He immediately stiffened.

"I mean, if you don't mind me asking." I looked down at the blanket, away from his stare.

His hand cupped my chin as he turned my face back toward him. I looked into his eyes and smiled, hoping he would notice just a fraction of the forbidden love I'd allow to seep past my defenses.

"It happened a long time ago, Sage. It's not really important anymore."

He smiled, but I could tell it was a sensitive subject for him.

"The scars don't disgust you, do they?"

His voice was quiet, his demeanor nonchalant, but I could feel the intensity of his gaze. My answer was important to him. I reached over and ran my hand through the thick, black hair at his temple; my fingers traced the scar running from his eyebrow down to his cheek. I leaned over and kissed his temple gently.

"There is nothing about you that could ever disgust me, Aldwin. You are absolutely perfect." A strong arm grabbed me, pulling me flush against his chest. His kisses were urgent and passionate, and I reveled in the rightness of it.

"Sage, the only thing I regret is not having two perfect eyes to see your beauty even more clearly. If I had a choice to have my eye working again or to be with you… I'd choose you every single time. I have never felt more whole than the day you came into my life; you complete me like no other could."

I felt a tear trail down my cheek. I didn't feel like I deserved such beautiful words. Aldwin wiped the tear away gently just as we heard the clop of horse hooves close by.

Aldwin helped me pin my wild hair in a loose bun at the base of my neck. I shoved my stockings into my pocket and put my boots back on. We held hands as we walked slowly back to the carriage, and both of us refused to acknowledge the fact that we would not be enjoying another day like that for a very long time, if ever. I didn't want to dwell on the negative, so I tucked away every single, beautiful memory we had made that day into a corner of my heart—a corner that had never been touched.

Little did I know, I would need those memories to keep me sane during the chaos in the following days.

CHAPTER
Twenty-four

SOREN AND I FELL INTO A PATTERN OVER THE NEXT few days. We attended every house party and gathering in the Charleston area, turning heads and setting tongues on fire with the spicy gossip of a supposed scandal. Soren performed his part well, playing the jealous, forbidding lover by hovering over me everywhere I went and staring down any man who came within a ten-foot radius. I almost believed him myself. Unfortunately, we hadn't found out anything useful, nor had we come across the smallest whisper of an underworld plot brewing.

We were seated for dinner at yet another house party hosted by the chief of police and his wife, when Soren leaned over to whisper in my ear. "Our host has been drinking more than usual tonight, and I've heard that he has been under a lot of pressure. I had his office at the station searched earlier this evening, but nothing was found." I was surprised at how much Soren had effortlessly accomplished.

"Perhaps a little peek into his personal library and desk is warranted," I replied, excitement starting to bubble at the thought of finally doing *something*.

Soren's eyes scanned mine, probably to see if he could talk me out of going with him. I narrowed my eyes, daring him to suggest it. His eyes dilated ever so slightly, and his nostrils flared. I swallowed. He reminded me of a wild animal some idiot had just poked with a stick. *Oh wait, I am the idiot.*

"Please, Soren, I need to *do* something. I'm going insane."

He gazed at me just a second longer, his eyes back to vampire normal, and nodded, an almost imperceptible movement.

I smiled brilliantly at him, thanking him without speaking for not making me piss him off later by ignoring his wishes. When we finished our dinner, we followed the rest of the party back into the ballroom to wait for the perfect time to make our escape and break into the chief's personal study.

It wasn't very much later when we slipped away separately from the party and met in the foyer. We made our way back to the library and slid inside the dimly lit room. It would have been much cooler if we had both been wearing black leotards, face paint, and little black beanie hats. But our vampire-warper team was still pretty badass. We made our way over to the enormous desk and started searching. There was a file in the top drawer, so I withdrew it and skimmed the various documents it contained.

Soren opened and closed several drawers before finding the bottom one locked. I interrupted my illegal perusal to see if he would pull some high-tech lock-picking device out of his pocket. Much to my disappointment, vampires didn't need to pick locks. Why pick a lock when you were strong enough to pull the drawer free, lock and all, without so much as flexing a muscle? I shook my head.

Soren looked at me quizzically, but I simply waved my hand at him and continued searching the file.

"Did you find anything?" I whispered to my partner in crime.

"Just a stack of unsolved murder cases. Unfortunately, all these seem to be the exact thing we have been trying to prevent."

I looked up to see his jaw clenched in anger. His eyes were close to lighting up the entire room with their golden glow.

"They are all preternatural killings," he murmured, confirming what I had already figured out. Soren shoved the files back into the drawer and shut it as quietly as possible. "How about you?" he asked.

I shook my head in frustration. "No, I haven't…" I stopped suddenly when my eyes roamed over the sheet of paper in my hand. It couldn't be. *My God.*

"What is it, Sage?" Soren stepped closer and looked over my shoulder to read the paper I clutched in my shaking hand.

"It seems the president of the United States will be giving a speech here in Charleston in less than forty-eight hours." The paper was a correspondence between the White House and the chief of police concerning security.

I turned to Soren and met his eyes. "You know what this means, right?" I barely whispered.

He looked like he wanted to kick someone's cat, but he nodded once and muttered, "Someone, probably a preternatural, is going to try to assassinate President Roosevelt in broad daylight in two days. That is, unless we do something to stop it."

I frowned at the offending paper. Why hadn't we

heard of the president's planned speech before tonight? I shoved the letter back into the folder just as Soren grabbed my arm and spun me in front of him.

"Do you trust me?" he whispered quickly into my ear.

I could feel his body rigid and tense, and my own stiffened in response. I nodded my head in one quick movement before Soren propelled us into the air to land on a settee several feet away from the desk. Soren landed on his back, and I landed on top of him. Before I could question what was going on or process how Soren had moved so quickly and gracefully, he had his hands buried into my hair and his mouth ravaging my shocked one.

I automatically stiffened in his arms and put my hands on his chest to push away, but the soft sound of the library door opening stopped me. Soren ran his hand up my back, encouraging me to relax and make our tête-à-tête believable. I relaxed my body, melting into the vampire underneath me. I felt Soren's hand skim my side, leaving goose bumps in the wake of the trail of heat he produced with his experienced hand. I moaned as he slanted his mouth over mine to deepen the assault he led on my lips.

I fisted my hand in the cloth at his neck to keep myself grounded, and Soren made a sound of approval in the back of his throat. A rational part of my brain heard a giggle and a curse as the library door was quickly shut, but most of my mind was a puddle of mush while Soren worked his voodoo on my body. I slowly surfaced from the beautiful haze I had found myself in, only to find Soren's bewitching eyes searching mine.

I'm not sure how long I would have lain there with my emotions out of whack and my confusion coating the air if Soren hadn't broken the kiss and spoken up. "Perhaps we should go ahead and make our way out the back door now that they're gone."

I gazed into his eyes, willing myself to hate him as much as I hated the two female vampires I had met. If I hated him, then I couldn't have any feelings at all for him. Wait... I had feelings for him? I was pretty sure I was in love with Aldwin, and here I was, splayed on top of a freaking vampire and wondering about what *feelings* I had for him?

It was that thought that had me jumping off Soren as quickly as possible. I felt so conflicted—how could someone have feelings for two guys at the same time? I wasn't the type to mess around with guys' heads, playing games with them, so what was my problem?

I shook my head as I tried to clear my jumbled thoughts. Maybe I was just sexually attracted to Soren. I mean, no woman in her right mind *wouldn't* be attracted to him. He was totally lickable, for crying out loud! That was it. If it had been under normal circumstances, we wouldn't have ended up locking lips... and that would have been an excellent excuse if I hadn't felt the same zing of power shoot through me, just like the first time we'd kissed.

We made it to Soren's home late that evening to send correspondence to Cerberus and the preternatural leaders. I had stayed over at Soren's large estate twice before, but it felt a little different after what had happened between us earlier. Soren was supposed to have gone to Dwennon's without me, but he changed his mind at the last minute and decided to accompany me back to his place first.

As soon as the carriage stopped, Soren started to get out, but I spoke his name softly, and he became eerily still. "Soren, I wanted to talk to you about what happened tonight." He turned around, and I blinked, startled by the golden light that shone from his eyes.

"There's nothing to talk about," he stated in clipped tones.

I reached over to touch his sleeve, but he flinched away from me. "I think there is," I said softly, not breaking eye contact as he stared me down.

I sighed in annoyance when it was evident that he didn't want to talk. Leaning over, I came nose-to-nose with him and spoke as softly as possible, bottling up all my frustration for later use. "Fine, Soren. We won't talk about this right now, but we *will* talk soon."

I stepped from the carriage feeling in control, getting the last word in and all. I guess I should have been paying more attention to my surroundings instead.

CHAPTER
Twenty-five

I HAD BARELY TAKEN A STEP AWAY FROM THE CARRIAGE when I caught a slight movement in the shadows to my left. My hand reached into my pocket for my dirk just as a figure lunged toward me with a small dagger in their raised hand. I just barely missed being slashed through as I dove out of the way, my legs becoming tangled in my pale-green evening gown. I pushed myself off the dirt and swung around to find Soren with his knee in the back of my attacker, who was face-down on the ground. Feeling a burst of pain in my left wrist, I looked down and saw that I had been cut during the scuffle. Sweat broke out on my forehead as I made my way over to Soren.

I wasn't prepared to see the face of my attacker. Soren flipped the person over, and the earth shifted slightly beneath my feet when I looked into a pair of familiar, gray eyes. "Phoebe?" I sucked in a pained breath and dropped to my knees, more worn out than I cared to admit. Phoebe looked at me through the tears tracking down her dirty face.

"I'm… so… sorry, Sage."

A gurgling sound came from her chest. I glanced up at Soren. "What's wrong with her?" I asked, dismissing my own pain.

"I don't know. She only has a small, superficial cut from her own knife that she got when I wrestled it away from her." He narrowed his eyes at the woman on the ground.

Phoebe made a choked sound, and her eyes widened with fright. "Poison," she rasped out as a coughing fit wracked her body.

My world tilted slightly on its axis again, and my eyes flew to Soren's. His nostrils flared delicately, and his gaze landed on my wrist.

"Phoebe, who are you working for? Whose orders were you carrying out?" I asked quickly, before my pain could incapacitate me.

I grabbed her shoulders and shook one hard time. Her pale face looked drawn and defeated. Her lips moved slightly, and a small sound escaped as she tried to form words. "Please, Phoebe, you must tell me," I begged.

She opened her mouth, and blood trickled out. Her words were barely audible. "I... had... to... I love... him."

Travis.

I felt Soren pull me off the ground and away from Phoebe. "She's dead," he whispered.

I looked back down into her lifeless, gray eyes, and all I could feel was pity.

"So am I," I muttered, feeling fire licking my wrist. I felt Soren lift me into his arms like I weighed no more than a child and march up the steps of his grand home. I felt so tired that by the time Soren laid me on a large bed, I could have sworn it had taken us hours to walk up the single flight of stairs.

"Soren, if I die, will you miss me?" I whispered. Heat encompassed my body, and an invisible fire licked my skin.

I prayed someone would put it out before it consumed me.

"You're not going to die, Sage. I won't allow it."

I snorted and immediately regretted the action when pain shot through my skull. I cried out. Soren hissed in a breath and wiped my brow with a damp cloth.

"Listen to me, Sage. I need to get the poison out of your blood. In order to do that, I am going to have to suck the wound and hope I get all the infected blood out." He spoke urgently, and I knew time was against us.

"I bet you just can't wait to sink your teeth into me, vampire." I tried to smile, but I'm pretty sure it was a grimace that adorned my face.

"You wish, warper," Soren quipped.

I looked into his eyes and spoke from my heart. "I trust you." It came out a whisper, but I knew my vampire employer would be able to hear me. I had some bizarre faith that he would be able to save me, as well.

Soren didn't waste any time. He took my left arm gently in his hands and sank his razor-sharp fangs into the cut at my wrist.

I flinched at the sharp pain. My right hand shot out to grasp a handful of his hair out of reflex. My body began to feel weightless as I slowly relaxed my grip. I stroked his head and neck to encourage him to continue, to let him know I was okay. A shudder ran through his body, and its vibrations shook my equilibrium.

Floating away bit by bit, I was soon unable to open my eyes. I drifted in and out of consciousness and caught only tiny glimpses of what was happening around me— Soren speaking to me with fangs peeking out of his mouth and blood dripping from his chin; Soren puking somewhere close by, ridding his body of my tainted blood;

Soren's shaky voice, telling me he was going to discard my dirty dress. I couldn't have cared less if he had stripped me naked—as long as I got to sleep in peace.

Sometime later, I woke in my shift with my heart pounding and a vampire lying deathly still next to me. I guessed I'd survived the night.

Throwing my legs over the side of the bed, I tried to stand but found myself weak as a kitten.

"Do you need something?"

My heart almost stopped. *Now, that would have been a waste.* I turned to Soren and tried to act natural. It wasn't very often a girl found herself in bed with a vampire.

"I was just going to find a drink of water. My throat is parched." I realized how pale he looked, and it hit me how much he'd put himself through to save me. I crawled over to him and placed my hand on his clammy brow. "Are you okay, Soren? Is there anything I can get you?" I furrowed my brow in thought. What if he hadn't rid his body of all the poison he'd taken from my blood? I couldn't let him die because of me.

"Sage, stop thinking so much. I'm fine, I'm just... thirsty," he rasped out.

"Well, why didn't you say so? Let me get you some wa—oh."

I searched his eyes and found the answer he didn't want me to see. He had spent all night throwing up the blood he had sucked from my body to make sure he didn't become poisoned. He was dehydrated. He needed blood. I got off the bed, went to the nightstand, poured myself a drink from the pitcher sitting there, and gulped it down.

I got back into the four-poster bed and crawled over to Soren's side. "You saved my life, Soren. Please let me help you in return."

I didn't give him time to argue. I lay down next to him, and he allowed me to pull him onto his side to face me.

"Sage, this isn't necessary... you're still weak from last night's blood loss."

I put my finger over his lips, and the ring around his eyes began to glow softly. "Don't talk, just nod your head. Can you take only a little blood for now?"

His eyes narrowed. He wasn't used to taking orders. *Tough luck.*

He nodded his head one time in a jerky movement.

"Good. I want you to take it from me, no arguing. I owe you, and I'll be sure to eat a ton of iron-filled foods later today. My wrist is very sore, so can you take from my neck without leaving nasty marks?" I asked the last a bit shyly. I was pretty sure there were no vampire etiquette classes that could help me in this situation.

My finger was still on his lips when he nodded again. I gulped and tried to regulate my breathing to show Soren I could handle the whole situation. Then, I removed my finger from his lips and moved in a little closer to my vampire. As I started to lift my hand to move my hair out of his way, he caught it and pulled it down to rest on his chest. I gulped in a breath as Soren reached over, grasped my tangled mass of hair into his large hand, and moved it over my shoulder to clear a pathway to the pulse point at my neck.

He took my chin in his hand and searched my eyes for any hesitation. Finding none, he angled my head to the left and leaned into me. His chest brushed mine, and his hair caressed my face. I had prepared myself for the

161

pain, but I didn't realize I should've also prepared myself for pleasure.

My gasp echoed through the room when I felt the sharp pain of Soren's fangs biting into my neck, but the pain didn't last long before a euphoric sensation swept through my body. Between the friction of our two bodies rubbing against each other and the pulling of Soren's mouth at my neck, I felt like I would forever be marked by the experience. Only a moment later, I felt him pull away from my neck, and his tongue swept out to seal over the two puncture wounds he'd created. I was breathing heavily and realized that my hand had a death grip on his white nightshirt. Loosening my grip, I smoothed out the shirt before I met his gaze.

I had no idea what to say. Thank you? *Wow* hardly seemed appropriate...

Before I could ponder the correct thing to say any longer, Soren leaned over and softly kissed the corner of my mouth. "Go to sleep, Sage. A vampire needs his rest, you know."

I smiled and settled next to him to go to sleep. I didn't even have to try. I was asleep before I could remember to worry about the upcoming evening.

CHAPTER
Twenty-six

WHEN I WOKE UP, IT WAS TO AN EMPTY BED. AFTER stretching my stiff body, I caught sight of a platter of fruit, cheese, and bread sitting on the bedside table. With a grumbling stomach, I made my way over and devoured half the contents of the platter before I noticed a clean outfit draped over a large chair near the fireplace. Munching on an apple, I walked over and found not only an outfit with an ecru-colored, high-necked blouse and a deep red skirt, but also a set of my undergarments and even a bar of my favorite lemongrass soap. I shook my head. Soren certainly was efficient.

After satisfying my hunger, I quickly washed in the adjoining bathroom and then paused to check the cut on my wrist and the bite marks on my neck. The puncture wounds were barely visible, and the cut on my arm was healing nicely. I bandaged my wrist lightly and dressed in the fresh set of clothes Soren had procured for me. The long-sleeved, high-necked blouse hid both of my recently acquired wounds. As I was braiding my hair loosely down my back, Soren knocked softly at the door before entering with a glass of wine for me.

The whole situation felt a bit awkward; I fidgeted and cleared my throat in the silence. Fortunately, Soren decided to proceed as if nothing out of the ordinary had happened. Maybe for him, it hadn't.

"I took it upon myself to write to Cerberus and Dwennon about last night's events."

I raised my brow, hoping he'd left out *some* of the details.

"Travis has been detained and will undergo extensive questioning. As of right now, he is denying any involvement in the string of deaths and in the assassination plot. He seemed genuinely distraught to learn of Phoebe's death. Some of Cerberus and the preternatural leaders will be coming here within the hour to meet and determine how we will proceed tomorrow when the president gives his speech."

And just like that, we were walking downstairs to meet with everyone and discuss a course of action to save the president of the United States.

Dwennon and his mate were the first to arrive, but not long after, Elaine and Aldwin joined our little meeting. I was standing with Soren in the foyer, greeting everyone as they entered, when Aldwin walked through the door. I smiled and started to hug him before I realized something was happening. I heard a warning hiss come from the vampire at my side and immediately found myself wedged between Soren with his fangs fully extended and Aldwin with a dagger drawn. *What the hell?*

Before I could even blink, everyone else had filed into the foyer and had begun yelling at each other. I had a hand on each man's chest, and I was beginning to feel quite claustrophobic and beyond pissed off. I tried to yell at everyone to get them to shut up and act like the adults they were supposed to be instead of animals. Well, not the shifters, of course; no one could blame them for acting like animals.

I let my anger build in my chest and then focused it—and my warper energy—into my hands, shoving the two pigheaded men across the room. Silence descended as everyone stared at me.

"You can have a pissing contest later, boys. Right now, we need to figure out a way to save both the president, who will be speaking in less than eighteen hours, and all of our asses." I narrowed my eyes at the two men who were still staring daggers at each other until they both nodded in my direction.

I let out a relieved breath and waved a hand in the direction of the library. "Okay. Let's get started, then." I brushed back the hairs that had escaped my braid and strode down the hall, hoping everyone would follow me without incident.

When we were all inside and seated, I made sure not to sit too close to Aldwin or Soren. As if nothing had happened, Soren began giving everyone an overview of the previous night's events, including us finding out about the president and the files of unsolved preternatural murders. He told everyone about Phoebe's attack and death as a result of the poison from her own blade. I saw Elaine flinch and pale as she heard Soren speak of Phoebe. I couldn't imagine the pain she must be in; she had known Phoebe much longer than me, and I still hurt to think of her and Travis' betrayal.

I unconsciously touched my left wrist, remembering the pain of the poison working its way into my bloodstream. If I hadn't been a warper, I would have died just as quickly as Phoebe had. I guessed some good things did come along with being a warper. I glanced up and realized Aldwin was watching me. I quickly put my hands in my lap and refocused my attention on what Soren was saying.

We all hashed out the worst- and best-case scenarios and came to a reluctant decision. I would get as close to the president as possible since I was the one with the powers to freeze time and possibly save the president if all the preternaturals failed to scope out and diffuse any potential threats.

I cleared my throat. "Is it possible for me to get that close to the president?" I asked.

Dwennon spoke up. "It shouldn't be a problem since the government is aware of Cerberus and the importance of the society. They'd listen to Mrs. Howell if she were to tell them it was in the best interest of the president to have you close by him during his speech."

I glanced over at Elaine, who looked distracted.

"Do you really think we should put Sage in that dangerous of a position?" she asked through clenched teeth.

I furrowed my brow. She wasn't acting like herself, but then again, she had just lost someone close to her, and she was probably scared to lose me as well.

"I'll be fine, Elaine." I tried to give her a reassuring smile. "Besides, we don't have much choice. If the preternaturals don't succeed in diffusing the situation, I'll be the only one able to save the president. This is what I was sent here for."

She cleared her voice and met my eyes. "You're right, of course. I'm sorry, I'm just not feeling very well. I'll make sure to contact our person in the president's security staff first thing in the morning."

Dwennon, Soren, Aldwin, and about a dozen other preternaturals were going to be patrolling the area surrounding City Hall tomorrow, hoping to find and take out any threats from the thousands of people who would be gathered to hear the president speak. I prayed they would be successful.

We all left shortly after making the final arrangements for the next day. Luckily, I didn't get a chance to talk to Aldwin or Soren before I left to go back to my townhouse; I didn't want to get distracted by any drama, and I needed more rest before the next day since I was still feeling a little weak from blood loss. The next day, I'd be rubbing elbows with President Theodore Roosevelt.

CHAPTER
Twenty-seven

NERVOUS WAS AN UNDERSTATEMENT.... I WAS scared as hell that I'd mess this whole thing up. I mean, what was riding on my success? Only the life of the president of the United States. Countless lives would also be lost if the president were assassinated publically by creatures that no one even knew existed; and let's not forget that the events today could alter the time stream if I failed. No pressure, really.

On top of everything else, I wasn't so sure I wanted to warp back to my time any longer. I had friends here. I also had Aldwin and Soren. I had so much more than I'd ever had in my own time. I couldn't fail, but I could only hope that once we succeeded, I would be allowed to remain in 1904.

I finished pulling my hair back into a bun and secured it tightly with pins, strapped my dirks in place, and laced up my black-heeled leather boots. I wore a long, simple black skirt with a black, long-sleeved lace blouse. Pinning on a small, black hat with a black, see-through veil that fell over my eyes, I looked like a black widow, especially when I added my black, kid-leather gloves. I would blend in as much as possible with the men wearing their black suits, and that was all that mattered. I didn't want to draw attention to myself.

I left my townhouse on foot, hoping everyone else was in place. The streets were already filled with people heading to Town Hall to hear President Roosevelt's speech. My boots thumped out a steady rhythm as I walked and kept an eye on the people I passed. It would have been nice to be able to take care of the problem before it ever got close to the president. But, of course, that would have been too easy.

I arrived at Town Hall just as officials were shuffling the crowd toward the designated spectator area. Once I reached the front doors, a man in a black suit and hat motioned for me to head in the other direction. "I'm here as part of the president's party," I stated, stepping into his personal space so I could speak quietly because I didn't want to make a scene.

His eyebrow rose, almost touching his non-existent hairline, and he smiled at me like a child who was entertaining him.

I stepped even closer, making him retreat a step, and his smile slipped in the process. "Perhaps you'd like to inform the president that you are keeping a member of Cerberus from doing her job—the one member who could very well save the president's life... and keep the world from plummeting into absolute chaos."

I'm not sure how I sounded to him—I didn't have time to check my attitude or deal with anyone's crap—but his eyes became as big as saucers, and he stepped back enough for me to enter the building. I followed him to the back of the building, where a large group of men were huddled around a small, round table, talking.

My reluctant companion walked over to the group

and spoke into the ear of a ginormous man. He glanced in my direction and ran his eyes over me in a purely academic perusal before he walked over. I gawked at the giant standing before me and held out my hand, which he reluctantly shook with his much larger paw.

I cocked my brow at him. "I am going to assume that you are the head of President Roosevelt's security, and I'm also going to assume that you didn't get the position just because of how large you are. Nor am I going to assume you got it because of how intimidating you are. No... I prefer to believe that you earned this position because you are the *best* at what you do." I clucked my tongue. "I would hate to make assumptions based on appearances, wouldn't you?" I looked up at him, keeping my eyes wide and innocent.

He cracked a grin. "Touché, Ms. Hannigan."

"Please, call me Sage. I'll have to be close to the president during the entire speech, and just to let you know, I have three weapons on me and a unique ability that may also come in handy."

I waited a second while he digested this info. His gaze quickly raked over me again, and I smirked as he tried to figure out where I could have hidden so many weapons. "You may want to rethink your disregard of women being capable enough to be a threat in the future. Luckily, I'm on your side."

"Indeed." This time, he looked at me with a bit of admiration when he held out his arm to me. I was suddenly nervous as he took me to become a bodyguard to the twenty-sixth president of the United States.

President Roosevelt didn't waste any time. Everyone was briefed on the situation and the part I would play as a female bodyguard. If there was any shock from the other bodyguards over my sex, or the fact that I'd be acting as second to the president's head bodyguard, I didn't notice. I was way too busy focusing on the task ahead of me. I barely registered anything that was said around me, and before I knew it, I was flanking President Roosevelt as we headed out the front doors of City Hall to stand in front of a crowd of thousands of spectators… thousands of potential assassins.

As I stood on the patio in front of Town Hall, it hit me how hard it would be to spot a suspicious person. All the women wore long skirts; all the men wore suits in varying shades of gray, black, and brown. 1904 was just a little too perfect for someone trying to blend in.

The president approached the banister, which overlooked the audience packed into the area to hear his speech, and began addressing them in a booming voice. I stood back, a few feet to his right, and scanned the crowd. I was amazed at how quiet the huge group was as they listened to him.

An abrupt movement in my peripheral vision caused me to take a step toward the president. I saw several people standing around a figure on the ground, and two men lifted her up as if she had fainted. I watched as they moved through the crowd, and a man with gold-rimmed eyes turned and winked at me. Soren. The woman had been a threat.

I stepped back into my original position and continued to scan the crowd for anything peculiar. A few minutes later, there was a scuffle close to the steps of the patio where we stood. It looked like a drunken fistfight, and I caught a glimpse of a scarred face before he grabbed the drunk by the scruff of his neck and led him away.

So far so good. My body began to relax just a little. The president's speech would be over any moment, and his bodyguards would get him quickly and safely out of Charleston. There was no doubt in my mind that two preternaturals had been taken care of by Soren and Aldwin, and I could only hope that they were the only ones dispatched to try to assassinate President Roosevelt.

Just as the president was wrapping up his speech, I saw a glimmer of bright yellow in the front row of spectators. I stepped closer to the president and put my hand lightly on his elbow. He didn't act like anything out of the ordinary was happening, but my stomach lurched when I saw a pair of elongated eyes staring in my direction. Dear God. For some reason I had expected a vampire, but if a shifter began shifting in front of everyone here, it would be beyond explanation.

President Roosevelt's chief security guard followed my line of vision, and his eyes widened when he found whom I was watching. The man's face had already begun elongating, his eyes looked more animal than human, and his teeth had already lengthened into deadly fangs.

It seemed that luck was on our side—only the head of security and I had noticed the change taking place. I had to scramble to come up with a way to handle the shifter without drawing attention to him or myself. He didn't give me the luxury of overanalyzing the situation, though. His eyes narrowed as he lunged toward the stairs leading up to the president.

A few people around him gasped when a growl erupted from his chest, but very few could track his inhumanly fast movements. Without thinking, I did what

I was meant to do. I did what I was brought to 1904 to do. I warped.

My left hand was still on the president's elbow as I ripped the power from deep within myself and hurtled it toward the crowd to encompass as far as it could reach. I bit my lip to keep from screaming out; it felt like my soul was being torn from my body. A warm trickle of liquid slid over my upper lip, and I quickly wiped the blood away with my gloved hand. I looked around myself and out into the crowd, nearly dropping to my knees when I saw the sea of people standing frozen like freaky, lifelike pieces at a wax museum. My power was stretched so far that I couldn't track its edges. I had no idea how much I could encompass with my time-freezing powers, or how far those powers could reach.

I removed my hand from the president's elbow and swung my eyes around to the shifter, who was frozen halfway up the stairs. I walked over to him and flinched. He had progressed at least halfway through his change. When I looked at his face, I felt like punching him. Moving the frozen half-wolf was going to be a difficult task. I pressed down on the center of my butterfly bracelet until I heard a little release *snick*, then jabbed the poisoned pin into the side of the shifter's neck and began the foul-language-inducing task of hauling the half-furry man away.

Sweat poured down my face and back by the time I had maneuvered the creature's body around the other frozen spectators and into a broom closet in the back of the building. Aldwin had told me that the poison coating the needle would knock out anyone—human or not—for several hours, but I wasn't taking any chances. I ripped off the ruffled hem of my underskirt and gagged and trussed the shifter like a Sunday goose before I headed back to the patio.

CHAPTER
Twenty-eight

B Y THE TIME I REACHED THE PRESIDENT'S SIDE, I could barely stand up straight, and I had to discreetly palm a piece of my underskirt for my bloody nose. I could feel my power shivering unsteadily around myself and the city, so I placed my left hand back on the president's elbow and let the power I'd unleashed snap back into my battered and weak body.

The president began mid-sentence where he had left off, and the eerie silence was once again filled. It took everything I had not to buckle under the backlash of power as it poured back into my body. My head spun, and visions of passing out danced in my head. I pressed the cloth to my nose and noticed how pale the president's head security guard had become as he stared at me and then at the spot where the shifter had been standing. He swallowed and raised a brow at me. I gave him a slight nod.

The president finished his speech, and we all once again flanked him as we headed back inside the building. When we made it safely inside, President Roosevelt took my arm and gently led me to a chair before he motioned to someone.

"Get this young woman a drink; I am fairly certain

she just saved my life."

I quirked my brow at him, but he just smiled down at me through his glasses and placed a glass of liquor in my hand. Thank God for someone who knew exactly what I needed right then.

A few moments later, Aldwin came in, escorted by a few of the president's security guards. He knelt down beside me so I could whisper in his ear where to find the shifter and what had happened. His eyes roamed over me, assessing me for any damage, and I smiled into his concerned face. I shooed him away to take care of the shifter mess and promised to meet him at Howell Home as soon as the president was safely on his way out of Charleston.

As the president's entourage prepared to leave, the mammoth-sized head security guard came over to shake my hand and make sure I would be okay.

"You have done your country a great service, Ms. Hannigan. I don't need to know all of what happened, or what, exactly, your abilities are; I am just very glad you were here when we needed you most."

I blinked at him, and for the first time I felt like everything I had endured had been worth the end result. "I am glad to use my abilities for good," I said, smiling up at the gentle giant.

"Well, we are heading out, then. If I hadn't seen the way you looked at that scarred gentleman earlier, I'd be asking to see you again sometime, but it looks like I'm too late to have a chance at winning your heart." With a roguish wink, he strode off, barking orders to the rest of his party.

Standing on shaky legs, I made my way out of the

building, unable to wait any longer to get home and sink into a hot bath.

I walked slowly back to the townhouse in the crowd still dispersing from the president's speech. People were talking and milling about, completely oblivious to the disaster that had just been averted. A small smile played at my lips when I thought of how I'd had such an important role in an event that would never be recorded in history. I didn't mind.

My thoughts drifted back to the bodyguard's assessment of my feelings for Aldwin. Could I be in love with him? I hadn't let myself truly and fully consider the possibility since I had always believed I'd warp back to my own time when my mission was over, but it looked like I was very much stuck in this era. I'd have plenty of time later to examine my feelings once all the excitement of our victory settled down.

About a block away from my townhouse, I felt a bee sting my neck. I slapped the stinging spot and felt a thin needle fall away from the tiny puncture wound, swinging around just in time to see the buildings around me blur and spin out of control. I didn't even have time to cry out before the darkness embraced me.

CHAPTER
Twenty-nine

MY BODY WAS SO TIRED, AND THE ONLY THING THAT mattered was rest. I tried to shake off the foggy mist that surrounded my mind. Wasn't there something important I was needed for? My eyes wouldn't open, and I couldn't lift my arms. The daze I struggled with drained what little energy I had left, but I fought against the fog, knowing my life was in jeopardy. I didn't want to die, especially not now.

Very slowly, I emerged from the haze in which the drug had held me. When my eyes finally opened, I squinted against the glare of a nearby oil lamp. I was lying on a bed in my shift, my arms tied above my head to the iron bedposts. My feet were secured to the footboard.

My mind spun. Travis must have gotten free; it was the only explanation. If he had escaped, that meant Aldwin and Soren would find me soon. I would just have to survive until help came.

I never thought my heart could get ripped out, or that some little part of me could die, but that's exactly what happened next. A low laugh echoed through the room, bouncing off the rock walls, causing a chill to slither into my heart.

"You, of all people, shouldn't be surprised, Sage.

Someone who has shut everyone out of her life, who has so many personal demons and well-kept secrets…"

I almost gagged on the bile that rose in my throat.

"I didn't want all of this to happen. I had hoped to use you and your powers a little longer, but I miscalculated how strong you would become and how you would side with those filthy creatures even though they'd almost killed you twice."

The lamplight reflected in her crazed eyes, and I flinched when I finally recognized her achingly familiar face. Elaine looked down at me with a disgusted sneer on her face, and the wounded beast inside me wanted to howl in denial. Not Elaine.

"Why?" The word slipped through my dry lips before I could stop it.

Her eyes went wild. "*Why?*" She paced back and forth at the foot of the bed, and I caught a glimpse of the long knife she gripped in her hand. "I loved him! I loved him, but it wasn't enough. My love wasn't enough to make him stop dealing with the preternaturals or Cerberus. He poured everything he had into them, and when he was done, he had nothing left for me." She pounded a fist against her chest.

"And then, how did the vile creatures repay him?" She looked at me, her eyes wide in question. "They killed him, that's how. He died because he dealt with demons and other spawns of Satan." She spat the words as if the act of saying them would rid the world of their filth. "I will make every one of them pay, one way or another. I have enjoyed using Cerberus' money and resources to wipe out the very creatures it's supposed to be protecting. Even though you stopped me today, the inevitable will happen;

they will be exterminated. It will be so much easier when you are gone."

My body went very still as I searched the face of the woman in front of me for any sign of the person I had once counted as my only friend. God, I had wanted her friendship so badly. The pain from this wound would never fade. What were my options? I only saw one exit, but what would freezing time accomplish if my hands were bound?

"Don't even think about time freezing," she spat. "I put enough of the neurotoxin into your bloodstream to make it impossible for you to draw on your little power."

I tried to tug on my power to test it. "*Crap.*"

She grinned. "This once, I'm in total agreement with your word choice."

If looks could kill, I'm pretty sure she would have exploded in an oozing mass on the floor.

"Like I give a damn what you think. So, what are you going to do, just kill me while I am tied up?" I asked.

She smiled as if I had finally asked the right question, but it didn't make me feel all happy inside.

"No, I have plans for you, Sage. You'll love it; it's very sporting." Her tone put me on edge, but before I could respond, she leaned over and pricked me on the leg.

"Oh, hell," I mumbled as the darkness claimed me once again.

CHAPTER Thirty

I JERKED MY HEAD BACK HARD ENOUGH TO CRACK IT on the stone wall I was now chained to, gulping in air around the icy water that had been thrown into my face. My hands were still bound above my head, and I doubted I'd ever get full feeling back in them. I shook my head to dislodge the wet hair plastered to my cheeks and found myself eye-to-eye with a feral vampire. My heart nearly plummeted to my feet when I reached inside myself and found a useless vapor where my power had once been. The vampire smiled, sniffing the air, smelling the fear that roiled off me and hearing the racing of my heart. I probably turned the bastard on.

I looked down at my feet and was shocked to find I still had my sgian-dubh in my boot holster. *Why would Elaine have left that on me?*

The vampire took a step forward as if he couldn't help himself, but he quickly recoiled when someone entered the chamber. Elaine strode into the room with another vampire and a shifter. I watched the trio enter but kept my mouth shut. She knew she was calling the shots, so I'd let her make the first move.

The trio from hell stopped directly in front of me, and a fair-haired vampire with a small piece of his left earlobe missing grabbed my chin in his iron grip. I tried to jerk out of his grasp but quickly gave up. I'd only tire myself out more and end up with bruises. Meeting the vampire's red-tinged stare, I lifted my chin slightly.

"So, this is the powerful time warper?" he hissed as his tongue swept over his lips and fangs, tasting my scent.

"So, this is the pathetic, piece-of-shit vampire?" I shot back when he released my chin.

His hand shot out so fast my eyes didn't register the movement. I tasted blood in my mouth, and my jaw felt dislocated.

Elaine cackled. "Come now, children, let's not get ahead of ourselves."

I met her gaze unflinchingly and had to stop myself from spitting in her face. Her smile slipped just enough to make me grin in triumph.

She snapped her fingers. "James, Colton, unchain her, and let's get this over with."

I tried to school my features, but my mind was racing through dozens of different scenarios. I was led from the room with my tingling arms pinned behind me in an unbreakable grip, trailing Elaine and her two vampire buddies. Of all the scenarios my mind could have come up with, I would never have envisioned what awaited me behind lucky door number three.

I blinked in amazement when I entered the room and came to a complete halt before the shifter holding me gave me a shove into the arena. *Arena* was the only word that could describe the room that I found myself in. I looked up, and to my stupefaction, I saw the moon and stars shining down from where the roof should have been. The building looked like some sort of abandoned factory.

There were torches burning all around, and dozens of preternatural eyes were trained on me. Slowly, a bead of sweat trickled down my temple.

Elaine and company led me to the center of the large room. She looked around, into the faces of all the creatures that she loathed—her deadly little minions—and then gave a nod of her head. The blond vampire left the three of us alone in the middle of the arena. Elaine began what only could be described as a pep talk to her followers. She went on about how today was only a setback, and once I was disposed of, their quest for a war would come to pass.

Yadda freaking yadda.

I looked around the room, searching faces and eyes for anyone that might be able to help me, for anyone that wasn't under the spell Elaine wove. My heart plummeted at the realization that there wasn't going to be any help coming from anyone except me. I gingerly wiggled my fingers behind my back, pleased to feel needle-like sensations accompany the movement; feeling was returning to my hands and arms. My ears picked up on something Elaine was saying, and I turned my attention back to her to see if I could make sense of her insane babbling.

"I will take care of the warper myself, to show you all that I am worthy to be your leader. Tonight, we will fight to the death for your entertainment." She smiled at the raucous burst of applause and cheers that came from the crowd surrounding us.

She had truly lost her ever-loving mind! A cold sweat broke out on my brow, and I felt like people do right before they throw up all over themselves. Surely, she didn't mean for us to fight one-on-one to the death. I licked my parched lips as she walked over to me with a sly grin painted across her face.

"This should be a fair fight since I've trained in combat and defense just as much as you have, perhaps a little more. You can't use your warper powers for at least another twelve hours, so it will be an even match."

I blanched at her casual disregard for my life. "Elaine, you don't mean to go through with this, do you?" I knew I sounded desperate, but I would swallow my pride if she'd only change her mind.

She looked into my eyes, and I saw determination and a thread of insanity lodged there. Why hadn't I seen it before?

"I won't feel the slightest remorse when I cut your throat and your life spills onto the floor tonight; you will be nothing more than another dead creature on my checklist."

I flinched from the venom in her voice.

"Let her go, and get out of the circle."

The shifter abruptly released my arms, and I rubbed each one slowly to get the blood flowing back into them. Elaine watched me from a few feet away as she removed her blouse, leaving only her shift and skirt to face me. A man approached her from behind, carrying something wrapped in velvet cloth. My stomach lurched when she pulled a dirk almost the exact same size as mine from the folds of the cloth.

I looked down at my shift with its missing hem and felt for the small knife strapped to my thigh. It was gone. I pulled the dirk from my boot and swiftly cut a slit up both sides of my shift to my thighs. To hell with appearances.

Elaine made a few lunges and practice jabs, getting

used to the feel of her dirk as I scanned the area surrounding me, looking for exits and trying to formulate a plan.

"You won't get away, Sage. I have given orders to have you killed instantly if you try to leave this arena."

I focused my eyes on the woman I had hoped to become close friends with and saw nothing in her to leave me any hope of avoidance. I shook my head and ignored the human-sized weight that had squatted on top of my chest. I didn't want to kill her, but I would do what I had to in order to survive. I centered myself and tightened my grip on the sgian-dubh in my hand. A ripple went through the crowd surrounding us, but I didn't have time to care about our morbid audience.

Elaine lunged toward me with her dirk raised in a forward-thrust motion aimed directly for my chest. She wasn't pissing around.

I leapt out of her way and barely avoided being skewered by the tip of her knife. I cried out when the blade sliced across my left arm. A hiss echoed throughout the room. Great, I was bleeding in a room filled with bloodsuckers. Now wasn't that just the icing on my crap cake.

Elaine and I circled one another, sizing each other up for our next move. This time, she swung her knife toward my neck just as I swung my dirk low. I bent backward far enough to allow her blade to pass over my head and immediately straightened and spun, ready for her next move. Elaine stood in front of me wide-eyed with blood seeping through the side of her chemise. I smiled and saluted her with the edge of my dirk.

Her eyes glazed over, and she threw herself in my direction. I met her halfway, and our weapons rang throughout the arena as they glanced off each other. She grabbed my arm with more strength than I would have credited her. I kicked her as hard as I could when my dirk began slipping, knocking her to the ground. Elaine jumped to her feet so quickly I wondered for a split second if she had some kind of preternatural ability. The thought was wiped from my mind as she swiped my legs out from underneath me; I landed flat on my back, and all the air whooshed out of my lungs.

From somewhere in the arena, I heard what sounded like a sonic boom, followed by howls of fury. The sounds were the least of my worries, though; Elaine was on me before I could gulp in a breath.

She leaned all her body weight onto the dirk poised above my heart. My own weapon lay just a few inches away, but if I let go of her hands, she would have had no trouble thrusting hers through my heart. My arms started to wobble, and the dirk slipped down another inch, puncturing the skin above my left breast.

Time seemed to suspend around us, and even though I could tell there was some kind of battle raging around me, it all felt very far away and inconsequential. I raised my eyes to look into Elaine's crazed face and knew that if I died right that moment, I would die without ever having fully lived… without ever having allowed anyone to know the real me. I couldn't let Elaine steal that away from me.

I found a burst of strength hidden deep inside myself that had nothing to with my warper powers and everything to do with my need to survive. Bucking my hips hard enough to dislodge Elaine's body from mine, I rerouted her dirk away from my chest. With my right hand, I reached out and grasped the hilt of my sgian-dubh just as

Elaine's dirk came back down again and tore through my chest a mere inch above my heart. An anguished scream was torn from my lips as blackness veiled my vision.

I turned my head just in time to see a body fall close to me, his eyes open but not seeing. As I glanced up, I could see Elaine's wild eyes and was sure she, too, was oblivious to the war going on around us. She only had my death on her mind.

My fingers involuntarily flinched around the dirk still in my hand, and something inside me snapped. Running on adrenaline, I swiped my dirk across the front of her chest, and she stumbled off me in shock. She was bleeding from shoulder to shoulder as she got to her feet.

Gathering every ounce of strength I possessed, I heaved myself up off the floor. Reaching up with my left hand, I jerked out the knife that was protruding from my chest. The bloody weapon clanged to the ground, and the searing pain nearly buckled my knees.

Elaine looked over at me, seething with hatred. I shook my head, pleading with her to just stop, but she charged me anyway. Everything happened so quickly, but it seemed at the time to play out in black-and-white movie stills. She charged, and I lifted my dirk just at the right moment for her to run directly into my blade. I couldn't have stopped it if I'd wanted to.

Her eyes widened in shock as the hidden knife she had retrieved fell to the ground. She landed on her knees, and I went down with her in an unwilling embrace. I jerked the dirk free from her chest, and she slid to the ground in front me. Her eyes swung around wildly, taking in the massacre going on around us, and a trickle of blood escaped her mouth.

As Elaine's eyes slowly dimmed in defeat and then finally closed in death, I felt tears streaming down my face, but there was nothing I could do to stop them. No matter the reason, I had taken a human life.

I looked down at my blood-soaked shift and staggered to my feet, even though my legs felt like they wouldn't hold me for long. The battle around me had died down, and dozens of bodies littered the arena. I looked across the floor and saw Aldwin shouting across the arena at someone I barely recognized. Soren stood there, covered in blood and looking like a dark, avenging angel. He glanced over in my direction, his eyes widened, and then he looked back at Aldwin.

I smiled at my guys and gave a little wave with my finger. Aldwin was running in my direction and saying something I couldn't make out when I toppled forward into oblivion.

CHAPTER
Thirty-one

SOMEONE CARRIED ME—EITHER THAT OR I FLOATED— out to the carriage. Whatever the case, I was sprawled across the lap of one very angry vampire. The carriage swayed back and forth, and I hoped I wouldn't throw up all over anyone. Aldwin was kneeling on the floor, hovering near me and arguing with Soren. I absently wondered what they were angry about—*must be something important*, I thought. I felt light as a feather and wondered how I could feel so wonderful after I'd lost so much blood; maybe the hole in my chest wasn't as bad as I had thought. I tried to lift my hand to smooth out the worry lines creasing Aldwin's face, to tell him it would all be okay, but my arms were as heavy as lead. Maybe I was having an out-of-body experience or something.

Someone slapped my face.

Really? After the day I'd had, they had to go and slap me? My eyelids were so heavy. Was it so bad to just sleep? Another slap, and my eyes cracked open to see whom I'd have to kill as soon as I was up to the task.

Aldwin was saying something; his lips were moving, but his words were echoing around somewhere in a far-off tunnel. His expression was urgent. Soren shook me, and my head lolled back. Words I couldn't piece together came from Soren or Aldwin... or both, I couldn't be sure.

"Blood... dying... consequences..."

Aldwin grabbed Soren by the throat, and with a wild look in his eyes, screamed at him.

I wished I could figure out what was going on. Maybe they'd tell me later. My eyes fluttered, and everything blurred again. I felt so peaceful and serene. I could have stayed like that forever, surrounded by the two people who meant the world to me.

Someone grasped my jaw, and the scent of wet pennies assaulted my nose. *Funny, I don't remember licking any pennies.*

I swallowed to get the taste out of my mouth, but instead, I choked on something sliding down my throat. I tried to close my mouth, but my jaw was once again pried open and more of the warm, metallic liquid invaded my mouth. I squirmed, trying to get free. The hand that had forced my mouth open let go to hold my arms down.

From somewhere far away, a familiar voice spoke, "Her heart is beating faintly."

And another voice, "She will be okay now, I'm sure of it. Thank you."

A pause. "I didn't do it for you."

"I know, but I am still thankful you did, no matter your reasons."

I tried to open my eyes, but the sea that I was floating on swept me further toward total abandon and merciful peace. Who was I to fight the tide?

The first thing I saw when I woke up was the face of Dr. Aldwin Blake asleep next to me. I closed my eyes and counted to ten before opening them again. He was still there. How did I go from a bloody fight to being in bed with the man who was possibly the love of my life? I hoped I hadn't missed any action. I reached over to push his hair away from his face as a contented sigh escaped me. I could get used to waking up to this sight.

Aldwin nearly catapulted off the bed when I touched him. Wow, he was a light sleeper. I jerked my arm back and felt a pain in my chest. Oh yeah, Elaine had run me through with a dirk. I grasped my chest at the fresh wave of pain her memory invoked.

Aldwin took my hand and kissed the back of it almost reverently. "You nearly sent me to an early grave worrying about you. It took us almost eight hours to find where Elaine had taken you! I'm not sure we ever would have if we hadn't had help from a coven of witches."

I smiled at him. "But you did, and just in time. Thank you."

Aldwin helped me sit up and propped two pillows behind my back.

"Tell me everything," I demanded as soon as I was comfortable.

He sat on the bed next to me and began to tell me all the things I'd pretty much figured out, but it helped to hear the truth spoken out loud. All the deaths Elaine had caused, all the chaos that had ensued. None of it made me feel better about having to take her life, but one day I hoped to be able to come to terms with it.

Zachary had alerted Aldwin when I hadn't shown up at the townhouse, and an all-out manhunt had begun. Evidently Aldwin, Soren, Travis, Dwennon, and about two dozen other preternaturals joined in the search. At first, it had been assumed that Elaine was missing, too; but a witch told them answers would be found in a trusted servant's room. It wasn't long before a diary was unearthed from under a loose board in Phoebe's closet.

Phoebe had kept a meticulous accounting of Elaine's treachery and also detailed how Elaine had blackmailed Phoebe into doing things against her will by threatening to harm Travis if she refused. Elaine had played on Phoebe's love. I shook my head in disgust. Phoebe named several places that Elaine used for meetings, and after finding two of them abandoned, they discovered the warehouse where I had been kept prisoner.

I held up my hand. I didn't need to hear any more; I knew the rest of the story.

Aldwin looked pained, and I reached out to touch his arm when he spoke in a whisper.

"There's something else."

I grasped onto my blanket. His bleak tone sent chills up my spine, and I wasn't sure I could handle much more. My mind raced with possibilities. I knew Soren had made it out alive—I had a vague recollection of him and Aldwin in the carriage... I wondered if Travis had made it out okay or not. Swallowing, I asked him to tell me.

He stood up and paced to the window and back to the bed again, his eyes pleading with mine to understand.

"Aldwin, please. I need to know what happened. Is Travis... all right?" I blinked back tears at the thought of losing someone else.

"No... I mean, yes. Yes, Travis is fine. This is something else."

My heart thumped irregularly, and I put my hand over it. I looked up at Aldwin, ready for whatever he had to say.

"You were dying."

I blanched at the bald-faced statement.

"You were dying. Soren heard your heart slowing, and I felt your soul leaving me." He said it in such an anguished voice that I longed to hold him tight and make promises that it would never happen again.

"But I didn't die, Aldwin; I'm right here in front of you. It all worked out." His pained expression chilled my heart.

"You are here because I begged Soren to save you." He swallowed and dropped to his knees beside the bed. "I couldn't live without you, Sage. You were seconds from being beyond even his help when I had him give you his blood."

The metallic taste. Vampire blood had healing properties, I knew that, but how much blood had I consumed to be brought back from the brink of death? I opened my mouth, but nothing came out. I cleared my throat and tried again.

"Will I become a vampire?" I didn't feel like a vampire. At least, I didn't have a sudden urge to bite into his neck... that was good, right?

"No, you won't become a vampire; the whole process is more complicated than that. It's just with you being a warper, we are not sure if there will be unforeseen consequences. Also... we are not positive, but you and Soren may form some sort of bond."

A bond? I shook my head, too many *ifs* and *maybes* for my taste.

Aldwin looked like he had told me a car had hit my favorite pet.

"Aldwin, you saved my life. No matter what happens as a result, I would rather deal with those consequences than be dead. I owe you my gratitude."

He searched my eyes, hoping what I said was true, and the next thing I knew, I was at the receiving end of a toe-curling kiss. I must have made a noise when he pulled me closer to him because he broke away and apologized for manhandling the patient. I winked at him and told him I'd love to be manhandled like that any day.

Aldwin finally left to tell everyone that, after almost eighteen hours of rest, I had come to, and to have someone prepare me a bath. Even though he had suggested I stay in bed, I was itching to get up and brush my hair. I made my way as slowly as a ninety-year-old woman over to my dresser, sat down in front of the mirror, and looked at my pale reflection.

Turning my head to the side, I saw a fading bruise on my jaw. I frowned at my reflection; the bruise looked nearly healed. Unbuttoning my nightgown to examine the wound above my heart, I gasped when I saw the two-inch scar was barely pink around the edges. It looked weeks old. If the only consequence of consuming vampire blood was super-fast healing, well then, I had nothing to complain about. I closed my eyes as I brushed the tangles from my hair. It felt good to do something so normal.

A few minutes later, Aldwin came back to check on me, and I asked him to have a dinner prepared for several people. He argued that I needed my rest, but I got my way. I wanted to see everyone—to make sure they all looked healthy and to show my appreciation for everything they had done for me.

After I had soaked about thirty minutes too long in my bath, I dressed in a loose-fitting, Roman-inspired dress and decided to defy popular fashion and wear my hair flowing down to the center of my back. I only wore my sgian-dubh in my boot and my stone pendant. I had lost my smaller dirk and the butterfly cuff bracelet.

When I made my way downstairs, a slight flutter in my chest alarmed me, and my eyes were instantly drawn to the door just as someone used the knocker. Zachary appeared and opened the door to admit Soren. His eyes found mine instantly. I made my way down the last few steps to meet Soren for the first time since the night of the battle. I had so much to say to him, so much to be thankful for.

He looked so intently at me that I unconsciously put my hand over my heart. I stopped directly in front of the vampire; he held out his hand for mine and brought my hand to his lips to kiss it. Meanwhile, his eyes never left mine.

"I'm glad to see you looking just as beautiful as ever." His eyes roamed over my hair and my black gown as if he were soaking in my features for future reference.

"I felt you right before you knocked," I whispered, watching his face for a reaction.

"Did you?" he asked without so much as a hint of what he thought about the situation.

I reached up and touched his face tentatively. He grabbed my hand and rubbed his cheek against it like a cat rubbing its body against his owner. Suddenly, he closed his eyes as if the contact brought him pain.

"Soren, I can never thank you enough for saving my life. I will be forever in your debt."

He looked into my eyes and then tucked my hand into the crook of his arm, murmuring, "There is no debt, Sage. My reward is having you on my arm and in my life for however long we have."

I frowned over his choice of words, but Soren led me into the dining room where Aldwin, Travis, Dwennon, and his mate all waited to celebrate our victory.

CHAPTER
Thirty-two

THE NIGHT WAS FILLED WITH FRIENDS LAUGHING and making plans for the future. Even though there had been deaths on both sides of the fight, we had been victorious. Only a few rogue preternaturals escaped, and Dwennon was confident they'd be found and taken care of. We all enjoyed each other's company until late into the night before everyone began going home.

A profound sadness was tugging on my heart, and I wondered where the feeling was coming from. I felt like I'd found the place where I belonged, I felt at home. When I saw Soren to the door, I realized the melancholy I was experiencing was coming from my brooding vampire. I reached out my hand to stop him, to ask him what was bothering him, but he jerked his arm away from me abruptly and muttered something about the bond being a nuisance. I let him leave without smacking some sense into him, but I promised myself I'd talk to him the next day.

Leaning against the front door after the last guest had left, I yawned into the back of my hand.

Aldwin walked over to me, flashing a crooked grin. "You are dead on your feet. Up to bed, Miss Hannigan."

I raised a challenging brow at him and crossed my

arms over my chest. "Make me." I thrust my chin out. The gauntlet had been thrown.

I shrieked as Aldwin pinned me against the door and then scooped me into is arms before I could even pretend to have had a fighting chance. I stuck my bottom lip out in a pout. "No fair! I'm wounded. It wasn't an even match."

His laugh boomed off the walls and warmed my heart. "You never had a chance, Sage," he boasted. He carried me all the way into my room and gently set me back on my feet.

I threaded my hand through his thick, ebony hair and felt a thrill shoot through me when his body shivered ever so slightly. I got up on my tiptoes to gently kiss him.

"Sage, you are injured. I don't want to hurt you further."

His husky voice cut through my haze of desire, and I looked into his concerned gaze and knew beyond a shadow of doubt that I wanted him more than I had wanted anything else in my life.

"Aldwin, I need you tonight. Please don't deny me again."

His eyes widened slightly. Instead of saying anything, he lowered his mouth to mine and answered me passionate kiss for passionate kiss.

After several moments, he broke away reluctantly and rested his forehead on mine. "I need to tell you something… before we—"

I put my finger across his lips and breathed in the scent of honey and spices.

"Whatever it is won't matter to me. Tonight is just about us. Save it for tomorrow," I said breathlessly.

He seemed a bit torn, so I made the decision easier for him. Turning around and looking over my shoulder at the man who made me feel complete, I asked, "Undo my dress for me, please?"

His pupils dilated, and I hid a small smile. His hand brushed my hair over my shoulder, and I felt his breath a second before he kissed my neck. I groaned out loud.

His fingers expertly unbuttoned the back of my dress, lowering it down past my shoulders and just above my breasts. His mouth skimmed the back of my neck, and then he kissed the sensitive skin where the mark of Amerach was.

I hissed in a breath at the contact, feeling a sizzling current travel throughout my body. Aldwin groaned as I let the dress drop to the ground. Stepping out of the puddle of fabric and turning to face him, I suddenly felt unsure of myself.

I reached over and tugged at the fabric around his neck; Aldwin took the hint and disposed of his shoes, tie, and vest. I smiled and crooked my finger at him. His eyebrows rose, but he didn't deny me. I reached up and slowly unbuttoned his shirt, exposing more and more of his muscular chest. When I pulled the fabric off and he stood shirtless in front of me, a jolt of red-hot desire shot through me.

I kicked my boots off and set my sgian-dubh on the bedside table. With my back still to Aldwin, I unclasped the hooks at the front of my corset. Suddenly self-conscious, I held on to it for a moment longer; I had never been completely bare in front of a man before. With a deep breath, I let the corset fall away, crossed my arms over my chest, and turned to face him.

Aldwin stepped forward and lifted my chin gently with his finger. "You are absolutely beautiful."

I released a breath as his mouth descended to mine again, saying what words never could and wiping away all my inhibitions.

Later that night, my head lay on Aldwin's bare chest, and I listened to his even breathing while he slept. I wondered why I hadn't said what had been in my heart since I had woken up next to him earlier that day. I shifted to look at his face and knew more certainly than anything in my life that I had begun to fall in love with him. I smiled to myself. My heart was swollen with love and happiness.

Dislodging myself from his embrace, I turned over to sleep on my side. A smile split my face when Aldwin unconsciously adjusted himself to wrap around me from behind. I fell asleep in a cocoon of warmth and contentedness with the smile still on my face.

I wish with all my soul that I had slept dreamlessly.

CHAPTER
Thirty-three

THE FOREST WAS FAMILIAR SOMEHOW. AN OWL HOOTED IN *the distance, and the faint ticking of a clock echoed in the darkness that surrounded me. I glanced around the forest, sure that I was missing something. I was certain I had been here before. My heart began to race; this place made me uneasy, and I didn't want to be here. A breeze blew past, and I caught a whiff of spices, herbs, and... honey. My heart filled with joy, and I was sure I could almost lift off the ground from the power that coursed through me. I shook my head and tried to connect all my thoughts. Why would that scent make me feel this way?*

I walked down an overgrown path, wondering where it would lead. I kept trying to place the tantalizing scent that lingered in the air around me. A man stepped onto the path, and I stopped to contemplate pulling on the thread of power I felt nestled inside of me. His gaze met mine, and my heart fluttered wildly when his gold-rimmed eyes penetrated the darkness that surrounded us. I knew those eyes. I raised a hand to him, but he just scowled at me.

Brooding vampire. *I touched a hand to my temple and wondered where the thought had come from.*

Another man stepped onto the path a bit further down, and I squinted to see if I could make out his features. The longer

I stared, the hazier the air around the man became, and the scent that hung in the air thickened, coating my tongue. I started walking toward the men, and both turned away from me to walk farther down the path. I moved quickly and soon caught up with the first man. He immediately reached out and took my hand. It seemed so natural that I didn't question it.

I tried to call to the man on the path in front of us, but nothing came out of my mouth. I started to run, and the vampire holding my hand ran with me. No matter how quickly we ran, though, the man in front of us never got closer. We ran around a bend and came to an abrupt halt at the edge of a large pool of water. The full moon reflected in its inky surface, and the man we had been trying to catch stood on the other side of the pool, his face half-hidden by shadows and the aura that surrounded him.

The vampire clasped my hand as I walked to the very edge of the pool's surface. The man across from me mirrored my movements. I reached out my hand to him even though I knew the chasm was way too wide for our hands to meet. He held his out, too, and I felt a gap in my heart, knowing I was not able to touch him.

I took a step into the water, and the vampire came with me. The man also took a step in. I smiled and wondered how deep the pool of water was. When we had all taken a couple more steps, I realized we would all be in over our heads by the time we reached one another. I looked back at the vampire holding my hand and wondered how far we would be able to go or even if the waters were safe. We were all standing in the water up to our waists, and I didn't know what to do next. There was just too much space between us.

The man I felt a connection to stepped forward, and the water sloshed up to his chest. I tried to cry out, but no sound escaped my lips. Panic started building in my chest; this was all wrong. I yanked on the vampire's hand, but this time he didn't budge. I jerked my hand harder, but I couldn't free it from his grasp. I tried to dive forward when the man took a step that brought him into deep water sloshing up to his neck.

I screamed a wordless scream, but the vampire held me by the waist, keeping me from helping my mystery man. When the man lunged forward again and was swallowed up by the icy black waters, I felt a part of my heart plummet with him. I kicked, hit, and tried to get away, but the vampire held me tightly in his arms. When my body was too tired to fight and my heart was filled with nothing but loss, the vampire embraced me gently like a lover and then dragged me under the murky depths of the water. As I sank to the bottom of the pool, a single shimmer of silver snagged my dimming vision. I reached out and grasped the hilt of a dagger. Mine, I thought.

CHAPTER
Thirty-four

ICAME OUT OF THE DREAM NONE TOO GENTLY. Coughing up a small pond, water leaked from my nostrils as I grabbed a sheet off the bed and wiped my face. Pushing my sopping wet hair out of my eyes, I stopped in mid-motion as the sounds and sights around me came rushing in.

No!

My heart threatened to stop altogether. I almost wished it had. Anything would have felt better than it breaking into a million pieces. I vaguely recalled setting my sgian-dubh, which I had in a death grip, next to the lamp on my bedside table. Standing up on autopilot, I walked over to the window and pulled the curtain back so I could look out. Cars swarmed the streets, horns honked, people on the corner talked loudly, and I could hear a television blaring through the wall from an apartment next door.

I walked into the bathroom and looked at my reflection in the large mirror hanging over the sink. I still had a faded bruise on my cheek and an almost-healed scar above my heart. Too bad my inner scars wouldn't heal that fast. My heart constricted when I thought of the night I had just spent with Aldwin, of all the things I never got to tell him, and how the night we had just shared had really happened a hundred years ago.

I grabbed onto the sink, my knees shaking, and stared at the stone pendant hanging around my neck. I loathed the day I'd picked it up at the antique bookstore. I fingered the mark of Amerach, remembering how Aldwin had so lovingly kissed it. A tear leaked out of the corner of my eye as I grabbed a large, glass bowl of seashells off the counter and smashed it into the mirror, shattering both into thousands of tiny pieces. Stumbling into my bedroom, I wrapped my cut hand in a sheet and curled into a ball, letting sobs wrack my body.

Never again would I allow myself to love. Never again would I allow myself to trust. The only friend I had trusted tried to kill me, and the only man I had ever loved was ripped from me by the fates. I wasn't going to let fate control my destiny any longer… fate could kiss my ass.

From here on out, I would make my own destiny.

ABOUT THE *Author*

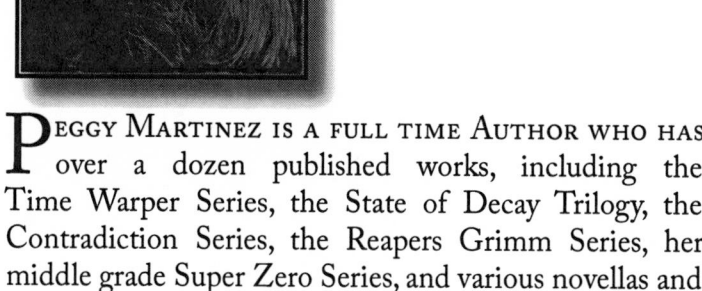

PEGGY MARTINEZ IS A FULL TIME AUTHOR WHO HAS over a dozen published works, including the Time Warper Series, the State of Decay Trilogy, the Contradiction Series, the Reapers Grimm Series, her middle grade Super Zero Series, and various novellas and serials.

When not writing, Peggy can be found homeschooling her teen son and four daughters. You may also find her packaging hundreds of boxes for her monthly box subscription business she founder just for readers! (Lit-Cube) She could also be spotted reading, making soap, dabbling in aromatherapy, watching gangster movies, prepping for the zombie apocalypse, or downing insane amounts of Twizzlers and Kazoozles. Oh yeah... and day dreaming about owning a small homestead or taking a dream vacation to Greece, Scotland, & Ireland... she could totally be doing that.